Laurie Fullerton

Laurie Fullerton was born in Marblehead, Massachusetts and began travelling at the age of 18. She has worked in publishing, as a freelance journalist and travel writer, since the early '80s. Her travels include a journey across the former Soviet Union, a tour of China, Tibet and the Philippines, a lengthy stay in Hong Kong, Australia and the UK, and a tour of the South Pacific.

Leanne Logan

First tasting Europe at the age of 12, Leanne has long been lured by travel. She completed a journalism degree at the Queensland University of Technology before exploring her homeland as a reporter for several newspapers and Australian Associated Press.

In 1987 she set off through Asia and the Middle East to London where, as deputy editor of a travel magazine, her wander lust was temporarily fed but never sated. Eventually she succumbed to it and bought a one-way ticket to Africa. Leanne returned to Europe to write the Benelux chapters for *Western Europe on a shoestring*. While conducting research into Belgium's 350-odd beers, she met a local connoisseur, Geert Cole. The pair have been a team ever since and together worked on the new *France tsk*.

Geert Cole

Having most of his roots in Belgium, Geert swapped university and social work studies for a discovery of broader horizons and other cultures. Each trip resulted in an extra diary being put on the shelf and another job experience being added to life's list.

In recent times, when not running his stained-glass studio close to hometown Antwerp, Geert has been found sailing the Pacific, sorting Aussie sheep and, amongst other challenges, trekking through Alaska and diving tropical reefs.

The most recent spark of destiny saw this artist, traveller, writer, cook, builder, landscaper...linked to companion, Leanne, with whom he researched *France tsk*. Together they continue fossicking around this lovely planet.

From Geert & Leanne

A great deal of assistance and enthusiasm was given to this project by many people, both in New Caledonia and outside. For their insight and generous gift of time, our special thanks go to Jeff Lalié on Lifou; Isabelle Kongouleux on Ouvea; Hilary Roots and Albert Thoma on Île des Pins; Andrea Schaefer and Jacky Sorin in Noumea; and Andrea Barnard and David Atwood from the South Pacific Commission. An ultra-special thank you to Phillida Stephens in Noumea who became an invaluable contact and friend.

Our sincere appreciation also goes to Raymond Prevot from Air Calédonie International; the staff of Destination Nouvelle Calédonie, including, in Noumea, Hélène Touret, Laurent Bernut, Isabelle Adrian and Sylvie Coquelet and, in Sydney, Donna Pegum; those at the Agence de Développement de la Culture Kanak, particularly Ledji Bellow and Odile Audrain; Jean-Pierre Garnier from Club Med; Claire Garrigue and Mr Chazeau from ORSTOM; and Pascale Joannot from the Noumea Aquarium.

Other people who provided information or lent a valuable hand just when it was needed were Susi Newborn, Trudi Hoogerbrugge and Narelle Logan-Werder. Jeanie & James Douglas, we thank you for looking after the herd. And then, special mention and our deepest thanks must go to Nev & Dee Logan for all the time they spent proofreading and for 'erring on the safe side'.

And lastly, thanks to the LP staff in the UK and the USA offices who assisted with information and to all those in the Melbourne office who welcomed us and worked on this book.

This Book

The first edition of this book was written by Laurie Fullerton. This edition was revised and greatly expanded by Leanne Logan & Geert Cole.

From the Publisher

This edition of *New Caledonia – a travel survival kit* was edited by Sally Steward. It was proofread by Adrienne Costanzo, Samantha Carew, Rowan McKinnon and Steve Womersley. Rowan also prepared the index with a bit of help from Sharon Wertheim. Margaret Jung designed the cover and Jacqui Saunders chose the photos, produced the maps and drew the illustrations. Ann Jeffree did the layout and additional illustrations.

Thanks

A big *merci beaucoup* to the travellers who used the first edition of this book and wrote to LP with information and suggestions:

Joanne Brown (Aus), Ian Diddams (UK), David Furrows (UK), Norma Glanfield, Cathy & Peter Houlihan (Aus), Michael Jasper (NZ), Karl & Patricia Juik, R McLean (NZ), Sophie Masson (Aus), Michael Mathew (Aus), L Nekstraat (Neth), Sue Nichols (Aus), M Schraag (Neth), George Spark (NC), Michael Speck (Aus), Cherilyn Taylor (Aus), K Tomaslevsky (USA), Wilfried Wadehn (G) and Mary Weaver (USA).

Warning & Request

Things change – prices go up, schedules change, good places go bad and bad places go bankrupt – nothing stays the same. So if you find things better or worse, recently opened or long since closed, please write and tell us and help make the next edition better.

Your letters will be used to help update future editions and, where possible, important changes will also be included in a Stop Press section in reprints.

We greatly appreciate all information that is sent to us by travellers. Back at Lonely Planet we employ a hard-working readers' letters team to sort through the many letters we receive. The best ones will be rewarded with a free copy of the next edition or another Lonely Planet guide if you prefer. We give away lots of books, but, unfortunately, not every letter/postcard receives one.

New Caledonia

a travel survival kit

Laurie Fullerton
Leanne Logan
Geert Cole

New Caledonia – a travel survival kit

2nd edition

Published by
Lonely Planet Publications
Head Office: PO Box 617, Hawthorn, Vic 3122, Australia
Branches: PO Box 2001A, Berkeley, CA 94702, USA
                  12 Barley Mow Passage, Chiswick, London W4 4PH, UK
                  71 bis rue du Cardinal Lemoine, 75005 Paris, France

Printed by
Colorcraft Ltd, Hong Kong

Photographs by
Geert Cole (GC)   Laurie Fullerton (LF)
Leanne Logan (LL)   Destination Nouvelle Calédonie (DNC)

Front cover: Yet another idyllic beach (DNC)

First Published
June 1990

This Edition
May 1994

Although the authors and publisher have tried to make the information as accurate as possible, they accept no responsibility for any loss, injury or inconvenience sustained by any person using this book.

National Library of Australia Cataloguing in Publication Data

Fullerton, Laurie.
   New Caledonia – a travel survival kit.

   2nd ed.
   Includes index.
   ISBN 0 86442 201 6.

   1. New Caledonia – Guidebooks. I. Cole, Geert II. Logan,
Leanne, 1964- . III. Title. (Series : Lonely Planet travel
survival kit).

919.59704

text & maps © Lonely Planet 1994
photos © photographers as indicated 1994
climate charts compiled from information supplied by Patrick J Tyson, © Patrick J Tyson, 1994

Contents

DEPENDENCIES OF NEW CALEDONIA.. **264**

ALTERNATIVE PLACE NAMES **268**

GLOSSARY **269**

INDEX **274**

Map Legend

BOUNDARIES

— · — · — · —	........International Boundary
——— · · — · · —	................Internal Boundary
+++++++++++++	....National Park or Reserve
— — — — — — —	........................The Equator
················	.........................The Tropics

SYMBOLS

◉ NATIONAL	...........................National Capital
● PROVINCIAL	........Provincial or State Capital
● Major	..............................Major Town
● Minor	..............................Minor Town
■	............................Places to Stay
▼	..............................Places to Eat
✉	....................................Post Office
✈	....Airport
i	.......................Tourist Information
⬤	.............Bus Station or Terminal
66	............Highway Route Number
☾ ✝ 🕌 ✝	...... Mosque, Church, Cathedral
∴	..........................Temple or Ruin
✚	......................................Hospital
☀	......................................Lookout
⚐	.... Camping Area
⌐	..............................Picnic Area
⌂	............................Hut or Chalet
▲	......................Mountain or Hill
+—+—■—+	..........................Railway Station
⩵	.... Road Bridge
+—+—+—+	..........................Railway Bridge
⇒ ⇐	..............................Road Tunnel
→→ ←←	...........................Railway Tunnel
⌇⌇⌇	....................Escarpment or Cliff
‿	....Pass
⊓⊔⊓⊔	............Ancient or Historic Wall

ROUTES

———————	.......Major Road or Highway
- - - - - - -	.... Unsealed Major Road
———————	.... Sealed Road
- - - - - - -	..... Unsealed Road or Track
═══════	...........................City Street
+++++++++++	...............................Railway
●—■—■—●	...............................Subway
- - - - - - -	.......................Walking Track
- - - - - - -	..........................Ferry Route
++++++++++++	.... Cable Car or Chair Lift

HYDROGRAPHIC FEATURES

	.....................River or Creek
	..............Intermittent Stream
	........Lake, Intermittent Lake
	...........................Coast Line
	...................................Spring
	...............................Waterfall
	.................................Swamp
	.... Salt Lake or Reef
	................................Glacier

OTHER FEATURES

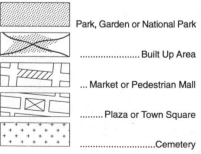

	Park, Garden or National Park
	.... Built Up Area
	... Market or Pedestrian Mall
	.........Plaza or Town Square
	...............................Cemetery

Note: not all symbols displayed above appear in this book

Introduction

New Caledonia is a South Pacific archipelago which goes by several names. The French call it Nouvelle Calédonie, to English speakers it's New Caledonia, while to many of the indigenous inhabitants it is Kanaky – the land of the Kanaks.

You have only to look at this collection of titles to get some clues as to what makes up contemporary New Caledonia. Sitting in the south-west of the Pacific in a region where the lingua franca is predominantly English, it is a French-speaking territory ruled partially by France and where the local Melanesian population, the Kanaks, are seeking independence. All this makes it one interesting little melting pot of Pacific and Western cultures.

New Caledonia has been part of France for about 150 years. Despite adverse conditions during this period, the Kanaks' tribal customs are still alive, and in recent years their culture has been going through a mini-renaissance, particularly amongst the younger generation. On the flip side, French traditions are also quite strong, brought to this far flung island first by convicts and later by French settlers. Their present-day descendants, many of whom have never seen metropolitan France, are called Caldoches. They are a unique people, having retained certain aspects of the distinct culture of their forebears, while also forging their own folkways.

Unlike some of its Melanesian and Polynesian neighbours who tally up hundreds of tiny islands, New Caledonia is made up of only a handful of islands. The main island, Grande Terre, is the largest – a lush and mountainous strip of land surrounded by one

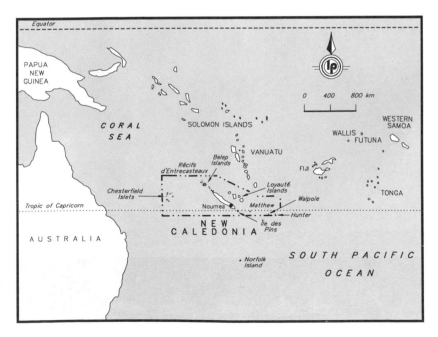

of the world's biggest reefs, second only to the Great Barrier Reef in Australia. Relatively close by are the blissfully beautiful Loyauté islands and Île des Pins, while, far away in the territorial waters, a few coral cays and old volcanoes make up the uninhabited dependencies.

Despite its few islands, New Caledonia is linguistically diverse, with some 28 indigenous languages spread over the pockets of land. Amongst the different Kanak clans, the Europeans, and the sprinkling of Polynesians and Asians who immigrated here over the years to work in the profitable nickel industry, French is the contact language. The capital, Noumea, is the meeting place for all these people, a multicultural city with a balmy climate, fine restaurants and a laidback atmosphere.

New Caledonians have an expression for everything outside Noumea. They call it *la Brousse*, which means the 'outback' or the 'bush', an appropriate term considering the rest of Grande Terre and the islands are a world apart from the sophistication of the capital. Though many visitors are content to stay in Noumea, those with the urge and the time to explore nature's pure delights away from it will find themselves on a memorable adventure. Perhaps they'll take away one of the age-old legends told by folk on the Loyauté islands, or the intoxicating habit of greeting every person they pass on the street. Maybe it'll just be the memory of strolling along sublime white sandy beaches lined with palms, or snorkelling through warm, limpid waters coloured the most stunning turquoise ever imagined. If nothing else, they'll have a taste of the infectious Pacific and its people that will never fade.

Facts about the Country

HISTORY
Early Settlers

Common belief is that the western Pacific was first populated by hunter-gatherers, people some historians now call the very old Oceanians, who came from South-East Asia at least 50,000 years ago. This was the Pleistocene period, or Great Ice Age, a time when the lowered sea level opened an easy migration route through Indonesia and Papua New Guinea, and possibly as far as the Solomons. Then, in about 10,000 BC, the earth warmed up again and the sea rose, inundating lowlands and forming isolated islands. Without the knowledge of seafaring, these people were restricted to their islands.

Between 7000 and 5000 BC, Austronesian-speaking, proto-Melanesian migrants from South-East Asia brought agriculture, pottery and canoe building to the area. As

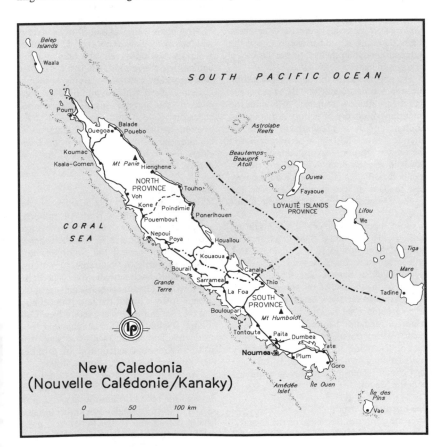

New Caledonia
(Nouvelle Calédonie/Kanaky)

their knowledge of navigating and farming increased, they expanded and settled over the Melanesian archipelagos, including the Solomon Islands and Vanuatu, before eventually arriving on New Caledonia's main island, Grande Terre, and its smaller Loyauté islands and Île des Pins. Some of these people then continued to western Polynesia.

The only archaeological evidence of this culture's existence in New Caledonia are tumuli (burial mounds) on Grande Terre and Île des Pins and petroglyphs on Grande Terre. Petroglyphs are designs, such as circles and spirals, carved in stone and found throughout the Pacific. Their meaning or purpose remains a mystery, as does their age. No organic materials were used to make them, therefore it's not possible to use the radiocarbon dating method to pinpoint their position in history.

The appearance of the Lapita culture took place sometime around 2000 BC. The people and their culture were named following the important discovery of pottery at Lapita, an ancient site near present-day Kone on Grande Terre. The Lapita people explored the western Pacific, leaving their elaborate, pin-hole incised pottery on coastal settlements from Papua New Guinea all the way east to Samoa. (For more details see the Lapita Pottery section in the West Coast chapter.)

From about the 11th century AD right up until the 18th century, there was another wave of migration to New Caledonia, this time essentially from western Polynesian islands such as Samoa, Tonga and Wallis. Forced by the threatened over-population of their islands to seek new lands, groups of 50 or so islanders set sail in long canoes in search of small uninhabited islands or larger islands with a population they could dominate or live with. In New Caledonia, they landed mainly on northern Grande Terre and the Loyauté islands, where they intermarried with the Melanesian tribes.

Pre-European Times

Over the centuries, the bulk of the islands' inhabitants settled on the coast and, in the case of Grande Terre, along nearby river valleys and at mountain foothills. Clan groupings varied in size, from as few as 50 up to 5000, depending largely on what the local environment supplied and the success of their own agriculture. They cultivated yams, taro, manioc and other crops; the terraced fields they once worked are still visible on Grande Terre.

With no domesticated beasts or large four-legged animals living on the islands, the locals relied for protein on fish, *roussettes* (flying foxes) and cannibalism. Inter-clan wars were common and eating the flesh of the enemy was an important ritual believed to enhance the power of the victorious clan.

Most clans were isolated from each other and thus many dialects evolved. Life centred around the *grande case*, the clan's largest conical hut where the chief lived. This hut was topped by a wooden carving known as a *flèche faîtière*, which symbolised the presence of the ancient, highly worshipped ancestors. Rule within the clan was by a revered tradition known in French as *la coutume* (custom), and recalled by the tribal elders. (See Traditional Kanak Culture, later in this chapter.)

European Arrival

In the late 16th century, the Spanish sent out expeditions in search of Terra Australis, the great southern continent that was believed to exist to counterbalance the northern hemisphere. They located the Solomons and islands in northern Vanuatu but nothing farther south. Each new discovery gave rise to the myths of Pacific paradise and the noble savage. It wasn't until the late 18th century that the first Europeans arrived in New Caledonia. By that time it was inhabited by a productive and strong race of Melanesians and Polynesians estimated to number 60,000; some figures put it even higher.

The English explorer Captain Cook spotted Grande Terre in 1774 when midway through his second scientific expedition in search of Terra Australis (it was this trip that finally put an end to the belief in a great southern continent). He named it New Caledonia as it had a slight resemblance to the highlands of Scotland, once called Caledonia by the Romans.

Cook and his crew, aboard the Royal Navy ship HMS *Resolution*, anchored at Balade on the north-east coast on 4 September 1774, just in time to record an eclipse of the sun two days later. They stayed one week as guests of the Kanak chief Ti-Pouma and his clan, and studied the ethnography and geography of the island's north-eastern region. Gifts were exchanged, including two pigs and two dogs, the island's first such creatures. Cook was later to report a favourable introduction, commenting that the natives were 'robust and active, courteous and friendly, of honest nature and the women modest'.

The *Resolution*, bound for New Zealand, then sailed down the east coast of the main island (without sighting the Loyauté islands) until Cook noted and named the beautiful Isle of Pines (Île des Pins). He was fascinated by the towering araucaria pines that lined the shore, describing them as 'the masts of a naval fleet at anchor'. However, gales and a treacherous reef made it impossible for him to land.

French interest in New Caledonia was sparked 14 years later when Louis XVI sent Comte de La Pérouse to explore its economic potential. But La Pérouse and his crew aboard the *Astrolabe* and the *Boussole* disappeared during a violent cyclone on the reefs off Vanikolo in the south-east of the Solomon Islands. A mission set out from France on 28 September 1791 to find them. Led by Admiral Bruny d'Entrecasteaux and Captain Huon de Kermadec, the *Espérance* and *La Recherche* landed at Balade on 17 April 1793, having sailed past Vanikolo where, unbeknown to them, two survivors of La Pérouse's expedition were still living.

Shortly after arriving in New Caledonia, Huon de Kermadec died. As the expedition had already discovered that the locals were cannibals, he was secretly buried on the islet of Poudiou in the hope that he wouldn't be found and eaten. D'Entrecasteaux and members of his crew carried out an exploration on

Jean-François de Galaup, Comte de La Pérouse

foot of northern New Caledonia, crossing from the east to the west coast and back again. They stayed a month but their reaction to the islanders was very different from Cook's. The admiral was to report them as aggressive thieves and cannibals, and the women prepared to sell themselves. D'Entrecasteaux made the first sighting of the northern Loyauté island of Ouvea and died during the return journey to France in 1793.

In the same year, the English captain Raven on the *Britannia* sighted the southernmost Loyauté island, Mare, and reported the presence of sandalwood. It wasn't until 1827 that the islands were correctly charted by the French explorer Dumont d'Urville, thus making the entire archipelago accessible to shipping.

Hunters & Traders

British and American whalers were the first commercial seafarers to make landfall on the islands. The British whalers set out from the small Australian settlement of Port Jackson (now Sydney) and by 1840 had set up an oil extraction station on the largest Loyauté island, Lifou. However, they were not generally welcomed by the islanders and the first skirmishes between locals and Europeans took place here. When a band of escaped convicts from Norfolk Island, Britain's isolated convict prison off Australia's east coast, landed on the island in the early 1840s, they were massacred.

The whalers were followed by sandalwood traders, who were the first Europeans to have any real impact on the islanders. They came in search of sandalwood trees, whose sweet-smelling roots and core were traditionally burnt as incense in Chinese temples. As supplies in the northern Pacific had already been severely diminished by the 1920s, their attention turned to the many islands to the south. New Caledonia took its turn between 1840 and 1850, during which time traders operating out of Australia stripped first Île des Pins, then the Loyauté islands and finally Grande Terre's east coast. They also collected *bêches-de-mer* (sea cucumbers), which, when dried and pulverised, have traditionally been used in Cantonese cuisine and considered by some an aphrodisiac. The traders gave the islanders metal tools such as axes, nails and fishhooks, or tobacco and alcohol in return for the sandalwood. With their ships loaded, they sailed to China where the fragrant wood was swapped for tea, which was brought back to Australia.

As the Chinese market expanded and sandalwood supplies diminished, the traders' tactics and behaviour grew more threatening and arrogant, and tensions developed because of cheating and the abuse of local customs. But more insidiously, the traders introduced diseases like smallpox, measles, influenza, syphilis and leprosy. The indigenous people and their medicinal men had no answers for these afflictions and vast numbers of people died. Eventually, fierce confrontations broke out between the locals and the traders. In 1849, the crew of an American vessel named *Cutter* was massacred and eaten by the Pouma clan living between Balade and Pouebo.

Later that century, another type of trade affected the clans, in particular those on the Loyauté islands, as Kanaks were taken to work on foreign plantations in what was known as 'blackbirding' (see the Loyauté islands chapter for an explanation).

The Missionaries

Although their aims were ultimately the same – to bring 'Christianity' to the 'heathen' islanders – Catholic and Protestant missionaries were great adversaries. They personified not just two branches of faith but more so two highly competitive nations – France (Catholic) and England (Protestant). The battles that ensued, especially on the Loyauté islands, wreaked havoc on their converts.

Two Protestant Samoan missionaries from the London Missionary Society (LMS) were the first to arrive, sailing into Ile des Pins in 1841. The LMS had learnt elsewhere in the Pacific (at the cost of the lives of several of their European brethren), that it was safer to send Polynesian converts first into unknown territory to break the ice, so to speak. If they survived the hostility and cannibalistic practices of the locals, the Europeans could follow. Though soon driven off Île des Pins by unreceptive locals, the British missionaries successfully established themselves on Lifou in 1842.

Meanwhile on Grande Terre, seven French Marists, sent out by the Société de la Propagation de la Foi (Society to Propagate the Faith), established a mission at both Pouebo and Balade on the north-east coast in December 1843. The mission was demolished four years later by angry locals suffering from drought, starvation and exposure to disease. A few of the Brothers were beheaded and eaten, but the majority were rescued by the ship *La Brillante* which was anchored offshore. In retaliation, the French military arrived and destroyed the tribal settlements, driving the locals into the mountains as punishment for the deaths of the men of the cloth. The next time the missionaries stubbornly attempted to establish themselves at Balade and Pouebo in 1851, they brought the French military with them for protection.

The missionaries profoundly changed

Kanak culture and daily life. Their 'word of God' was the word of a dominant culture imposing its values on the local people. Nakedness was considered offensive and 'proper' clothing – flowing missionary-style dresses which obliterated any suggestion of female form – was introduced, while children were sometimes separated from their parents in order to live and go to school at the mission. The British missionaries introduced the game of cricket, at the same time stamping out traditional games. Converts were made to sleep on beds, drink tea and, above all, to stop eating one another. Polygamy, along with cannibalism, was customary to some tribes and the missionaries staunchly campaigned for the eradication of these practices.

One of the major stumbling blocks between the missionaries and the Kanaks was the concept of land ownership. The missionaries believed they had 'purchased' a block of land from the local clan and therefore what that land produced was theirs. Melanesian custom did not have such an idea of private land ownership. When communal crops were ripe, they were harvested and distributed amongst the clan. When the Melanesians tried to take yams from the missionaries' fields, the latter branded them as thieves and eventually used dogs to guard their stores.

However, the relative success of early missions is attributed in part to the threat posed by the French military and its colonisation strategy. The missions offered protection to displaced tribes and, as long as they maintained their authority over the clan, local chiefs were ready to compromise with the missionaries. But as the missions became more powerful, customary life began to break down. People were forced to choose between the mission's leadership and its dualistic good against evil doctrine, or the rule of the clan's chief and their traditional beliefs. On top of this, tribes were soon divided along religious lines and wars broke out. It was not until the later part of the 19th century that these holy wars were suppressed by the French military.

French Annexation

In the early 1850s, with fewer South Pacific islands for Britain and France to choose from and the London Missionary Society becoming more influential, there was growing concern in France that Britain would take possession of New Caledonia. The French were looking for a strategic military location, as well as an alternative penal settlement to their notorious Devil's Island off French Guyana in South America, which was riddled with malaria. When New Caledonia was recommended, the new emperor, Napoleon III, did not hesitate.

In 1853, he ordered the annexation of New Caledonia, under the pretext of protecting France's floundering Catholic missions. British missionaries were perceived as the 'Trojan horse of English influence' and, after annexation, the French military closed the colony and ousted the British. When the French flag was raised at Balade on 24 September 1853, Britain did not react as it was too busy with the newly acquired possessions of New Zealand and Australia. In 1862 the first governor was appointed and, for the second half of the 19th century, New Caledonia was governed by a military regime.

The Penal Colony

Following the British example in New South Wales, New Caledonia was founded as a penal colony and the first shiploads of convicts arrived in May 1864 at Port-de-France, or present-day Noumea. It took four months to sail from France to New Caledonia around the Cape of Good Hope. Conditions were miserable and hundreds of convicts died at sea. Those who survived the voyage were kept in large huts on Île Nou off Noumea harbour. They were soon put to work on the construction of a chapel and the penitentiary and settlement that would eventually house them and thousands of others. Many of the colony's public works were carried out by these prisoners, including Noumea's St Joseph cathedral and most of the roads on Grande Terre.

As labourers spread out in work teams,

they became difficult to supervise. Disciplinary measures were established and carried out mercilessly. The most difficult convicts were sent to Camp Brun, referred to as the 'slaughterhouse', where men were put to hard labour, housed in dungeons and beaten for the least misdemeanour. The guillotine was brought to New Caledonia in 1867 and, in the next 21 years, about 80 heads rolled. Before being executed, a condemned prisoner was offered one last cigarette and a glass of rum.

Deportation

All up, almost 21,000 male and female convicts were sent from France for various felonies. Political prisoners were high on the list and, in the eight years following the 1871 Paris Commune uprising, some 4300 Communards were deported. Mainly working class Parisians, the Communards were radical Socialists and revolutionaries who seized power from the monarch-controlled French government for two months. But the government troops crushed the Commune's National Guard – the people's army – and thousands were killed in the battle, while some 20,000 people were later summarily executed. Others were rounded up, given life sentences and deported.

Most Communards were sent to Île des Pins but a few of the more 'dangerous' ones were incarcerated on the Ducos peninsula across the harbour from Noumea. Amongst the more famous Communards was Henri de Rochefort, a radical newspaper editor who was a member of parliament in 1869. He was sent to Ducos from where he and a few others escaped to Australia on 19 March 1874, on board a cargo ship captained by a sympathetic Australian seaman. The escapees swam across Numbo Bay to the awaiting ship anchored near Île Nou and hid in the hold until they were safely out of New Caledonian waters. Rochefort then went to the USA and the UK, campaigning for the release of his compatriots in New Caledonia.

Another well-known deportee was the 42-year-old feminist and anarchist Louise Michel, who was also imprisoned at Ducos.

She had earned the name the 'Red Virgin' during the Paris Commune riots and refused any special treatment on Ducos. After the general amnesty in 1879, she worked in Noumea, sympathising with the Kanaks' struggle against the colonial rule, and later returned to France. She wrote a book, a collection of Melanesian legends, entitled *Légendes et Chantes de Gestes Canaques*.

The deportees on Île des Pins suffered from isolation and homesickness and many young poets and artists gave up life. These artisans and intellectuals had philosophies that helped disrupt much of the zealous missionary work going on at the time. They shared a collective hatred for the bourgeoisie and especially the clergy, and must have clashed with the stoic Marists.

In the same year as the Paris Commune riot, 20,000 Arab warriors in Algeria, France's North African colony, revolted against the past 40 years' colonisation and France's recognition of the many Jews who were settling in the country. The rebellion was crushed and the Berber leaders captured and sent to New Caledonia. They too were imprisoned on Île des Pins and Ducos. Many spent 50 years in the colony before their sentences expired and they were able, as old men, to return to their homeland. Others simply settled here.

By 1879, a series of pardons for the Communards was granted, allowing many of them to return to France. No amnesty was given to the Arab prisoners. Meanwhile regular criminals continued to flow into the territory until the governor of New Caledonia begged France to 'turn off this tap of dirty water'; this was finally done in 1897.

Once freed, the ex-convicts were encouraged to stay and settle in New Caledonia, and women prisoners were shipped out from France to find husbands amongst them. The experiment was not entirely successful as the women preferred the *colons*, free settlers who were migrating to the territory. Many of the convicts returned to France; however, some of today's New Caledonian-born French, known as Caldoches, are related to the original convicts.

All photographs by LL

Top Left: (LL)
Top Right: (LL)
Middle Left: (GC)

Middle Right: (LL)
Bottom Left: (LL)
Bottom Right: (LL)

The Revolt of 1878

While freed convicts were encouraged to settle in New Caledonia, there was also a programme in the 1860s and 1870s, aided by the discovery of nickel in 1864, to bring settlers from France. Hostilities began between Kanaks and the French when these settlers started to encroach on tribal lands. The process of taking Melanesian land began in earnest when the governor Guillain introduced the system of *cantonnement*, which gave him the right to sell land to French settlers at a fixed price with unlimited grazing rights, and to appoint or dismiss Kanak chiefs. As the colony grew, demand for beef increased and large tracts of land were gradually taken over for cattle. This destroyed the Kanaks' taro and yam beds and wrecked their irrigation channels. As a result, in the two years prior to the rebellion, the Kanaks were in real fear of famine. Another grievance was the settlers' deliberate desecration of tribal burial grounds in their search for native skulls and artefacts, which were prized in Paris.

Finally, some of the best land was taken from local leader Chef Ataï to be used for a women's prison farm at Ponwhary near La Foa. To voice his dismay, Chef Ataï met the then governor, Olry, at nearby Fort Teremba. He produced two sacks, one filled with fertile soil, the other with rocks, and told the governor 'this is what we used to have, and here is what you are leaving us'. His words fell on deaf ears.

The revolt broke out around La Foa early in the morning of 25 June. It was sparked off when local gendarmes arrested several innocent chiefs and took them in for questioning over the murder of a Kanak woman. Led by Ataï, the Kanaks attacked the gendarmerie and killed the police. From here it snowballed, with settler families and workers in La Foa and Bouloupari areas being killed in surprise assaults. The Kanaks then marched in an unsuccessful attack on Fort Teremba. In the first two days about 120 Whites, including women and children, were killed. The revolt went on for seven months, involving clans all the way from Bouloupari to Poya, 140 km to the north. Cattle stations were destroyed and grazing land was burned. In all, 200 French and 1200 Kanaks were killed, including Ataï and other chiefs. As a result of the rebellion, 800 Kanaks were exiled to the Belep Islands or Île des Pins. Others were sent to Tahiti, never to return. The repression which followed damaged the Kanak culture and way of life forever.

Establishing the Colonial Order

Full-scale colonisation began at the end of the 19th century. Governor Paul Feillet came to Noumea in June 1894 and initiated a rigorous campaign to recruit free settlers from France. Families with 5000F and farming knowledge were given free passage and 15 to 25 hectares of land on arrival, on the sole condition that they had to grow at least five hectares of coffee. As the governor hoped, coffee exports soared during the late 1890s.

When the flow of convicts stopped in 1897, the settlers' free labour supply was extinguished (though the Kanaks were soon brought in to fill their place). The metallurgical industry, whose mines had previously been worked by hundreds of convicts, faced the same labour crisis. Recruits were sought and people from Indonesia, Vanuatu, Vietnam and Japan answered the call. The Société Le Nickel (SLN) was established in 1910, financed by the Rothschild corporation, and, for a time, New Caledonia became the world's largest nickel supplier.

But the most damning aspect of colonisation was the *indigénat* system, instituted by the French soon after the 1878 revolt. This system put Kanaks outside French common law, legally giving them a subordinate status. It subjected them to the whims of the ruling colonial administration and made segregation between Kanaks and Europeans legal. The locals were forced into reservations in the mountainous highlands which they could leave only with police permission. Interisland trading routes amongst Kanaks were halted and religious or ancestral ties to sites and places were ignored. In the end, only 11% of the land on Grande Terre, mostly hilly regions in scattered areas, was left to the Kanaks. They were forced to work for settlers or the colonial authorities and a 10F reward was offered to anyone capturing a 'native in an irregular situation'.

The Kanak population began to decline from 42,500 in 1887 to only 28,000 in 1901. A later Kanak leader, Jean-Marie Tjibaou, described their demise: 'The tribes had nothing to do but die because there was nothing left to eat because there were no people left to work at growing things to eat'.

The indigénat system was reviewed and renewed every decade until WW II, with the French authorities inevitably deciding on each occasion that the natives hadn't reached sufficient moral or intellectual standards to run their own affairs. Not until 1946, when the system was abolished and Kanaks received French citizenship, were they allowed to leave their reservations without permission.

The World Wars

During WW I, 5500 Caldoche and Kanak men were recruited to form the French Pacific Battalion, which fought in North Africa, Italy and southern France. At least a quarter of the battalion died and the colony again suffered from a loss of labour. The Kanaks had been forcibly recruited, unable by la coutume to disobey the command of their chief, who in turn was pressured by the colonial authorities to provide fighters. In all, 372 Kanaks died for France, leading to the 1917 revolt in the Kone-Hienghene area when Chef Noël called on Kanaks to fight the French at home as ably as they were fighting the Germans abroad. Two hundred Kanaks and 11 French died in the uprising, including Chef Noël. A reward of 2000F had been offered by the colonial administration for his head, which was dutifully cut off by his killer.

The Kanak population reached its lowest point shortly after WW I. In 1923, the teaching of French in schools became compulsory and the practices of Kanak medicine men were outlawed, with the threat of jail for anyone practising 'wizardry'. During the '20s and '30s, the country became economi-cally isolated, settlement slowed down and the colony stagnated; this situation did not change until WW II.

The majority of French people in New Caledonia chose to support President de Gaulle and the Free French Forces as opposed to the collaborationist Vichy regime, which took over France in WW II. The colony's US allies were given permission to set up a military base on Grande Terre and, in early 1942, 40,000 American, and a lesser number of New Zealand, personnel arrived. Admiral Halsey, whose strategies helped win the Solomon Islands offensive, set up headquarters near Anse Vata beach in Noumea, from where attacks were launched against the Japanese in the Philippines and in the Battle of the Coral Sea. When the Americans departed, they left behind US$3 million worth of equipment.

The Kanaks have good memories of the US presence. For the first time, they were employed for their labour and received good wages. They were also impressed by what they saw as relatively easy interaction between Black and White American soldiers, something that was lacking between people living in the French colonial system. This taste of a different Western culture would change the lifestyle of many Kanak families.

The Post-War Period

New Caledonia's status was changed from a colony to a French overseas territory after WW II and, straight away, Kanaks began to formulate their own political and social demands. Chef Naisseline of Mare prepared a 'native bill' and argued that, as Mareans and other Kanaks had fought and died under the French flag during the world wars, they were entitled to the rights of French citizens. In 1946, Kanaks were given French citizenship and the more privileged, such as chiefs, priests and former soldiers, became eligible to vote (the bulk of Kanaks didn't receive the right to vote for another 11 years). The authorities finally abolished the demoralising indigénat system, though by this time they had virtually achieved their aim, with few improvements to the Kanaks' situation, save the questionable benefits of the partial Westernisation of their way of living. As Wilfred Burchett, an Australian journalist, wrote during a visit in 1941: 'The administration has now taught the native to build more hygienic huts (than the *case*) or bungalow-type housing, with neat whitewashed stone walls, plenty of light and air space and wide verandahs supported by niaouli poles – and, in some deluxe residences, glass windows'.

In 1953, the first political party involving Kanaks was formed. Called Union Calédonienne (UC), it was a coalition of Kanaks, White small-scale landowners, the missions and union supporters. It was led by Maurice Lenormand, a Frenchman who had been sent to the colony for military service 20 years earlier and had never left. Under the banner 'two colours, one people', they campaigned for equality of pay and improved housing, medical facilities and education. The UC won 25 seats in the Territorial Assembly elections in that same year, becoming the majority party on the General Council. Nine seats were held by Kanaks, including one by Roch Pidjot, the man who became known as the 'grandfather of the independence struggle'. He went on to become the first Kanak elected to the French National Assembly.

The nickel boom of the '50s and '60s brought prosperity but it also caused an imbalance in the country's way of life. Mines appeared everywhere, farmers became miners and Kanaks left their reservations, lured by work in the mines and the money it would bring in. The door was open for their entry to the industry, as Japanese workers had been forcibly expelled from the colony following the attack on Pearl Harbor and many of the Vietnamese and Indonesian workers had gradually been repatriated. By the late '60s a new wave of immigrants – neighbouring ni-Vanuatu (citizens of Vanuatu) and Polynesians from Wallis and Tahiti – arrived on the nickel bandwagon and Noumea went through its own population boom. Speculation on the housing market started and apartment blocks rose like rabbit

boxes, while away in the villages there was still no running water or electricity. Schools and offices were now open to Kanaks, but segregation and discrimination continued in other areas of society.

The boom harvested bitter fruits. The Kanaks wanted their land back while the Caldoches wanted to be free from a growing state administration run by people they didn't know. The administrators' Pacific paradise and privileged life was slipping away, and the stage was set for the violent political struggles of the next two decades.

The Independence Movement

Political consciousness was raised by the first Kanak university students, who returned from France in 1969 having witnessed the student protests in Paris the year before. One such student was Nidoish Naisseline, the son of the Chef of Mare, who formed the Foulards Rouges (Red Berets), a group which revalued Kanak culture and broke traditional taboos by such actions as walking into all-White cafés. They also reclaimed the word 'Kanak', until then used as a term of insult.

New political groups formed and, having witnessed independence in nearby Fiji and Papua New Guinea, they wanted more than the limited autonomy to which the UC had previously aspired. In 1975 the Caledonian Multi-Racial Union (UMNC) was the first party to demand total independence from France. Two years later, it changed its name to the Front Uni de Libération Kanak (FULK) and, with another pro-independence party, Parti de Libération Kanak (PALIKA), put independence and the important issue of restoration of Kanak land squarely on the agenda for the elections of 1977.

But by now, Kanaks were a minority in their own land. The immigration influx of the previous decade, coupled with the Kanaks' decline in population since European arrival meant that even if they were united for independence, they were still outnumbered.

The election of Socialist François Mitterrand to the French presidency in 1981 brought shock and fear to New Caledonia's

Caldoche community. Most Caldoches were supporters of the right-wing ruling party Rassemblement pour Calédonie dans la République (RPCR), set up in 1977 and led by multi-millionaire mining mogul Jacques Lafleur. It is affiliated to the French party Rassemblement pour la République (RPR). For the Kanaks, Mitterrand's rise looked like the end of 'the long night', to quote French historian Jean Chesneaux when he visited the same year. Prior to the 1981 election, the Socialists had promised that the Kanaks' right to self-determination would be respected once Mitterrand came to power.

By this stage, the Kanaks' lobby for reclaiming traditional land was well underway and had received a mixed reaction from the Caldoches. Some were prepared to sell out if the government instituted a plan and paid attractive prices, while others simply dug in. Sporadic violence between the settlers and Kanaks broke out. In September 1981, the UC general secretary, Pierre Declercq, was assassinated. Just over a year later, two members of the *gardes mobiles* (riot squad) were killed in a confrontation over the polluting of a local water supply by a sawmill. In 1983, round-table talks were held in France between the government and independence leaders, at which France accepted the 'innate and active right to independence of Kanak people'. In turn, the movement's leaders recognised that other communities in the territory, principally the Caldoches, were 'victims of history' and had as much right to live in New Caledonia as the Kanaks.

Les Évènements The turning point for the independence movement was 1984, the year in which *Les Évènements* (the Events), as the French refer to the next two years of widespread chaos, began.

1984 In this year, France mooted its Lemoine Plan, designed to give the territory five years of internal autonomy before a vote on self-determination in 1989. Thoroughly disillusioned with the French Socialists'

empty promises, several pro-independence parties merged to form a new movement, the Front de Libération Nationale Kanak et Socialiste, commonly called the FLNKS. Including the FULK, PALIKA and its largest single component, the UC, the FLNKS was seen as a legitimate mouthpiece for Melanesian *indépendantistes*, although it did not represent the opinions of all Kanaks. The UC president, Jean-Marie Tjibaou, was its first leader.

The party immediately decided to boycott the forthcoming territorial election and wage a militant campaign to disrupt it. On polling day, November 18, coconut trees were felled for roadblocks, two town halls were burnt down, ballot boxes were stolen, and Kanak elders summoned the rains to prevent voters from reaching polling stations. Voter turnout stood at 50%, a drop of 25% from the previous election, with the RPCR winning 34 of the 42 seats. A week later, the FLNKS proclaimed the Provisional Government of Kanaky, presided over by Tjibaou.

Just 10 days after the provisional government was set up, mixed-race settlers ambushed and massacred 10 Kanaks, including two brothers of Tjibaou, near the coastal village of Hienghene. Grief and tension was so great that the quadrennial Festival of Pacific Arts, due to be held in December in the capital, had to be cancelled. With Kanaks and Whites provoking each other and taking the law into their own hands, the whole country was on the brink of civil war.

1985 On 7 January, Edgard Pisani, the Special High Commissioner of New Caledonia, outlined French policy on the future of the territory. Known as the Pisani Plan, it included a referendum on independence in July 1985 and self-government 'in association' with France from 1986. All adults resident in the territory for the past three years would be able to vote. The plan was immediately rejected by the independence movement.

A few days later, a 17-year-old Caldoche youth was shot by Kanaks. The following day, one of the most radical FLNKS leaders,

Eloi Machoro, was killed by paramilitary marksmen near La Foa. Machoro, together with 200 supporters, had taken control of the entire nickel-mining town of Thio for three weeks just after the 1984 election and he was intensely hated by the right-wing. With the news of his assassination, pandemonium broke out and street riots spread all over New Caledonia. Paratroopers were flown in from France and a six-month state of emergency was declared, the first time such measures had been taken in a French-ruled territory since the 1961 insurrection in Algeria. A bomb ripped through central Noumea and the tensions between French and Kanaks began to seriously affect tourism.

Following these events, Pisani's plan was torpedoed and in April the French Prime Minister, Laurent Fabius, ushered in a new programme with land reforms and increased autonomy for Kanaks. Four regional councils were to be established at an election set for September. The main right-wing parties, the RPCR and the Front National, condemned the plan, saying that the distribution of seats would favour the indépendantistes. Prior to the election, they waged a strong political campaign, aided by French opposition heavyweight Jacques Chirac, and Jean-Marie Le Pen, the leader of France's ultra-right Front National, who both made flying visits to the territory. In general, Fabius' plan was well received by the FLNKS and, at the election, they won the three regional seats, while the RPCR kept control of the large Noumea-based electorate.

The Calm before the Storm

The French legislative elections were held in May 1986 and Chirac was made the new conservative prime minister. An uneasy calm prevailed as the new minister in charge of the territory, Bernard Pons, released his plan for New Caledonia's future. Some described it as paternalistic, others simply said it was patronising. It stripped the territory's four regional councils of much of their autonomy and abolished the office which had been buying back land for Kanaks. A referendum on the question of independence was sched-

uled for late 1987. The FLNKS wanted eligible voters to consist only of Kanaks and those people who were born in the territory with one parent also of New Caledonian birth. With a United Nation's resolution backing this demand, they decided, if France would not agree to it, that they would boycott the referendum. Bernard Pons described the demand as 'ridiculous'.

By now rifts had begun to appear in the FLNKS, and the leader of the militant FULK faction, Yann Uregei, went on a highly controversial visit to Libya to attend an international conference on liberation movements. However, the party received important backing in August 1986 when the South Pacific Forum's 13-member nations met in Suva, Fiji, and decided to support the FLNKS's bid to get New Caledonia re-inscribed on the UN's decolonisation list (from which it had been removed in a unilateral move by France in 1947). In December of the same year, the UN's General Assembly voted 89 to 24 in favour of the territory's re-inscription. It was an important step towards independence, as it gave international credence to the territory's 'inalienable right to self-determination' and, moreover, required France to supply reports to the UN on moves towards self-rule. France interpreted the UN vote as interference in its territorial affairs and, in anger at the outcome, expelled the Australian consul general from New Caledonia on the grounds that he had played a leading role in the affair.

On 13 September 1987, the referendum on independence was held and was boycotted by 84% of Kanaks. Of the 59% of eligible voters who cast a ballot (which included everyone who had lived in the country for more than three years, such as all the nickel boom immigrants of the '60s and '70s, 98% were against independence. The referendum was trumpeted as a resounding victory by loyalists in the territory and the conservative French government. But both the Australian and New Zealand governments issued public statements against jubilation, the former warning that 'as a significant proportion of the population did not express their views, the referendum could serve to deepen the divisions between the territory's communities'.

What certainly did deepen the division was the result of the preliminary trial of the seven men charged with murdering the 10 Kanaks at Hienghene in 1984. In October, the examining magistrate ruled that they had acted in 'self-defence' and would not stand trial. In December, the FLNKS deputy leader, Yeiwene Yeiwene, was arrested on charges of inciting violence and murder after he made a 'call to arms' following the release of the seven men. His call was meant as a warning for Kanaks to arm themselves for self-defence and, after a public outcry, Yeiwene was released.

The Storm

The French National Assembly approved a new Pons plan for the territory put forward by Chirac's government in January 1987, and called an election for 24 April 1988, the same day as the first round of voting for the French presidency. The new plan redefined the four regional council boundaries so that the Kanaks were likely to lose one region and be left with the country's most underdeveloped and resourceless area.

After years of trying to preach a policy of peace, and the rejection of their proposals by France, the FLNKS announced its 'muscular mobilisation' campaign. Tjibaou explained the Kanaks' decision to turn to violence: 'We are on a battlefield and we are just dead people awaiting our turn to die. The balance of power is such that if we didn't have international support, the colonial power could wipe us out'.

The Ouvea Crisis

In April 1988, a group of militant Kanaks seized the gendarmerie on the tiny Loyauté island of Ouvea. Four gendarmes were killed and the rest taken hostage. They were kept in a cave while negotiations were carried out. Three days before the French presidential election, the military launched an assault on the cave, leaving 19 Kanaks dead. The assault was widely condemned as a political 'adventure'

Jean-Marie Tjibaou

We are from here and nowhere else. You are from here but also from somewhere else.
– Tjibaou, 1983, addressing RPCR leader, Jacques Lafleur

Jean-Marie Tjibaou was a contemporary version of past great Kanak chiefs. As tradition in their ancient oral culture demanded, he was first and foremost a man of words. To go into violent confrontation was something he agreed to as a last resort. His belief in peace, as with many martyrs of this genre, is what cost him his life.

Born in the village of Tiendanite on Grande Terre's north-east coast in 1936, Tjibaou was exposed early to the repression of colonialism. Under the indigénat code, people of his village were forced to work on road gangs or in settlers' fields. 'The gendarmes regularly took a certain number of men each month...there was a guard with a truncheon and a gun to make the people work'.

Like a few of his contemporaries in the independence movement, Tjibaou went to university in Paris in the late '60s to study sociology. Already a Catholic priest, he abandoned the

by Jacques Chirac in a last-minute bid to gain popular public support for his challenge to Mitterrand's presidency. It failed. The Socialists were returned to power in France and a concerted effort was made to end the bloodshed in New Caledonia.

The Matignon Accords On 26 June, 1988, the newly elected French Prime Minister, Michel Rocard, brokered the Matignon Accords, an historic peace agreement signed in Paris by the two New Caledonian leaders, the FLNKS's Jean-Marie Tjibaou and the RPCR's Jacques Lafleur. 'Peace at last or a recipe for ruin?' is how one media headline voiced the question on everyone's lips following its signing at the Hôtel Matignon, the Prime Minister's office.

Under the accords, it was agreed that New Caledonia would be divided into three regions – the Noumean-based South Province and the North and Loyauté islands Provinces. The latter two would both be likely to come under Kanak control in an election. Economic development would target Kanak

areas and amnesty was granted for all political offences (excluding murder) carried out before the accords were signed. The accords stated that referendum on self-determination would be held in 10 years' time, with all New Caledonians established on the territory by 1988, and their descendants, eligible to vote. With this freezing of the electoral role, Kanaks could be in the majority by 1998, but that is not a certainty, just as the accords are no guarantee of independence.

The big difference between the accords and previous agreements is that a change of government in France cannot mean the scrapping of the planned 1998 referendum, as one of the accords' demands was that a referendum on the issue be held in France. If successful, the French government would be locked into the 1998 referendum. Four months after the accords were signed, a very lethargic one-third of French voters went to the ballot box – 80% of them voted 'yes' to the accords.

Back in New Caledonia, the Matignon Accords were both hailed and cursed. Many saw them as a trade-off, with the FLNKS

priesthood on his return home. 'You cannot take up a stand for your brothers without questioning the role of the official church', he explained. He worked with young people in training programmes and promoted Kanak culture. As the elected mayor of Hienghene, one of his goals was to instil an entrepreneurial spirit into Kanaks. His town benefited from experiments such as a catering school, cultural centre and a co-op store. In 1975 he organised Melanesia 2000, a landmark cultural festival which gathered 2000 Kanaks from clans all over New Caledonia to Noumea.

With Yeiwene Yeiwene, Eloi Machoro, Pierre Declercq (all killed) and François Burke, Tjibaou entered national politics in 1977, when the Union Calédonienne stopped calling for greater autonomy and instead started demanding independence from France. In 1984 he was elected first president of the FLNKS, a party calling for immediate independence and one which was prepared to act more radically than any of those in the past to achieve it. The personal toll to Tjibaou was heavy. Two of his brothers were killed in the Hienghene massacre late that year and, a month later, his fellow leader, Eloi Machoro, was gunned down by French police.

Tjibaou's signing of the historic Matignon Accords in 1988 brought relative peace to the troubled territory. But a much-publicised photo of Tjibaou and fellow signatory, Jacques Lafleur, shaking hands was to sow the seed of discontent and, on 4 May 1989, Tjibaou was assassinated with his deputy, Yeiwene Yeiwene. The two leaders were given state funerals attended by foreign dignitaries, including the then prime minister of France, Michel Rocard. Their coffins were draped with FLNKS flags. Tjibaou was buried at Tiendanite alongside his tribal and blood brothers who were killed in the Hienghene massacre. Yeiwene was buried at Tadine, his hometown on Mare.

Known amongst his friends as a poet and a fine singer, Tjibaou, the father of four boys and an adopted daughter, was often described by journalists as a 'spiritual man, a visionary'. As one correspondent wrote: 'No matter how turbulent and violent the events around him, he seemed an oasis of calm and inspiration. He was determined to achieve independence...but with the least sacrifice for his people'. ∎

accepting a delay in its desired timetable for independence and the RPCR almost admitting to the inevitability of New Caledonia's being cut off from France.

The Assassinations On 4 May 1989, Jean-Marie Tjibaou and his second in command, Yeiwene Yeiwene, were assassinated. They were shot while attending a tribal gathering on Ouvea to mark the end of the mourning period for the 19 Kanaks killed during the hostage crisis. Their murderers were local Kanaks, supporters of FULK, who believed that the FLNKS leaders had sold out by signing the Matignon Accords. This time the shock and grief did not promote violence. Instead, throughout the country tears flowed. The two men were given a state funeral attended by many foreign dignitaries.

Towards Kanaky
The assassinations were the last acts of political violence to shake New Caledonia. With the loss of its leaders, the FLNKS went through turmoil and the FULK, which had continually opposed the Matignon Accords, left the umbrella organisation. Eventually Paul Neaoutyine, a PALIKA member from the tribal village of St Michel near Poindimie, was elected to replace Tjibaou as FLNKS's president, a position he still holds. The new leadership expressed the FLNKS's continued support for the Matignon Accords, but reiterated the movement's long-standing demand that the 1998 referendum be conducted in accordance with UN principles – that is, only Kanaks and long-term settlers be allowed to vote. These days, the party is highly fractured and Neaoutyine faces the task of keeping them together long enough to work on New Caledonia's becoming an independent Kanaky.

One of the biggest recent threats to the Matignon Accords was the ADRAF Scandal which surfaced in 1989, uncovering loyalists corruptly using the territory's Land & Rural Development Agency (ADRAF). Set up in 1986 under the Fabius plan, the agency was to negotiate land claims by Whites and Kanaks after many Caldoches, with compen-sation from the government, agreed to sell their properties. While most Whites' applications were settled, the majority of Kanak claims were not. In addition, and the focus of the scandal, one of the men involved in the Hienghene massacre sold his property through the agency for 42% more than its estimated value and then received a discount to relocate on land close to Noumea.

As agreed in the accords, France has been pouring money into construction and infrastructure in an attempt to 'rebalance' the territory's economy and give a greater share of resources to Kanaks. Electricity and telephones have started being installed in remote villages and 400 'mostly Melanesian' public servants have been sent to France for training. At grass-roots level, many Kanaks believe they're being paid off to keep the status quo. The lull imposed by France is designed to maintain the calm while the real power stays with the French. Discrimination and exploitation still exist. Secondary and higher education teaching and white collar jobs are still generally reserved for or accessible only to Whites, and many Kanaks working in the nickel smelter in Noumea live in polluted low-income housing ghettos.

With several years still to go before the promised referendum, its reality is already in review. The buzz word now in right-wing and even some pro-independence circles is '*consensus*', a vague term introduced in 1991 by Jacques Lafleur when calling for the abandonment of the 1998 referendum. A consensus solution would give New Caledonia greater autonomy while retaining links with France. It is modelled on Pacific nations such as the Cook Islands, an internally self-governing island territory of New Zealand.

Political camps are no longer split on racial lines. Some Whites and Kanaks want independence, others don't and there are fears on both sides about what will happen once France turns off the financial tap. That tap is dependent on nickel, which seems to be the main reason France won't let go of the territory. Conservative calculations say there's enough nickel to mine for at least another 10 to 15 years. Will Kanaks have to wait for New Caledonia to be stripped clean before it becomes Kanaky?

GEOGRAPHY

New Caledonia is in the south-west Pacific Ocean, just north of the Tropic of Capricorn. It is made up of an archipelago comprising the main island, Grande Terre (16,350 sq km), which is surrounded by the world's second-largest reef; Île des Pins (152 sq km); the Loyauté islands (1980 sq km); and the tiny Belep Islands. Scattered round it at considerable distances are various dependencies – the Entrecasteaux and Chesterfield reefs, Walpole Island and the small volcanic Matthew and Hunter islands (both disputed territory) – in all totalling four sq km. The whole of New Caledonia covers a land area of 18,580 sq km.

The territory is located roughly between the latitudes of 18° to 23° south and longitudes of 158° to 172° east. Some 900 km separate the northern Entrecasteaux reefs from Walpole Island in the south-east, while 1000 km lie between the Chesterfields in the north-west and the easternmost Loyauté island, Mare.

New Caledonia's closest neighbour is Vanuatu (its capital, Port Vila, is 527 km north-east of Noumea). The two are separated by the Vanuatu Trench, which reaches depths of around 8000 metres. Further north are the Solomon Islands, while Fiji sits 1200 km east towards Polynesia. West across the Coral Sea is Australia's nearest town, Bundaberg, 1500 km from Noumea; Sydney is 1978 km south-west. About 800 km to the south is the Australian territory of Norfolk Island; another 1000 km farther south is New Zealand's nearest port of call, Auckland. Paris sits past the horizon more than 18,000 km away.

Grande Terre

This cigar-shaped mountainous island, 400 km long and 50 km wide, is the fourth largest in the South Pacific, after the islands of New Zealand and Papua New Guinea. The shape has been compared to a sea mammal followed by her young – the little Île des Pins.

In contrast to many Pacific islands, Grande Terre was not created by volcanic activity. One of the oldest Pacific islands, it was part of Gondwanaland, the ancient continent that held present-day Africa, South America, Antarctica, the Indian subcontinent, Australia and New Zealand together. Grande Terre and New Zealand broke away from eastern Australia about 140 million years ago and, 80 million years later, Grande Terre went its own way. About 40 million years ago the actual geological structure was laid when the Indo-Australian plate dived under the Pacific tectonic plate. Grande Terre began slowly to submerge, reefs built up and a huge lagoon was created.

The island lies at a south-east to north-west angle and is divided by central mountain ranges. The rugged interior has dense vegetation and fog-bound peaks, the highest being Mt Panie (1628 metres) on the north-east coast between Hienghene and Pouebo, and Mt Humboldt (1618 metres) in the south-east. From this mountain chain, numerous rivers make their way to the sea, causing sudden floods in the wet season.

Grande Terre's two long coasts couldn't be more different. The east coast is wet and lush, untamed and rocky, with waterfalls and fast-flowing rivers tumbling down the mountain sides and a shoreline cut by narrow but deep estuaries. In contrast, the west coast is dry and windy, with wide, grassy coastal plains stretching from the mountain foothills to large but shallow coastal bays. The bays are lined with mangrove forests and inaccessible, mosquito-infested beaches. Southern Grande Terre is mainly an iron plateau, 250 metres high, with small natural lakes and marshes linked by streams.

Grande Terre is rich in minerals as it is partly covered by peridotite, a green bedrock layer normally found 30 to 60 km below ground, which contains much chrome, nickel and platinum ore.

Offshore Islands

The Loyauté islands and Île des Pins originated from a chain of submarine volcanoes, inactive for the past 10 million years, which were situated on the eastern border of the Australian plate. All are now highly porous, uplifted coral islands created after the old volcanoes sank and the reef rose around them. The Loyauté islands are essentially flat and have no rivers. Freshwater is caught in water tables and does not mix with the surrounding seawater because of the difference in their densities. Île des Pins has a few low hills and some streams.

The Reef

Second in size only to Australia's Great Barrier Reef, New Caledonia's main barrier reef *(récif* in French) encompasses Grande Terre. Its western side is 600 km long while the eastern flank extends for 540 km. In all, the reef measures 8000 sq km and encloses a magnificent 23,500-sq-km turquoise lagoon, around 25 metres deep on the west coast and averaging 40 metres in depth on the east. Occasionally the barrier reef is interrupted by underwater valleys, the remains of old river beds, which can drop to 80 metres. These breaks expose the shore to the ocean's swell, resulting in some interesting coastal rock formations. In addition to the barrier reef, close-to-shore fringing reefs surround all the smaller outlying islands.

Even during the lowest tides, the living coral reefs are covered by 10 to 20 cm of water. In cases where the reef has grown up and eventually broken above the water level, the coral dies, marine debris collects on the

flat surface and what is known as a coral cay is formed. Over the years, waves pound the coral and break it down to sand. Once these sandy cays are stable, birds nest on them, providing the fertiliser for hardy plants to take hold and grow. Some, such as coconuts, are washed ashore; others are inadvertently transported as seeds by birds.

CLIMATE

Sitting on the edge of the tropics, New Caledonia is sometimes referred to in tourist brochures as the 'land of eternal spring'. It has a temperate, oceanic climate and seasons alter little as ocean breezes level the temperature. From mid-November to mid-April it is warm and humid, with tropical depressions sometimes developing into cyclones.

Maximum temperatures vary between 22°C and 28°C, and minimums range from 11°C to 17°C. The average is around 23°C. February is the hottest month while the coolest are July and August. Grande Terre's mountains and the plateaux of Mare, Lifou and Île des Pins can cool off to 5°C or 8°C on clear winter nights. Humidity sticks to around 75% for most of the year, peaking between February and April, when it can rise to 80%. It is at its lowest in the early afternoon and highest in the early morning and late afternoon.

Both torrential rains and drought have been known to strike at any time of the year. There is no dry season, as rain is adequate all year and abundant from February to late April. This is when the clouds can hang low and threaten for much of the day and the mosquitoes rage. From May it's drier and gradually becomes cooler, with more clear days. In mid-September temperatures start to pick up.

Rainfall is not uniform throughout Grande Terre. The central mountain chain plays an important role in determining how much rain the different areas get. The windward east coast receives twice as much rain (up to 4000 mm a year) as the west coast, which lies in a 'rain shadow' and annually records less than 1000 mm. The average rainfall is 1413 mm per year.

Moderate-to-strong trade winds blow for more than 200 days a year while the sun's schedule varies little, rising at about 6 am, setting around 6 pm and shining, on average, for 2575 hours per year.

Cyclones

Tropical cyclones are low pressure systems that build up into highly devastating forces, with winds rotating clockwise around an 'eye', heavy seas and torrential rain. The ocean temperature must be around 28°C to generate a cyclone (called hurricanes or typhoons in some parts of the world). Therefore, the cyclone season is mainly in summer from December to March, but they can show up a month on either side of this. Usually gaining momentum over the Coral Sea to the north-west of New Caledonia (though they can also come from east of the Solomons), they move south to south-east, ending up either on the Australian coast or anywhere in the Pacific from New Caledonia to Samoa.

Unlike neighbouring Vanuatu and Fiji, New Caledonia has been spared the devastation of a major cyclone during the past decade. However, every year at least one cyclone comes close enough to make its presence felt, such as in April 1989, when Bourail was flooded. When these storms do cross land, nature is at its most fierce. Niaouli trees are stripped of their bark, and falling coconuts and flying sheets of corrugated iron pose great dangers, as do the huge waves that pound the coastline. Any vessel in the region moves to the shelter of Noumea's protected harbour.

When a cyclone is heading towards the country, a rating one warning is issued 24 hours before it is due to strike. Within four hours of crossing land, a cyclone warning two is announced over radio and TV. Most recently, in April 1993, Noumea was up to a 'cyclone two' alert when Cyclone Prema approached with gusts of up to 250 km per hour. It miraculously changed course only 100 km offshore from the Loyauté islands and headed out to sea. At times like this, shops and industries must close, some houses are evacuated and many residents fix diagonal strips of tape to their windows to lessen the chance of flying glass should a pane smash.

FLORA & FAUNA

New Caledonia's flora & fauna originated in eastern Gondwanaland. When Grande Terre became separated 80 million years ago, they evolved in isolation and, as a result, the country has a noteworthy number of unique species of plants, animals and, especially, birds. From the 35 araucaria tree species recorded worldwide, 13 are endemic here. The nautilus (a type of mollusc) which lives

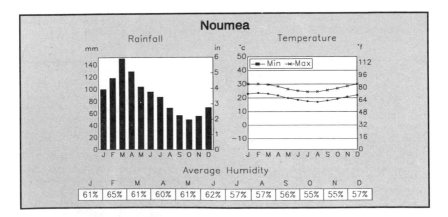

in the waters here is native, as are 30% of the country's birds, some spiders, geckos, freshwater snails and shrimps.

Botanists claim that the vegetation resembles, as closely as possible, that which existed in tropical regions in the beginning of the Tertiary Era (60 million years ago). The extreme biodiversity is caused by Grande Terre's central mountain range. It has created a variety of niches, landforms and microclimates where endemic species thrive, and sometimes a species will be confined to a small mountainous area with only a single known population.

Flora

Despite its small size, New Caledonia is exceptionally rich in original flora. Of the 3250 flowering plant species, 80% are native.

Forests

A great deal of New Caledonia has been stripped of its virgin forest and, sadly, certain species of trees have disappeared forever. At present, 400,000 hectares, or 20% of the land, is still covered by indigenous forest.

The exploitation began in the 1840s with sandalwood hunters. In a 15-year peak period, about 8000 tonnes were cut. Over the last 50 years 1000 tonnes of sandalwood have been removed. Another tree used commercially was the kauri *(kaori* in French), the gum of which was used as a component in varnishes until it was superseded by synthetics. Kauris were taken from the Rivière Bleue region and shipped to Australia. After WW II, bulldozers and cables were imported and forests were logged at a fluctuating rate, averaging 10,000 cubic metres per year. In 1993 five work sites were in operation.

Reforestation is often obstructed by discussions over land ownership. When a company has finished its operations, whether it be forestry or mining, the Kanaks claim back the land. In general, the company gives it back in the damaged state. In the past, small-scale, unsuccessful reforestation was carried out with pine, but the soil proved unsuitable and the climate too warm and wet.

Trees

Some noticeable trees you'll come across include:

Araucaria columnaris From the araucaria family, this columnar pine can stand an impressive 60 metres in height and has a diameter of two metres. Its natural habitat is the coast, and it was this tree which prompted Captain Cook to name the island south of Grande Terre the Isle of Pines. Used for making pirogues and in carpentry, it was planted in many Kanak villages; isolated patches of these trees in mountainous regions point to old settlements. In Kanak symbolism this tree has male status.

Banyan (Ficus prolixa) Typical of the tropics, this huge tree from the fig/rubber family has a wide canopy and big aerial roots. A banyan starts as a seed dropped by a bird or the wind into another tree. Its roots descend from the branches to the soil, encircling and eventually strangling the host tree. The roots are used for pirogue floats, while cricket balls are made from its sap.

Niaouli Tree

The *niaouli* tree *(Melaleuca quinquenervia)* is predominant along Grande Terre's west coast. This melaleuca is a common tree in Australia, where it is called the paperbark. It is part of the myrtle family and akin to honey myrtles, tea trees and bottle brushes. This white-flowering tree needs fire to propagate, but at the same time resists the flames thanks to its multi-layered paperbark. It is credited with preserving soil in a land threatened by bushfires and erosion. Not a dominant tree, it will disappear when there's competition, and dry conditions limit its growth. It can flower when only 20 cm high.

The tree's pliable bark peels off easily and is used to insulate the walls and roofs of traditional Kanak huts. The leaves contain essential oils, often used to treat bronchitis. *Gomenol*, a local medicinal essence, is also made from it. About 130 kg of leaves are needed to extract one litre of essence. The leaves brew into a fragrant herbal tea when steeped in boiling water. ■

Black tree Known in French as *arbre noir*, this tree used to be grown as shade covering for coffee plants to protect them from the harsh summer sun which caused a leaf disease. The slender trunk is fanned by a wide canopy that is very reminiscent of African acacias.

Coconut tree (Cocos nucifera) This tropical palm grows in regions where the average temperature does not drop below 20°C. It predominates on islands and along coastlines and can bear 80 to 125 nuts a year. The very large nut is embedded in a fibrous husk and when harvested, its flesh is used to make copra. It is just one of the 30 palm species growing in New Caledonia.

Gaïac (Acacia spirorbis) This little tree is found in the upper level of low-altitude sclerophyll forest. Its heart wood is very hard and is often used for making fence poles.

Ironwood (Casuarina collina) This tree has a very hard heartwood that is heavier than water.

Kauri (Agathis lanceolata) From the araucaria family, this conifer is heavily forested for its good-quality wood which is supple, light and without knots. It's one of the giants of the forest.

Niaouli (See the aside on Niaouli trees.)

Pandanus From the Malay word *pandan*, these trees are mostly found along the seashore and on rocky cliffs. The trunk is rarely forked but has many stilt-roots. Some species have edible nuts. Its leaves are used for weaving hats, mats and baskets.

Tamanou (Calophyllum montanum) An endemic tree with very hard and heavy timber, it is impervious to water and therefore used for wharf construction.

Plant Communities Some types of vegetation found on Grande Terre include:

Coastal flora Mangroves, found mostly on the west coast, cover nearly half of the island's shoreline. Found in shallow water, these trees grow in tidal zones and have special adaptations, such as aerial and stilt-roots with minimal evaporation. Behind the mangroves, or alternatively the beach, is a small protective band of casuarina, acacia, pandanus and pine, while the estuary forests have rosewood, sandalwood, vines, pines, kohu and bluewood.

Savane à niaoulis Also called a woody or niaouli savannah, this type of open grassland, predominant on the west coast, was established with human help when the land was cleared and burned to make cattle country. The tree most frequently found growing here is the niaouli but, without human intervention, the more dominant gaïac, ironwood and gum oak would take over. These savannahs are sometimes cut by rainforest in river valleys or along estuaries.

Humid evergreen forest Found at a middle-to-high altitudes (300 to 1500 metres), these regions are exposed to dominant winds and contain kauri, pine, araucaria, tamanou, houp, oak, beech and acacia. Though they are fragile environments rich in endemic species, these forests are still the main source of timber.

Sclerophyll forest This is a low forest found along the west coast (but much replaced by cattle farming) where dry conditions prevail. Their leaves are hard, thereby minimising evaporation. Ouen Toro in Noumea is one good example of this forest.

Maquis minier Also known as serpentine scrub, this diverse community covers 30% of Grande Terre and consists of a variety of trees and shrubs which thrive in soils that are poor in major elements but have an abnormal concentration of heavy minerals. This is especially so in the south, where the mineral-rich soil has created an adapted flora where few other species can compete.

Land Fauna

So far, 4500 species of terrestrial animal life have been identified in New Caledonia, mainly consisting of birds, reptiles and some mammals.

Mammals Of the few land mammals, only roussettes (members of the flying fox or fruit bat family) are indigenous. Found on all the islands, roussettes are large nocturnal creatures that live in trees and fly out at sunset. They are a traditional Kanak food source, although hunting is restricted in all areas and is illegal at nesting or sleeping sites.

All other creatures have been introduced. The first pigs and dogs to set foot here were given as gifts by Captain Cook to his tribal hosts. Their numbers were later reinforced with the arrival of missionaries, who also brought donkeys to carry their supplies. These days, donkeys are found only on Mare. The English trader James Paddon is thought to have introduced the first horses and cattle to Grande Terre, while deer were imported from the Philippines in 1870, as the governor's wife had a penchant for hunting. Polynesian rats and feral cats have also made their way in.

Birds With an estimated 68 species of birds, about 20 of which are indigenous, New Caledonia holds the interest of ornithologists and simple bird lovers alike. The most renowned indigenous species is the cagou.

The native bird most in danger of extinction is the Ouvea crested parakeet *(Eunymphicus cornutus uveansis)*, numbering a meagre 10 couples. Its brilliant green/yellow plumage is crowned by a splash of deep red just above the beak, and a green crest. Living only on Ouvea, the bird is highly prized by international bird collectors and, despite laws protecting it against capture and a ban on its commercial sale, authorities have been unable to stop them from being smuggled out, either on yachts or in the hand-luggage of plane passengers. Unless a much publicised anti-smuggling campaign launched in 1993 is successful, this beautiful bird will go the way of many other now-extinct species.

Another bird that you may (with luck) see is the rare peregrine falcon, capable of reaching speeds of 350 km/h when diving after prey.

Huge groups of magnificent frigate birds glide above the coastline forewarning the villagers below of bad weather. With the longest wingspan (229 cm), in proportion to weight, of all birds, they are somehow reminiscent of the prehistoric pterodactyl.

Other birds include doves and pigeons, such as the large indigenous *notou* or imperial pigeon *(Ducula goliath)*, whose numbers are becoming 'vulnerable'. More common are bastard nightingales *(Megalurulus)* and black honeyeaters *(Meliphagus)*, egrets, rails (marsh birds), red-beaked finches and various types of green parakeets. Small turquoise kingfishers perch on power lines. Turkeys were introduced.

Reptiles New Caledonian snakes are mainly of the marine variety (though one sea snake species is amphibious – see the Sea Snakes section). On land, there are two blind snake species and a rare harmless boa, found only on the Loyauté islands and introduced as a food source by Polynesian immigrants in the 16th century.

When swimming, there's no need to worry about crocodiles. Only one salt-water croc

---

The Cagou

A stocky, flightless bird with soft, silky-grey plumage, the cagou or kagu *(Rhynocetos jubatus)* is New Caledonia's national bird. Sadly, like the Ouvea crested parakeet, it has made the endangered species list, as dogs and feral cats can easily outrun and kill it, while wild pigs disturb its food habitat. In 1993, only an estimated 700 birds existed; however a successful breeding programme is being carried out in the Rivière Bleue park east of Noumea and it's hoped their numbers will rise. You're unlikely to see one in the wild.

Standing 50 cm tall, this plump nocturnal bird with red eyes and an orange beak is most noted for its cry, which is reminiscent of a dog's bark and made only in the early morning usually around 4 am. When startled or protecting their young, cagous spread wide their wings, which are laced with dark grey-and-white stripes, and raise their silky top-knot crest.

Living in isolated pairs in damp rain forest or at slightly higher altitudes, they feed on worms, snails and insects. Once or twice a year, one egg is laid. It takes a month to hatch, after which both parents raise the baby. ■

has ever found its way to New Caledonia and that was a little guy from the Solomons who apparently lost his direction during a storm.

Several species of skinks get around but the one you're most likely to encounter is the gecko – the name comes from GEC-KO, the sound made by a common African species. An insectivorous nocturnal lizard, it has little affixing disks with microscopic hooks (unlike tree frogs with suction pads) that help it to master walls and ceilings. These friendly little creatures, with pale skin and wide eyes, come out in the evening to feast on moths and mosquitoes and are frequent guests in hotel rooms. Consider yourself lucky to have one as they do their best to catch everything that moves.

Another gecko, though one you're much less likely to spot, is the endemic giant gecko *(Rhacodactylus leachianus)*. Some 35 cm long, excluding its tail, it takes the world title for the biggest gecko. The only larger known species was a gecko (extinct but skeletal remains have been found) that lived in New Zealand up until the 18th century. New Caledonia's giant gecko lives in rainforest areas and is active at night.

Other Creatures Possibly the most noticeable of all New Caledonia's land creatures is the Giant African snail, a huge introduced mollusc which is now in plague proportions (take note: it's illegal to take their shells into Australia). Another, much less abundant, mollusc is the edible snail found only on the forest floor of Île des Pins.

Only one frog species exists. Something else to watch out for is the coconut crab *(Birgus latro)*. These large blue-grey crabs have been eaten to extinction on some Pacific islands and are considered rare in New Caledonia. However, this doesn't prevent them from being on many tourist menus on the Loyauté islands and Île des Pins. Slow growers, they can take 30 years to reach a weight of two kg. They live close to the water, in coral outcrops or in burrows, and come out at night to feed on the flesh of coconuts. How they crack open a coconut is something of a mystery. Some people say

they simply use their enormous pincers to crack the nut, while others believe they climb a coconut palm and cut off a few nuts, some of which will crack open when they hit the ground. While both scenarios seem incredible, one of them must be true. The crab then spends hours prising open the split nut and a day or two to devour it. This devotion to coconut has made them easy pickings. Loyauté islanders simply halve a coconut, attach it to a stick that's firmly dug into the ground and come back to collect the crab at night when it is feasting.

Marine Life
In what has been described as the world's largest lagoon, New Caledonia's waters are rich with sea fauna in what can only be described as an amazing spectacle of colour and form. As ocean life has few restrictive boundaries, about 80% of the species found here also exist along Australia's Great Barrier Reef. Reef sharks, stingrays, turtles, dugongs, dolphins, colourful gorgonian coral, sponges, colourful sea cucumbers and a multitude of diverse molluscs, including trocchus *(troca* in French), cowrie and cone shells, giant clams, squid and the beautiful nautilus, all thrive in these waters.

Marine Mammals Many large ocean creatures live in or pass through the lagoon at various times of the year. Humpback and mink whales are sometimes seen with their young in winter months, having come up to escape the harsh Antarctic waters. They migrate along the Vanuatu Trench and appear occasionally in the southern part of the lagoon and around Île des Pins and the Loyauté islands. In the 19th century they were heavily hunted for their blubber, which was used as lamp oil until it was replaced by kerosene.

The gentle, seemingly overweight dugong (or sea cow, as it's also called) is an endangered animal protected, except for limited hunting by Kanaks, by New Caledonian laws. Dugongs feed on seaweed and sea grass. Attempts are being made to count their population by enlisting the cooperation of fishers and pilots, the people most likely to see these timid creatures.

Fish Only underwater guidebooks would attempt to go into the stunning variety of 2000 fish species that thrive in New Caledonian waters. Schools of small but intensely colourful species stay close to coral outcrops, while at high tide many bigger, less vibrant-looking mullet, trevally and garfish ride in on the swell.

Common and very comic are the several species of clownfish *(Amphiprion)*, most often orange with white or blue stripes but sometimes a deep blue with white stripes. They hide between the waving, poisonous tentacles of sea anemones, watching and waiting until, if you come close enough, their curiosity overcomes them and they dart at you in a humorous display of daring ferocity. A veritable rainbow of parrot fish *(Scarus)* and clown triggerfish *(Balistoides)* can be seen propelling themselves rapidly through the water. You may see the flat yellow butterfly fish *(Chaetodon)*, which often have a false eye to fool attackers. Be aware of the perfectly camouflaged stonefish *(Synancea)*, which dwells in muddy water and has 13 spines that inject a potentially fatal poison if stood upon. Closely related, equally as venomous but much more beautiful is the flashy lionfish *(Pterois lunulata)*.

Sea Snakes New Caledonia's 12 species of sea snakes are oxygen-breathing reptiles that are often sighted on the water's surface or on land. Well adapted to the sea, they have a flattened, paddle-like tail and airtight nostrils and can stay underwater for up to an hour searching for food. Their poison is particularly potent. Luckily for divers and snorkellers, they're generally curious but not aggressive, unless they are deliberately provoked or when protecting their nest.

The one you'll come across the most, and also the most poisonous, is the amphibious *tricot rayé* or striped jersey *(Laticauda semifasciata)*. It has black and beige stripes and spends as much time in the water as out,

curled up near a rock or under a bush. Divers are known to touch them but their poison is deadly (and there's no serum), so if you see one it's best to heed a local saying: 'Leave them alone and they'll do likewise. If you kill one, it'll bring bad weather'.

A much bigger and intensely curious sea snake is the beige snake *(Aypisurus laevis)*, which can grow up to two metres long. Divers sometimes find them peering in their masks with the tip of their tongue persistently investigating the rim.

Other Sea Creatures Three sea turtle species live and nest throughout the territory – the loggerhead, green and hawksbill turtles (for details see the aside on Sea Turtles). Unfortunately these rare and threatened creatures still crop up on tourist menus on Île des Pins despite being restricted as food sources for Kanaks alone.

Green Turtle

With a smorgasbord of preferred food, sharks in New Caledonian waters rarely pose problems to swimmers or divers. They'll watch you and, depending on how you interpret their look, may appear hungry, but it's likely there'll be no problem as long as you don't threaten them. Species which stay in relatively shallow waters include blacktipped and white-tipped reef sharks, usually about 1½ metres long, and larger grey reef sharks. Across the reef in deeper waters are whale and tiger sharks; you don't want to come too close to the latter.

Though their feeding habits are different, rays are basically steamrollered sharks and they're often seen by snorkellers or divers. Indeed, for divers, the ultimate experience can be a close encounter with a colossal manta ray as it wings past in search of small fish. Stingrays hover or lie on the sand in shallow lagoons and are well camouflaged. They move away as soon as they sense your presence, but be careful not to tread on one as you're walking out to snorkel, as they can whip their tail around and strike you with its poisonous barb.

Moray eels *(Muraena)* peer out from dark coral cavities, while last but not least there are marvellously gracious sea horses *(Hippocampus)*, seen mainly by night divers.

Coral Coral is what makes a reef and, though thought for many centuries to be some form of flowering plant, it is in fact an animal. Both hard and soft corals exist, their common denominator being that they are made up of polyps – tiny cylinders ringed by waving tentacles that sting their prey and draw it into the stomach. During the day, corals retract into this tube and only at night do they display their real colours. Hard coral is distinguished by its external skeleton of excreted lime – this is what actually forms the reef. When one polyp dies, another builds on top of its skeleton and gradually the reef grows.

There are many different coral types: brain corals are big, round and bulbous, staghorn corals have many extending arms, while sheet, commonly called plate coral, grows wide and flat. A huge coral outcrop is known as a 'bommie'. To exist, coral needs saltwater that never drops below 17.5°C, and it must be clear in order for the sun to penetrate. Coral can't grow below 30 metres as it lives in symbiosis with algae, which transform sunlight into a substance used by the coral to build up its skeleton; the algae then eliminate the coral's waste.

Once a year, at the beginning of summer, all the corals spawn, releasing their eggs which rise to the surface in a spectacular array of colour – the Caledonians call this time the 'season of the flowering coral'. One of the special places in New Caledonia for large, fragile corals is the sheltered Baie de Prony, a favoured site amongst divers.

Molluscs The mollusc family is wide and diverse, ranging from sea shells to clams, squid, octopus, nautili and nudibranches. Combined, they form some of the most colourful elements on the reef.

Shell collectors will feel in paradise. That said, they can be disruptive to the reef's fragile environment, so please, tread carefully and don't remove any shells – enjoy them where they are. Pick up only those that are empty, as even shells abandoned by their original inhabitant may now house a little hermit crab.

Cowries, strombs and volutes are the most common shells, but prehistoric nautili often wash up on the beaches after a storm. Beware of picking up any cone shells (marine snails), in particular *Conus geographus*, which has a lethal sting. Many local people dive for shells such as the whirled trocchus, and eat the mollusc inside. Big Triton's shells (commonly called conches), are the ones found impaled on the flèches faîtières. There is one endemic shell, the highly prized black cowrie, renowned for its abnormally dark coloration and found in the southern parts of the west coast.

Nudibranches are naked sea slugs that discard their shells in favour of a riot of colour. Australian underwater specialist Neville Coleman refers to them as either 'gaudy little sea slugs' or 'butterflies of the sea'. They are found in the country's southern waters.

Clams are twin-lobbed shells. The best known is the giant clam *(Tridacna gigas)*, the largest known bivalve mollusc, capable of reaching one metre in length and weighing more than 200 kg. The mouth flesh is of fantastic fluorescent colours – often green, purple and blue. Clams are poached throughout the Pacific for their edible flesh and valuable adductor muscle, considered a delicacy and aphrodisiac in the Orient.

Echinoderms These creatures belong to the *Phylum Mollusca* group and are characterised by a five-armed body structure, numerous little tube feet and a skeleton of plates. Probably most noticeable are starfish *(Asteroidea)* such as the stunning blue *Linckia leavigata*, abundant on the east coast, and the *Protoraster nodosus* or rhinoceros starfish, covered with red-black horns. Luckily, the infamous crown-of-thorns starfish is not posing a devastating threat to the reefs here as it does in other areas.

Also a member of this family are the fat, colourful sea cucumbers *(Holothuroidea)*, also called bêches-de-mer. These vacuum cleaners of the sea are still collected for export to Asian markets, where they become part of the cuisine. Spiky sea urchins *(Echinoidea)*, two species of which are poisonous and rare, abound in local waters. The waving feather stars *(Crinoidea)*, the group's most primitive members, seem to resemble a plant more than an animal.

Crustaceans Crabs, lobsters, shrimps and crayfish were all once abundant in New Caledonian waters but greedy overfishing is severely depleting numbers. Lobsters are especially scarce around Île des Pins and areas close to Noumea. New Caledonia has four kinds of lobster, capable of growing up to 10 kg. As they never enter traps, divers swim at night with underwater lamps and collect them by hand or spear them (even though the latter activity is illegal).

The Nautilus

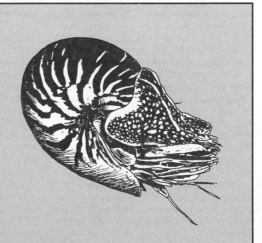

Unchanged for more than 100 million years, nautili are living fossils, the only survivors of a family which was common 450 million years ago and included ammonites (whirled shells like a ram's horn). It's a mystery to geologists why most of this group suddenly disappeared 70 million years ago. There are six remaining species of nautili living in the south-west Pacific, although in earlier times they were more widespread. One species is found only in New Caledonia.

The nautilus is a mollusc; however it is the only cephalopod (those molluscs with a well-developed head and eyes, and a ring of sucker-bearing tentacles) to have an external shell. All others such as cuttlefish and octopus have an inner 'shell'.

Never growing larger than 30 cm, the nautilus' ivory-coloured, curled shell has red-brown stripes and, inside is lined with mother-of-pearl. Its shell is divided into about 36 chambers, formed one by one as the nautilus grows and moves forward, each time closing off the preceeding chamber. The oldest segments are filled with a gas while the newest and biggest are filled with water and air. It moves by water expulsion through a siphon and can vary its buoyancy by changing the levels of gas and air in the individual chambers. It has a slightly negative buoyancy, meaning it will slowly sink when motionless. As it is sleepy during the day, it avoids light and warm water and therefore usually lives on the external slopes of the barrier reef at extraordinary depths of up to 500 metres. It feeds on crabs, shrimps and all kinds of dead bodies, using its many tentacles (about 90 around the mouth) to feed and protect itself. The nautilus' strange big eyes are undeveloped and its reproduction system is unknown. ■

Insects

While sea slugs may be the butterflies of the sea, New Caledonia has an equally impressive array of the real thing. At least 65 types of butterflies *(Lepidoptera)* fly around, the most striking being the blue *Papillon Montrouzieri*, which is similar to the Ulysses butterfly in Australia, and is abundant on Ouvea. At night, the air is even more alive, with an estimated 516 different species of *papillons de nuit* or moths.

Also of note is a giant endemic grasshopper and a reddish-brown centipede, which sometimes enters homes. About six cm long, its bite is poisonous enough to make you feel ill. Don't confuse it with the harmless common black millipede, which rolls itself up in a ball when disturbed. Apparently, local custom requires that if you don't want centipedes in your room, you politely ask them to leave – if you ask often enough they may just do so.

ENVIRONMENT
Natural Parks & Reserves

In general, New Caledonians don't show much environmental awareness. Since the Matignon Accords, conservation measures have been the responsibility of each of the three provinces. To date, there are no fully protected reserves on any of the islands (though there are tribal reserves where fishing is limited). While a few relatively small reserves, confined to mountain tops or forested slopes, have been established, they are mostly inaccessible to nature enthusiasts and only the Parc de la Rivière Bleue and Plaines des Lacs openly welcome hikers and campers.

Land Protection Three types of reserves exist – nature reserves, special botanical or fauna reserves, and provincial parks. The level of protection offered varies, but only the former have strict measures limiting access by people. In fact, there is currently only one nature reserve, the 6000-hectare Montagne des Sources, north-east of Noumea.

Special botanical reserves are the Chutes de la Madeleine and seven other areas on the Plaine des Lacs, as well as Mt Mou, Mt Humboldt, Mt Panie, Mt Ninga, Mt Do and the Saille Forest. Special fauna reserves, mainly protecting birds, are the Upper Yate reserve, Léprédour Island, Mt Aoupinie and Pam Island. These total 30,000 hectares.

Two provincial parks have been created, the larger and more accessible being Parc de la Rivière Bleue (see the Southern Grande Terre chapter) and Ouen Toro in Noumea. The Monts Koghis just north of the capital are listed as a tourist site, but this area, despite having a diversity of flora, has no protective classification.

In addition to these reserves and parks, there are some 323,000 hectares where mining is 'regulated' and a meagre 30,000 hectares where it is forbidden. More alarmingly, simply because the areas mentioned here are said to be 'protected', it doesn't mean they are safe from future mining.

Marine Protection Much could be done for marine protection in New Caledonia, particularly around touristic hot spots where the lagoon and the reef suffer from overuse by humans. Unfortunately, up to now it has been all talk but little action. In 1992, for example, Noumea's most popular tourist beach was temporarily closed only after swimmers found they were covered with rashes after bathing there. It was only then that those responsible for pumping under-treated sewage into the sea were induced to change their ways.

At present, only 53,000 hectares (530 sq km) of marine area is protected. The heaviest restrictions apply to the 17,000-hectare Yves Merlet Reserve, between the southern tip of Grande Terre and Île des Pins. Except for scientific research, entry and all activity is strictly forbidden.

Other than this, there are 'special marine reserves' where limitations are imposed on touristic and commercial activities and where it is illegal to remove or disturb minerals, flora or fauna. Into this category falls the Parc Territorial du Lagon Sud (South Lagoon Park), which takes in six islets

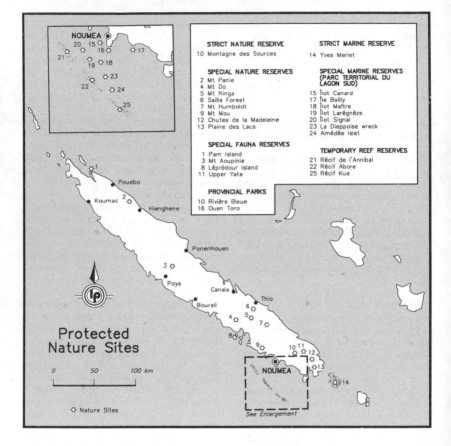

STRICT NATURE RESERVE
10 Montagne des Sources

STRICT MARINE RESERVE
14 Yves Merlet

SPECIAL NATURE RESERVES
2 Mt Panie
4 Mt Do
5 Mt Ninga
6 Saille Forest
7 Mt Humboldt
9 Mt Mou
12 Chutes de la Madeleine
13 Plaine des Lacs

**SPECIAL MARINE RESERVES
(PARC TERRITORIAL DU
LAGON SUD)**
15 Îlot Canard
17 Île Bailly
18 Îlot Maître
19 Îlot Larégnèze
20 Îlot Signal
23 La Dieppoise wreck
24 Amédée Islet

SPECIAL FAUNA RESERVES
1 Pam Island
3 Mt Aoupinie
8 Léprédour Island
11 Upper Yate

TEMPORARY REEF RESERVES
21 Récif de l'Annibal
22 Récif Abore
25 Récif Kue

PROVINCIAL PARKS
10 Rivière Bleue
16 Ouen Toro

Protected
Nature Sites

0   50   100 km

◇ Nature Sites

around Noumea; the wreck of *La Dieppoise* and everything within a 300-metre radius; and three temporary reef reserves – the Récif de l'Annibal, Récif Abore and Récif Kue. This trio, running roughly parallel to Grande Terre from Noumea south to Île Ouen, work on a rotational basis, each closed to fishing for three years once every nine years.

Environmental Hazards

Mining and smelting, urbanisation around Noumea and bushfires are the predominant dangers to nature in New Caledonia. Traditionally, the Kanaks had a very sensible relationship with the environment, considering it their *'garde-manger'* (food safe), which meant the territory had to be saved in order to provide a sustainable food supply. This contrasts greatly with modern-day White attitudes and practices in which deforestation and cattle farming exhaust the mountains and promote the formation of deserts on the plains.

Opencast nickel mining is the supreme perpetrator of deforestation, erosion, river or stream pollution and reef damage. The latter occurs particularly along the mid-section of the east coast, as the run-off from the stripped mountains pours down the rivers straight into the sea after torrential rain. Water pollution from nickel mines and other sources has been a controversial issue for years. In 1978 there was a public demonstration against an east coast nickel mine that was polluting a particular village's stream. Then in 1983, two gendarmes were killed during what started as a peaceful protest against a sawmill which was polluting the drinking supply of the Koinde and Ouipoint tribes near Sarramea.

The emissions released from the Doniambo nickel smelter in Noumea are another serious issue. International health and environmental agencies, including the World Health Organisation (WHO) and the American Environmental Protection Agency (EPA), have classified nickel as a carcinogen and have recognised that it can induce asthma. The EPA lists it as an 'extremely hazardous substance', while the EU (European Union, formerly known as the European Community) has directives covering its handling and smelting, its emissions into the soil, air and water, and workers' occupational health. However, New Caledonian legislation for smelting has set standards far below those accepted by these bodies.

The effect it is having on the people, especially those working in the industry or living in the low-cost housing communities nearby, is great. In 1992, the head of the emergency clinic in Noumea's main hospital revealed that the country holds the world record for asthma-related deaths. WHO data has shown that New Caledonia holds the Central and South Pacific's lung cancer record, with three to seven times more cases than in other countries in the region.

The only body checking mining pollution is the state-run Mining Pollution Control Commission. Industry regulations forbid smelter emissions when winds are blowing from the north-east towards the south-west, that is, in the direction of Noumea's city centre. But in 1991 a wind change covered tourist beaches in smelter dust and Société Le Nickel, which owns the smelter, was forced to issue a public apology in the national newspaper. Normally the emissions go west out over the lagoon where they settle on the water surface and eventually suffocate plankton and kill the reef.

Fishing

Fishing may not be a big money-making industry for New Caledonia but there are enough amateurs and professionals indulging in it for there to be regulations.

The spearfishing of fish, turtles and lobsters is illegal but it still goes on in order to cater to the thriving restaurant market, mainly in Noumea. With fish, the hole can be camouflaged or the fish simply filleted. Turtles are prohibited for consumption by anyone but Kanaks, but unfortunately restaurants on Île des Pins blatantly cater to tourist demands. Crabs can't be caught in January and at other times must be a minimum of 15 cm (excluding the legs), while lobsters must be a minimum of 7½ cm along the breast. The fishing season is between 1 January and 30 September and only rods and handlines are allowed (not dams, poisons, harpoons and explosives, as have been used in the past).

At one stage, trout were unsuccessfully introduced into rivers where conditions were thought to be perfect, but the water was too warm.

GOVERNMENT

Since 1956, New Caledonia has been classed as a French Territoire Outre-Mer (TOM) or overseas territory, the same as French Polynesia (including Tahiti) and Wallis & Futuna. In contrast to the status of overseas Départements (DOMs), such as Guadeloupe and Martinique, New Caledonia has some laws and a currency that differ from France; however, its national anthem and flag are those of France and its inhabitants are French citizens. They vote in national elections and elect representatives (two deputies and one senator) to the French National Assembly (which has 577 members) and Senate (317 members) in Paris. Once every seven years, New Caledonians vote for the president of the French Republic, or the 'State' as it's often called.

The French government controls many of the main sectors of society: the territory's defence and justice system, law and order, secondary and higher education, broadcasting, currency, and trade and mining regulations. At territorial level, the state is represented by a high commissioner, at present Alain Christnacht, who has executive authority.

Since the signing of the Matignon Accords in 1988, New Caledonia has been governed by a 54-member Territorial Congress. It is made up of three Provincial Assemblies – the Loyauté islands (seven seats), the North (15 seats) and the South (32 seats). The Loyauté islands Province takes in all four islands and is controlled by the FLNKS. The North Province, also dominated by the FLNKS, includes everything from the Belep Islands to Poya on the west coast and Nakety on the east. The South Province encompasses the remaining half of Grande Terre and Île des Pins. Centred in Noumea with its strong European majority, the South Province is in the hands of the RPCR.

Despite the FLNKS's governing two provinces, the RPCR has overall control of the territory, having won 27 seats to the FLNKS's 19 in the 1989 election. The two New Caledonian delegates elected to the French National Assembly (whose most recent election was in 1993) are also RPCR faithful – Jacques Lafleur is one and Maurice Nenou, the chief of Napoemien, a tribal village near Poindimie, is the other.

The three Assemblies, whose members are elected by popular vote every six years, act as local parliaments with independent budgets and administrations. They have direct control of customary law, primary education, provincial road networks, local medical services, tourism, housing and urban planning. At local government level, New Caledonia is divided into 32 *communes*, each with an elected mayor and municipal council.

A referendum on the future of New Caledonia will be held in 1998.

Political Parties

While 15 political parties contested the 1989 territorial election, there are just two main adversaries now: the right-wing Rassemblement pour Calédonie dans la République (Rally for New Caledonia within the Republic), otherwise known as the RPCR, and the pro-independence Front de Libération National Kanak Socialiste (Kanak Socialist National Liberation Front), or FLNKS. Since its founding in 1977, the RPCR has been presided over by a Caldoche, Jacques Lafleur, a land and mine owner reputed to be France's fifth-richest man. The FLNKS, formed in 1984, groups together various parties, including the Union Calédonienne (UC), Parti de Libération Kanak (PALIKA), Parti Socialiste Kanak (PSK) and Union Progressiste Mélanésienne (UPM).

The FLNKS's trademark is the blue, orange/red and green flag with, at its yellow centre, a flèche faîtière signifying unity. The colours of the flag stand for the sky, the sun, the blood of the Kanaks, and the land.

Some of the other larger parties include former FLNKS member, Front Uni de Libération Kanak (FULK), which split from the FLNKS after the assassination of Tjibaou and Yeiwene. Still led by its founder, Yann Uregei, FULK has changed name to the Congrès Populaire. Union Océanienne (UO) is a grouping of different factions from the Wallisian and Tahitian communities. Formerly part of the RPCR, the UO split in 1989 and is led by Michel Hema. The Front National (FN), affiliated with France's ultra right-wing party, has a fairly strong following in New Caledonia. It's driven by Guy George and has as its logo a flame with the French colours emblazoned over a blackened Grande Terre. Its fascist slogans call for a military solution to the territory's problems and the suppression of the independence movement. Calédonie Demain, a right-wing party comprising former members of the RPCR and the FN, is led by Bernard Marant.

The moderate Kanak Socialist Liberation party is headed by Nidoish Naisseline, the Grand Chef of Mare, and is popularly supported on that island.

Military Presence

Some 4000 military personnel, mainly soldiers from metropolitan France, are stationed in New Caledonia. The French government has repeatedly stated that, as Noumea was a strategic base for US and Allied forces during WW II, it is necessary to retain a significant garrison to ensure the territory's security. Their mandate is also to assist in the case of a natural disaster or possible disorder. New Caledonian men over the age of 18 years are required to do one year's compulsory military service. There are 400 full-time uniformed national gendarmes, made up primarily of officers recruited from France, and 200 uniformed *municipales*, an auxiliary unit comprising many Kanaks.

ECONOMY

Captain Cook was spot on when he assumed that Grande Terre could 'conceal great mineral potential'. Indeed, the country's economy centres around mining and the metallurgy industry, and their profits contribute to the Western-style life that many people lead. Tourism is the second greatest money spinner, while agriculture, fishing and aquaculture contribute to a lesser degree.

The country's GDP in 1989 was 253 billion local francs (CFP) or US$2.5 billion. Imports, accounting for some 90 billion francs, more than doubled the value of exports, of which 90% come from refined minerals and nickel ore. Although licences and taxes have been eased on Australian goods, France is still the major trading partner and supplies half the imported consumer products, mainly food, machinery and transport equipment. On top of that, the trade balance gap is largely bridged by enormous French funding. It is predicted that France will pump $US600 million into New Caledonia between 1992 and 1997 in accordance with the Matignon Accords, much of which will be used by the three provinces as they see fit. Housing, job creation and highway construction are some of the areas that have been earmarked. Already, new provincial government headquarters have been built and electricity systems are being expanded.

Inflation fluctuates between 3% and 4%. Wages are generally higher than in France, but with steep accommodation and food expenses, some of the French who pass through looking for work become discouraged and stay for only a few months. The minimum wage is 413.50F per hour (about US$4) or 69,879F for a 169-hour month. From this, an average 7.35% is taken out for income tax, which was first introduced in 1982. The workforce is around 55,000; the unemployment rate in 1989 was 16%, made up predominantly of Kanaks. There was 12% unemployment in the South Province, 21% in the North and 36% on the Loyauté islands.

Far away from the market economy, many rural Kanaks continue to grow modest subsistence crops. The average income of a Kanak couple living in *la Brousse* (the bush) is half the amount they would earn in Noumea, and only a quarter of what the average European couple in the capital brings home. Some Kanaks collect unemployment benefits after brief periods of work; others get old-age pensions and the clan then takes care of their basic needs. Only in the last few years, since job training facilities and programmes have been inaugurated in the wake of the Matignon Accords, have Kanaks entered service industries and started to climb administrative and bureaucratic ladders. One such highly publicised scheme was the Quatre Cents Cadres, which saw 400 young people, 80% of them Kanaks, sent to France for administrative training. Vocational, public service, mining and teacher training institutes have all opened in New Caledonia, but it will still be some time before the bulk of civil servants, secondary school teachers, doctors, engineers, etc, are not recruited from France.

Mining

Grande Terre has the world's largest known nickel deposits, accounting for 30% of world reserves, and is the second-largest cobalt producer. It also has large deposits of other sought-after minerals such as iron, manganese and chrome. Copper, lead, zinc and gold are found in smaller quantities.

Nickel was found at Dumbea in 1864 by the Irish-born colon John Higginson and in the same year by engineer Jules Garnier at the Diahot River. It has been mined since 1875, with New Caledonia dominating world supplies until 1905 when Canada took over the lead role. In 1877, chrome was discovered in the north at Tiebaghi, and a chrome mine, which grew to be the world's largest, was started in 1902.

The largest mine sites are around Thio, Poro and Kouaoua on the east coast and Koumac and Nepoui on the west coast. They're worked mainly by Europeans, Kanaks and Wallisians. There are 12 mining centres, variously owned by Société Le Nickel; wealthy families such as the Pentecost family and, formerly, the Ballandes; and the Société Minière du Sud Pacifique (SMSP). The latter was owned by RPCR leader, Jacques Lafleur, until 1990 when he sold 85% of his holdings to the North Province. In 1993, the SMSP was set to become the country's leading exporter of nickel to Japan, the world's biggest nickel consumer.

Nickel Anti-corrosive and an excellent heat resistor, nickel is a vital resource for the steel and armaments industries of industrialised Western countries, and is also used in the production of money and electronic goods.

New Caledonia is the third-largest nickel producer in the world after Canada and Russia, with 96,000 metric tonnes of nickel mined in 1989. The last nickel booms were in 1963 and from 1969 to 1971, after which the industry went into crisis as international markets dived, largely due to Russian oversupply. The situation has eased somewhat in the last few years and prices are again relatively high.

France regards nickel as a strategic metal and has maintained strict control over mining. As New Caledonia controls 9% of the world market (a drop compared with 15% some 30 years ago), nickel is the primary reason why France wants to hold on to the territory. According to one mining engineer, New Caledonia has enough reserves for mining to continue well into the 21st century.

Mining for nickel is opencast, as it lies between the base rock and the scraped-off layer of top earth. Bulldozers generally work on the tops of mountains and the ore is carted down to the coast, from where it's shipped to a smelter in Noumea, or exported to France or Japan. In the 1940s, nickel and chrome were still coming down the mountains by flying fox, which was eventually superseded by trucks. Now, at some mine sites, kilometre-long conveyor belts carry the ore straight into the holds of awaiting ships.

Société Le Nickel SLN, as it's better known, was formed in 1880 by the nickel discoverers Higginson and Garnier, the latter also credited with mastering the nickel fusion process. They were financially backed by the international mining corporation Rothschild. The SLN monopolises all processing as it owns the sole smelter, Doniambo, just north of central Noumea. It's the country's largest single employer, with a workforce fluctuating between 2000 and 3000, and it injects considerable sums of money into the local economy via salaries, wages, taxes and energy consumption. At its peak in the 1971 nickel boom, SLN employed 1200 miners – French, Kanak, Wallisian and other nationalities – and 3500 workers at the Doniambo plant where Europeans outnumbered Kanaks by five to one.

Tourism

After dramatically nose diving for several years as a result of the Events, the tourist industry got back on its feet and these days directly creates about 2250 jobs. However, in many circles it's still considered the country's most under-exploited industry.

Since 1988, the number of foreign tourists has continued to grow, to what was an all-time high of 122,000 in 1992. Just over a quarter of these were from Japan, followed by Australians, French and New Zealanders. On average, tourists arriving by air stay for 14 days, while the 44,000 cruise ship passengers who arrive each year are in Noumea for a 'flying' one-day visit. Many Japanese come to the capital to get married, and it's not unusual to see them being photographed in their wedding gear in front of the old bandstand on Place des Cocotiers.

While Noumea has traditionally monopolised international tourism, the policy since the Matignon Accords has been to decentralise facilities, and several new hotels and resorts have opened outside the capital. Large-scale promotion in overseas markets is being carried out by Destination New Caledonia, a government-run 'economic interest group' set up in 1990.

Agriculture

About 28% of the population derives a living from agriculture. However, there are two styles of rural existence which are vastly different: west-coast settlers own huge tracts of land, while the Kanaks often have little more than small plots on the outskirts of their villages. The latter scenario is particularly the case along the east coast and on the Loyauté islands, where four in every five families rely heavily on subsistence farming. The cultivation of traditional crops like banana, taro and yam is declining, to be replaced by rice or experimental fruit such as oranges, avocados and pineapples.

The successful coffee plantations so enthusiastically cultivated along the west coast and in the south in the late 1890s were almost totally destroyed in 1910 by a parasite which affected the Arabica variety. On the east coast, many settlers sold their plantations to Kanaks who switched to the Robusta crop (Robusta is richer in caffeine, while Arabica has a stronger aroma and is the preferred drink of connoisseurs). In 1990, there were some 1200 growers producing 250 tonnes per year.

Copra (dried coconut flesh) is an important revenue for the Ouveans as this Loyauté island has almost half the country's coconut groves. Processed in a small factory near the island's wharf, the extracted oil is used to make copra cakes (cattle feed), soap and margarine.

Cattle & Venison While 12% of the country is arable, 93% of this (230,000 hectares) is used only for cattle grazing and fodder production. Once the country's second most important industry, it has slowly declined over the years, and today cattle account for only 2.5% of the GDP. Drought has been a major factor in the industry's decline (in 1973, two-thirds of all the cattle on Grande Terre perished on rain-starved land), as has lack of government subsidies and assistance. While 125,000 head of cattle now roam the west coast, demand is so great that beef must still be imported from Australia and New Zealand.

Deer have roamed Grande Terre's western foothills since last century, introduced as prey for weekend hunters who enjoyed a slab of venison. In the last few years, 20 commercial deer-farming projects have been started.

Fishing & Aquaculture

Despite abundant marine life, New Caledonia still has a small, albeit expanding, fishing industry. The country's 'fleet' is made up of small boats operating mostly in the sheltered lagoon that surrounds Grande Terre and catering mainly to the specific needs of a family or clan. Tuna destined for Japan is the main target of the few commercial Noumean-based operators. An estimated 6000 tonnes of fish is caught per year. On top of that, 150 million francs' worth of fresh and frozen fish, shrimps and oysters are imported annually.

Aquaculture experiments over the past decade are now reaping benefits. The six shrimp farms dotted mainly along the west coast occupy nearly 200 hectares and, in 1992, produced 700 tonnes both for local markets and to export to France, Australia and Japan.

POPULATION

The last census, carried out in 1989, tallied the population at 164,173. The Kanaks are the largest cultural group, making up 44.8% of the population or 73,600 people. Europeans (mainly New Caledonian-born or metropolitan French) are the second-largest group at 33% or 55,000. Wallisians account for 8%, Indonesians 3.2%, Tahitians 2.9%,

Vietnamese 1.5%, and ni-Vanuatu, Indians, West Indians, Arabs and others make up the remaining 4%.

New Caledonia's population dropped dramatically soon after the Europeans set up in the 1850s, only starting to pick up in the 1930s. In 1887, there was estimated to be 62,500 people, comprising 68% Kanak, 30% European and 2% other. A count taken in 1921 showed a large drop to 47,500, of which Kanaks accounted for 57%, Europeans 29% and others, mainly made up of indentured miners, 13%. This period was the all-time low for the Kanaks, their population having been decimated in the previous 70 years by disease, war and the indigénat system. By 1969, the continued tide of immigrants seeking labour, the growth in European families and the revival of the Kanaks took the population up to 100,000, though by now Kanaks were a minority (46%) in their own land. Further rapid growth has meant that about 53% of the population is now under the age of 24. Predictions for the year 2000 set a figure of 172,000, made up of 47% Kanak, 37% European and 16% other.

New Caledonia's population is largely confined to what is referred to as 'Greater Noumea', including the capital and nearby towns of Dumbea, Paita and Mont Dore. This conurbation accounts for 60% of all inhabitants. Those from outside here are collectively known as *Broussards*, that is, someone who comes from la Brousse. Though the total density for the country is a very comfortable 8.8 people per sq km, regional figures tell a different tale, with 2.75 people per sq km on the west coast, 3.5 on the east coast, 7.5 on the Loyauté islands and a huge leap to 1335 per sq km in Noumea.

PEOPLE
Kanaks

Kanaks or *Ti-Va-Ouere*, meaning 'Brothers of the Earth' as they sometimes call themselves, are Melanesians (from the Greek word *'melas'* meaning 'black' and *'nesos'* meaning 'island'), the group of people who inhabit many of the islands in the southwestern Pacific. Although in anthropological terms they are often referred to as Melanesians, the country's indigenous people prefer to be called Kanaks, and many already call their country Kanaky (Kanaké in French) rather than New Caledonia.

Generally very courteous, Kanaks also tend to be rather shy and often hesitant or even seemingly disinterested in being the initiator of contact. However, once you've passed the reservation façade, you'll find they are warm people filled with natural good humour. Repression and the erosion of their customs, however, have led to a general resentment of the French. When walking through a village they tend to greet every passer-by with 'bonjour' and, when being introduced, usually shake hands lightly. However, other than this brief contact, they are not normally very tactile and only a tiny minority have adopted the French greeting of kissing on both cheeks.

Since 1946, Kanaks have automatically been French citizens. The large majority live in clan communities inland or along Grande Terre's east coast, on Île des Pins and on the Loyauté islands, where they make up 98% of the population. Before colonisation, tribes kept mainly to the coast, but during the discriminatory indigénat system they were forcibly moved off their traditional lands and relocated. Today, many tribes live in foreign areas distant from their birthplace and natural homeland, making the controversial issue of defining land rights an even stickier problem. Since the early '80s, the French research body ORSTOM has endeavoured to pinpoint the traditional land of today's clans.

In recent decades, Kanaks have felt compelled to forsake their tribal life in search of work and education in Noumea. Since the Matignon Accords, the imbalance of facilities throughout the country has been recognised. Consequently, the French government is now pumping in substantial funds to provincial areas in an attempt to create local employment and to build secondary and technical schools so that people are not forced to leave their families and communities. But as one indépendantiste, Susanna Ounei-Small, wrote in a recently released book, *Tu Galala – Social Change in the Pacific*: 'One of the weaknesses of our movement is that it has never resolved the issue of what kind of development we want – what kind of future society we want to build. Talk about the development of Kanaky is always about making our country more like France'.

French

The French are divided into three main groups – the Caldoches, the *métros* and the *pieds noirs*.

The Caldoches are those who were born in New Caledonia, with ancestral ties that go back to the days of the convicts, or to the early French settlers, who were known as colons. They generally settled on Grande Terre's west coast, where many continue to run large cattle properties. While some Caldoches also set up on the east coast in the late 1800s during the coffee boom, most sold up and left prior to or around the Events, re-establishing themselves in the south or west. Some bought land in Australia and talked about emigrating, but it was a reality few achieved as Australia severely curtailed its immigration policy in the 1980s.

The French who come to New Caledonia to work for a few years with the benefit of high wages are called *métros* (short for *métropoles*, meaning from metropolitan France). Another term sometimes used for them, though one that is not appreciated, is *zoreilles*. This name, derived from the French term *les oreilles* (the ears), originated in convict times when, as the story goes, the guards used to cup their hands behind their ears in order to eavesdrop on the prisoners' talk. Noumea, sometimes called the 'Paris of the Pacific', is the chosen home for most métros.

Lastly, there's a small community of about 2000 pieds noirs (literally, 'black feet') as Algerian-born French colonialists are called by their fellow French. They preferred to move to New Caledonia rather than France after the fall of Algiers in 1962.

Other New Caledonians

The other races of people now making up the country's population arrived for work reasons at various times in New Caledonia's history. At the turn of this century, indentured labourers from Indonesia, Vanuatu, Vietnam and Japan arrived to work the mines. Their families now make up close-knit communities, centred mainly in Noumea, though a few of the more intrepid have set up shops and businesses elsewhere on Grande Terre. The Japanese are the sole exception, as they were arrested en masse and expelled after the attack on Pearl Harbor. These days, Japanese in New Caledonia are tourists or employees of companies catering exclusively to them.

Coinciding with the nickel boom of the 1950s, Polynesians from the French-controlled islands of Wallis (known as Wallisians) and Futuna, both north-east of Fiji, and Tahiti began to arrive in Noumea. In the late '60s and early '70s, they boomed again along with the nickel.

EDUCATION

Education is one means of moulding people's ideas into a desired frame and, as such, the French education system operating in New Caledonia has come up against opposition in recent years. Rebel schools were set up in the early 1980s and, with the signing of the Matignon Accords, France recognised that school curricula must be adapted to reflect local conditions.

While a formal education is now compulsory for all New Caledonians between the ages of six and 16, it wasn't until 1956 that *lycées* (secondary schools) were opened to Kanaks. Five years later, the first Kanak student attained a secondary school certificate, known in the French system as *le Baccalauréat*, or *le Bac* for short.

In a 1989 survey, 48% of the total population over 14 had a primary level of education, 39% had secondary-level education, 6% had been to university and 7% had no formal education. Taken province by province, these figures change significantly, with more people in the South (French-populated) Province having continued to secondary level and 8% to university. In contrast, on the Loyauté islands, 15% never attended school and only 2% went on to tertiary education. Overall, 10% of the population is illiterate.

The System

There are 280 primary schools, 43 secondary, 31 technical and six higher education institutions, controlled by the provinces, the state or the Church.

Primary education is in the hands of each province. English is now taught at this level (rather than at secondary as in the past) and, in a few places like Mare and Lifou, the local Kanak languages are now taught (for only one or two hours a week, depending on the availability of a teacher). Secondary schools are under state control and their teachers, mostly from France, are handsomely subsidised to move to New Caledonia. As well, they receive double the salary they would get back home.

The French University of the South Pacific, built in Papeete (Tahiti) in 1987, has had a second campus in Noumea since 1988. With 700 students, it concentrates on English, modern literature, law and history, together with 'local' programmes for mining, public works and aquaculture. Students can do only two years at the university, after which they are obliged to finish their studies elsewhere. This is when difficulties arise, as it is expensive to go to France (about 100 students attend university there each year), and degrees from other countries such as Australia are not given equal recognition in New Caledonia, thereby diminishing work and career opportunities.

EPK Schools

In 1984, Écoles Populaires Kanaks (Kanak Popular Schools), otherwise known as EPK schools, were started in various regions such as Canala on Grande Terre and Gossanat on Ouvea in a bid to 'decolonise' Kanak children. These schools rejected both the French curriculum and the idea that all knowledge must come from France. Not surprisingly, they encountered pressure from the government, which refused to recognise them and cut off family benefits to parents who actively favoured the EPK schools. Many have since folded. The teachers were a mixed lot, from young indépendantistes with qualifications but no jobs to teachers who had resigned from government schools to work without pay in an EPK. Resources were pooled and children were taught in their native tongue.

TRADITIONAL KANAK CULTURE

The clan, not the individual, was *the* important element in traditional Kanak society. Life was based on communal principles achieved through village living, a system sometimes labelled by Westerners as 'tribal socialism'. No-one was better or worse off than someone else, as equality was a cardinal rule. Village life ensured that nobody went hungry or was uncared for – everyone contributed in some aspect whether it was fishing, gathering food, tending fields, sculpting wood or repairing huts. In return, everyone reaped the rewards. The ancient Kanak code of la coutume kept this system alive and it provided a common bond and understanding between all Kanaks.

Westerners introduced the ideas of individualism and private ownership and, as they forced Kanak culture to its knees, their new ways replaced the old – to a degree. But they didn't manage to repress la coutume. Today, while it may be up to the village elders to tell the old stories and sing the traditional songs, the cultural renaissance amongst the younger generation appears to be strong enough to ensure that traditional Kanak culture will live on.

La Coutume

La coutume is the essential component of Kanak identity. This code for living encompasses rites, rituals and social interaction between and within the clans, and maintains the all-important link with their ancestors. Nowadays, politics often clashes with la coutume and, with young people still leaving their clans to go to Noumea, it is under threat. Some Kanaks fear la coutume is becoming a thing of the past, though others believe it is too ingrained to be lost.

The exchange of gifts is an important element of la coutume, as it creates a much-revered network of mutual obligations. The one who offers a gift receives prestige from this action while placing an obligation, which is never ignored, on the receiver to respond. In all the important stages in life, such as birth, marriage and mourning, a gift is given, symbolic offerings are made and discussions are held. After that, dance, food and laughter take over.

When Kanaks enter the home of a chief, they will offer a small token as a sign of respect and to introduce themselves. Food, a few metres of textiles, money, or a packet of cigarettes are the traditional and contemporary offerings and, if you're given the rare privilege of being invited to a tribal home, you should respect la coutume by bringing a gift. When you want to camp on a clan's ground or visit a site, it's wise and courteous to introduce yourself to the chief, if possible, or at least to someone in the clan.

The Clan

Some 300 clans are believed to have existed when White people arrived. The missionaries coined the term 'tribe' to describe a clan or sub-clan (Moaro in one Kanak language, la tribu in French). Each clan lived in its own village and had its own totem from which its name was often derived. The clan's lineage continued through the bloodline of one person and was linked or related to a spiritual ancestor. Relationships with these ancestors and the spirit world were strong, and were demonstrated by symbolic festivals and dances. Each clan had its own traditions and legends. Bridal exchanges and polygamy inter-related villages. The clan's activity was centred around the largest hut, the grande case, where the chief lived.

The Chief The spirit of the clan, handed down through generations of ancestors, was embodied in the chief (Orohau or le chef). In daily life he was the visible presence of the ancestors and the living link to them. He was considered the clan's oldest son and was its memory. Men became chiefs either on a hereditary basis or were appointed for their skills. Either way, when a new chief was presented, a huge celebration followed during which he had to recite the clan's entire genealogy from memory. In this oral society, eloquence was highly revered and the greatest chiefs were those who could best use the power of words. Traditional wood sculptors portrayed this by carving faces with protruding tongues.

Essentially responsible for conservation of the clan, the chief administered justice and, when necessary, declared wars (though this did not mean he led the warring party into battle). Assistance was given to him through a council of elders, made up of the oldest men of each family in the clan, who were tuned to the spirits through visionary dreams.

As with the word 'tribe', the missionaries also introduced the term 'chief', implying a false, more powerful status than the head man originally had. Previously, all clan members were treated equally, and the head man was singled out only to receive a few special foods, such as turtle and the first yams of the annual harvest. It was, in fact, the council of elders who traditionally held more sway than the head man. The colonial authorities took the missionaries' lead a step further and invented the titles of Grands and Petits Chefs – the 'big' and 'little' chiefs. The latter rose to this status often in exchange for their cooperation, and the whole notion artificially modified the social structure of the clan.

Today, the chief represents or speaks for the local community. On the Loyauté islands and Île des Pins, they tend to play a greater role in society, acting as a monarch with the help of ministers. This promotion is partly explained by the Polynesian influence on the islands and because of a greater concentration of indigenous people living there.

The Women's Clan Kanak women have a special status in the family. A woman generally becomes a member of her husband's family after marriage, and children are named after the father. However, when a child is born, it is permanently linked to its mother's clan through the mother's brother, known as the 'maternal' or 'uterine' uncle; *Kanya* in one Melanesian tongue. The Kanya takes on a role in the child's life that is more important than that of the father, because he is the child's guardian. The family's ancestral totem is also believed to live in his neck and he blows its spirit into the young child. This link to the life and blood of the mother's clan protects the child and enhances the role of the wife, as her clan is respected within her husband's household through this link. All disciplinary action is carried out by the Kanya, who will serve as the child's mentor throughout his or her life. A woman whose husband has died can expect her husband's brother to marry her. Polygamy was customary before the missionaries frowned on it and stamped the practice out.

Sadly, women in modern Kanak society face the contemporary problems of women in many countries. Because of the long-reaching influence of religion, contraception is something which is not often discussed, while excessive alcohol use has been identified as one of the causes of domestic violence and rape.

The Life Cycle
Traditionally, life for most Kanaks started in a smoky hut. The mother had worked until that day and gave birth alone. She bathed the child and called the Kanya, who would blow the *Rhevana*, the breath of the totem, into the ear of the child. The mother breast-fed for about 18 months, during which time her husband lived in the men's hut.

Education came gradually, always with respect towards the Kanya. Traditional knowledge was passed on orally through poems, legends and stories. Children went naked until the age of seven or eight, when girls were given a kind of skirt and boys received a *bagayou* or penis sheath. Once clothed, they were fully part of the community and could assist in hunting and fishing.

In certain regions, at around 15 to 18 years, boys would be circumcised. For this important ritual they had to stay in a special hut topped with a yam, a virility symbol, and fast for a certain time. Afterwards, it was a good occasion to hold a memorable celebration. Girls had no such initiation rites.

Marriage was sealed through a simple act of sitting together on a mat and sharing a meal, followed by an elaborate festival. The parents would give a *case* (hut) as a wedding present. And so life moved along, through often demanding years in a land where nature could be capricious and food was not always available. In comparison with today's Western norms, most Kanaks died quite young. At the day of death, traditional money would be brought to the Kanya and the funeral initiated. It would last for 20 days; the mourning period lasted a year. The body would be buried in foetal position in a basket or dug-out tree trunk, or laid in a cave or a tree.

Earthly Relations
As with the Aborigines of Australia, the Kanaks have a mystical connection with time, space and the land. All dances, custom rites, totems and sacred sites refer back to this 'space notion' in which the clan connected through a particular rock, tree or island. It is said that on Grande Terre and the islands there are 'no empty spaces or virgin land'. When a clan loses its land, their collective personality is also lost.

Cultivating plants is seen as the perpetuation of the clan's life and all plants in Kanak society are given either male or female status. The Kanak's two principal crops are yams and taro which, aside from being staple foods, greatly influence cultural beliefs. Taro is grown in shallow terraces watered by irrigation works; terraces of early tribes can still can be seen on Grande Terre.

But it is the humble yam *(igname* in French) that really holds a special place in society as, having grown in the ancestral soil, it is sacred. Yams hold men's virility, thus ensuring that the clans continue their lineage. They also determine the Kanak social calendar, and the cultivation and harvesting of

---

Festival of the Yam

The Festival of the Yam takes place at harvest time, generally in mid-March, about six months after the yams are planted. However, unlike harvest festivities in many other countries, this is not a huge public affair with singing and dancing. Instead it's a calm gathering of the clan and a sharing of the blessed yam which is treated with the reverence normally reserved for a grandfather or ancestor. Many Kanaks living in Noumea return to their villages for this event.

The elders decide when it is time for the harvest, and traditionally watch nature for signs indicating that the yam is ready. These include the appearance of certain stars, such as the Southern Cross, the call of a buzzard or the flowering of a particular tree. The official start of the harvest comes when the first yams are pulled from a sacred field and presented to the older clansmen and the chief. The next day, which is more often than not March 19, everyone gathers in the local church (this part, of course, has occurred only since the missionaries arrived) and the pile of yams is blessed by the priest. The roots are then carried out in procession form to the grande case, from where they are distributed amongst the tribe. Out of respect, the yam is never cut, but broken like bread. ■

---

yams are filled with rituals designed to thank the spirits. Elders pray to them to ensure that what has been planted will 'spring up again' in a plentiful crop.

Traditional Religion

Kanak religion was traditionally a form of ancestor and spirit worship and had a universal view with spiritual ideas. There were no temples or other places of worship and no written texts. Then, 150 years ago, missionaries brought the 'Word of God' and the concept of heaven and hell. Initial resistance, rivalry and, ultimately, religious wars ensued to the point that proselytism had to go on under the military's protection. Protestants were very successful on the Loyauté islands, while Marists (Catholics) dominated Grande Terre and Île des Pins.

Ancestors & Spirits The ancestors are the spirits of humans receiving power after death. They are present in tribal life in the form of sacred stones used in ceremonies, in the living presence of the chief, or in the carving on top of the grande case – the flèche faîtière. Other spirits, which had never been living creatures, are the guardians of the fields and forests, or simply a source of tribal strength. Notions of the sacred and the forbidden, the visible and invisible worlds (the ancestors and spirits) all exist. Offerings are given to the invisible world, as a healthy life depends on its support. Certain places are the domain of the spirits and thus considered sacred and taboo. Burial grounds are one example – bodies were buried in caves or in a tumulus (burial mound) while the skull was left at the cave entrance or above ground. Medicine men had special mythical powers and could influence war, natural elements and health. The colonial authorities outlawed their practices early on, though their knowledge lives on in contemporary Kanak society.

Taboos & Totemism Taboos are normally, though not always, related to a totem. Totemism is the belief in a special relationship between a certain animal, plant or thing and the clan or person. This belief has a mythical character, the unity of which creates rites and taboos – powerful rules and restrictions which must be respected. If broken, illness and even death are believed to follow. It is forbidden to kill or eat your own totem. Things directly related to the totem are affected by it, so the bank of a river, for example, may be taboo because the eel totem is sleeping there.

In traditional Kanak society, siblings are not allowed to have a sexual relationship and tribal members cannot have sex during menstruation and pregnancy. The head of the chief may not be touched and a person who has cleaned the body of a dead tribal member must fast, let his hair grow and must not touch a woman until the taboo is lifted. Tribal burial sites are out of bounds as they are where the ancestors lie, and old housing sites protected by spiritual powers are also taboo.

Ceremonies

Many celebrations and ceremonies are held, but some of the most important are for marriage, to honour the chief and to start the yam harvest.

The clan begins marriage preparations months in advance. The groom's family gathers gifts which they will present to the bride's family as a kind of exchange. During the wedding, traditional *bougna* (a Kanak meal) is roasted on a heap of red-hot stones. There is usually a great deal of singing, with traditional songs that tell the clan's stories, and *pilous*, dances regarded as the supreme expression of tribal culture.

The *fête du chef* (chief's feast) is held at the beginning of the year and reaffirms the unifying bonds between the clan and the chief. The chief receives the support of the total clan and in return gives it strength and courage for the new year.

Cases

The thatched round hut, known as a *case* in French and pronounced 'kaahz', is the Kanaks' traditional architecture and the most enduring, visible artefact of their culture. When Polynesians arrived on the Loyauté islands they brought with them the design for rectangular *cases*. Families there then often built two homes – a rectangular one with living quarters and the beehive-shaped hut for sleeping. These days, you'll find *cases* alongside modern-style houses, the latter enforced by the colonial authorities.

Construction materials were obviously whatever the local environment offered. On Grande Terre, clans on the west and north-east coasts used strips of niaouli bark for the *case's* walls and sometimes the roof, while on the islands the main material was grass. In both areas coconut palm fronds were used for waterproofing and vines for binding. All these materials are still used in contemporary *cases*.

Grande Case This 'big hut' is one of the strongest symbols of the Kanak community. Having followed the same building pattern for centuries, it is the widest and tallest *case* in each clan settlement and traditionally home to the chief. Today, the chiefs all have modern homes, called *chefferies*, located close to the grande case where the tribal gatherings and discussions still take place.

The craft involved in the building of a grande case is impressive and the job requires many hands. Every aspect of the construction has symbolic importance, such as the origin of the building materials, the chosen site, the building techniques and the cooperation of the tribe.

Where possible, the hut is built on a knoll above the rest of the village. The central pillar, an immense trunk of a carefully chosen tree, is erected first. It will support the entire *case* and symbolises the chief (in the case of a normal *case*, it represents the family's head man). A stone hearth is laid between this post and the door and constantly burns during the cool months. A regular fire is essential, as without it the hut will be invaded by insects and will soon rot away. Even so, the thatching of most *cases* is replaced every five years or so.

The entrance to the grande case is via two low doorways flanked by wide wooden boards. These are often carved in the form of a face and called *katara*, meaning 'the sentinel who reports the arrival of strangers'. Inside, the walls and ceiling are lined with wooden posts or beams, lashed to the frame with strong vines and all of which lean against the central pillar, symbolising the clan's close link with the chief. Finally, a flèche faîtière is erected on the roof and a magical packet and traditional money are hung or buried nearby, providing the important link with the ancestral and spiritual world.

Avoiding Offence

It is part of tribal life to greet passers-by, even if you're inside a vehicle going past pedestrians; you'll soon find you do a lot of handwaving. When being introduced,

Top Left: *Flèches faîtières* in the museum, Noumea (DNC)
Top Right: Sculptured palisade on Île des Pins (LL)
Bottom: Pilou dancers re-enacting a traditional story (DNC)

Top: The wreck of the *Ever Prosperity* off Amédée Lighthouse (DNC)
Bottom Left: Medu cave, Mare (LF)
Bottom Left: Amédée Lighthouse south of Noumea (LL)

Kanaks usually shake hands but, out of politeness, they often do not look directly into the eyes of the person they're meeting. If you are being introduced to a Kanak, you should do the same.

It is part of ancient Kanak customary laws to offer visitors food and it is a tradition that has not slipped away. Arriving in a village, you may be invited to share a cup óf tea or coffee or even an entire meal in the house of someone you met only 10 minutes earlier in the back of a pick-up truck. Nothing more than a 'thank you' is expected in return if you are just passing through. However, if you stay a day or so, out of politeness to their custom you should present your host with some food.

Kanaks these days do not get around scantily clad so, no matter how hot it is, you should not enter villages wearing just swimwear or revealing shorts. Women should make sure their skirts or pants are of a 'decent' length and men shouldn't be bare-chested. You'll have no problem dressing in revealing clothes around the beach suburbs of Noumea, but everywhere outside the capital it's frowned upon and on Île des Pins, by decree of the chief, such clothes are strictly illegal (except on Kuto and Kanumera beaches). Much the same goes for nude swimming and sunbathing – on Noumean beaches going topless for women is fine but outside the capital, if it's a beach or waterfall visited by locals, they'll consider it very rude if you're there starkers.

FRENCH CULTURE

French culture is firmly implanted in Noumea – but not in New Caledonia as a whole. This dichotomy is primarily a result of a country whose population includes two very different groups of so-called 'French' people: the Caldoches and the métros.

The Caldoches are quintessentially rural folk who enjoy the occasional rodeo and country fair, the latter complete with a beauty pageant. Though of French descent, the Caldoches' forebears (mainly convicts) chose to stay in New Caledonia when freed, rather than returning to the mother country.

In so doing, they basically turned their backs on French culture. Over the years, little has replaced it, as the Caldoches are too few in number and live too far apart to forge a distinct culture of their own. These days, they're still more or less culturally adrift and are neither part of the renaissance in Kanak culture nor akin to their French-loving counterparts, the métros.

Métros epitomise the most renowned aspects of French culture: cuisine, clothing, art and sport. As they hold dear the finest of French ways, they brought them to their homes in New Caledonia. Hence, Noumea has a bounty of restaurants specialising in French cuisine and serving traditional Burgundian dishes. Likewise, fashion is observed and, in recent years, more and more small art galleries have popped up in the capital. On the sporting front, soccer is avidly followed, while cyclists race around Noumea's waterfront boulevards as if in competition with the many windsurfers streaming across the bays. On weekends, métro families pack up and drive to one of the less touristic beaches on Noumea's out-skirts (or sail to a nearby deserted island) for a spot of sunbathing. As on the French Riviera, going topless is, of course, in vogue.

ARTS

Increasingly, Kanaks are concentrating on preserving and safeguarding their ancient crafts and artefacts. Coming from an oral tradition, they were masters of speech, while the written word was nonexistent. Writing, therefore, has never been a recognised art form and, though it's slowly changing, there are only a few contemporary Kanak authors.

In other areas, Kanaks are skilled and handy craftspeople, using natural materials for a wide range of purposes. Their art is part of the rich cultural heritage of the Pacific, which has been nicely described in a perma-nent inscription on a wall of the South Pacific Commission in Noumea:

Pacific artists were great creators of forms. They could express themselves the most in sculpture and sometimes in drawing. Pacific design is revealed in tattoos, the paint strokes on *tapa* bark, the figurines carved in wood and in petroglyphs. At first sight, Pacific sculpture and design show an extreme variety in styles, although this opinion is not shared by the ethnologists. The Pacific artists, especially the wood-carvers, are an admired class, their social and material rank comparable to that of the greatest chiefs. The magic of being connected with the supernatural world is as essential for a perfect creation as manual skill or the inventing mind is.

Unlike in other Pacific regions, Kanak art is not a big business. Perhaps this is because of the people's reserved nature and the fact that, traditionally, most art forms were private or for use within the clan. These days you'll never be accosted by street hawkers selling crafts, and even established locations for viewing or buying true Kanak works of art, as opposed to pieces made for tourists, are few and far between.

Pottery

Pottery dates back to New Caledonia's earliest known civilisations, the Lapita culture of around 1500 BC. Later, it was essentially a woman's craft, and finished pots traded with other clans for more desirable goods. Locally made traditional pottery is no longer produced.

Made from clay deposits found around the islands, the pottery was simple. The clay was kneaded and rolled into strips, which were joined by beating the clay with a wooden spatula. The pots were then wrapped in grass and baked in an open fire. While still hot, they were covered with kauri-gum varnish for waterproofing.

Carvings

Wood In older times, spirits were carved in wood, and today the art of sculpture embodies the spirit of the Kanak culture. The most important wooden sculpture is the flèche faîtière, which resembles a small totem pole with symbolic shapes. It adorns the top of the grande case and is the home of ancestral spirits.

The flèche faîtière has three main parts. In the centre is a flat, crowned face representing the ancestor. Above this is a long, rounded pole run through by conch shells, which symbolise the ancestor's voice. The base is planted into the *case's* central pole, thus connecting it with the clan through the chief. At either end of the central face are pieces of wood which fan out to sharp points – these tips are barriers that prevent bad spirits from going up or down into the ancestor.

Flèche faîtière

Other wooden carvings resembled hawks, ancient gods, serpents and turtles. They were often carved from tree trunks and placed as a palisade around important objects such as the grande case. One such set of carvings stands like a mini Stonehenge at Vao on Île des Pins, surrounding a religious memorial.

War clubs were carved from the strongest trees and fashioned with a phallic head, known in French as a *casse têtes* (head breaker), or as an equally lethal bird's beak club or *bec d'oiseau*. In conflicts, spears made from niaouli trees were lit and thrown into the enemy's hut to set it alight.

Stone The most important stone artefact in New Caledonia is the ceremonial axe, a symbol of the clan's strength and power. It is generally used to decapitate enemies during a battle or to honour ancestors during pilou celebrations. The stone of this axe, usually green jade or serpentine, is polished smooth until it resembles a disk. Two holes are drilled, like eyes, into the central area of the stone, and a handle made of flying fox fur is woven through these holes and fastened. The bottom of the handle is adorned with stones and shells, with each pendant serving as a symbolic reference to a particular clan.

Bamboo Engraving

At the end of the 19th century, anthropologists started collecting intricately engraved bamboo canes from Kanak communities. As most of them date from around the arrival of the Europeans, it's unsure whether cane engraving was a form of traditional art dating back many centuries or simply a fad of the time.

The canes averaged a metre in length and were used by Kanaks in dance ceremonies or when entering a village. They contained magic herbs that warded off evil spirits and were covered with designs which had been carved into the green pole with a quartz tip. The themes were mostly geometrical, though real images were sometimes portrayed, ranging from the pilou dance to agricultural motifs and village scenes like fishing or building *cases*. The canes were held over fire to give the engraved areas a black patina.

Dance

Kanak customary gatherings were always accompanied by dances designed to strengthen the relationships within the clan and with the ancestors. They were mimic dances that conveyed a message or told a legend, often regarding aspects of everyday life – fishing, a turtle swimming, a *case* being built. Dancers painted themselves to appear beautiful before the gathered clans and to please the watching ancestors. The steps were powerful and the feet pounded the earth energetically. Wooden masks adorned with local materials such as bark, feathers and leaves – physical links with the invisible world – were exhibited or worn only by the chief.

These days the odd dance workshop is held where Kanaks learn traditional movements or newly created dances, usually to perform them at large events such as the Festival of Pacific Arts.

Pilou The pilou is a dance that tells the stories of the clan and is unparalleled as a physical expression of Kanak culture. Although the steps may appear similar in each dance, they are in fact quite different, each telling a story about a birth or marriage, the destruction of a church by a cyclone, or preparations for battle. Sometimes a pilou will tell of the arrival of the missionaries and the subsequent conversion to Christianity.

Pilous were staged at important ceremonies, for instance, when a new chief took over or after young males had been circumcised and had to be presented to the rest of the tribe. Other tribes would be invited to a pilou and, after the exchange of gifts, it was a festive occasion of dance and food. Even greater than a normal pilou was the pilou-pilou, staged to commemorate the death of a chief. Events like this could take a year just in planning and preparation. Human flesh was sometimes eaten during the feast and, realising this, the missionaries assumed these dances were cannibalistic rites and denounced them. Later, colonial authorities took it a step further by banning pilous because of the high energy and trance-like state they induced. The last great pilou was staged in 1951.

Music

Music-making was an important element of every intense ceremony such as initiation, courting or the end of mourning, and always accompanied dance and song. Sometimes instruments were played simply for the clan's entertainment. Above all, however, Kanak music is vocal.

Instruments There are no Kanak words for music or musical instrument. Rather, their terminology is more appropriately translated as 'sound-producing' instruments, the classic example being the conch shell which, when blown, represents the call of the chief or the voice of an ancestor. Many instruments were made for a specific occasion; string instruments did not exist. Rhythm instruments, called *bwanjep*, were used during ceremonies and were played by a group of men. More melodious instruments, known as *hago*, were played solo by both sexes simply for everyday entertainment. Amongst some of the 27 instruments used in ancient Kanak culture were (with anglicised names) the:

Jews'-harp (*wadohnu* in the Nengone language where it originated): made from a dried piece of coconut palm leaf held between the teeth and an attached segment of soft nerve leaf. When the harp is struck, the musician's mouth acts as an echo chamber, producing a soft, low sound.

Coconut leaf whizzer (*maguk* in Pijé): a piece of coconut leaf is attached to a string and twirled, producing a noise like a humming bee.

Oboe: made from hollow grass stems or bamboo.

End-blown flutes: made from a 50-cm-long hollowed pawpaw leaf stem. The pitch varies depending on on the lips' position and how forcefully the air is blown through the flute.

Bamboo stamping tubes: struck vertically against the ground and played at main events, usually by two or more men.

Percussion instruments: these included hitting sticks, palm sheaths which were strummed or hit, and clappers made from a hard bark filled with dried grass and soft niaouli bark, tied together and hit against each other. They are called *doobwe*, meaning 'crab's back' in Xârâcùù, as they were originally made from a crab shell.

Rattles: worn around the legs and made from coconut leaves, shells and certain fruits.

Conch or Triton's shell: used like a trumpet on special occasions and played by a special appointee.

Bead Money

Kanaks' ancient bead money was not a currency in the common sense of the word, for it was never used for buying or exchanging. Instead, it was given as a customary exchange of respect at a birth, marriage, funeral or other ceremonial event, and as a 'seal' to support and maintain relationships and alliances that had somehow been previously damaged. The money needed long and careful preparation. It was made in the form of the ancestors, with a carved or woven 'head' from which hung a string of pendants, either of bone, shell or herbs, resembling the 'spinal cord'. Sometimes a metre-long string or 'leg' of flying fox fur was attached.

Clothing

The days of grass skirts and bagayou are long gone, as the missionaries found such nakedness offensive. They did a thorough job of covering women up by introducing the so-called 'Mother Hubbard' dress. This shin-length, loose-fitting dress, adorned with a stripe or two of lace and worn without a belt in order to camouflage all feminine form, is still the preferred dress of many Kanak women today. At least, unlike some of the clothing missionaries brought into Africa, this dress is cool.

Boats

Canoes made from hollowed-out tree trunks and huge double-hulled outriggers with triangular sails, known as *pirogues*, were the traditional transport for those tribes living on the islands. In these, the tribes – especially those from Lifou and Île des Pins – explored and conquered or simply brought in the daily catch. The art of building these ships has declined though there are still people on Île des Pins and around Yate on the east coast of Grande Terre who have the expertise.

Contemporary Art Festivals

While there are very few Kanak art festivals at grass-roots level, two relatively recent international events have lifted the all-round awareness of Kanak art. The first, held in Paris in 1991, was called *De Jade et de Nacre – Patrimoine Artistique Kanak* (Jade and Mother-of-Pearl – Kanak Artistic Heritage). The largest exhibition of Kanak art ever staged in Europe, it was a tribute to the Kanaks' past. It was also an expression of hope that the ancient culture would continue to flourish. Kanak art, from museums all over Europe and the Noumea museum, was gathered for the exhibition. Following in its footsteps came *Ko i Nèvâ*, an exhibition of modern-day wood sculptors and painters from which the first book on contemporary Kanak art was produced.

A huge quadrennial event is the Festival of Pacific Arts, which gives the indigenous people of all Pacific nations and people from many other places awareness of the Pacific's cultural heritage. This festival was set to be held in Noumea in late 1984 but was cancelled because of political turmoil. New Caledonia hopes to get another chance at hosting it in the year 2000. The most recent festival was staged by the Cook Islands; the next one, in 1996, will be held in Western Samoa.

Films

Little has been produced in English on Kanak culture although the ADCK (see Useful Organisations in the Facts for the Visitor chapter) sells a range of videos in French. Culture and the struggle for independence were the subjects of a documentary entitled *Kanaky au Pouvoir* (Kanaky in Power) made in 1988 by New Zealand film maker, Kathy Dudding. Screened at the International Short Film & Video Festival in France, the document, according to one report, 'caused a stir'.

SPORTS
Cricket

This British game has been the favourite sport of Kanak women since the missionaries introduced it to the Loyauté islanders in the 1850s. It caught on all over the country, predominantly as a women's game, though in recent years men have also taken to it. However, it in no way threatens the popularity of soccer, the number one sport. Caledonian cricket is raucous and rowdy, with Mother Hubbard dresses and matching headbands making up the riotously colourful team uniforms.

The rules of cricket have been altered over the decades to suit the Kanaks, making it a faster and more exciting game than the staid Western version. Each team has 13 players and four reserves, including two bowlers and two batters. There is no such thing as 'high' or a 'wide' and, in grandmothers' matches, young girls called 'horses' do the running. Bats and balls are chunky, village-made items, the former carved by a tribal sculptor and the balls made from the curdled sap of banyan trees. The season varies from place to place, but from March to November you can count on a few matches being played either on Saturday or Sunday afternoon in Noumea and on all the Loyauté islands.

Pétanque

Another sporting idiosyncrasy, this time inherited from the French, is *pétanque*. Sometimes called *boules* (bowls), it too is a special version of the original game and in no way can be confused with traditional bowls where white-clad men and women stand around an immaculate green lawn in the heat of the midday sun.

Instead, this much-loved men's game is played in the cool of the late afternoon on a rough but flat gravel pitch (a *boulodrome*), scratched out under the shade of large trees. The aim is for you and your partner to throw, with much flair and style, large metal bowls at a small target ball, the 'jack'. The bowl that lands closest to the jack wins. Pétanque is played passionately by both French and Kanaks in Noumea and elsewhere, and the New Caledonian champ has the honour of going over to compete in the annual French title, which is held around June.

Soccer

As in France, soccer is the country's most popular sport. It is played and avidly supported throughout the country by both Kanaks and Caldoches, with games usually held on Saturday or Sunday. In Noumea, there's a well-used soccer field just north of the Anse Vata beach area. On the Loyauté islands, every village has its own field, usually located close to the church or school, where the whole village from tribal elders right down to young children congregates to enthusiastically cheer on the home team.

RELIGION

For details on traditional Kanak religion see the previous Culture section.

As a result of the missionaries' work, there is not a single town in New Caledonia which does not have at least one church. However, the role of religion is losing importance as younger Kanaks are preferring to revive their ancient customs. That said, on any given Sunday, the Noumea cathedral and little churches all over the country are filled to capacity with an elderly Kanak congregation. The missionary zeal that converted the islanders to Christianity makes priests and ministers in remote areas conduct five services on the Sabbath, driving from one small church to another or, if necessary, being delivered to their flock by motor boat.

Almost two-thirds of the population is Catholic, accounting for 92,000 people. Of these, just over half are Europeans and the remainder are Kanaks, and some Wallisians. Protestants make up one-quarter of the population; Kanaks form the majority of followers, far outweighing the Tahitians and Europeans who also follow this faith. Other religious groups include about 4000 Muslims, generally of Indonesian descent, Mormons from Tahiti, and Buddhists, Baha'ists, Seventh-Day Adventists and Jehovah's Witnesses.

Saint Louis Mission Church

LANGUAGE

French is the official language of New Caledonia. It is widely spoken and understood, unlike English which is limited to some French people, those in the tourist industry, and the new generation of Kanaks who are now receiving more English education. In addition, Tahitian, Wallisian, Indonesian and Vietnamese are also spoken, mainly in Noumea.

A host of Kanak languages exist but, unlike neighbouring Vanuatu, Kanaks have no unifying indigenous language. (Vanuatu, which has considerably more Melanesian languages than New Caledonia, has adopted a ni-Vanuatu pidgin called Bislama, thus enabling all people to speak to one another.) Therefore, when independence comes, French will probably remain the lingua franca, because of the lack of consensus on what tribal language to use. This is hardly surprising considering that the French have long discouraged or ignored Kanak languages. They would never have allowed the emergence of another language, as it would have threatened French, which they felt was already battling for survival in a region where the majority of countries and islands use English as their international language.

Kanak Languages

An estimated 28 distinctly different Kanak languages coexist in New Caledonia and are part of the 1200 known Melanesian languages spoken throughout the Pacific. The Melanesian dialects are an eastern subdivision of the huge widespread Austronesian language family. Other spoken languages in this family include Malagasy (from Madagascar), Tagalog (Philippines) and the Polynesian and Malay-Indonesian languages. The many Melanesian dialects are not only the result of the isolation of the different communities but also reflect the multiplicity of the clans and of their contacts.

Within the 28 Kanak language groups there are also many dialects, with most Kanaks being able to speak their own language as well as neighbouring dialects. While all Kanaks know French and use it in particular situations, the majority of rural Kanaks use their own language within the sphere of their family and clan. The language spoken by the largest number of Kanaks is Drehu. It comes from Lifou and is mixed these days with some Polynesian, French and English. Iaai and a Polynesian language, Faga Uvea, are spoken on Ouvea while the sole indigenous language of Mare is Nengone and that of Île des Pins is Nââ Kwênyii. On Lifou and Mare, in addition to the everyday languages, there are respectful, ceremonial dialects used only when talking to the chief or the ancestors. They are called Miny and Iwateno respectively, but are rarely practised these days.

On Grande Terre there are numerous languages, the one most spoken being Ajië which links clans on both coasts. The north is dominated by Yâlayu; in the south it's Xârâcùù. A type of pidgin dialect called Tayo exists in the Saint Louis area near Noumea as people from differing tribes were once brought to this region and needed a contact language. Some languages such as Zirë, spoken around Bourail, and Arhâ, near Poya, have as few as 250 speakers.

Before the missionaries arrived, literature was nonexistent. The missionaries translated the Bible and a few other religious works into a couple of the Kanak languages, but little else happened until French ethnologist Maurice Leenhardt arrived early this century and started studying the languages. The Kanaks' linguistic diversity has long been used by the French government as an excuse not to teach local languages in school. The few EPK schools that still exist teach their students in their native tongues while, in a very recent initiative, government schools on the Loyauté islands and around Houailou have started teaching the local language for a couple of hours each week. In a private lycée in Noumea, students can get training in Drehu and Ajië. At higher levels, both the government-run and private teachers' train-

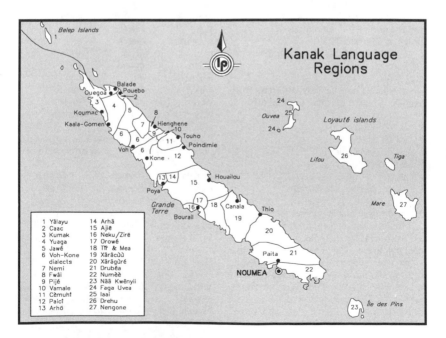

Kanak Language Regions

1	Yâlayu	14	Arhâ
2	Caac	15	Ajië
3	Kumak	16	Neku/Zirë
4	Yuaga	17	Orowé
5	Jawé	18	Tîrî & Mea
6	Voh–Kone dialects	19	Xârâcùù
		20	Xârâgùré
7	Nemi	21	Drubéa
8	Fwâi	22	Numèè
9	Pijé	23	Nââ Kwênyii
10	Vamale	24	Faga Uvea
11	Cêmuhî	25	Iaai
12	Paicî	26	Drehu
13	Arhö	27	Nengone

ing colleges in Noumea offer students the option of studying Melanesian languages and literature. This small movement to reintroduce the indigenous languages comes at a time when many Kanak languages are in danger of being lost.

Pronunciation While many features of the various Kanak languages are similar, they do not have identical pronunciations. In some languages, for example Drehu and Nengone, nasal vowels do not exist, while others, including Paicî and Ajië, are very tonal. Long vowel sounds formed by the doubling of vowels is frequent but double consonants are not. Many aspirated consonants exist and are always preceeded by an 'h'.

Although many consonants sound similar to those used in English, the following hold a few surprises:

c   as 'ch' in 'cheque'
dr as 'd' in 'day'
g   as 'ng' in 'camping'
j   as 'j' in 'June'
hw as a normal 'w' but aspirated
ny as 'n' in neuter
x   a guttural sound as the 'ch' in the Scottish 'loch'

Vowel sounds can be very different from English. A few of the more unusual are:

â   as 'o' in 'on'
ë   as 'an' in 'land'
ö   as 'ou' in 'about'
ô   as 'o' in 'long'
u   as 'oo' in 'too'
û   as 'oo' in 'too' but shorter

Grammar In Kanak languages there is often no difference between a noun and a verb. The Iaai word *han*, for example, means either 'a meal' or 'to eat'. There are no features like nouns with genders: instead, in Ajië, the terms would be *mèyë bwè* (female chicken) and *mèyë wi* (male chicken). With pronouns, one word suffices, and therefore in Nengone, the word *inu* means 'I', 'me', 'my' and 'mine'. There are also no verb endings to indicate

present, past and future tenses. To show that something is plural, a pluraliser is used in front of the word, for example, in Drùbea, *mwà* is 'house' while *ma mwà* is 'houses'.

Some Useful Words A few Drehu words which may come in handy are listed here:

English	French	Drehu
banana	*banane*	wshnawa
beach	*plage*	hnangöni
bed	*lit*	göhnë
boy	*garçon*	nekö trahmany
bread	*pain*	falawa
dance	*danser*	fia
dinner	*dîner*	xeni hej
to eat	*manger*	xen
English	*anglais*	papale
father	*père*	kem-kakaa
French	*français*	wiwi
language	*langue*	qene hlapa
mother	*mère*	thin-nenë
rain	*pluie*	mani
sky	*ciel*	hnengödrai
to speak	*parler*	ewekë
sun	*soleil*	jö
to swim	*nager*	aj
tree	*arbre*	sinöe
when	*quand*	eu
where	*où*	kaa
which	*quel*	kau
who	*qui*	drei
why	*pourquoi*	némen

Some Useful Phrases The following phrases, also in Drehu, may prove helpful:

English	French	Drehu
Hello.	*Bonjour.*	Bozu.
Goodbye.	*Au revoir.*	Dréé.
please	*s'il vous plaît*	sipone
until tomorrow	*à demain*	e lanyié
What is your name?	*Comment t'appelles-tu?*	Dréi la éjé i éö?
How are you?	*Comment allez-vous?*	Tune ka epun?
What do you want?	*Qu'est-ce que vous voulez?*	Epun a aja nemen?
I would like to buy...	*Je voudrais acheter...*	Eni a itö...

Drehu-Tahitian Comparison

This short list shows the communal roots of two branches of the Austronesian language family – one Polynesian (Tahitian), the other Melanesian (Drehu).

English	Tahitian	Drehu
ancestor	tupuna	xo trapan
arm	rima	im
beautiful	lele	lolo
breast	ouma	mano
to be able	mana	men
to cut	tapahi	thapa
day	lai	drai
fish	ika	i
leave	rau	dron
light	malama	melem
mother	tina	thin
mouth	vaha	whe
to need	fia	pi
old	tua	what
plant	tanu	tan
tooth	niho	nyo
two	lua	lue
water	miti	tim
with	ma	me
work	ohipa	huliwa
you	oe	eo

English & French

Most New Caledonians do not speak fluent English and many have no knowledge of that language at all. Some of the French living here have the age-old prejudice against all things British and will rarely bother speaking the language. On the other hand, Kanaks recognise that English is the predominant language in the Pacific region and regard it as important to learn.

French is spoken and understood by 97% of the population. It would be wise to carry and use a good French phrasebook as outside Noumea not very much English is spoken. You'll find the French are most likely to use their English if you have at least attempted to speak their language. Start out with a few words of French and when they see you're making the effort (or murdering their language, depending on how they interpret it), they are likely to volunteer their English.

The following list of French expressions may be helpful in the short term. For better comprehension of French, there is the CREIPAC school in Noumea which teaches French to tourists and visiting students (for details see the Language Courses section in the Facts for the Visitor chapter).

Greetings & Civilities

Good morning.	*Bonjour.*
Good evening.	*Bonsoir.*
Good night.	*Bonne nuit.*
Goodbye.	*Au revoir.*
No.	*Non.*
Yes.	*Oui.*
Yes, please.	*Oui, volontiers.*
Please.	*S'il vous plaît.*
Thank you/thanks.	*Merci.*
Thanks very much.	*Merci beaucoup.*
Excuse me.	*Excusez-moi.*
Sorry.	*Pardon.*
How are you?	*Comment allez-vous?*

Some Useful Phrases

Do you speak English?	*Parlez-vous anglais?*
I understand.	*Je comprends.*
I don't understand.	*Je ne comprends pas.*
How much is it?	*C'est combien?*
Can I...?	*Je peux...?*
Can I have...?	*Je voudrais...*
I'd like to...	*J'aimerais...*
We'd like to order...	*Nous aimerions commander...*

Signs

camping ground	*camping*
YHA hostel	*auberge de jeunesse*
hotel	*hôtel*
entrance	*entrée*
exit	*sortie*
information	*renseignements*
open/closed	*ouvert/fermé*
prohibited	*interdit*
right/left	*droit/gauche*
toll	*péage*
toilets	*toilettes, WC*
ferry terminal	*gare maritime*
bus station	*gare routière*

Around Town

I'm looking for ...	*Je cherche ...*
a bank	*une banque*
the town hall	*la mairie*
the ..., embassy	*l'ambassade de ...*
the post office	*le bureau de poste*
a bookshop	*une librairie*
a tobacconist/	*un tabac*
little shop	
a swimming pool	*une piscine*
the hospital	*l'hôpital*

Around the Countryside

Where is (the) ...?	*Où est ...*
beach	*la plage*
waterfall	*la cascade*
cave	*la grotte*
cliff	*la falaise*
chief's house	*la chefferie*
flying fox	*la roussette*
turtle	*la tortue*
(water)hole	*le trou*
mountain pass	*le col*
community clinic	*le dispensaire*

Some Useful Words

shell	*le coquillage*
rock	*la roche*
the outback	*la brousse*
custom	*la coutume*
arrow	*la flèche*
room	*la chambre*

Getting Around

Where is the bus station?
Où est la gare routière?
Is it far from here?
C'est loin d'ici?
I am hitchhiking.
Je fais de l'autostop.
How far are you going?
Jusqu'où allez-vous?
I'm heading for...
Je vais à...
How do I get to...?
Comment peut-on aller à...?
We're just travelling around.
Nous visitons la région.
I'd like to rent...
J'aimerais louer...

a car/bike/moped	
une voiture/un vélo/une mobylette	
bus	*le bus*
mail bus	*le courrier*
ferry	*le bac*
plane	*l'avion*

Food

breakfast	*le petit déjeuner*
lunch	*le déjeuner*
dinner	*le dîner*
set dish of the day	*le plat du jour*
set meal of the day	*le menu du jour*
bread	*du pain*
cheese	*du fromage*
sandwich	*le sandwich*
seafood	*des fruits de mer*
cheese omelette	*une omelette au fromage*
chips/French fries	*des frites*
yam	*l'igname*
waffle	*la gaufre*
pancake	*la crêpe*
snack	*le casse-croûte*
a slice	*une tranche*
shop	*le magasin*
grocery store	*l'épicerie*
food shop	*l'alimentation*
bakery	*la boulangerie*
pastry shop	*la pâtisserie*
butcher	*la boucherie*
café-style snack bar	*la brasserie*
service charge (not) included	*service (non) compris*

Drinks

beer	*une bière*
wine	*du vin*
jug/pitcher	*un pichet*
orange juice	*un jus d'orange*
milk	*du lait*
pub	*un bistro*

Health

I'm ...	*Je suis ...*
diabetic	*diabétique*
asthmatic	*asthmatique*

I'm allergic ...	*Je suis allergique ...*
to antibiotics	*aux antibiotiques*
to penicillin	*à la pénicilline*

Emergencies

Help!	*Au secours!*
Call a doctor!	*Appelez un médecin!*
Call the police	*Appelez la police!*

Times & Dates

At what time?	*À quelle heure?*
What time is it?	*Quelle heure est-il?*
What's the date?	*Quel jour sommes nous?*

today	*aujourd'hui*
tomorrow	*demain*
yesterday	*hier*

Monday	*lundi*
Tuesday	*mardi*
Wednesday	*mercredi*
Thursday	*jeudi*
Friday	*vendredi*
Saturday	*samedi*
Sunday	*dimanche*

Numbers

1	*un*
2	*deux*
3	*trois*
4	*quatre*
5	*cinq*
6	*six*
7	*sept*
8	*huit*
9	*neuf*
10	*dix*
11	*onze*
12	*douze*
13	*treize*
14	*quatorze*
15	*quinze*
16	*seize*
17	*dix-sept*
18	*dix-huit*
19	*dix-neuf*
20	*vingt*
30	*trente*
40	*quarante*
50	*cinquante*
60	*soixante*
70	*soixante-dix*
80	*quatre-vingts*
90	*quatre-vingt-dix*
100	*cent*
1000	*mille*
2000	*deux mille*

Facts for the Visitor

VISAS & EMBASSIES

All visitors must be able to show a return or onward air ticket and, of course, must have a valid passport.

European Union and Swiss nationals may stay for up to three months without a visa. Citizens of Canada, Japan, New Zealand and the USA are allowed entry for one month without a visa; however, if you're planning to stay longer than a month, you should consider getting a three-month maximum visa before leaving home. You'll probably have to pay for it but it'll save the hassle of trying to get an extension in Noumea, where they're not always given. On the other hand, if Noumean officials do grant an extension, it will be free.

Australians need a visa as do all citizens from countries not previously mentioned. Australians can get a 30-day maximum visa free of charge by applying to a French embassy or consulate. You'll need a good reason, such as a work contract, for a longer visa to be granted.

Only in exceptional circumstances, such as cyclone season for yachties, when weather conditions impede departure, or if you have an accident, will visas be extended for more than three months. For all enquiries contact the Haut Commissariat, Bureau des Étrangers (☎ 27.28.22), Rue Paul Doumer, BP C5 Noumea. It is open weekdays from 7.45 to 11 am and 12 to 2 pm.

French Embassies & Consulates

Following is a list of French embassies and consulates in some major cities around the world.

Australia
> French Consulate General, 492 St Kilda Rd, Victoria 3004 (☎ (03) 820 0921)
> French Consulate General, 20th floor St Martins Tower, 31 Market St, Sydney, NSW 2000 (☎ (02) 261 5779)

Canada
> French Embassy, 42 Sussex Promenade, Ottawa, Ontario K1M 2C9 (☎ (613) 232 1795)

France
> Ministère des Affaires Étrangères, 21bis, 23 & 34 Rue la Pérouse, Paris 75775 (☎ (01) 40.66.66.99)

Japan
> French Embassy, 11-44, 4 Chome, Minami, Azabu, Minato-Ku, Tokyo 106 (☎ (3) 5420 8800)
> French Consulate General, 24th floor Ohbayashi Building, 4-33 Kitahama-Higashi, Chuo-Ku, Osaka 540 (☎ (6) 946 6181)

New Zealand
> French Embassy, 1-3 Willeston St (PO Box 1695), Wellington (☎ (04) 472 0200)

UK
> French Consulate General, 21 Cromwell Rd, London SW7 2DQ (☎ (071) 581 5292). The visa section is at 6A Cromwell Place, London SW7 2EQ (☎ (071) 823 9555)

USA
> French Embassy, 4101 Reservoir Rd NW, Washington DC 20007 (☎ (202) 944 6000)
> French Consulate General, 540 Bush St, San Francisco, CA 94108 (☎ (415) 397 4330)
> French Consulate General, 934 Fifth Ave, New York, NY 10021 (☎ (212) 606 3621)

Foreign Consulates in New Caledonia

All nations represented in New Caledonia have their offices in Noumea.

Australia
> Immeuble Foch, 19-21 Ave du Maréchal Foch, BP 22 Noumea (☎ 27.24.14)

Belgium
> 13 Rue Jules Ferry, BP 2683 Noumea (☎ 28.46.46)

Indonesia
> 2 Rue Lamartine, Baie de l'Orphelinat, BP 26 Noumea (☎ 28.25.74)

Italy
> 1 Rue des Frères Vautrin, Vallée du Tir, BP 4046 Noumea (☎ 27.67.53)

Japan
> 45 Rue du 5 Mai, Magenta, Noumea (☎ 25.37.29)

New Zealand
> 4 Blvd Vauban, BP 2219 Noumea (☎ 27.25.43)

The Netherlands
> Route de la Digue, BP L2 Ducos, Noumea (☎ 28.57.20)

Papua New Guinea
    The Australian Consulate acts as the PNG representative
Switzerland
    18 Rue Jim Daly, BP 2352 Val Plaisance, Noumea (☎ 26.11.59)
Vanuatu
    1st floor, Shop Center Vata, 101 Route de l'Anse Vata, Noumea (☎ 25.90.85)

Work Permits

Only French citizens can immediately work in New Caledonia. All other nationalities need a work permit and they are nigh on impossible to get once you're there. The government gives them out only to people with skills that are highly sought after. For such positions all the paperwork is usually arranged long before you arrive in the country.

That said, it is not impossible to pick up work on the spot if you have the right expertise and can find an employer who is willing to overlook the work permit regulation; that is, hire you 'in the black'. Highly qualified technical jobs are available as there is a surplus of bureaucrats but not enough skilled workers. Computer experts and English teachers fit this bill. Wages for computer personnel, especially those with knowledge of systems other than IBM, are high, typically between US$25-40 per hour. Teaching English has long been the domain of the métros, but if you're qualified you may be able to get some private work in the black.

The main body aiding in the search for a job is the Agence pour l'Emploi on Rue du Général Gallieni in Noumea.

CUSTOMS

For any enquiries about customs regulations, contact the Office de Douanes (☎ 28.57.32), 7 Rue du Général Gallieni in Noumea.

Concessions

Travellers arriving from Europe, America, Africa or Asia (with the exception of Indonesia) are allowed to bring in 200 cigarettes, 50 cigars or 250 grams of tobacco, two litres of wine or one bottle of spirits or liqueur, and a 'reasonable' quantity of perfume for personal use. There is no restriction on cameras and film as long as they are for yourself.

Regulations

It is strictly forbidden to bring in firearms or ammunition, drugs, birds such as parrots, parakeets, pigeons or turtledoves, or cats and dogs. Animals found will be quarantined. Plants and seeds must be declared to customs who will have them checked by the Health Department and possibly given a sanitary certificate for entry. Up to A$10,000 can be imported without being declared.

When leaving, the export of anything that appears on the Washington Convention list (regarding the commerce of endangered wild flora and fauna) is prohibited. This includes rare indigenous birds such as the cagou and the Ouvea parakeet, and turtles and dugongs. Objects of ethnographic interest are also not to be taken out of the country.

If you're taking home a bucket of shells, there is one that is forbidden in Australia and New Zealand and will be hunted out and confiscated by customs there. It is the shell of the big land snail seen all over the country, known as the Giant African snail. This voracious eater can lay eggs in the tip of its shell, and therefore is prohibited.

MONEY

Currency

The currency used in New Caledonia is the CFP (Communauté Française du Pacific) franc. Though banks and other formal institutions use that abbreviation, it is most commonly shortened to an 'F' written after the numeral, which is the method used throughout this book. The same currency is used in French Polynesia and, although the money may have the mint mark of Noumea or Papeete, the two are interchangeable.

Banknotes come in denominations of 500, 1000, 5000 and 10,000F. Coins come in units of 1, 2 and 5F (very lightweight coins) plus standard 10, 20, 50 and 100F.

Exchange Rates

The CFP is tied to the French franc (FFr) at a fixed rate, with 1CFP equal to 0.055FFr (hence the occasionally used expression *'faire du cinq cinq'* which literally means 'to make five five' but freely translated is 'to make a lot of money'). The value of the CFP in relation to some other international currencies is:

US$1	106.67F
UK£1	158.98F
A$1	74.56F
NZ$1	60.47F
CA$1	81.40F
Y100	95.68F
1FFr	17.94F
100VT (Vanuatu)	88.82F
SGP$1 (Singapore	66.57F
DM1	60.77F

Banks

Five banks have their headquarters in Noumea but the only ones with a few branches around the country are Westpac and Banque Nationale de Paris (BNP). Also in la Brousse you'll sometimes come across the Banque Calédonienne d'Investissement (BCI), a development bank created following the Matignon Accords. It generally does not handle foreign exchange. The only bank doing exchange on the Loyauté islands is the BNP on Lifou. There is no bank on Île des Pins.

All banks charge a 500F commission on all cash or travellers' cheques transactions. The only place without this fee is the American Express office in Noumea. The exchange counter in the arrival hall of Tontouta Airport asks 400F commission but its exchange rates are lower than those of the banks. There's a new Westpac branch at the turn-off from the highway to the airport.

Banking Hours Most banks are open Monday to Friday, non-stop from 7.20/7.45 am to 3.30/3.45 pm. All are closed on weekends with the sole exception of a BNP branch in the Noumean suburb of Sainte Marie. The exchange counters in the arrival hall and departure lounge at Tontouta Airport are open only when there are flights.

Credit Cards

Major credit cards are accepted by hotels, restaurants, duty-free shops and airline offices in Noumea, but only at more expensive hotels outside the capital. Money can be drawn on American Express cards at the company's Noumean office, on Visa cards at BNP, and on Diners Club, Visa and MasterCard cards at Westpac. The Société Générale bank has automatic tellers for Visa cash advances but they work only with Visa cards issued in France.

If you arrive in New Caledonia on a Friday evening with only a credit card in hand, it'll be very difficult to get local currency before Monday morning. You can get cash advances through some of the top-end hotels but they'll charge through the nose. Alternatively, the BNP bank at Sainte Marie can organise an advance (Visa only) on Saturday mornings but you must get to the bank by 9.30 am to give them time to arrange it.

Costs

New Caledonia is expensive, both in the capital and around the country. Like many South Pacific islands, most of the goods are imported, usually from France but also from Australia or New Zealand, and therefore are pricey. Even the cost of local produce like fish, fruit and vegetables follows the artificially pepped-up trend. Accommodation bills are extremely high for what you get.

In Noumea, if you stay in the YHA hostel, live on bread, cheese and fruit and do nothing but hitch to the beach, you'll still go through 1500F (around US$15) per day. Step up to a bottom-end hotel, a *snack* bar meal and a few sights and you'll be looking at 6000F (US$60). From here, your wallet or credit card's ceiling is the limit.

On the other hand, in a beautiful setting away from the capital there's less need to spend lots of money. A night's camping will cost less than 1000F or, on the Loyauté islands, can often be free. The tropical life outside Noumea lends itself to finding solitary places, snorkelling for hours or hiking in the forests. Without a tent though, accommodation and meals will still be the major costs.

There is no value-added tax (VAT) in New Caledonia.

Tipping & Bargaining

Neither of these practices is very common in New Caledonia. Tipping is discouraged as, according to Melanesian custom, it is considered a gift and creates the obligation that the receiver must reciprocate. On the flip side, if you round up the bill or simply leave change in a European-run café or restaurant, it's unlikely your gesture will be declined.

WHEN TO GO

Weatherwise, the best time to visit is from September to November when the days are not too hot or sticky and there's less likelihood of rain. June and July can also be pleasant and not overly hot.

WHAT TO BRING

Dress in New Caledonia is casual. Kanak women wear their light, cool Mother Hubbard dresses, while men generally stick to short-sleeved shirts and shorts or trousers. The French community, particularly in Noumea, are pretty much immaculate in their choice of clothing and style.

Comfortable cotton clothing is best and you'll need to bring a pullover or cardigan in late autumn or winter as temperatures drop at night-time. In the wet season, you may want to toss up between a collapsible umbrella or a light raincoat (the latter can tend to make you feel sweaty and sticky). A hat and sunscreen are the bare necessities for protection from the intense sunrays, and insect repellent is essential during the February-April mosquito season.

Stout walking shoes are a prerequisite for getting across the razor-sharp coral tracks and cliffs on Île des Pins and the Loyauté islands. A Swiss-style army knife is also handy for uncorking a bottle of wine at picnic time and for prising open coconuts for their sweet milk during long walks (that said, it's not an easy task and, once you've succeeded, you'll then need a straw to drink it!). Those into exploring caves will need a torch (flashlight).

For reef walking, either plastic shoes or an old pair of slippery sneakers will do in the short term but the best protection and durability comes from diving boots (which are quite pricey). Keen snorkellers must bring their own mask, snorkel and, if possible, fins – otherwise they'll miss most of the beauty as rental outlets are few and far between (though you can buy reasonably priced gear in Noumea).

Depending on your intended activities, a final 'essentials' checklist would include the following: comfortable cotton clothing, swimsuit, sweater, sandals or thongs, walking shoes, first-aid kit, hat, sunscreen, insect repellent, camera, film, snorkelling gear, international diving certificate, torch, water bottle, sleeping bag or sheet and tent.

SUGGESTED ITINERARIES

Depending on the time and money you have to spend and your talent at organising, the following itineraries could be considered:

Three Days
Spend one day in and around Noumea, take a day trip or diving excursion to Amédée Islet, Île Ouen or Île des Pins (though divers would have to be careful about flying afterwards if they went to Île des Pins) and one day to the Rivière Bleue park or the Yate/Goro area (you'd need to hire a car or take an organised tour to do these in a day).

One Week
There are plenty of options with this amount of time. As an example, you could spend two days in Noumea, one day diving and snorkelling on Amédée Islet or Île Ouen, a day's hike in the Rivière Bleue park, one day exploring around Yate/Goro and two days on Île des Pins. Alternatively, cut out Yate/Goro, drop Île des Pins to one day and then spend three days on the Loyauté islands or up along the north-east coast (the latter would be possible using local buses).

Two Weeks
This is a good amount of time to start exploring all of New Caledonia. For example, you could have two days in and around Noumea and a day on Amédée Islet or a hike around Monts Koghis. Then take off for five or six days in a car around Grande Terre, spending a night in La Foa or Sarramea, two or three nights in gîtes along the east coast, one night in the north and another around Bourail. At a more hectic pace this is also possible using buses and your thumb. The last six days can then be divided between the Loyauté islands and Île des Pins.

TOURIST OFFICES

Since the Matignon Accords, New Caledonia's three provinces have been responsible for their own tourism strategies and, as a result, there's no coordination. The main tourist office in Noumea caters predominantly for visitors to the capital and the South Province, though it has a little information on the whole country. The North Province Tourist Office, also in Noumea, can assist with general information and accommodation lists for its region. Various other agencies in the capital may prove to be helpful – these, as well as the two offices previously mentioned, are detailed in the Information section in the Noumea chapter.

Probably the best, all-round sources of information are the government tourist offices in your home country. In Japan, Australia and New Zealand (New Caledonia's biggest tourist markets), offices of the highly efficient Destination Nouvelle Calédonie, a promotional agency established following the accords, have been set up.

Overseas Reps

Overseas addresses of New Caledonian government tourist offices are:

Australia
    Destination Nouvelle Calédonie, 11th floor, 39 York St, Sydney, NSW 2000 (☎ (02) 299 2573; fax (02) 290 2242)
Canada
    Soft Montreal, Suite 490, 1981 Ave McGill College, Montreal, Quebec H3 A2 W9 (☎ (514) 288 4264; fax (514) 845 4868)
France
    Maison de la Nouvelle Calédonie, 7 Rue Général Bertrand, 75007 Paris (☎ (01) 4273 2414; fax (01) 40.65.96.00)
Japan
    Destination Nouvelle Calédonie, Akasaka Park Bldg No 2, 10-9 Akasaka 2-Chrome, Minato-Ku, Tokyo 107 (☎ (03) 3583 3280; fax (03) 3505 2873)
New Zealand
    Destination Nouvelle Calédonie, 3rd floor, 57 Fort St, PO Box 4300 Auckland (☎ (09) 307 5257; fax (09) 379 2874)
USA
    French Government Tourist Office, 9454 Wilshire Blvd, Beverly Hills, Los Angeles, CA 90212 (☎ (310) 271 7838; fax (310) 276 2835)

USEFUL ORGANISATIONS

Some organisations which may prove useful include:

Agence de Développement de la Culture Kanak (ADCK)
    BP 378 Nouville, Noumea; agency to promote Kanak culture in New Caledonia and around the world.; open weekdays from 7.30 to 11.30 am and 1 to 4.30 pm (☎ 28.32.90; fax 28.21.78)
Association Calédonienne des Handicapés
    Route Parc Forestier, Montravel, Noumea; organisation for handicapped people (☎ 27.60.65)
Association pour la Sauvegarde de la Nature Néo-Calédonienne
    37 Rue Georges Clémenceau, BP 1772 Noumea; flora & fauna protection group (☎ 28.32.75)
Organisation de Recherche Scientifique du Territoire Outre-Mer (ORSTOM)
    Promenade Roger Laroque, BP A5 Noumea; the overseas French office for scientific research on the South Pacific (☎ 26.10.00; fax 26.38.18)
SOS Violences Sexuelles
    12 Rue des Frères Vautrin, Vallée du Tir, Noumea; rape and sexual violence assistance centre; open weekdays from 7.30 to 11.30 am and 1.30 to 5.30 pm (☎ 27.83.43)
Université Française du Pacifique Sud
    59 RT14 Magenta or BP 4477 Noumea; French University of the South Pacific (☎ 25.49.55)

Emergency Telephone Numbers

The following are emergency numbers you can call anywhere in the country:

Police	☎ 17
Fire	☎ 18
SAMU (medical aid)	☎ 15

BUSINESS HOURS & HOLIDAYS
Business Hours

New Caledonians generally observe the Mediterranean tradition of closing for at least a couple of hours at lunch time. Sundays are extremely quiet throughout the country. All businesses, most shops and many restaurants are closed.

Offices Government offices and most private businesses are open weekdays from 7.30 or 8 am to 4 or 5 pm but close for a two-hour siesta between 11.30 am and 1.30 pm. Banks are the only formal institutions which do not indulge in this lunch-time tradition.

Shops In general, shops are open weekdays from 7.30 to 11 am and 2 to 6 pm and Saturday from 8 or 9 am to noon. However, some supermarkets and small convenience stores have much longer hours. They often don't close for lunch, extend trading until 7 pm or later and are open all day Saturday and Sunday morning.

Village trade stores are generally open Monday to Saturday from sunrise to sunset, though proprietors usually shut up shop for the two-hour lunch. They may open for a few hours on Sunday prior to the morning church service and then again for a couple of hours in the late afternoon.

Note that it is not permitted to sell alcohol from shops anywhere around New Caledonia between noon on Saturday and 6 am on Monday. This law is quite stringently enforced in Noumea (though if you're a good talker and can produce a brown paper bag, you'll probably find your way around it) but elsewhere, particularly along Grande Terre's north-east coast and on the Loyauté islands, it's ignored.

Holidays

When a national holiday falls on a weekend, the accompanying public holiday is usually taken on the following Monday. New Caledonia follows France in all its major public holidays.

1 January	*New Year's Day*
March/April	*Easter Monday*
1 May	*Labour Day*
May/June	*Ascension Day* – 40 days after Easter Sunday
	Whit Monday – the eighth Monday after Easter
14 July	*Bastille Day*
15 August	*Assumption Day*
24 September	*New Caledonia Day*
1 November	*All Saints' Day*
11 November	*Armistice Day*
25 December	*Christmas Day*

CULTURAL EVENTS

France's national day, 14 July, commemorates the storming of the Bastille prison by a Parisian mob in 1789. While that event is far removed from contemporary New Caledo-

nia, a military parade is still held in the morning in central Noumea. Unlike Tahiti, which is famous for its festivities marking Bastille Day, in Noumea the only fun event is held the preceding evening, when families and children carrying pretty lighted lanterns gather at dusk and form a procession that winds through the streets to Place des Cocotiers. Here, in some years, dance floors are set up and bands entertain until late in the evening.

New Caledonia Day commemorates the day in 1853 when Admiral Auguste Febvrier Despointes claimed New Caledonia for France. It's simply a public holiday and no celebrations are held. The Kanaks have traditionally considered this to be a day of mourning, despite attempts by contemporary Kanak leaders to reverse that idea and make it, instead, a day to celebrate their culture.

Other events held around the country include:

March
> *Festival of the Yam* – The most important Kanak festival marking the beginning of the harvest. The date varies from village to village and year to year, but it's generally around March 19. For details see the aside on the Festival of the Yam in the Facts about the Country chapter.

April/May
> *Giant Omelette Festival* – Dumbea; a huge skillet and many hands are used to make a free-for-all omelette

Mid-May
> *La Régate des Touques* – Noumea; people build decorative floats from empty oil barrels and paddle furiously in a race along Anse Vata

Late August/Early September
> *Agricultural Fair* – Bourail; features a rodeo

Late October/Early November
> *Sound & Light Show* – Fort Teremba, near La Foa; light shows are staged over a fortnight before the mosquito invasion begins

POST & TELECOMMUNICATIONS

There are post offices throughout Grande Terre and the outlying islands. Officially called Office des Postes et Télécommunications (OPT), they use a symbol of a startled-looking blue cagou on a yellow background. Internal postal deliveries are frequent, with small postal buses carting mail back and forth across Grande Terre in the early hours of the morning.

The main post office in Noumea is at 9 Rue Eugène Porcheron. Its office hours are weekdays from 7.45 to 11.15 am and 12.15 to 3.30 pm, and Saturday from 7.30 to 11 am. Branches around Noumea, as well as those all over New Caledonia, generally have the same hours except that they close at 3 pm.

Many people and organisations use a PO Box, written in French as BP (short for *boîte postale*).

Sending Mail

Airmail letters up to 10 grams cost 80F to Australia, New Zealand and France. To North America and Asia they cost 95F, to the UK and Europe 105F.

The estimated delivery time to New Zealand and Australia should be about four to seven days but letters have been known to take a fortnight to get to Brisbane, the closest Australian city. To Europe and North America count on at least seven to 10 days.

Receiving Mail

Most post offices have a poste restante service where mail sent to you can be picked up for a 50F-per-letter charge. Holders of American Express cards or travellers' cheques can have mail addressed to them at American Express, 27bis Ave du Maréchal Foch, BP 50 Noumea. There's a set 100F pick-up fee for any number of letters. Those staying at the Noumea YHA Hostel, Route Château d'Eau, BP 676 Noumea, can get mail delivered to their doorstep for no extra charge.

Philatelic Bureau

Many of New Caledonia's stamp issues are beautifully designed and some are sought after by collectors. They are sold from a special counter at the far end of the main post office in Noumea.

Telephone

The phone service throughout the country is quite good. *Télécartes* (telephone cards) cost 1000F (25 units), 3000F (80 units) or 5000F (140 units) and are available from post offices and a few *tabacs* (tobacconists' shops) in Noumea. To get directory assistance *(renseignements téléphoniques)*, dial ☎ 12.

Local Calls Local telephone calls are charged according to the sort of phone you use. The cheapest way to telephone locally is to buy a phonecard and head to an appropriate phone box where your call will be calculated at 40F per unit (which lasts about five minutes). Local calls made from a coin-operated telephone box cost 70F per unit. A few tabacs and cafés have cream-coloured public phones which cost a minimum of 100F. The disadvantage with the first method is that the cheapest phonecard you can buy costs 1000F, so it's tough luck if you want to make only a few calls. The problem with the second method is that there are very few public phones in Noumea which accept coins. Around la Brousse, however, most public booths take coins only.

International Calls The least expensive way to make an international phone call is to buy a phonecard and use a public box. Dial the international access code 00; then the country code, city code and your number. Off-peak discount rates apply only on calls to France.

To phone Australia or New Zealand you'll be looking at 285F per minute. To France/Japan it's 427/530F and to the USA/UK it costs 570/640F per minute.

Operator-connected international calls can also be made from the main post office in Noumea. You must ask the teller at counter 17, hand over your passport and pay when you've finished. It's calculated on the unit rate plus a tax of 32F per unit (depending on the destination, a unit can be as little as six seconds), which makes it expensive. This counter is open weekdays from 7.45 am to 6 pm and Saturday from 7 to 11 am.

To call New Caledonia from overseas, the country code is 687.

Telegram & Fax

Sending a *télégramme* is cheaper than a fax only if you have a very short message. Both can be made from counter 17 at Noumea's main post office. To Australia and New Zealand, a half/full-page fax will cost 700/900F. To the USA, Canada or the UK it's 1400/1600F, and to France it costs 1000/1250F.

Should you want someone to contact you, faxes can be transmitted to the main post office on its fax number: (687) 28.78.78. You pick it up the fax from counter 15.

TIME

New Caledonia is 11 hours ahead of UTC (Universal Time Coordinated), which makes it one hour ahead of Australian Eastern Standard time (Sydney, Brisbane and Melbourne) and one hour behind New Zealand and Fiji. Local time is the same as in Vanuatu. It is 11 hours ahead of London, 10 hours ahead of Paris and 16 hours ahead of New York. Thus, at noon on Sunday in New Caledonia it is 1 am Sunday in London, 2 am Sunday in Paris and 8 pm Saturday in New York. No daylight-saving time system operates.

The 24-hour clock is commonly used; however, you'll soon find that the notion of time is quite changeable, especially on the Loyauté islands where 'island time' operates. When there, just go with the groove.

ELECTRICITY

The current throughout New Caledonia is 220 V, 50 cycles AC, using plugs with two round prongs. Occasionally, in a few hotels or, for example, the Noumea YHA Hostel you'll see three-prong bayonet sockets of the Australian type.

The electricity authority, Enercal, operates the large hydro-electric installation at Yate Dam, which supplies Noumea and some of the main island with power. About 55% of the country is supplied by thermal power stations. In the most remote areas of Grande Terre and the islands, generators are still used. They start up at around dusk and lights go out at 10 pm. However, the days of these noisy beasts are numbered as Enercal is rapidly meeting needs by extending a wired network to every village.

LAUNDRY

Laundries (called *blanchisseries* or *laveries* in French) are found only in Noumea (see the Laundry section in that chapter for details). For those staying in middle or up-market hotels, it should be no problem getting your washing done on the premises, but you'll pay dearly for it – 1300F for one dress, 750F for trousers.

WEIGHTS & MEASURES

New Caledonia follows the metric system, hence distances travelled are measured in km. In New Caledonia as in France, decimals are indicated with commas and thousands with points.

BOOKS

English and French writers, explorers and romantics wrote profusely about French Polynesia but, in comparison, little has been penned on New Caledonia. Until very recently, most tomes on the country were academic and historical, or written in French with no English translations. However, the Events of the 1980s have led to some very readable, English-language analyses of the country's history and the independence movement.

Kanak authors are still in a fledging era as, having been part of an oral society, they felt no need to express themselves in the written language. That too is changing and, since the setting up of the somewhat crudely named Agence de Développement de la Culture Kanak (Agency for the Development of Kanak Culture; ADCK), several books on Kanak culture, written by Kanaks and translated into English, have been published.

History & Politics

There are two excellent books which trace New Caledonia's history from the original Kanaks to the 1980s. *The Totem and the Tricolour* (New South Wales University Press, 1986), by Martyn Lyons, covers the country's history up to the 1984 crisis but not the Events themselves. A university lecturer of history, Lyons examines the earliest contacts between Kanaks and Europeans and the catastrophic consequences for the former. Alternatively, there's John Connell's *New Caledonia or Kanaky?* (Australian National University, 1987) which takes it a step further up to the French government's Fabius Plan.

Connell, together with Michel Spencer and Alan Ward, also worked on *New Caledonia: Essays in Nationalism and Dependency* (University of Queensland Press, 1988). According to one member of the literati, this is the 'first book presenting the point of view of Europeans as well as the indigenous people'. It reads like an academic thesis at times, but there are some very interesting insights into French policy throughout New Caledonia's colonial period.

One of the best books written on the impact of colonialism in the South Pacific is Alan Moorehead's *The Fatal Impact – The Invasion of the South Pacific 1767-1840* (Harper & Row Publishers, New York, 1966). Also on this subject is *The South Pacific – an introduction* (University of the South Pacific, Suva, 1973) by Ron Crocombe. This book discusses the potential of Pacific nations as independent countries and the changes to their cultures and identities since White settlement.

They Came for Sandalwood (Melbourne University Press, 1967), by Dorothy Shineberg, is the best account of the turbulent times of the sandalwood trade in the southwest Pacific from 1830 to 1865.

For those into tales of adventure, *Everlasting Hurricane* (Angus & Robertson, Sydney, 1937) by Walter Coulter, is a narrative on the escape of two convicts, one of whom was a Communard from New Caledonia, and their journey through the Pacific.

One of two recent books to look at France's more contemporary role in the Pacific is Stephen Henningham's *France & the South Pacific* (Allen & Unwin Pty Ltd, Sydney, 1992). This very readable paperback deals individually with New Caledonia,

Vanuatu, French Polynesia, Wallis & Futuna and, also, French nuclear testing. The book looks at two eras in New Caledonian history – post-war 1945 to 1978, and the rise of the independence movement from 1979 to 1989.

The other book in this genre is *France's Overseas Frontier* (Cambridge University Press, 1992), by Robert Aldrich & John Connell. This hardcover claims to be the first full-length study in English of the 'confetti of an empire', the 10 former French colonies (now called departments or territories) which have not gained independence.

The Cross of Lorraine in the South Pacific (Australian National University, Canberra, 1982) by John Lawrey examines the Free French movement of 1940 to 1942. As the Australian government representative in Noumea during WW II, Lawrey studied the Free French movement in the Pacific.

In the same era, *Danger! Marines at Work* (Random House, New York, 1959), by Robert G Fuller, is the reminiscences of a US marine based in New Caledonia during WW II. This is something of a collector's item and sells for about A$100.

Politics in New Caledonia (Sydney University Press, 1984), by Myriam Dornoy, deals successfully with New Caledonia's contemporary political history from 1945 to just before the start of the Events.

In a similar vein, though with more bite, is *The Kanaks of New Caledonia* (Minority Rights Group, London, 1986), by Ingrid A Kircher. This report discusses the history of New Caledonia as a colony and the growing independence movement. It also has statistics on the inequalities and discrimination that Kanaks face in New Caledonia today.

The Events For a pro-independence account of the Events, get hold of Helen Fraser's hardcover *Your Flag is Blocking Our Sun* (ABC Books, Australia, 1990). This book tells of Fraser's time in New Caledonia as an Australian journalist, starting with her arrival in 1981 to cover the funeral of Pierre Declercq. Her lucid prose graphically charts the growth in tension and violence up to

1985 while also telling of her dualistic role as a journalist and mother. The book concludes with the funerals of Tjibaou and Yeiwene in '89. Its title is a variation of a quote once made by Yeiwene: 'Pull down this red, white and blue flag for it's blocking our sun'.

Blood on their Banner: Nationalist Struggles in the South Pacific (Pluto Press Australia, 1989), by David Robie, is an illustrated paperback which covers the 'legacy of traumatic colonialism' using Fiji as the highlight. His examination of New Caledonia is based on his own experiences as a New Zealand reporter in the '80s. It recalls some of the poignant moments in the Kanak's struggle for independence, such as the killing of Eloi Machoro and the assassination of Tjibaou and Yeiwene.

Penelope's Island (Hodder & Stoughton, 1990) by James MacNeish tells the story of people, mainly Caldoches, living on the north-east coast of Grande Terre at the time of the 1984 Hienghene massacre. According to a reliable source, it accurately retells the ambush and is 'a good read...but don't think it's a true and balanced picture'.

People & Culture

Kanak Writers Produced just after the Melanesia 2000 festival, *Kanaké – the Melanesian Way* (Les Éditions du Pacifique, Papeete, 1978; 2000F), by Jean-Marie Tjibaou, was a landmark book to mark the festival. Tjibaou used colour photos, poems, legends and imagery to explain what Kanak culture is all about. The impact of modernism on his people is discussed and an outline for the future drawn. As he says in the foreword: 'Through this book, we want to resume the dialogue, to rebuild, to tell the world that we are not survivors of prehistory, still less archaeological fossils, but men of flesh and blood'.

Tu Galala – Social Change in the Pacific (Bridget Williams Books Ltd, New Zealand & Photo Press, Australia, 1992), edited by David Robie, is a collection of essays by indigenous writers, many of them activists and leaders in their own countries. The book's title means 'freedom'. It covers various Pacific nations and describes the impact that growing poverty, nuclear testing, independence struggles, militarisation and social dislocations are having on their people. On New Caledonia, Susanna Ounei-Small, a Kanak living in exile in New Zealand, writes about the Matignon Accords or, as she describes it, 'the peace signed with our blood'. She says the accords were designed to shut out the 'extremists' and to divide the independence movement.

A very enjoyable booklet which offers an insight into the legends of the people of Hienghene is *Hwanfalik – Sayings from the Hienghene Valley* (ADCK, Noumea, 1987), by Kaloombat Tein. It's an anthology of expressions used amongst the people in their own dialect, with explanations in English.

An illustrated booklet, *Pue thawe* (ADCK, Noumea, 1992), explains the myth behind the origins of traditional Kanak money. It's told by Timothée Daahma Le We, from the Tiendanite clan near Hienghene.

Other Writers *Pacific Treasure Island* (F W Cheshire Pty Ltd, Melbourne, 1941), by Wilfred G Burchett, is a novel filled with interesting titbits of information and B&W photos which together depict a rather paradoxical New Caledonia. An Australian journalist, Burchett travelled around New Caledonia prior to the Pacific War, after being invited to leave his home country because of his communist leanings. Burchett explains that he wrote the book because: 'It's high time that all we Pacific neighbours began to know each other a little better'. Hear! Hear!

A decade and a half later, a Swiss couple, May and Henry Larsen, passed through New Caledonia and produced *The Golden Cowrie* (Oliver & Boyd, Edinburgh, 1961), which describes the daily life of Kanaks and settlers they encountered in the '50s.

More local stories are told in *Legends from the Isle of Pines* (1984) written by Hilary Roots, a warm-hearted New Zealander who has lived on Île des Pins for many years. She has gathered together a booklet of tales, with illustrations done by her young students on the island.

Hilary Roots' next work was *Île des Pins – Where Nature Dreams* (1990), a coffee-table style book which beautifully portrays the idiosyncrasies of Île des Pins and the Kunies. It contains exquisite photos by Pierre-Alain Pantz.

Cultures in Conflict (Polity Press, 1989), by Urs Bitterli, is an encounter between European and non-European cultures, giving reconstructions of the experiences of both. The chapter entitled 'Cultural contacts as a scientific challenge' describes England's and France's overseas efforts to 'test' their knowledge in the 18th and 19th centuries.

On the same wave-length, but in French, is *La vie quotidienne en Nouvelle Calédonie de 1850 à nos jours* (Hachette, 1985), by Jacqueline Sénès. A journalist who lived in Noumea for more than 30 years, Sénès goes in search of Melanesian traditions and myths while looking for essential keys to the current conflicts.

An interesting collection of essays is *Religious Movements in Melanesia Today* (Melanesian Institute for Pastoral & Socio-Economic Service), edited by Wendy Flannery. It is written by an assortment of people ranging from anthropologists to missionaries. The general topic deals with Christianity, but pagan beliefs are also discussed in relation to modern-day Melanesians.

Art

Ko i Nèvâ – Sculpteurs et Peintres Kanak Contemporains (ADCK, Noumea, 1992) is the first book to be written on contemporary Kanak art. It's in French but has an English translation insert; the title means 'The Spirit of the Country'. Published after the recent 'Ko i Nèvâ' exhibition, featuring 45 Kanak sculptors and painters, it's a beautiful hardcover book with commentaries by the artists.

Ancient Kanak pottery styles and shapes are outlined in Jean-Christophe Gallipaud's *Kanak Pottery* (ADCK, 1985).

Flora & Fauna

Birds of New Caledonia & the Loyauté Islands (Éditions Cardinalis, Noumea, 1980), by Hannecart & Lennocart, has everything you ever wanted to know about the cagou, notou and many of the country's other endemic species. It's a large, detailed book with colour photos.

Two excellent books on marine fauna are *Fishes of the Great Barrier Reef and the Coral Sea* (Crawford House Press, Bathurst, 1990), by Randall-Allen & Steene, and the big *Encyclopedia of Marine Animals* (Harper & Collins, New York, 1991), by Neville Coleman. Both give exhaustive lists of information with photos and descriptions of each species covered.

Nudibranches of the South Pacific (Sea Australia Resource Centre, 1989) and *Shells of New Caledonia* (Les Éditions du Pacifique, Papeete, 1988) are both pocket-sized books which peer into what you may or may not see on the reef. For a more comprehensive picture there's the *Underwater Guide to New Caledonia* (Les Éditions du Pacifique, Papeete, 1979), by Pierre Laboute & Yves Magnier. It gives a general introduction to the reef, the lagoon, its flora and fauna and all the dangers and countermeasures.

Travel Guides

The selection of travel guides specifically about New Caledonia in English is very limited. One book that gives a general rundown on the archipelago is *New Caledonia* (Les Éditions du Pacifique, Papeete, 1975; 2450F), by Mike Hosken. It is a small coffee-table book with nice photos but scant practical or factual information. In French there's *En Nouvelle Calédonie* (Guides Hachette, Paris, 1991), better known as the 'blue guide', by Marie-Pierre Levallois & Armelle de Moucheron.

Yachting Guides

For details on yachting books, see the Yachtie's Guide in the Getting Around chapter.

Bookshops & Libraries

Bookshops Noumea is the only place in New Caledonia where you'll find bookshops *(librairies* in French) with English-language literature, but such books don't come cheap. You can expect to pay around 2000F for a current paperback novel – double what you'd pay in Australia. The major towns around la Brousse – Koumac, Bourail and Poindimie – also have small bookshops but they do not stock anything in English except the odd magazine.

Noumea has one exclusively English-language bookshop and several French bookshops with small stocks of English novels or guides. For details, see the Bookshop section in the Noumea chapter.

Some of the books detailed in the previous section are available from Jean-Louis Boglio (☎ (075) 34 6065), PO Box 72 Currumbin, Qld 4223, Australia. This mail-order bookdealer specialises in new and old books about the sea but, as a former resident of New Caledonia, he also has a penchant for literature on the territory and, to date, has a nine-page list of titles. He'll send a copy of this list free of charge.

Libraries There are several options in Noumea for those with an exploratory nature. The Bibliothèque Bernheim, the main library in Noumea, stocks some English-language magazines as well as ORSTOM's monumental atlas of New Caledonia, in part translated into English.

The ADCK (see the Useful Organisations section) has a specialised library open for public perusal with books, magazines and anthropological studies and essays on Melanesian culture or the Pacific in general. Many works are in English. The ADCK publishes and sells its own books about Kanak heritage, some of which have been translated into English.

Both the Australian and New Zealand consulates have small libraries where you can browse through books, national newspapers and magazines, though the papers are usually a week out of date.

MAPS

The Noumea tourist office gives out a free blue map of New Caledonia and Noumea. It's called a road map but you wouldn't want to put it to the test. It also sells a large tourist map of the capital (500F) detailing its bus routes as well as national tourist sites (described in French).

The best maps of New Caledonia are produced in France by the Institut Géographique National (IGN). Its *Nouvelle Calédonie* map No 514 (scale 1:500,000) gives an overview of the entire Grande Terre, Loyauté islands and Île des Pins, with places of interest and hotels marked. The map includes a large-scale inset of Noumea and its environs. It sells for about 880F from most bookshops in the capital.

IGN also publishes the '*Série Orange*', a collection of 45 maps covering every area in the country in greater detail (scale 1:50,000). The range is sold in Librairie Montagne (see Bookshops in the Noumea chapter).

MEDIA
Newspapers & Magazines

The only daily newspaper, *Les Nouvelles Calédoniennes*, is a pro-French tabloid that focuses on local and international news, with a heavy emphasis on sports and recreation. It costs 120F. All major French newspapers

– *Le Monde*, *L'Express*, and *Le Figaro* – and magazines *(Paris Match)* are regular features on bookstore shelves in Noumea. The only English-language newspapers sold here is the *International Herald Tribune*.

A newsletter for the Kanak community, *Bwenando*, was published for several years in the '80s and was used as a powerful tool in the independence movement. Sadly, it died in 1989 along with Tjibaou and Yeiwene. Nothing similar has replaced it.

Noumea Newsline is a four-page 'summary of commercial news and basic information for the business traveller', produced by an American lawyer living in Noumea. It is distributed in mid-range and top-end hotels every three or four months.

Australian current affairs magazines such as the *Bulletin/Newsweek* (740F) and the Australian edition of *Time* (550F) are sold but are usually a week out of date. The range of 'special interest' Australian periodicals includes the Women's Weekly (815F) and fishing, gardening and home-maker magazines.

Two English-language magazines circulate around the Pacific and are available in New Caledonia. *Pacific Islands Monthly* (PIM; 250F) is an excellent monthly publication committed to independence issues. It's almost an institution in the region, having been around since the 1930s. Its address is PO Box 1167 Suva, Fiji (fax (679) 303809). *Island Business Pacific* is the other monthly magazine published in Fiji which attempts to cover business and current events.

Radio & TV

TV in New Caledonia is controlled by the French government and operates through RFO (Radio & Télédiffusion Française d'Outre-Mer), the overseas arm of the French broadcasting service. Noumea has had TV since 1965, though it took another decade to be relayed to the Loyauté islands. A second TV channel started in 1984. Most of the TV programmes are dispatched directly from metropolitan France; all are in French or dubbed into French.

There are several radio stations and programmes tend to have more of a local slant

than does TV. One of the favourite radio stations for younger French people is Radio Rythme Bleu (RRB), a private, non-commercial station. The government-run RFO has a large slice of the audience and, together with RRB, broadcasts 24 hours a day, only in French. RRB (102FM) has two minutes of English headline news at 8.30 am Monday to Saturday. Radio Djiido at 97.4FM is the station preferred by many Kanaks.

With a short-wave radio it's also possible to tune into English-language radio programmes from the Australian Broadcasting Corporation (ABC).

FILM & PHOTOGRAPHY

Film, developing and photographic accessories are all available but they are very expensive. Film supplies in the capital include 64 to 200 ASA 35 mm colour slides and 100 to 400 ASA colour prints, as well as B&W material. As an example of prices, you'll be looking at 1050F for a Fuji 100 ASA, 36-exposure slide film and 1000F for a Kodak 100 ASA, 36-exposure print film. Development costs are 950/1200F for 24/36 slides and 2560/3640F for a 24/36 exposure colour print film.

The intensity of the coral sea, the blue sky, the white sand and the green, green hills all look like magic in the camera's eye but the result can be disappointing because of overexposure. You should avoid the midday sun when taking photos – the ideal time is from sunrise to about 9 am and after 4 pm. If that's not possible, then slightly underexpose the shot to avoid the tropic's harsh glare. Using skylight and polariser filters is also a good move.

Always keep film dry and cool and your camera clean. Excessive handling in tropical elements – salty air, sand and humidity – can ruin the film. If you will be passing through a succession of airports, it is recommended you buy a laminated lead bag to protect your film from X-ray machines. If you ask, customs personnel at Tontouta Airport will usually let you carry your camera without its having to go through the machine.

When photographing local people, always ask permission first. Mostly, your subjects will not mind though they may be shy initially. Taking random close-ups of people who are unwarned is asking for trouble, not to mention rude.

HEALTH

New Caledonia is malaria-free and has no tropical diseases. Inoculations are not required except for those arriving, within 14 days, from an area infected with smallpox.

Self-diagnosis and treatment can be risky, so wherever possible seek qualified help. Your hotel, consulate, a friend or the tourist office in Noumea will know of a good doctor. The standard of medical care in New Caledonia is not as high as in Europe, the USA, Australia or New Zealand, but it is available and you should not hesitate to see a doctor.

There are clinics in the towns and villages around the country but their medical supplies may be limited. If you're in an isolated area and you start feeling really sick, your best plan is to get aboard a plane and fly straight back to Noumea.

Health Care Facilities

New Caledonia's health services are administered by the government, which ensures that medical facilities are available throughout the country, including areas where private doctors may not choose to live.

There are two public hospitals in Noumea, various private clinics and many chemists. Each rural town has a *dispensaire* (community clinic), where you can receive emergency first-aid treatment, and even the remote Belep islands have one French doctor. The French surgeons and practitioners generally choose to come to New Caledonia when they are just out of medical school and are relatively young. At present, there are very few Kanak doctors.

Public medical and emergency care is good and inexpensive, but like many overcrowded institutions with underpaid staff, personal attention and hospital care can be minimal.

Scuba divers should note that there is no operational decompression chamber in New Caledonia; the closest is in Townsville, Australia or Suva, Fiji.

Travel Health Information

For personalised health advice in Australia, you can contact the Medical Advisory Service for Travellers Abroad (MASTA). It is in Brisbane (☎ (07) 253 5416) and Sydney (☎ (02) 905 6133) and has reliable, up-to-date information on prevailing patterns of diseases worldwide, necessary precautions and treatments.

Predeparture Preparations

Health Insurance You must pay for any medical attention you receive in New Caledonia so you'll need to take out travel insurance before you leave home, including adequate coverage for emergency health care.

Some policies specifically exclude 'dangerous activities' such as scuba diving, motorcycling and even trekking. If these activities are on your agenda, find another policy. You may prefer a policy which pays doctors or hospitals direct rather than you having to pay first and claim later. If you have to claim later make sure you keep all documentation. Some policies allow you to call (reverse charges) an international centre where an immediate assessment of your problem is made. Ensure your policy covers ambulances and an emergency flight home. If you must stretch out, you'll need two seats and somebody has to pay for them!

Medical Kit It is wise to carry a small, straightforward medical kit. A possible kit list includes:

- Aspirin or Panadol – for pain or fever.
- Antihistamine (such as Benadryl) – useful as a decongestant for colds, allergies, to ease the itch from insect bites or stings or to help prevent motion sickness.
- Antibiotics – useful if you're travelling well off the beaten track, but they must be prescribed and you should carry the prescription with you.
- Kaolin preparation (Pepto-Bismol), Imodium or Lomotil – for stomach upsets.

- Rehydration mixture – for treatment of severe diarrhoea; this is particularly important if travelling with children.
- Antiseptic, mercurochrome and antibiotic powder or similar 'dry' spray – for grazes and cuts, especially coral cuts which are hard to heal.
- Calamine lotion – to ease irritation from bites or stings.
- Bandages and Band-aids – for minor injuries.
- Scissors, tweezers and a thermometer – note that mercury thermometers are prohibited by airlines.
- Insect repellent, sun block, suntan lotion and chapstick.

Health Precautions Make sure you're healthy before you start travelling. If you're embarking on a long trip, have your teeth checked before you go. If you wear glasses bring a spare pair and your prescription. Losing your glasses or contact lenses can be a real problem, though new ones can be made up quickly in Noumea.

If you require special medicines take an adequate supply as they may not be available in New Caledonia. Take the prescription, with the generic rather than the brand name (which may not be locally available), as it will make getting replacements easier.

Note that New Caledonia is malaria-free but if you plan to visit a malaria-infected area before or after New Caledonia (Vanuatu for example), make sure you seek advice from your doctor about malarial prophylactics.

Basic Rules
Care in what you eat and drink is the most important health rule; stomach upsets are the most likely health problem but the majority of these upsets will be relatively minor. Don't become paranoid; trying the local food is part of the experience of travel.

Many health problems can be avoided by taking simple precautions. Wash your hands frequently, as it's quite easy to contaminate your own food, giving yourself diarrhoea or something worse. Constipation can be almost as common. You can easily avoid this by eating plenty of fresh fruit and vegetables. Salads, fruit and vegetables should be peeled or well washed. Thoroughly cooked food is safest but not if it has been left to cool or if

it has been reheated. Take great care with shellfish or fish and avoid undercooked meat.

Always be sure your diet is well balanced. Eggs, beans and nuts are all good ways to get protein. Peelable fruit, such as bananas or oranges, is always safe. They, along with coconuts and pawpaws, are a good source of vitamins.

Water The water in New Caledonia is deemed safe to drink, except on the Loyauté island of Ouvea where the water is saline. When you're there, ask for '*eau potable*' (drinkable water) from the owner of your accommodation or buy bottled water. For those skittish about drinking the water anywhere, there's an abundance of bottled water for sale, produced either from local springs or imported from France.

Make sure you drink enough during New Caledonia's hotter seasons and don't rely on feeling thirsty to remind you to do so. Not needing to urinate or very dark-yellow urine should be treated as a warning that you're not drinking nearly enough. Always carry a water bottle on long trips.

Because of the humidity, excessive sweating and therefore salt deficiency can lead to muscle cramping. If this occurs, extra salt with your daily food should help. Salt tablets are not a good idea as they cause some people to vomit.

Climatic & Geographical Considerations
Sunburn In the tropics you can get sunburnt surprisingly quickly, even through cloud. Use a sunscreen and take extra care to cover areas which don't normally see sun – eg, your feet. A hat provides added protection, and you should also use zinc cream or some other barrier cream for your nose and lips. Calamine lotion is good for mild sunburn.

Prickly Heat Prickly heat is an itchy rash caused by excessive perspiration trapped under the skin. It usually strikes people who have just arrived in a hot climate and whose pores have not yet opened sufficiently to cope with greater sweating. Keeping cool but bathing often, using a mild talcum powder or even resorting to air-conditioning may help until you acclimatise.

Heat Exhaustion Dehydration or salt deficiency can cause heat exhaustion. Take time to acclimatise to high temperatures and make sure you get sufficient liquids. Salt deficiency is characterised by fatigue, lethargy, headaches, giddiness and muscle cramps and in this case salt tablets may help. Vomiting or diarrhoea can deplete your liquid and salt levels.

Anhydrotic heat exhaustion, caused by an inability to sweat, is quite rare. Unlike the other forms of heat exhaustion it is likely to strike people who have been in a hot climate for some time, rather than newcomers.

Heat Stroke This serious, sometimes fatal, condition can occur if the body's heat-regulating mechanism breaks down and the body temperature rises to dangerous levels. Long, continuous periods of exposure to high temperatures can leave you vulnerable to heat stroke. You should avoid excessive alcohol or strenuous activity when you first arrive in a hot climate.

The symptoms are feeling unwell, not sweating very much or at all and a high body temperature (39°C to 41°C). Where sweating has ceased, the skin becomes flushed and red. Severe, throbbing headaches and lack of coordination will also occur, and the sufferer may be confused or aggressive. Eventually the victim will become delirious or convulse. Hospitalisation is essential, but meanwhile get patients out of the sun, remove their clothing, cover them with a wet sheet or towel and then fan them continually.

Fungal Infections Hot weather fungal infections are most likely to occur on the scalp, between the toes or fingers (athlete's foot), in the groin (jock itch or crotch rot) and on the body (ringworm). You get ringworm (which is a fungal infection, not a worm) from infected animals or by walking on damp areas like shower floors.

To prevent fungal infections wear loose,

comfortable clothes, avoid artificial fibres, wash frequently and dry carefully. If you do get an infection, wash the infected area daily with a disinfectant or medicated soap and water, and rinse and dry well. Apply an antifungal powder like the widely available Tinaderm. Try to expose the infected area to air or sunlight as much as possible, wash all towels and underwear in hot water and change them often.

Motion Sickness Eating lightly before and during a trip will reduce the chances of motion sickness. If you are prone to motion sickness try to find a place that minimises disturbance – near the wing on aircraft, close to midships on boats, near the centre on buses. Fresh air usually helps, but reading and cigarette smoke don't. Commercial anti-motion-sickness preparations, which can cause drowsiness, have to be taken before the trip commences; when you're feeling sick it's too late. Ginger is a natural preventative and is available in capsule form.

Diseases of Insanitation
Diarrhoea A change of water, food or climate can all cause the runs; diarrhoea caused by contaminated food or water is more serious. Despite all your precautions, you may still have a bout of mild travellers' diarrhoea but a few rushed toilet trips with no other symptoms is not indicative of a serious problem. Moderate diarrhoea, involving half a dozen loose movements in a day, is more of a nuisance. Dehydration is the main danger with diarrhoea, particularly for children, so fluid replenishment is the number one treatment. Weak black tea with a little sugar, soda water, or soft drinks allowed to go flat and diluted 50% with water are all good. With severe diarrhoea a rehydrating solution is necessary to replace minerals and salts. You should stick to a bland diet as you recover.

Lomotil or Imodium can be used to bring relief from the symptoms, although they do not cure the problem. Only use these drugs if absolutely necessary – eg, if you travel. For children, Imodium is preferable, but do not use these drugs if the patient has a high fever or is severely dehydrated.

Antibiotics can be very useful in treating severe diarrhoea especially if it is accompanied by nausea, vomiting, stomach cramps or mild fever. Ampicillin, a broad-spectrum penicillin, is usually recommended. Two capsules of 250 mg each taken four times a day is the recommended dose for an adult. Children aged between eight and 12 years should have half the adult dose; younger children should have half a capsule four times a day. Note that if the patient is allergic to penicillin, ampicillin should not be administered.

Three days of treatment should be sufficient and an improvement should occur within 24 hours.

Dysentery This serious illness is caused by contaminated food or water and is characterised by severe diarrhoea, often with blood or mucus in the stool. There are two kinds of dysentery. Bacillary dysentery is characterised by a high fever and rapid development; headache, vomiting and stomach pains are also symptoms. It generally does not last longer than a week, but it is highly contagious.

Amoebic dysentery is more gradual in developing, has no fever or vomiting but is a more serious illness. It is not a self-limiting disease: it will persist until treated and can recur and cause long term damage.

A stool test is necessary to diagnose which kind of dysentery you have, so you should seek medical help urgently. Tetracycline is the prescribed treatment for bacillary dysentery, and metronidazole that for amoebic dysentery.

With tetracycline, the recommended adult dosage is one 250 mg capsule four times a day. Children aged between eight and 12 years should have half the adult dose; the dosage for younger children is one-third the adult dose. It's important to remember that tetracycline should be given to young children only if it's absolutely necessary and only for a short period; pregnant women should not take it after the fourth month of pregnancy.

With metronidazole, the recommended adult dosage is one 750 mg to 800 mg capsule three times daily for five days. Children aged between eight and 12 years should have half the adult dose; the dosage for younger children is one-third the adult dose.

Viral Gastroenteritis This is caused not by bacteria but, as the name suggests, by a virus. It is characterised by stomach cramps, diarrhoea, and sometimes by vomiting or a slight fever. All you can do is rest and drink lots of fluids.

Hepatitis Hepatitis A is the more common form of this disease and is spread by contaminated food or water. The first symptoms are fever, chills, headache, fatigue, feelings of weakness and aches and pains. This is followed by a loss of appetite, nausea, vomiting, abdominal pain, dark urine, light-coloured faeces and jaundiced skin; the whites of the eyes may also turn yellow. In some cases there may just be a feeling of being unwell or tired, accompanied by loss of appetite, aches and pains and the jaundiced effect. You should seek medical advice, but in general there is not much you can do apart from resting, drinking lots of fluids, eating lightly and avoiding fatty foods. People who have had hepatitis must forgo alcohol for six months after the illness, as hepatitis attacks the liver and it needs that amount of time to recover.

Hepatitis B, which used to be called serum hepatitis, is spread through sexual contact or through skin penetration – it could, for instance, be transmitted via dirty needles or blood transfusions. Avoid having your ears pierced, tattoos done or injections if you have doubts about the sanitary conditions. The symptoms and treatment of type B are much the same as for type A, but gamma globulin as a prophylactic is effective against type A only.

Giardia This intestinal parasite is present in contaminated water. The symptoms are stomach cramps, nausea, a bloated stomach, watery, foul-smelling diarrhoea and frequent gas. Giardia can appear several weeks after you have been exposed to the parasite. The symptoms may disappear for a few days and then return; this can go on for several weeks. Metronidazole, known as Flagyl, is the recommended drug, but it should only be taken under medical supervision. Antibiotics are of no use.

Worms These parasites are most common in rural, tropical areas and a stool test when you return home is not a bad idea. They can be present on unwashed vegetables or in undercooked meat and you can pick them up through your skin by walking in bare feet. Infestations may not show up for some time, and although they are generally not serious, if left untreated they can cause severe health problems. A stool test is necessary to pinpoint the problem and medication is often available over the counter.

Diseases Spread by People & Animals

Tetanus This potentially fatal disease is found in undeveloped tropical areas. It is difficult to treat but is preventable with immunisation. Tetanus occurs when a wound becomes infected by a germ which lives in the faeces of animals or people, so clean all cuts, punctures or animal bites. Tetanus is known as lockjaw, and the first symptom may be discomfort in swallowing, or stiffening of the jaw and neck; this is followed by painful convulsions of the jaw and whole body.

Bilharzia Bilharzia is carried in water by minute worms. The larvae infect certain varieties of freshwater snails that are found in rivers, streams, lakes and particularly behind dams. The worms multiply and are eventually discharged into the water surrounding the snails.

They attach themselves to your intestines or bladder, where they produce large numbers of eggs. The worm enters through the skin, and the first symptom may be a tingling and sometimes a light rash around the area where it entered. Weeks later, when the worm is busy producing eggs, a high fever may develop. A general feeling of being unwell may be the first symptom; once the disease is established, abdominal pain and blood in the urine are other signs.

Avoiding swimming or bathing in freshwater where bilharzia is present is the main way to prevent the disease. Even deep water can be infected. If you do get wet, dry off quickly and dry your clothes as well. Seek medical attention if you have been exposed to the disease and tell the doctor your suspicions, as bilharzia in the early stages can be confused with malaria or typhoid. If you cannot get medical help immediately, Niridazole is the recommended treatment. The recommended adult dosage is 750 mg (1½ tablets) taken twice daily for a week. Children aged between eight and 12 years should be given 500 mg (one tablet) twice daily for a week.

Rabies Rabies is caused by a bite or scratch by an infected animal. Dogs are a noted carrier. The most reassuring aspect of travel in remote parts of New Caledonia is that dogs are friendly and seldom bite. The incidence of rabies in the country is low, but don't take any chances if bitten and demand that the dog be checked by a vet. If it is rabid, get the proper shots immediately.

Dengue Fever In 1989, there was concern in New Caledonia over an epidemic of dengue, a fever carried by a certain kind of mosquito that looks translucent and slightly green. There is no prophylactic available for this disease and the main preventative measure is to avoid mosquito bites. Symptoms are flu-like chills, with a sudden onset of fever, and bodily pains. Although it's rarely serious, it's no fun either. When mosquitoes are rampant (the worst time is February to April) try a repellent and, if your accommodation is not well screened, sleep, if possible, under a mosquito net or use an electrical insecticide vaporiser. The latter are sometimes provided in mid-range hotels and gîtes in New Caledonia.

Ciguatera Ciguatera (*gratte* in French or 'ichthyosarcotoxicosis') is a form of poisoning acquired by eating toxic fish. It has been reported in parts of the Pacific, including New Caledonia and northern Australia. A toxin called ciguatoxin forms in algae-eating fish if they feed around 'stressed' reefs. These are reefs where coral has been killed or damaged either by storms, the intervention of people, silting or heavy rainfall. These fish are then eaten by predatory tropical reef fish which are the ones to avoid as the toxin concentrates in them. Fish living on the outer side of the reef between depths of 200 to 400 metres are free of ciguatera.

Ciguatera's symptoms include vomiting, diarrhoea and cramps, alternating fevers and chills, joint aches, and tingling in the skin and mouth. If you experience any of these symptoms after eating fish, contact a doctor immediately.

Eating fish served in a restaurant is as safe as a seafood meal anywhere. If you're catching your own fish, especially from the lagoon or around the reef, get the opinion of a local before cooking and eating it (cooking will not kill the toxin).

Sexually Transmitted Diseases (STDs)

Sexually transmitted diseases such as gonorrhoea and syphilis are a problem throughout the Pacific, including New Caledonia. Common symptoms include sores, blisters or rashes around the genitals, and discharges or pain when urinating, though these symptoms may be less marked or not observed at all in women. The symptoms of syphilis eventually disappear completely, but the disease continues and can cause severe problems in later years. Treatment of gonorrhoea and syphilis is by antibiotics so, if you suspect you have an infection, get to a hospital quickly. Condoms give the best protection against infection.

AIDS Being an international problem, AIDS (SIDA in French) has no boundaries. The number of AIDS cases in the Pacific is relatively low compared with many regions worldwide, and STDs are considered a more common and pressing problem here. However, according to an Australian survey in mid-1992, French Polynesia and New Caledonia had the highest incidence of AIDS in the Pacific. In New Caledonia, there were 77 known cases of people with HIV (Human Immunodeficiency Virus), 22 of which had been diagnosed with full-blown AIDS.

There is currently no cure for AIDS, which is most commonly spread through male homosexual activity, but is also common amongst heterosexuals around the world. Using condoms is currently the most effective preventative.

AIDS can also be spread through infected blood transfusions (most developing countries cannot afford to screen blood for transfusions) or by using dirty needles – vaccinations, acupuncture and tattooing can potentially be as dangerous as intravenous drug use if the equipment is not clean. If you do need an injection, always insist on a new needle, or buy a new syringe from a pharmacy and ask a doctor to use it.

Information to increase public awareness about AIDS in New Caledonia and to fight against its spread is handled by the Comité de la Lutte contre le SIDA (☎ 28.63.38), BP J5 in Noumea. The South Pacific Commission also publishes a bulletin entitled *Pacific AIDS-STD Alert* (known as PASA), in English and French, which is distributed to health and education authorities around the Pacific.

Cuts & Scratches

Skin punctures can easily become infected in hot climates and may be difficult to heal. Treat any cut right away with an antiseptic solution and mercurochrome. Where possible avoid bandages and Band-aids as they can keep wounds wet.

Coral cuts must be cleaned right away as the coral injects a weak venom into the wound and they are notoriously slow to heal, especially in humid conditions. Avoid coral cuts by wearing shoes on reefs.

Bites & Stings

Marine Creatures Certain varieties of cone shells found in the Pacific are so poisonous that their sting can be fatal. They fire a barb to kill their prey and, while they may be very pretty, they should be handled with great caution.

Sea urchins are also dangerous if you stand on one. Their spines are long and sharp, and easily broken off but difficult to remove from your foot once embedded. As their name says, stingrays have a poisonous barb which they can use should you be unlucky enough to stand on one; doing the same to a stonefish can be fatal.

All coral is poisonous and brushing against certain types can give you a painful sting and an itchy rash. Anemones are also poisonous and should be left to the clownfish.

New Caledonia has a dozen different sea snakes but the one you're most likely to encounter is the black-and-beige striped jersey. Their venom is deadly and there is no known serum. They are not commonly aggressive so it's best just to leave them alone.

Bees & Wasps Bee and wasp stings are usually painful rather than dangerous. Calamine lotion will give relief and ice packs will help reduce the pain and swelling.

Women's Health

Gynaecological Problems Poor diet, lowered resistance through the use of antibiotics for stomach upsets and even contraceptive pills can lead to vaginal infections when travelling in tropical areas. Maintaining good hygiene, wearing cotton underwear and skirts or loose-fitting trousers will help to prevent infections.

Yeast infections, characterised by a rash, itch and discharge can be treated with a vinegar or even lemon-juice douche or with yoghurt. Nystatin suppositories are the usual medical prescription. Trichomonas is a more serious infection; symptoms are a discharge and a burning sensation when urinating. Male sexual partners must also be treated and if a douche is not effective medical attention should be sought. Flagyl is the prescribed drug.

Pregnancy Most miscarriages occur during the first three months of pregnancy so this is the most risky time to travel. The last three months should be spent within reasonable distance of good medical care as quite serious problems can develop at this time. Pregnant women should avoid all unnecessary medication, but vaccinations and malarial prophylactics should still be taken if possible. Additional care should be taken to prevent illness and particular attention should be paid to diet and nutrition.

WOMEN TRAVELLERS

To find out about what's happening in women's issues and events in New Caledonia and all round the Pacific, you can subscribe to *Women's News*, a quarterly, 16-page newsletter of the Pacific Women's Resource Centre published by the South Pacific Commission, BP D5 in Noumea.

Generally speaking, women should have few problems travelling solo around New Caledonia. However, as in any city, there have been reported cases of sexual harassment in Noumea, both during the day and at night-time, so it's best to be cautious if you are on your own. If walking alone late at night, try to stick to crowded areas and avoid dark streets. Hitching alone is not recommended for women either, although a New Zealander who hitchhiked by herself all over Grande Terre said she had an excellent, safe experience. Hitching with two people is ideal and there is very little chance of being threatened.

Unfortunately, it appears that incidents of sexual violence targeted at local women are on the increase. In 1992, SOS Violences Sexuelles, a crisis aid and counselling association, was set up in Noumea, the first of its kind to be established in the capital. It is presided over by Marie-Claude Tjibaou, the wife of the assassinated independence movement leader, Jean-Marie Tjibaou. Some 300 people met to discuss the establishment of the association. François Burke, a mixed-race politician and one of the founders of the Union Calédonienne, told the gathering: 'We must be united to fight this explosion (of sexual violence) that is amongst us'. The previous year, 21 cases involving sexual violence had been brought before the courts in Noumea, though this is believed to be only the tip of the iceberg.

DANGERS & ANNOYANCES

While thefts and attacks on tourists are not commonplace, they are also not unknown in Noumea. Take particular care when walking back to the YHA hostel at night as the route up the hill is poorly lit and there has been the occasional incidence of travellers' being held up at knife-point. In recent years, thefts have also occurred in a few remote spots like waterfalls or beaches on Grande Terre's north-east coast. We've mentioned in the relevant chapter where to be cautious.

On the roads, be wary of drunk drivers as New Caledonia has a high death toll from road accidents. Also, it may be prudent to avoid cardboard boxes lying in the middle of the road. According to one traveller who wrote to us, it's a favourite trick of Kanak kids to hide a large stone or dead animal in the box.

Something else to watch for is the odd falling coconut. According to local legend, the coconut is the reborn head of a snake or a mythical eel – you can see its eyes and mouth when you peel off the outer fibres. It can see you and will try to avoid crashing down on top of you when it falls from the palm. Of course, it may be wise not to tempt the devil.

The dearth of fauna makes it safe to walk anywhere in New Caledonia's mountainous regions or high plateaux without fear of stepping on something and being bitten. Along the coast or in the water, be aware of the the various venomous sea creatures (see Marine Creatures in the Health section for details). When swimming, snorkelling or diving, work out the local situation before plunging in and don't overlook one of the most underestimated marine dangers, the sea's current.

Marijuana is illegal in New Caledonia though it's around and is plentiful on Ouvea. Tourists caught in possession of a small amount of dope are likely to get an on-the-spot fine. For hard drugs, you'll go to court.

Political Stability

New Caledonia's political situation in mid-1993 was quite stable. There have been no violent incidents since 1989 and polling for the French National Assembly in March 1993 passed peacefully. Unlike during the events of the '80s, nowhere in the country nowadays is off-limits to tourists. In early 1993, a few roadblocks were erected on the Loyauté island of Lifou as part of a long-running internal political problem but the protest action was in no way designed to deter tourists. Despite the pervading calm, it would be wise to keep an eye on political developments in the country in the lead up to the independence referendum of 1998.

ACTIVITIES
Snorkelling

New Caledonia has the world's second-largest reef and the opportunity to take a look for yourself should not be missed. It's another world from the one you're used to and witnessing the endless parade of its beautiful inhabitants is something that never ceases to fascinate. The best sites are the reefs away from mud-polluted rivers and artificial disturbances, such as those around the Loyauté islands and Île des Pins.

Snorkelling off one or two beaches close to Noumea is OK but you'll find better visibility and range of marine life if you get out onto the lagoon. Unfortunately, this is not a cheap prospect, as all tourist operators running day trips to places like Amédée Islet or the Seahorse Pontoon on the outer reef charge through the nose. If you have the time, it would be better and cheaper to head down to the Yate/Waho region or up to the north-east coast or, better still, get to the islands.

Sites along the north-east coast are superb but you'll need to keep clear of areas where mountain streams meet the sea, as the mixture of fresh and salt water creates an oily effect in the water and visibility is decreased. Around river mouths with run-off from mining, particularly after heavy rains, there is zero visibility for at least a few days.

If you plan to spend a lot of time snorkelling it definitely pays to have your own equipment. Rental locations are confined mainly to Noumea while, around the country, only top-end hotels have equipment for guests' use. ABC Marine at 28 Rue du Verdun in central Noumea has a good selection of gear. Prices vary depending on quality but the cheapest you'll be looking at is 270F for a snorkel *(tuba)*, 250F for fins *(palmes)* and 650F for a mask *(masque)*.

Finally, a word of warning to novices or weak swimmers. Though there are few accidents with snorkellers in New Caledonia, you should be aware that water currents can be strong and that you'll rapidly tire when swimming against them. As a policy, you shouldn't snorkel without fins and, if you're a newcomer to the underwater world, it is wise not to touch anything. Stunning cone shells can be deadly and even brushing against coral can give you a nasty sting.

Scuba Diving

Despite its potential, New Caledonia has only a modest range of scuba-diving organisations. It has never been a thriving centre for divers like, for example, Fiji, which attracts many Australians and Americans each year. And, compared with neighbouring Vanuatu, diving in New Caledonia is expensive. Thus the industry has been left to a small community of enthusiastic locals, métros who want to make good use of their few years' living in the tropics, and some Japanese tourists on exclusive dive package holidays. Of course, the advantage of its underexploitation is that most dive sites and marine life are relatively undisturbed.

With reefs encircling Grande Terre, tropical fish of every colour abound. Many of the most popular dive sites are located in the marine reserve in the seas south of Noumea, including close to Amédée Islet. Here you can see sharks, including black or white-tipped reef sharks, grey reef sharks and whale sharks, gropers, moray eels and manta and eagle rays. The Baie de Prony at the main island's southern tip is also special, with nudibranches and a startling underwater *aiguille* or pinnacle, while the waters around

Gadji off Île des Pins are rarely visited, except by dolphins, and are totally unspoilt.

There are two internationally approved dive companies in Noumea, Amédée Diving Club and Noumea Diving. There is also the Pacific Diving Centre, which operates from the Malabou Beach Hôtel near Poum on Grande Terre's north-west coast, and the Nauticlub at Ouameo on Île des Pins (see the relevant chapters for details). They all run open-water diving courses and organise diving trips for those with certificates. At Poindimie and Hienghene on Grande Terre's north-east coast, and on the Loyauté island of Mare, there are people with air compressors and dive boats, but to arrange something with them you'd have to have the full kit and caboodle.

Water Temperature The sea temperature around New Caledonia peaks at a warm 29°C in February and drops to 20°C in August. During the summer months, it's warm enough to scuba dive without a wet suit, though most divers wear at least a lycra outfit to protect themselves against abrasions. From March, five-mm wetsuits are necessary.

Visibility Depending on the season and conditions, underwater visibility ranges from 50 metres on a calm windless winter's day, down to 15 or even 10 metres in summer when the water has been whipped up from the wet season run-off and is turbid. At the start of summer, coral polyps spawn in a mass of colour which reduces visibility.

Decompression Facilities There is a decompression chamber at Noumea's main Gaston Bourret hospital but it has not been operational for some years as a result of staff and funding cuts. The closest working chambers are in Townsville, Australia, or in Suva, Fiji.

Dive Courses It is possible to do an open-water certification course approved by either the Professional Association of Diving Instructors (PADI) or the French organisation, Fédération Française d'Études et Sports

Sous-Marines (FFESSM). They are offered by English-speaking instructors at all the dive clubs. You'll be looking at about 30,000F for a three-day FFESSM course or 42,000F for a four-day PADI course. The FFESSM course is not as widely recognised around the world.

Before starting, you'll need to get a medical certificate stating that you're fit to dive. This examination can be done for free by a doctor at the Direction Territoriale de Jeunesse et Sport at Magenta stadium; alternatively, ask your dive club to recommend a doctor.

Dive Sites Each club has its own special sites, but a few of the more popular include:

Around Amédée Islet

La Patate: 6½ km south of Amédée, isolated bommie south of the Récif Sournois where a few moray eels live

Le Tombant: 5½ km south, spectacular drop-off north of Récif Sournois

Passe de Boulari: 3½ km south-west, exposed but interesting for migrating fish, manta rays, cods, groups of reef sharks and the occasional whale shark

Inner reef of Passe de Boulari: good for white-tipped reef sharks and leopard rays

La Dieppoise: a special marine reserve, this wreck is behind Récif Tabou, two km west

Le Snark: another wreck on Snark Reef, six km north-west of Amédée

Around Southern Grande Terre

Seahorse Pontoon, 25 km west on Annibal Reef: just 15 metres deep with passageways and lots of fish

Passe de Dumbea, 20 km west-south-west of Noumea, north of Abore Reef: dramatic drop-offs

Canal de Woodin, between Grande Terre and Île Ouen: strong current, rich marine life, gorgonians

Aiguille de Prony: spectacular 'cathedral' pinnacle in the deserted Baie de Prony. It rises from 40 metres up to 1½ metres below the surface; sponges, moray eels, barracuda and, rather exceptionally, tiger and hammerhead sharks.

Grotte de Merlet: 60 km south-east at Passe de Vatio, 1½-hour boat trip; unspoilt fantastic diving

Other Water Activities

Noumea's beaches are well positioned to catch strong winds coming in over the sea, and windsurfing *(planche à voile)* has seen enormous popularity in recent years. Equipment can be rented at the main beach, Anse Vata. Catamarans, jet skis, canoes and kayaks are also available from here. A popular spot for canoeing is Dumbea, just north of Noumea, while plans are in hand to start canoeing and kayaking expeditions in the Rivière Bleue park east of the capital.

Swimming & Beaches New Caledonian beaches vary from fine white sand to coarse darker grains, the latter along the west coast. The stunning, white beaches have finely ground coral, shells and sand particles so minute they squeak under your toes. They are at their most sublime on the Loyauté islands and Île des Pins.

While various species of sharks are quite common in the deep waters outside the lagoon, those which may eat humans rarely cross the reefs; thus fatal shark attacks are rare. If in doubt, ask the locals their opinion of your chosen bathing spot. When swimming, stick to the calm, protected waters of a bay or the lagoon. Crossing an offshore reef means you'll suddenly encounter very strong ocean currents, breaking surf and perhaps a biting shark.

Sports

Noumea is host to most of New Caledonia's sporting facilities, although you can watch games of the two favourite sports – soccer and women's cricket – practically anywhere in the country on weekends.

Rugby union is played from April to October by seven teams – six of which are based in Noumea and one in Bourail. Games are held under lights with late kick-offs to avoid the heat. Teams are made up of French players and a few Wallisians.

The capital has the country's only squash court while several public tennis courts are located at Anse Vata. Some of the wealthier hotels, in Noumea and elsewhere, also have courts for their guests. The odd public swimming pool is dotted around the country, such as in Noumea and Poindimie.

With the influx of Japanese tourists, golf

has risen in status in New Caledonia. There are three 18-hole golf courses in the country, all in the southern part of Grande Terre. The course at Tina Bay in Noumea is a professional circuit with a par 69 rating. Other courses are located at Dumbea and at a hotel/golf resort at Ouenghi near Boulouparis.

Cycling is as manic here as it is in France. On any given afternoon the waterfront boulevards around Noumea are teeming with enthusiasts, most of whom are métros. In September, New Caledonia's version of France's famous Tour de France is staged, with cyclists from Tahiti, Australia, New Zealand and France competing.

In mid-November, the Round New Caledonia Auto Safari takes off, once again with an international line-up. Various prestigious yacht races include Noumea on their itineraries (see the Yachtie's Guide in the Getting Around chapter for details).

Hiking
During the cooler mid-year months, trekking in New Caledonia is superb. Paths lead to waterfalls, deep caves and caverns, lakes and old burial grounds, some of which should be visited only with permission from the local clan.

Two areas not far from Noumea that are increasingly popular with hikers are the Monts Koghis and the Parc Provincial de la Rivière Bleue (see the Southern Grande Terre chapter for details on both).

Along the north-east coast, many walking paths wind up to waterfalls or lead into the mountains from the end of a river valley. One such track is the Chemin des Arabes, an old footpath that links Hienghene on the north-east coast to Voh on the west, crossing the central mountain chain.

A word of warning to hikers – remember that it gets dark relatively quickly and quite early so unless you're prepared to spend a night in the bush, keep an eye on the time.

Horse Trekking
Horse treks will let you get to know Caldoche ways a little better and are quite popular along Grande Terre's north-west coast. Two or three-day safaris up into the mountains can be arranged at both Bourail and Kone. At Dumbea, close to Noumea, a horse ranch offers hourly rides for those wanting only a short stint in the saddle. The Rivière Bleue park authorities hope to introduce horse riding in 1994.

Bush Safaris
Several tour companies arrange safaris into the interior of Grande Terre or around its entire perimeter. For details, see the Organised Tours section in the Noumea chapter.

Speleology
Adventurous speleologists can have lots of fun exploring rarely visited caves (*grottes* in French). There are many on Grande Terre – Grottes d'Adio near Poya and the Koumac caves for a start – and a few good ones on Île des Pins and the Loyauté islands (such as the Grotte du Diable on Lifou). In some, a good torch is necessary and perhaps a roll of string to find your way back.

Ultra-Light Flying
About 70 ultra-light planes are registered in New Caledonia, making up supposedly the biggest club in the Pacific (after Australia). Club members have normal ultra-lights as well as little amphibians, the latter having the obvious added attraction of being able to land on solid ground or water. A flight in one of these is *the* most exhilarating way of viewing the countryside. As well, you get a fantastic overview of the reefs and can see the blurred outlines of sea creatures. From a total flying height of 1300 metres, the planes can drop down to skim across the aqua waters a metre or two from the surface.

The club, called the Association des Planeurs Ultra Légers, was set up in Dumbea in 1983. So far there have been no fatalities. Attached to it is a flying school (☎ 35.30.51) that planned to organise tourist flights by the end of 1993. You'd be looking at roughly 6000F for 15 minutes of ultra-light flying. Probable take-off strips close to Noumea will be Kuendu Beach and Îlot Ma tre. The school has qualified instructors to train beginners and also plans to make ultra-lights available for hire by visiting pilots.

Boat Hire
For yacht charters see the Sea section in the Getting Around chapter.

Language Courses
Individuals, as well as groups of Australian and New Zealand school students, are attracted to Noumea to learn French. Once there, private tuition can be arranged by contacting Mme Valette (☎ 26.38.56). Alternatively, you can tee up two to four-week French courses from home, organised by the Centre of International Cultural & Linguistic Exchanges in the Pacific, otherwise known as CREIPAC. Offered is a beginners' or refresher course (15 hours per week) for 22,500F and a more intensive course (25 hours per week) costing 30,000F. The courses include lectures, tours, lessons in cooking French cuisine and meals. There's a 2000F registration fee.

For more information, contact CREIPAC (☎ 25.41.24; fax 25.40.58), BP 3755 Noumea. Australian and New Zealand representatives include:

GET Education Tours
    1st floor 33 Bank St, South Melbourne, Victoria 3205 (☎ (03) 699 9044)
Leisure Pacific
    3rd floor 92 Pitt St, Sydney NSW 2000 (☎ (02) 231 4643)
Diamond Tours
    PO Box 46-015 Herne Bay, Auckland (☎ (09) 897 105)

ACCOMMODATION
There's no getting around the high prices of accommodation in New Caledonia, unless you bring a tent and stick to deserted beaches (which isn't such a horrible idea anyway!). Every type of hotel seems overpriced for what you get. The only real 'bargains' are package deals from Australia or New Zealand, whereby you get to stay at Club Med, for example, for a reasonable price.

The government extracts a room tax from every hotel with more than 10 rooms, which accounts for most places in Noumea. The tax is determined by the room price, so you'll pay either 140F, 280F or 380F per night on top of your bill, depending on the quality of hotel.

Camping
Camping is possible almost everywhere. You only have to ask the landowner's permission and, if required, pay a fee. One of the problems will always be a lack of drinking water, but villagers are usually generous with supplies. Official camping sites with running water and sometimes showers (rarely hot) also exist around Grande Terre and are usually free. Along the east coast and on the islands, many tribal *gîte* owners allow people to camp for between 700 to 1000F per tent per night. You then have access to their restaurant, shower and toilet facilities.

Hostel
New Caledonia's sole YHA hostel is in Noumea. It is highly recommended for those wanting to save on accommodation costs as it is the cheapest place to stay in the whole country (for details see the Noumea chapter).

Gîtes
Throughout the country, many families and clans have constructed gîtes for tourists. They are usually modelled on the traditional Melanesian *case* and generally set in an idyllic spot, overlooking a distant reef and an aqua lagoon. The huts range from being spartan to quite modern, and are generally clustered around a thatched restaurant which caters for guests and non-guests alike. Occasionally a row of very basic 'studio' rooms, with cement floors and perhaps a table, sits at the back of the property. You can rent one of these at a cheaper rate than a hut. The more expensive gîtes have private shower and toilet facilities in each bungalow but in the cheapies they're communal.

In some places, such as Île des Pins, Mare and Ouvea, gîtes are the only available accommodation and the domestic airline, Air Calédonie, has a large say in what owners charge. Most bungalows sleep up to three or four people and range in price from 1500F to 5000F for one person, 3000F to 5500F for two and 4000F to 6500F for three or four people. The double studio rooms are usually 1000F to 1500F cheaper than a bungalow.

Bookings can be made direct or, in Noumea, through Air Calédonie, the Maison de Lifou and the North Province Tourist Office.

Hotels & Resorts

Noumea has long dominated the hotel scene but in recent years hotels and resorts have popped up elsewhere around Grande Terre. The one and only top-end abode on the islands is found on Lifou.

Around la Brousse, the west coast has the healthiest share of hotels, though it could be wise to make a booking or two in advance as many of these are taken by local workers and travelling sales reps. Hotels are few and far between along the north-east coast; the only choices are the hotels at Poindimie and the new Club Med village at Hienghene. Some hotels take a 'pay-if-you-use' attitude towards air-conditioning (climatisation), meaning you could be up for an extra 800F or even 1500F for keeping cool. There is one hotel chain, Monitel, which in 1993 admitted to being in financial difficulty; however, it was attempting to keep its hotels in Bourail, Kone, Koumac and Poindimie open.

In Noumea the cheapest options, usually pretty basic and quite run-down hotels, start at 4000F for a single or double room. Some have kitchenettes, which can save you eating out every day, while others rent out double rooms on a weekly (26,000F) or monthly (90,000F) basis, though these are mainly taken by workers. In addition, there are two motels in the Anse Vata area and one is particularly nice (there is no difference in New Caledonia between a hotel and motel).

Stepping up to mid-range abodes, rooms generally cost 7500/8500F for a single/double though there are a few decent places costing less and some considerably more. Most Noumean hotels in this category (and of course in the top-end) have coffee and

tea-making facilities in each room, TV, private facilities, free air-con, etc. At extra cost is the continental or more expensive American breakfast. You get eggs, bacon, sausages and orange juice with the latter, while the continental version is strictly a typical French breakfast: *baguette* (French stick) or croissants served with butter *(beurre)* and jam *(marmelade)* plus tea or coffee.

If you enjoy a splurge, there are enough top-end options to keep you busy for a week or more. None of these hotel/resorts, however, really makes it to four or five-star comfort. On a luxury scale they rate below European-style extravagance but they're welcoming enough and offer a few extras, such as a free 1000F betting slip to Casino Royale and sporting facilities. The prices for single/double rooms climb from 9000/10,000F up to whatever it takes to pay for indulgence.

Many of the middle-range and top-end hotels and resorts can be booked as part of a package tour from Australia and New Zealand. If you're wanting to lie around in luxury, these deals are definitely the way to go – for details, see the Package Tours section in the Getting There & Away chapter.

FOOD

New Caledonia has a wide variety of cuisines but the most common restaurants are French, Vietnamese and Indonesian. You'll also find the odd Spanish, Indian, Mexican, Italian and vegetarian restaurant but these are limited only to Noumea. Outside the capital, restaurants are somewhat scarce and are usually attached to hotels though you don't have to be a guest to dine there. The islands and the east coast are your best bet for getting a chance to try Melanesian fare.

Dining Out

Thanks to the long midday break, as big a fuss is made over lunch as it is over dinner. Restaurants are generally open between 11 am and 2 pm and from 7 to 11 pm. On Sunday very few establishments are open.

French Cuisine French restaurants abound in Noumea. On one corner will be a little café with filling, but hardly what one would call fine food and, opposite, an extravagant à la carte place specialising in local *fruit de mer* (seafood), *escargots* (snails) from Île des Pins and gourmet dishes from France's noted Périgord region.

The best value for money comes with ordering either a *plat du jour* (dish of the day) which costs about 800F or, better still, a fixed-price *menu du jour*, usually referred to simply as a *menu*. For anywhere upwards of 1100F, a menu du jour generally entitles you to an entrée, main course, dessert, bread and chilled water (and sometimes even a small carafe of wine and an espresso). You may be given several choices with each course or you might just have to eat what you're given. Some restaurants offer a menu du jour at both lunch and dinner, while at others it's a lunchtime special only.

Many restaurants are exclusively à la carte, which means you must select dishes individually from the menu. A three-course meal composed in this way is considerably more expensive than a menu du jour.

For those with a taste for it, *venaison* (venison) features on menus along the west coast. Deer were imported to New Caledonia in the late 19th century and, when an Australian journalist visited in 1940, he commented that 'a braised venison steak is as common in New Caledonia as a lamb chop in Australia'. It's not quite like that these days, but it's still around.

Melanesian Cuisine Food prepared by Kanaks is served in most gîtes outside Noumea and in village *snack* bars. Often they cater to Western tastes so it doesn't mean the food is authentically Kanak, but it is closer to it.

The Melanesians have one special dish called *bougna*. It's a combination of chunks of yam, taro, sweet potato or cassava and banana with pieces of chicken, crab, lobster or meat. All this is mixed in coconut cream then wrapped in banana leaves, tied tightly with palm fronds and baked or steamed on hot coals or in an earth oven for about two hours. It is essentially meant for times of sharing, such as during tribal festivals and weddings or after a Sunday mass.

Bougnas are prepared for tourists on the Loyauté islands, Île des Pins and Grande Terre's east coast (and there's a family in Noumea who can also arrange one for visitors). One bougna generally feeds four people. In rainy weather they can still be made as the women cook them in large pots on the stove.

Other Cuisines Most of the Vietnamese, Indonesian and Chinese restaurants cater to their local populations. The meals are generally cheap (in comparison with French food) and filling. The few Indian restaurants in Noumea are run by families that have lived in French colonies, especially New Caledonia, for generations. According to a native of Bombay, the only thing authentically Indian about the food is the curry.

Snacks/Cafés The cheapest type of restaurant is called a *snack* or café. These establishments do a swift trade at breakfast and lunch and then close at about 2 pm; some reopen in the late afternoon until about 6/7 pm. They serve much the same sort of meals – *steak-frites* (steak & chips) for about 750F; *poulet au curry* (curried chicken) for 680F and *crevettes à l'ail* (garlic prawns) for 780F. Many of these meals are also available, in Noumea, from mobile vans that set up nightly in a car park.

Some takeaway specialities include *nems* or Vietnamese spring rolls, *bami*, a spicy Chinese or Indonesian dish based on noodles with chicken, pork or shrimps and vegetables and *Salade Tahitienne*, a favourite raw-fish salad from Tahiti. Nems are widely available – from snacks, the vans and even many small épiceries. Ice creams and sorbets, costing 160/320F for one/two scoops, can be bought from *glacières* in Noumea as can crêpes and *gaufres* (waffles).

Self-Catering
The morning market in Noumea is the

biggest of its kind in the country. All others are tiny events with a few women trading local produce; on Grande Terre's east coast there are also unattended roadside fruit stalls. Noumean supermarkets and village stores, the latter called either *épiceries* or *magasins*, sell crusty *baguettes* and croissants for 50F, *fromage* (cheese), some fruit and vegetables, tinned fish, corned beef, rice, coffee and other essentials. Supplies are quite limited on the Loyauté islands and Île des Pins, as stocks are dependent on the sporadic supply ships.

Local Foods

As in other Pacific countries, New Caledonia's staple foods are fish, coconut, banana, taro, sweet potato and yam, all available year round. Needless to say, their nutritional value is higher than much of their imported tinned counterparts but, unfortunately, traditional fare is being replaced more and more by expensive processed foods, as you'll see by the piles of canned beef and tins of coconut cream found in the shops.

Lobster *(langouste)*, coconut crab, dugong and turtle *(tortue)* are all traditional Kanak food sources, as is a wide array of fish. These days the number of turtles and dugongs which can be hunted for food is limited, and their killing for commercial purposes is prohibited, though turtle still appears on menus on Île des Pins to appease those tourists who want a bite of forbidden fruit.

Various local recipes exist for cooking *roussette*, a fruit-eating flying fox, but most commonly it's boiled, the skin taken off and then the flesh cooked again in coconut cream.

A variety of nuts, such as the candlenut (known as *tai* in Kanak) and pandanus nuts, are eaten, as are the seeds from breadfruit, pawpaw, watermelon and pumpkin.

One of the most famous nuts is the coconut, growing on trees *(Cocos nucifera)* which can reach 25 metres in height and live for up to 80 years. Coconuts usually take a year to ripen – they're ready when you can hear the juice (called either milk or water and

different from coconut cream, which is made from the grated flesh) shaking around inside. The less developed the coconut, the sweeter the juice, which is why many people cut off the tops when the outside husk is still green, and drink the milk. Even young, the soft coconut flesh is tasty though the flavour increases with age. The flesh contains oil which is pressed from the dried kernels, known as copra.

The following is an introduction to the most common staple root foods:

Yam *(Dioscorea, igname* in French): the yam is to Pacific islanders what the potato is to Westerners – an energiser. It has a high status in Kanak society and is treated with a reverence normally reserved for elders or the ancestors. It's nutritious (particularly in vitamins B & C and in minerals) and grows as a climbing vine, with long edible roots which can be roasted, boiled, used for fritters or in curries. Botanists have linked the introduction of the yam to the arrival of the first Melanesians.

Taro *(Colocasia esculenta)*: this root plant spread from South-East Asia long ago and is still used, although its cultivation is declining as rice takes over. The plant has big, edible leaves and stocky roots about 30 cm long. In the centre of Grande Terre you can still see the terraced fields where irrigation techniques for taro cultivation were mastered in the early centuries AD. It is an energy giver and is full of fibre, calcium and iron.

Taro plant

Cassava *(Manihot esculenta)*: also called manioc or tapioca, this plant has five to seven lobed leaves and is found in many vegetable gardens. It still grows where yam or taro fail and both roots and leaves are eaten.

Sweet potato *(Ipomoea batatas)*: originating in South America, this plant has nice-tasting tubers and grows in many varieties. It is associated with the arrival of Polynesians to New Caledonia.

Fruit

While there's a decent range of fruit, New Caledonia does not have the abundance of tropical delights you might expect of a Pacific island and, in large supermarkets, imported fruits sometimes outnumber local produce. Seasonal fruits include avocados, passionfruit, mangos, oranges, pineapples, custard apples, watermelons and citrus fruits such as pomelos. Bananas, coconut and pawpaw are available year round.

Unlike in Western countries, unripe pawpaw is used in New Caledonia for salads and in cooking. When used in this way, you must peel and soak it in water for an hour to extract the bitter white juice. It can then be grated and sprinkled with vinaigrette to make a tasty side dish.

Breadfruit trees bear large starchy fruit containing a lot of sugar. As the name suggests, the fruit can be baked or roasted and can replace flour when dried and pounded. The seeds and young leaves of the tree are also eaten.

Breadfruit

Guavas, originating in tropical America, grow wild along the roadsides in New Caledonia. The ripe yellow fruit tastes a little like a tomato and has many hard little seeds to spit out. It breaks the record for vitamin C content and also has a lot of pectin (used for making jam).

The jacquier, a sort of durian, grows up to 30 kg and has mushy, yellowish flesh. People either love this fruit or hate it. Its seeds can be roasted.

Recipes

For those with the means, here are a few local recipes (servings for four) to try:

Taro Leaf Soup
20 young taro leaves
3 cups water
1½ tablespoons oil
1 diced onion
2 cups milk
1½ tablespoons flour
Salt & pepper to taste

Add the taro leaves to the boiling water and cook for 10 minutes. Drain and set aside. Fry the onion in the heated oil for a minute then add flour and cook for another minute. Remove from heat, stir in the milk and bring to the boil. Add the taro leaves and simmer for five minutes, stirring often.

Boiled Yam in Coconut Cream
2 cups coconut cream
8 pieces of yam (150 grams each)
16 taro leaves

Coconut cream is the rich liquid squeezed out of grated coconut. To make two cups of it, grate the meat of two coconuts and add one cup of hot water. Let it stand for 15 minutes then pass it through a cheesecloth or a sieve to press out the cream. Peel the yams and chop into large cubes. Place the yams, coconut cream and taro leaves in a pot, cover and boil for 35 minutes or until cooked.

Green Pawpaw Curry
2 medium-sized green pawpaws
2 tablespoons butter
1 large onion, chopped
2 garlic cloves, crushed
2 green chillies
1 tablespoon curry powder
1 cup coconut cream
1 cup water
½ cup lemon juice
Pepper to taste

Peel the pawpaw, remove the seeds and soak in water for an hour to extract the bitter sap. Melt the butter and fry the onion and garlic for three minutes. Add the chillies and curry powder and cook for five minutes. Slowly stir in the coconut cream (see the previous recipe) and water. Chop the pawpaw into cubes and add them to the curry sauce; cook for 30 minutes then add the lemon juice and pepper.

Banana Rice
1 cup rice
6 sliced bananas
1 cup coconut cream

Put rice and bananas in a pot. Add water to five cm above the rice and boil gently until cooked. Make the coconut cream (see the yam recipe) and stir through the cooked rice.

DRINKS
Water
Throughout New Caledonia water is safe to drink, except on Ouvea, where it's saline. Should you prefer bottled water, several French brands such as Évian (150F per litre) are sold in shops or there's a local equivalent bottled from a spring at Mont Dore. On the Loyauté islands and Île des Pins, take care not to over-tap the locals' limited fresh-water supply.

Coffee
The French take their coffee-drinking seriously and it's a trait that hasn't disappeared just because they're now in the Pacific. Much of the coffee that is served is grown and roasted in New Caledonia.

A cup of coffee can take various forms but the most common is a small, black espresso called *un café noir*, *un express* or simply *un café*. Depending on where you buy it, you'll pay between 100F and 150F; you can also ask for the long *(grand)* version. A *café crème* is an espresso with steamed milk or cream, while a *café au lait* is a large espresso with steamed milk and costs between 200F and 250F. On the islands and in a few mainland places you'll have the choice of a *tasse* (cup) or *bol* (bowl). A bowl costs about 10F more and is designed to give you a double fix (though it's far from hot by the time you reach the bottom).

Alcohol
The preferred drinks in New Caledonia are *vin* (wine) and *bière* (beer). The local beer is simply called Number One and is brewed at the Grande Brasserie at Magenta in Noumea. The cheapest way to buy it is in the huge 58 ml bottles available from supermarkets. Pubs and bars serve Foster's, Heineken and Number One on tap or in cans. Nightclubs charge double the normal pub price for all drinks.

French, Australian and New Zealand wines are available in supermarkets, though the first far outnumbers the others. Expect to pay anything from 300F for a cheap bottle of *vin de table* (table plonk) to 4500F for a Laurent Perrier champagne. A four-litre cask of Australian table red costs 1000F. Restaurant prices for wine are double, sometimes triple, what you'd pay in a shop and, unfortunately, the concept of BYO has not caught on here.

Drinks are further divided in apéritifs like *porto* (port) and *pastis*, an aniseed-flavoured drink which was banned in New Caledonia up until 20 years ago. Essentially, it is the drink favoured by and associated with old men sitting under a plane tree in the south of France. Mixed with about five parts water, it's strong and refreshing.

Then there are *digestifs*, drinks to conclude the meal (though it's not unknown for a digestif to be taken during a meal, supposedly to make room in the stomach for the next course!). Typical choices are brandies (700F per nip) like armagnac or cognac. French liqueurs like Cointreau and Grand Marnier are readily available.

As a reminder, alcohol cannot legally be sold from shops in New Caledonia between noon on Saturday and 6 am on Monday. However, shopkeepers on the north-east coast and the islands don't bother enforcing this rule and even in Noumea, where it's more rigidly controlled, people find ways around it.

ENTERTAINMENT
Modern Kanak music has few ties with tradition and there is no one musical style which

instantly typifies the contemporary scene. The local live music arena contains many Kanak bands, playing everything from sentimental mush to reggae, but unfortunately none of the bands performs on a regular basis. If you're in the right place at the right time you might catch a local group – look out for Drui or Bwanjep. Reggae is very popular amongst Kanaks and, in recent times, international bands such as Lucky Dube, Burning Spear and Steel Pulse have performed here. However, the few who pine for the Western 'cultured arts' and classical music are not so lucky. It is difficult to lure those sorts of artists to such a far-flung island. Once or twice a year, however, usually in winter, there's an orchestral concert and a ballet.

Noumea has the country's only cinemas, but the large west coast towns hold monthly film nights in school halls or community centres. About 66% of the films shown in New Caledonia come from the USA and 17% are from France. All are exclusively in French (and the dubbing is often atrocious).

THINGS TO BUY
Curios

Some 50 curio shops, mostly laden with cheap imported junk, dot Noumea but they're non-existent elsewhere. One popular seller which is immensely handy for the tropics is the *pareo*, a colourful, hand-dyed sarong found waving in the breeze at the entrance to every curio shop. They are worn wrapped around the waist like a skirt and topped by a T-shirt, though only your imagination can limit ways of tying them.

Pareos are not a traditional dress of Kanaks. The concept comes from Polynesia where they're called *pareus* and are commonly worn around the house. Their origin explains why you can still see village men on Mare wearing pareos, though their wraps tend to be in earthy colours rather than the flashy fluorescent colours found in Noumea (the latter are used locally only as car seat covers). Prices range from 1300F to 1800F depending on the size and the intricacy of the design.

Natural Products
Carvings Wood carving is one of the oldest and most practised Kanak artforms; however, it has not spilled over into a thriving tourist-orientated craft. Sandalwood is available only on Île des Pins where rough but fragrant carvings are sold, as are bags of the leftover wood chips. A few sculptors along the north-east coast have roadside stalls and their works – usually replicas of a grande case, ceremonial axe or a *bec d'oiseau* (bird's beak club) – are considerably cheaper than pieces you'll find in Noumea. The same goes for hand-carved soapstone. A piece depicting an ancestor's face will sell for about 700F in la Brousse and 1700F in the capital.

Sand & Bark Unusual and very beautiful sand paintings of traditional Kanak scenes start at 4000F for a small painting and go up to 20,000F for a large one. Paintings made from niaouli tree bark sell for similar prices. Also in this genre are sand lamp shades, though they're not the easiest thing to carry around.

Minerals The country's many minerals are polished and sold as they are, or, in the case of nickel, made into clocks, key chains, fancy cigarette lighters, you name it. Nickel comes up a greenish-brown colour and can be mistaken for jade, which is also found in New Caledonia but not in the same quantity. Chunky little nickel clocks sell for between 3000F and 5000F.

Shells Many Noumean curio shops sell polished conch, trocchus and cowrie shells for ludicrous prices while roadside vendors along Grande Terre's north-east coast are not much better. You can pick up the same unpolished, salt-smelling specimens for free on east coast beaches and on the Loyauté islands.

Nautilus shells can be another rip-off. A perfect shell can sell for 4000F in Noumea; however, you should give it the once over if you want to be sure of buying a New Caledonian nautilus. Only one nautilus species is endemic – it can be recognised by the deep central cavity formed where the shell coils around. Most of those sold in shops do not have this concave section and are from the Philippines.

Music

Cassettes of local bands, more often than not from the Loyauté islands, are sold in music shops in Noumea and in grocery shops on the islands. If you're looking for a mix of contemporary New Caledonian bands, the CD/cassette *Mix Mangrove* was put out in '89 and blends reggae, soul and blues sung in both French and Kanak languages.

For more ceremonial-type music, *Kanaké* – *Songs and Dances of Kone, Gaica and Lossi*, was recorded during the Melanesia 2000 festival and includes music from Lifou and the mainland. Another cassette, *Cada and Ayoii*, features traditional, dual-voiced men's songs from Heinghene. Both these are available from the ADCK (for details see Useful Organisations in this chapter).

Duty-Free

Plenty of duty-free shops in Noumea sell imported French perfumes, jewellery, scarves and clothing. Prices are not cheap as they cater to Japanese honeymooners who hanker after French goods. You'll have to show your plane ticket when you go shopping.

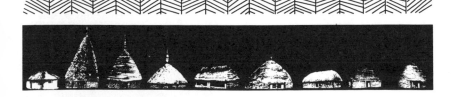

Getting There & Away

AIR

The major airline flying into the country is Air France, which took over the previous main carrier, UTA, in March 1993, though you may still see UTA signs up around Noumea. The other major airline, focusing more on connections with Pacific destinations, is the territory's international carrier, Air Calédonie International.

Other airline companies which fly into New Caledonia are Qantas, Air New Zealand, Air Nauru and Air Vanuatu. Because Air France controls the skies around New Caledonia, many other commercial airlines cannot get permission to fly to the French territory. Therefore, companies such as Thai International, Malaysian Airlines and Scandinavian Airlines (SAS) fly into either Australia or New Zealand from where the other carriers take over the final leg to New Caledonia.

Arrival

All international flights land at Tontouta International Airport, 45 km north-west of Noumea. It has duty-free facilities, an exchange desk, car rental outlets, a restaurant and bar, but no tourist information office. For details on the various options for getting between Tontouta and Noumea, see the Getting Around section in the Noumea chapter. Information on accommodation near the airport is outlined in the Tontouta section in the Southern Grande Terre chapter.

Round-the-World Tickets

With Round-the-World (RTW) fares offered by airlines, two or more carriers link up and permit you to fly anywhere you want on their global route systems so long as you do not backtrack. Since New Caledonia is on the other side of the world from Europe or the east coast of North America, it may work out to be no more expensive or even cheaper to buy an RTW ticket rather than an ordinary return ticket. However, as New Caledonia is

not on the major flight paths of most large airline companies, not a great deal of RTW tickets automatically include it, though it is possible to be routed through the country when mapping out your travel itinerary. Another option may be to buy a RTW ticket that includes a neighbouring Pacific nation which is on a major route, such as Fiji, and then buy a return ticket to New Caledonia from there.

Besides having to go in the same direction, other restrictions with RTW tickets are that you (usually) must book the first sector in advance and cancellation penalties then apply. There may also be a limit on how many stops you can make. Usually the tickets are valid for 90 days up to a year. An alternative type of RTW ticket is one put together by a travel agent using a combination of discounted tickets.

In the UK, an agent like Trailfinders can often come up with some interesting London-to-London RTW combinations usually with Qantas or Air France. Typical prices for these South Pacific RTW tickets are UK£1400 to UK£1500.

If you buy a RTW ticket in France which includes a stopover in Noumea, you'll be looking at about 18,890FFr for an Air France ticket valid from two weeks to six months. Other likely stops on this ticket would include Singapore, Jakarta, Sydney, Papeete and San Francisco.

Circle Pacific Tickets

Circle Pacific fares use a combination of airlines to circle the Pacific. This usually means travelling one way from Australia or New Zealand to North America, or vice versa, via either the South Pacific or Asia. As with RTW tickets, there are usually restrictions on booking, the number of stopovers you can have, and validity. In general, they allow you to fly for at least three months up to a year.

While an extraordinary range of combinations exists, once again New Caledonia unfortunately does not feature all that often. Your travel agent will know what's currently available.

From Australia, the only so-called Circle Pacific fare that includes Noumea is a regional ticket that does a loop from Sydney or Brisbane to Noumea, Auckland, Christchurch and Wellington and back to Australia. It costs A$1085, is valid from six to 60 days and you can stop in all three New Zealand cities.

Leaving from New Zealand, Air Calédonie International and Solomon Airlines have an Auckland-Noumea-Port Vila-Honiara-Port Moresby ticket that is valid for a year and costs NZ$1570.

To/From Australia

New Caledonia is a very popular destination for Australians. The majority of tourists, after the Japanese, come from Australia and thus it can be one of the cheapest jumping off points. Flights leave from Brisbane, Sydney and Melbourne and are shared predominantly by Air Calédonie International and Qantas. Air France has two flights per week from Sydney only. Note that flights to/from Australia are heavily booked during high seasons, which mostly coincide with school holidays in New Caledonia and in Australia.

Besides package deals, the cheapest way to fly to New Caledonia from any of the three cities is with a return excursion fare. They are ruled by a five-day minimum and 30-day maximum stay and vary in price depending on season – the more expensive, high season is roughly 30 June to 13 July; 15 to 28 September; and 15 December to 24 January. Buying a ticket this way is considerably cheaper than getting a standard return fare (which does not change with season when bought in Australia).

One of the best agencies that arranges low-cost travel is STA, whose head office (☎ (03) 347 6911) is at 224 Faraday St, Carlton, Melbourne. Full-time students should enquire about possible discounted fares. STA also has offices in all major Australian cities.

You can also book directly through Air Calédonie International, which has offices in the following Australian cities:

Brisbane
    8th floor, ANZ Centre, 324 Queen St, 4000
    (☎ (07) 221 2433)
Sydney
    World Aviation, 64 York St, 2000 (☎ (02) 239 1722)
Melbourne
    World Aviation, 541 King St, West Melbourne, 3003 (☎ (03) 321 6872)

Brisbane Qantas and Air Calédonie International share this route, each having one flight per week in both directions. The flight time is two hours. The return excursion fare (for conditions see above) to New Caledonia costs A$701/811 in low/high season; in contrast, standard one-way/return fares cost A$583/1166. A standard return ticket bought in Noumea to fly to Brisbane will cost 74,900/86,600F in low/high season.

Sydney There are three flights per week in either direction (one each with Qantas, Air Calédonie International and Air France) and the trip takes about three hours. The return excursion fare from Sydney costs exactly the same as from Brisbane – A$701/811 in low/high season. However, standard fares are slightly more expensive, with one-way/return tickets costing 632/1264F. If bought in Noumea, a standard return fare will cost 81,200/93,600F in low/high season.

Melbourne You can fly between Melbourne and Noumea (via Sydney) twice a week in either direction with Air Calédonie International or Qantas. A return excursion fare is A$952/1103 in low/high season. The standard one-way/return fares are A$853/1716. From Noumea, low/high-season standard return tickets cost 91,700/104,500F.

Australian Visas Except for New Zealanders, all visitors to Australia need a visa. They are generally valid for six months and must be applied for before arrival. There is an Australian Consulate in Noumea which processes visa applications.

To/From New Zealand

There are two flights per week between Auckland and Noumea, one with Air New Zealand and the other flown by Air France. Again, flights are heavily booked during high seasons, which generally coincide with school holidays in both New Zealand and New Caledonia. The flight time is 2½ hours.

As an example of prices, a 35-day return excursion fare costs NZ$635 while a standard return is NZ$1430. If you're buying the ticket in Noumea, low/high season return standard fares cost 60,900/66,600F. A highly recommended travel agency for tickets to New Caledonia is Flight Centre (☎ (9) 377 4655), Fort Street, Auckland, which has branches around the country.

Citizens of Australia, the UK, Canada, the Cook Islands, Japan and some western European countries do not need a visa for New Zealand. For those who do, there is a consulate in Noumea.

To/From the Pacific

Because of Air France's control of the skies around New Caledonia, most of the multi-stop, discounted 'air passes' offered by airlines of nearby Pacific countries do not include New Caledonia on their itineraries.

Vanuatu Port Vila's Bauerfield Airport in Vanuatu is New Caledonia's closest neighbouring airport. You can fly between the two with Air Calédonie International or Air Vanuatu about four times a week. The flight time is one hour. Bought in Noumea, a standard one-way/return ticket costs 20,500/41,000F.

A cheaper ticket is the 30,300F return excursion fare offered by both airlines which is valid for a seven-day minimum and 20-day maximum stay. Another option is Air Vanuatu's special weekend deal of 40,400F whereby you must leave Friday and return two days later. The price includes the airfare, two nights' accommodation and airport transfers. If you're considering seeing Fiji as well, see the details on the triangular fare in the following Fiji section. Air Vanuatu is represented in Noumea by Axxcess Travel

(see the Information section of the Noumea chapter for details).

Visas are not required by nationals of the British Commonwealth, most western European nations, Japan or the USA. Everyone else should enquire at the Vanuatu consulate in Noumea.

Fiji Air Calédonie International flies to Nadi (pronounced 'Nandi') once a week. The flight takes two hours. A return excursion fare is available for 63,700F while the standard one-way/return fares are 43,400/87,000F. With the excursion fare, you're limited to a minimum six days and a maximum of 14 days.

Alternatively, there is a triangular fare you can buy from Air Calédonie International which connects Noumea with Port Vila (Vanuatu), Nadi (Fiji) and back to Noumea for a good price of 66,400F. The only stipulation is that you must stop over in each place for at least 24 hours.

Nationals of the British Commonwealth and most western European countries, as well as those from the USA, Japan and several other nations, do not require a visa for Fiji.

Nauru Air Nauru has one flight in and out of New Caledonia from Nauru per week. It costs about A$260/520 for a one-way/return ticket.

Wallis & Futuna Twice a week, Air Calédonie International flies to Hihifo on Wallis Island (flight time four hours). The Wednesday flight then continues to Vele on Futuna (total flight time six hours). A 14-seat plane is used for these flights but, as many Futunians are quite sizeable people, it sometimes can take only nine passengers. The return fare for either is 71,000/78,200F in low/high season.

Like Tahiti and New Caledonia, Wallis and Futuna islands form a French territory, so similar visa requirements apply. For details, contact the Bureau des Étrangers in Noumea (see the Visas & Embassies section in the Facts for the Visitor chapter).

Tahiti Air Calédonie International flies via Wallis to Papeete's Faaa airport once a week for a return price of 109,000/121,500F in low/high season. Air New Zealand also has a service, via Auckland en route to Los Angeles and Paris, for the same price.

Visa requirements for Tahiti are similar to New Caledonia's except that New Zealanders, in addition to Australians, must have visas. For details in Noumea, contact the Bureau des Étrangers (see the Visas & Embassies section in the Facts for the Visitor chapter).

To/From Europe

The UK Most travellers from this side of the world don't travel directly to New Caledonia. They might stop in Noumea en route to Australia using a RTW ticket or buy a cheap ticket from one of London's low-cost 'bucket shops' (independent air ticket centres) to an east coast Australian city and then get reasonable fares to New Caledonia from there. Bucket shop one-way/return fares to Brisbane or Sydney on Australia's east coast range from UK£350/650 in low season to UK£575/950 in high. In contrast, British Airways' standard one-way/return fares are UK£600/860 in low season and UK£930/1400 in high.

Trailfinders (☎ (071) 938 3366) at 46 Earls Court Rd, London W8, produce a lavishly illustrated brochure which includes airfare details. STA (☎ (071) 581 4132) at 74 Old Brompton Rd, London SW 7 and (☎ (071) 465 0484) 111 Euston Rd, London NW 1, also has branches in the UK. Look in the listings magazines *Time Out* and *City Limits* plus the Sunday papers, or pick up one of the free news/travel magazines such as *TNT* which are widely available (mainly outside railway and underground stations) in London.

Most British travel agents are registered with ABTA (Association of British Travel Agents). If you have paid for your flight to an ABTA-registered agent who then goes out of business, ABTA will guarantee a refund or an alternative. Unregistered bucket shops don't have this guarantee and are therefore riskier, but also sometimes cheaper.

France Air France, Qantas and Air New Zealand are the major carriers between Europe and Noumea, with flights via either the USA or Asia. The USA route, flown by Air New Zealand or Air France, goes from Paris to Los Angeles, Papeete, Wallis, Auckland and finally Noumea (total flight time 31 hours) once a week. Standard economy one-way/return fares cost about 8000/11,000FFr. The Asian route (27 to 29 hours) via Singapore, Jakarta, Denpasar and Sydney is flown four times a week by Air France which offers a return excursion fare for 9990FFr valid for 45 days only. Qantas also flies this route – one-way/return tickets cost 8000/10,990FFr. A recommended travel agency in the French capital for tickets to the Pacific is Tours 33 (☎ (1) 43.29.36.50) at 80 Blvd Saint Germain, 75005 Paris.

There are several options if you're buying a ticket in Noumea to fly to France. Air New Zealand and SAS combine to fly Noumea-Auckland-Copenhagen-Paris, with a stop in either Singapore, Hong Kong, Honolulu or Papeete, for a minimum one-way fare of 121,000/133,000F in low/high season. Thai International has flights to Paris via Sydney or Melbourne and Bangkok for 150,000/240,000F for a one-way/return ticket. Malaysian Airlines has one flight per week to Paris via Auckland and Kuala Lumpur for 139,000/200,000F one way/return in low season. Qantas has a low season one-way fare of 123,000F. Air France sometimes has a discounted Apex fare of 180,000F return, otherwise its fares step up to an excursion return ticket of 252,000F.

To/From the USA & Canada

The major west coast cities for departure to the South Pacific are San Francisco, Los Angeles and Vancouver, while on the east coast departures are from New York, Boston and Toronto.

Another option from this end could be to buy a fare to Australia via Fiji and then, as New Caledonia is just a short hop from either, buy a separate ticket from Sydney or Nadi. Qantas flies between Los Angeles and Sydney via Nadi four times per week. Prices depend on the season, but you'll be looking at roughly US$3000 for a standard, return economy ticket and US$1100 for a return excursion fare valid for three months. Any time you are looking for an inexpensive way to travel, check the travel section in the *New York Times*, *Los Angeles Times*, *San Francisco Examiner* or *Toronto Globe & Mail*.

From New Caledonia to the USA, Air France has one flight per week via Auckland, Wallis and Papeete to Los Angeles. It costs 203,000/407,600F for a standard one-way/return ticket though occasionally return excursion fares valid for one-month only are available for about 188,000F.

To/From Asia

Depending on where you're coming from, a cheap way to get to New Caledonia could be to fly to South-East Asia and find a bucket ticket to New Caledonia via Australia or New Zealand. The only Asian destinations directly connected with New Caledonia are Singapore, and Denpasar and Jakarta in Indonesia.

Fares for Air France flights from Singapore, Jakarta and Denpasar to Noumea cost A$3000/3900 one way/return. Obviously, cheaper fares can be found within these countries.

From New Caledonia, Air France has two flights per week between Noumea and Paris which stop in Denpasar (seven hours), Jakarta (9½ hours) and Singapore (14 hours) and another two Paris-bound flights via Sydney (three hours), Jakarta (11½ hours) and Singapore (16 hours). The price from Noumea to either Indonesian destination is about 94,000F for a return excursion fare or 152,700F for a standard one-way fare. To Singapore, a return excursion fare is 95,000F and a one-way standard ticket is 163,000F.

All other Asian options mean flying via Australia or New Zealand. With a Thai International ticket you can fly from Bangkok to Australia and continue on Air Calédonie International to Noumea. From Noumea, it costs 115,000/170,000F one way/return. With a Malaysian Airlines ticket, you can fly Kuala Lumpur-Auckland-Noumea.

To/From Japan

Air France has two direct flights per week between Noumea and Tokyo (8½ hours). From Noumea, a return excursion fare is available for 178,000F, while a standard one-way/return ticket costs 125,000/251,000F. Qantas also flies from Noumea to Tokyo but it's a longer trip, going via Sydney. Return fares in low/high season cost 112,000/139,000F.

To/From South America

Lan Chile connects Papeete, Tahiti with Santiago, Chile via Easter Island. Air France and Air Calédonie International link Tahiti with New Caledonia, making it possible to travel from South America to the south-west Pacific, New Zealand and Australia. The round-trip fare between Papeete and Santiago is about US$1150.

SEA

Noumea's natural, deep-water harbour was the reason why France chose this spot to set up the capital. These days, it's New Caledonia's only official port of entry for international vessels.

The harbour has two distinct sectors. To the north lies the Grande Rade or, as it's also known, Anse de Tir. It's an industrial area, dominated by the bulky hulls of cargo ships as well as Société Le Nickel's smelter and adjoining nickel-loading wharf. To the south, entered through a narrow headland, is Baie de la Moselle where luxury cruise liners, visiting yachts and island supply ships dock. Both bays are used as shelters for vessels during cyclones.

Cruise Ships

Noumea has long been a port of call for luxury liners cruising the Pacific. While the Events of the 1980s turned many ships away for a few years, more recent world economic woes have led to Australian-based cruise companies restructuring their programmes to provide shorter, less expensive trips. As this is one of the closest foreign ports to Australian east-coast cities, New Caledonia has benefited from this change in attitude.

Whether you're watching from ashore or

Top Left: Putting on an underwater show (GC)
Top Right: Longing for the sea (LL)
Bottom: New Caledonia's striking nautilus shell (LL)

Top: Bonhomme de Bourail (DNC)
Bottom: Sunset (DNC)

from deck, it's a majestic sight to see a liner sailing silently into Noumea's protected harbour. On average there is one ship in town every week, sometimes more. While Noumea has the country's only harbour facilities, some liners also drop anchor at various spots around New Caledonia and then shuttle their passengers ashore to spend a day on the beach. Prime locations for this include offshore from Kuto Bay on Île des Pins, or Amédée Islet in Baie de Prony on Grande Terre's southern tip, or in Hienghene's bay on the north-east coast.

Gare Maritime All cruise ships dock in Baie de la Moselle, either at the old *gare maritime* (boat terminal) on Ave James Cook or at the new terminal, a cream-coloured building with impressive sails, close to the city centre on Rue Jules Ferry. In mid-1993, only the *Club Med 2* was fortunate enough to be able to drop anchor at the new gare maritime, as the water there was too shallow for other vessels. The *Fairstar* and *Michael Sholokhov* were still docking at the old terminal and transferring their passengers into town by bus. By the end of 1993, the new berth should have been deepened to accommodate all liners.

There is a small tourist office inside the new gare maritime, open only when ships arrive, and a postal agency but no foreign exchange facilities. The souvenir shops and bike rental outfit in this terminal will accept A$ and US$.

Cruise Companies The following companies have cruise liners regularly calling into Noumea:

Club Med
> 9th floor, 55 Market St, Sydney 2000 (☎ (02) 265 0500; fax (02) 265 0599) or at 41-43 Rue de Sébastopol, Noumea (☎ 27.43.79; fax 26.33.87). Club Med describes its new vessel, *Club Med 2*, as a 'ship with the soul of a yacht'. This deluxe 187-metre-long vessel has five enormous computer-controlled sails and is claimed to be the world's largest sailing ship. All the luxuries in life are on hand – a casino, bars with evening shows, two restaurants, a swimming pool, disco etc. The cabins are very comfortable, the crew is a hotchpotch of nationalities and all water sports such as scuba diving and water-skiing are free.

The *Club Med 2* spends roughly the first six months of the year plying continuously between Noumea, Île des Pins, Hienghene and Port Vila (Vanuatu) before setting sail north to Micronesia, where it sees the rest of the year out island hopping between Guam, Palau and Chuuk.

As an example of prices (when booked in Noumea), a five day/four night cruise around New Caledonia to Port Vila and back costs 32,000F for a single cabin or 24,000/20,000/17,000F per person in a double/triple/quad. In Australia, Club Med organises several 'fly/cruise' packages. The cheapest is a seven-night deal including return economy airfares to New Caledonia, three nights at Club Med's village in Noumea and the remainder on *Club Med 2*, plus all meals. Prices vary depending on season and the Australian city you fly out of but, as an indication, you'd be looking at about A$1700 leaving from Brisbane.

Cunard Line
> 146 Arthur St, North Sydney, 2060 (☎ (02) 956 7777; fax (02) 956 6229). This Norwegian company began sailing its new liner, *Crown Monarch*, in the waters of the Coral Sea and the South Pacific in late 1993. A 550-passenger, four-star liner built in 1990 and crewed by Filipinos, the *Crown Monarch* sails every three weeks from Sydney to Noumea, Île des Pins, either the Solomon Islands or Fiji, and Port Vila on 10-to-14-day cruises.

Pacific Cruise Company
> 10th floor, 109 Pitt St, Sydney 2000 (☎ (02) 235 0444; fax (02) 221 7584) or, in New Zealand, represented by Thomas Cook Holidays, (9) 96-98 Anzac Ave, Auckland (☎ (9) 796 800; fax 303 0266). The *MV Michael Sholokhov* and the *MV Russ* are both relatively small and old, Russian-crewed ships, catering for 250 passengers. Cruises to New Caledonia depart from Brisbane or Sydney every couple of weeks. Prices vary depending on season, the number of people you have in the cabin and whether you want a porthole or not. On a seven-nights' cruise from Brisbane, the cheapest twin/quad cabin would cost A$935/540 per person.

P&O
> P&O Booking Centre, 33 Bligh St, Sydney 2000 (☎ (02) 237 0333). The well-known, so-called 'funship' *Fairstar* regularly sails to New Caledonia and on to Vanuatu on nine to 14-night cruises leaving from Sydney. Once again, cabin prices are variable but you can expect to pay A$1180/1030 per person in a cheap twin/quad on a nine-night cruise.

From Noumea, it's possible to hitch a ride back to Australia on the *Fairstar* for about 30,000F. The company to contact for details is Compagnie Générale Maritime (☎ 27.33.21; fax 27.41.83) at 32 Rue Gallieni, Noumea.

Freighters

The romanticised times when you could make your way around the world on a cargo ship for little more than a song or dance have long gone. These days, few freighters accept passengers and those that do usually charge mightily for their service. If you're looking for a ride out of Noumea, your best bet is to be at the docks and personally ask the captains. If you go through most of the shipping companies, you'll repeatedly get a flat 'no'. Otherwise, you may want to try the following:

AMACAL
  5 Rue d'Austerlitz, Noumea (☎ 28.72.22); this company has ships sailing monthly to Wallis and Futuna. The voyage takes four days. For 22,500F you can have a 'bungalow', which is nothing more than a container, or for 28,000F a basic cabin. Once every two months, the *Moana II* sails from Noumea to Port Vila. This trip will cost about 12,000F.

Sydney International Travel Centre
  8th floor, 75 King St, Sydney 2000 (☎ (02) 299 8000; fax (02) 299 1337). This place handles bookings for Contship Container Lines Ltd, a seven-ship German fleet which sails from Melbourne and Sydney via New Zealand, New Caledonia, Taiwan, Hong Kong, Singapore and the Suez Canal to England. Roughly one ship per month makes the 55-day voyage, carrying 22,500 tonnes in some 1000 containers, and a maximum of 10 paying passengers (between February and April is the most popular time).
  On board there's a swimming room, sauna, lounge and restaurant (don't expect luxury) and double cabins with private facilities. They will accept passengers just wanting to travel from Australia to Noumea, but those making the full trip to England get priority. Melbourne-Noumea is four days' sailing and Sydney-Noumea is two days'; you'll be looking at a pricey A$200-250 a day.

Yachts

For all details on yachting to, from and around New Caledonia see the Yachtie's Guide in the following Getting Around chapter.

PACKAGE TOURS

Package deals to New Caledonia from Australia are big business and they can be good for people whose holidays are limited to a few weeks. In addition, in the case of an expensive destination like New Caledonia, a package holiday may end up being cheaper than doing it on your own tight budget.

Australia is the best place to pick up packages. Most deals include return economy airfares from Brisbane, Sydney or Melbourne, accommodation in high-class hotels and the possibility of many other incentives such as free air tickets for children, airport transfers, breakfast, casino chips, discounts on tours, water sports equipment and car hire.

While many packages used to be limited to hotels in Noumea, some now give the option of staying in the new resorts dotted around the country such as Malabou Beach near Poum, Poe Beach near Bourail, and Club Med's new village close to Hienghene. Others allow for a stay in Noumea plus a few nights on the Loyauté island of Lifou, Escapade Island Resort just off Noumea, or in a gîte on Île des Pins. Alternatively, you can combine a visit to New Caledonia with a taste of Vanuatu or Fiji.

One thing to watch out for when booking a holiday like this is the number of days your package advertises. Many flights from Australia arrive in New Caledonia in the late evening while departures can be mid-morning. This means, for example, that a so-called 'seven-day and five-night' package may in reality be only five days and five nights.

Also, prices are usually calculated on a single, twin or triple room basis. The more people you have, the cheaper the package costs per person. Those going solo can be up for an extra 20% or more on twin-share prices.

Travel agents have brochures detailing what's offered. A few agents specialising in New Caledonia and the Pacific include:

Air Calédonie Holidays
  These packages are booked through the offices of Air Calédonie International (see the previous Air – To/From Australia section for details). They have a wide range of deals in New Caledonia alone or in combination with Vanuatu. For example, a seven-night package in either Noumea's Hôtel Ibis or Le Surf Novotel will cost A$760/895 per person (twin-share) respectively while two nights in New Caledonia and five in Vanuatu is A$825 per person.

Club Med
  9th floor, 55 Market St, Sydney 2000 (☎ (02) 265 0500; fax (02) 265 0599); there are two Club Med villages in New Caledonia – the original Château Royal in Noumea and the new Koulnoue Village near Hienghene. Package holidays include accommodation, all meals, airfares, airport transfers and use of water sports equipment. As price examples, seven nights in Noumea will cost upward of A$1300 while a seven-night package staying at both villages starts at A$1500. Prices rise depending on the season and whether you leave from Brisbane, Sydney or Melbourne. Another package combines a stay in Noumea with one at Club Med's Vanuatu resort, or there are 'fly/cruise' deals including a few days on the *Club Med 2* (for details see the previous Sea – Cruise Ships section). You can get information from Club Med's offices in Brisbane, Sydney or Melbourne.

Connection Holidays
  Suite 21, 2nd floor, 110-116 Sussex St, Sydney 2000 (☎ (02) 262 2444; toll free (008) 22 1215; fax (02) 290 3159); this company organises four to 10-nights' stays at different locations including Noumea, Lifou, Île des Pins, Escapade Island Resort and others. It also combines packages with stays in Vanuatu or Fiji and has price-cutting self-drive deals and a meal voucher system.

Islands International Travel
  Suite 15, 7th floor, 428 George St, Sydney 2000 (☎ (02) 223 7966; fax (02) 221 4370) or Suite 1, 117 Bluff Rd, Black Rock, Melbourne, Victoria 3193 (☎ (03) 521 0133; fax (03) 597 0887); offers a selection of hotels in Noumea, Lifou or Vanuatu or gîtes on Île des Pins.

Orient Pacific Holidays
  132 Albert Rd, South Melbourne, Victoria 3205 (☎ (03) 690 1500; fax (03) 690 1942); this company has fly/drive packages on Grande Terre with the choice of several prime resort locations. Four nights' accommodation and airfare packages start at A$724 per person, based on twin-share prices and departures from Brisbane or Sydney. Extra nights will cost A$50 to $80 depending on the hotel, while car hire including unlimited kilometres and insurance costs A$124

per day (drivers must be over 25 years and you have to hire the car for a least three days).

LEAVING NEW CALEDONIA

No airport departure tax is levied when you leave. If you're buying an air ticket in New Caledonia, all travel agencies in Noumea have the same prices for airfares to neighbouring Pacific countries. The only destination worth shopping around for is France, as, at certain times, travel agencies offer discounted excursion fares.

You should remember to confirm your onward flight on arrival or at least 72 hours before your scheduled departure to avoid having your booking cancelled.

WARNING

This chapter is particularly vulnerable to change – prices for international travel are volatile, routes are introduced and cancelled, schedules change, rules are amended and special deals come and go. Airlines and governments seem to take a perverse pleasure in making price structures and regulations as complicated as possible and you should check directly with the airline or a travel agent to make sure you understand how a fare (and ticket you may buy) works. In addition, the travel industry is highly competitive and there are many lurks and perks. The upshot of this is that you should get opinions, quotes and advice from as many airlines and travel agents as possible before you part with your hard-earned cash.

The details given in this chapter should be regarded as pointers and are not a substitute for your own careful, up-to-the-minute research.

Getting Around

Using local buses, your thumb or feet, you can get around inexpensively on New Caledonia's various islands. If that's not quite your style, you can rent a vehicle or, alternatively, jump on a plane. To get between islands, the choice is limited to frequent planes or sporadic boats.

AIR
Air Calédonie

New Caledonia's only domestic airline is Air Calédonie. It uses a striking black flèche faîtière emblazoned on a golden sun as its symbol and is not to be confused with the international carrier, Air Calédonie International, whose logo is a red hibiscus.

Air Calédonie flies to the towns of Kone, Touho and Koumac on Grande Terre, to Wala on the Belep Islands, to each of the four Loyauté islands and to Île des Pins. Domestic flights operate out of Magenta Airport in Noumea; however they are not always direct. For example, on Grande Terre, a plane going from Magenta to Touho will often hop over to Kone before heading back to Noumea, while a flight from Magenta to the Belep Islands will stop also at Kone and Koumac on both the trip there and back.

For one-way fares between destinations, see the Air Routes map in this chapter. Return fares are simply double. As schedules for Grande Terre flights change often, the number of flights per week that service each destination has been detailed but not actual flight days or times. For Grande Terre details, see the Getting There & Away entry in each of the Kone, Koumac, Touho and Belep Island sections. For full schedules to the Loyauté islands and Île des Pins, see the Getting There & Away sections in those chapters. Remember that this sort of information changes periodically so check with Air Calédonie for the latest details.

The airline's fleet comprises two models – the 46-seater ATR 42-300 and the 19-seater turboprop Dornier 228. The latter is an excit-ing means of air travel, as no door separates the cockpit from the passengers so you have almost as vivid a view at take-off and landing as the pilot. Seat number allocations are non-existent so first on gets the pick of the places – the front is generally believed to be less noisy. Take note, as no flight leg is longer than 45 minutes, the toilets on board the planes are not used. Theoretically, you should be at the airport an hour before departure, but as long as you're there 20 minutes before the plane leaves they won't sell your ticket to someone else. There's a 10-kg limit for luggage going in the hold and excess may be charged at a rate of 100F per kg. A maximum of three kg of hand luggage is allowed.

The main office for Air Calédonie (☎ 28. 78.88; 25.21.77 for reservations only) is in Immeuble Manhattan, Rue de Verdun, Noumea. It is open weekdays from 7.30 am to noon and 1.30 to 5 pm, and Saturday from 7.30 to 11 am. If you need to change or rearrange your ticket outside Noumea, Air Calédonie agencies exist at all flight destinations around Grande Terre and on the islands. Bookings are generally easy to make, especially to the Loyauté islands and remoter parts of Grande Terre. However, Japanese day-trippers often pack the planes to Île des Pins so it's wise to reserve these flights in advance. Accommodation and airport transfers on the Loyauté islands and Île des Pins can be booked and paid for at the same time you reserve your flight.

For details on transport to/from Magenta Airport see the Getting Around section in the Noumea Chapter.

Charter Flights

Aviazur (☎ 25.37.09), BP 1116 Noumea, is a charter company which, at various times, has planes flying to local destinations from Magenta Airport. If there's a spare seat, they'll sell it to travellers. As a rough example of return fares to its most frequented

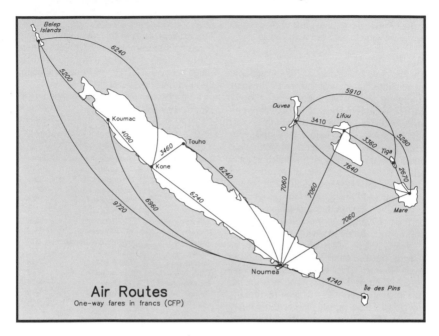

Air Routes
One-way fares in francs (CFP)

destinations, you would be looking at 14,000F to Île des Pins, 10,500F to Touho and 15,000F to Malabou Beach Hôtel near Poum.

Helicocean (☎ 25.39.49), based at Magenta Airport, has helicopters available for hire at 74,000F per hour. They hold four people and for that price you can, of course, choose your own routing.

LAND

Grande Terre's east and west coasts are connected by six roads which cross the central mountains over *cols* (passes). The most recent of these, a new crossing called the Kone-Tiwaka road opened early in 1994. It connects Kone on the west coast with Tiwaka, close to both Touho and Poindimie, on the east. It's commonly referred to as the 'H-road', as it provides the central link between the two north-coast roads, altogether creating a figure H. Crossing some 70 km of mountainous terrain, it used to be likened to a trans-Amazonian road because until it was sealed, this track was the domain of 4WDs only.

Grande Terre's northern half has one road (with various names such as the RT1, RT3, RT6 and RT7) that basically circumnavigates the entire top end above Bourail. In the island's central portion, the two coastlines are connected by a ring road comprising two mountain crossings (Bouloupari-Thio and La Foa-Canala) and the rather infamous Canala-Thio road. The latter is impassable for conventional vehicles after heavy rain. If you intend doing the full central circle, you should read the details of this road in the Canala section in the Southern Grande Terre chapter before setting off.

Unfortunately, unlike with the west coast, it is impossible to drive the entire length of the east coast as there are no roads linking the sections between Yate-Thio or Poro-Houailou. Therefore if you want to see the entire Grande Terre, you must make several trips between the east and west coasts.

Bus

The little old blue buses of New Caledonia are an island trademark and are used extensively throughout Grande Terre. Slowly they're being superseded by newer white buses with a red and a green stripe but it will still be a long time before they disappear from the roads. On the islands, the main blue buses you'll see are those transporting local school kids and, because of security and schedules, drivers won't usually pick you up. On Lifou and Ouvea, there are meagre bus systems but, as with the other islands, you'll basically have to rely of pre-arranged transport or your thumb to get around.

Nearly every town or large village on Grande Terre is connected by bus, all leaving from Noumea's bus station *(gare routière)* (☎ 27.82.32 or 27.25.81). This station has two distinct sections – as you're looking towards the blue-capped market, those buses on your left will be heading to destinations outside Noumea (into 'la Brousse' as locals would say), while the buses on the right shuttle around the capital. All buses carry a destination sign propped up against the front windscreen. Don't count on buses to stop automatically if you're standing at a bus stop or on the side of the road – you should always flag them down. Bourail is the island's central bus junction.

Roughly, for the normal buses, you can count on paying 100F to 150F per 20 km, the ticket price being relatively cheaper the further you go. The mail buses are cheaper again and are usually the first buses to leave Noumea each day, getting on the road around 4 or 5 am, bound for major destinations such as Koumac or Hienghene. After that, a variety of buses head up along the east and west coasts and one goes down to the southeast Yate/Goro area. In some cases, services double up – for example, if you're heading to La Foa you can get on any bus heading to either the north-east or north-west coasts. On Sundays, services to the two northern coasts are limited to about one bus per coast; to

other destinations services are practically non-existent. Only with a lot of spare time is it possible to complete the whole northern circle by bus, as services over the northern range between Hienghene, Pouebo, Ouegoa and Koumac are sparse.

Some places that can be reached from Noumea by bus are:

Destination	Time	Price from Noumea
Bouloupari	one hour	600F
Bourail	2½ hours	900F
Dumbea	30 minutes	220F
Hienghene	approx six hours	1450F
Kone	3¼ hours	1100F
Koumac	5½ hours	1450F
La Foa	1½ hours	700F
Paita	40 minutes	250F
Poindimie	approx five hours	1250F
Poum	six hours	1650F
Sarramea	two hours	750F
Thio	2½ hours	800F
Tontouta Airport	1⅕ hours	400F
Touho	5½ hours	1350F
Yate/Waho	1¾ hours	500F

Bus Schedules While the buses try to run to schedule, they often turn up early, late or sometimes not at all. Road and weather conditions play a large part in their reliability and, as both can sometimes be atrocious, you should expect the unexpected. For details on bus schedules to all destinations, see the relevant town or village. The small kiosk next to the main gare routière building in Noumea also has timetables.

Taxi

Taxis are confined to Noumea and the larger towns on Grande Terre. Sixty-five taxis roam the capital – one for every 1000 people.

Taxis run on a meter – you'll be looking at about 90F per km in the city; 150F per km if you go outside Noumea. On top, there's a 240F fee for jumping in and it's 100F extra if you book by phone. It's not wise to take a taxi between Noumea and Tontouta Airport as the fare is prohibitive. In the capital, they might be convenient in the evenings as buses stop running at about 6.30 pm.

Car

A great deal of Grande Terre can be seen in one or two days with your own wheels. At a leisurely pace, the whole tour can be done in a week or just over. Car rental companies abound, but unfortunately their rates are high and none will rent to anyone under 25 years. All companies are based in Noumea, but the larger ones also have desks at the airport, while Avis can also arrange for you to pick up a car from Malabou Beach Hôtel near Poum. Cars can also be arranged at Touho and Kone and on all the islands. You'll need to give rental outlets, especially those around Grande Terre and on the islands, a few days' warning so that they can organise a car.

The well-known companies on average charge about 3000F to 3300F per day for something like a small Fiat Uno and about 3500F for a larger Peugeot 205. On top, there's a charge of 30F to 36F per km, daily insurance and, of course, petrol. For the same cars, the smaller companies charge about 2500F to 2800F, or 3200F, and often offer good deals with unlimited km.

A valid driving licence from your own country is all that is needed, along with a sometimes hefty security deposit *(caution)* of 100,000F. Some of the rental companies include:

AB Location
    36 Ave du Maréchal Foch, central Noumea (☎ 28.12.12)
Avis Rent-a-Car
    Rondpoint du Pacifique, central Noumea (☎ 27.54.84)
    Tontouta Airport (☎ 35.11.74)
Budget
    Palm Beach Complex, Promenade Roger Laroque, Anse Vata (☎ 26.20.09)
Hertz
    113 Route de l'Anse Vata, Anse Vata (☎ 26.18.22)
    Tontouta Airport (☎ 35.12.77)
Mencar
    8 Rue Jean Jaurès, central Noumea (☎ 27.61.65)
Pacific Car
    9 Rue de Soissons, Faubourg Blanchot, Noumea; this lesser known company offers some of the best rates in town (☎ 27.60.60)
Pointe Rouge
    5 Rue Papin, Ducos; slightly out of town but this new company is well recommended (☎ 27.74.60)

Tour des Îles
    17 Rue Colnett, Motor Pool; specialises in rentals for the Loyauté islands and Île des Pins (☎ 26.41.42)
Visa
    Corner Rue de Sébastopol and Ave Auguste Brun, Latin Quarter (☎ 27.27.12)

Camper Vans

Camper vans for four people can be hired (two-day minimum rental) from Pacific Charters (☎ 26.10.55), 138 Route de l'Anse Vata in Noumea. The daily rate is 14,000F plus insurance and a 30F per km fee (the first 100 km are free). For a seven-day package including unlimited km and insurance, you'd be looking at 98,000F. Bed linen per person costs 1500F.

Motorbikes

The only motorbike rental outfit in New Caledonia is Noumea Car (☎ 27.56.36), 9 Rue Bichat, in the Latin Quarter. It has Honda 500cc bikes for 6000F per day plus 30F per km; there's a 60,000F deposit.

Bikes & Mopeds

Mopeds can be rented from just one place in Noumea and one on Lifou (see relevant chapters). Bicycles are more plentiful, with several outlets in the capital as well as a few on the Loyauté islands and Île des Pins. As well as conventional cycles, some places have VTT *(vélo tout-terrain)* or mountain bikes. For details, see the Getting Around section in each of the mentioned places. Bikes are also rented at Hienghene, Poindimie and Île Ouen – see those sections for information.

Road Formalities

Once outside Noumea, road signs are quite poor and sometimes non-existent, so a good map is essential. As in France, driving is on the right-hand side of the road and, except when you're on a major road, you must take care to give way to the right *(priorité à droite)*. The maximum speed limit on a main road is 110 km/h and in towns 60 km/h. Seat belts are compulsory though few people wear them. International Driving Permits are not required. There is only one *péage* (toll) road in the country, which is just as you enter Noumea coming from the north; it costs 150F for the 17 km.

New Caledonia has a high number of deaths from road accidents, and drink-driving is a problem. The maximum permissible blood alcohol concentration is 0.08% and random breath testing is carried out. Also, take care if you see a cardboard box on the road as, according to one visitor, Kanak kids like to test motorists by hiding a rock or dead animal in the box (though we never saw or came across such a trick). Be wary at creek crossings as they're prone to flash flooding in the wet season.

Each town or large village will have one petrol station or at least a pump, but in remote areas they can be few and far between so take care not to run too short. Petrol stations are generally open Monday to Saturday from 6 am to 6 or 7 pm, closing for a couple of hours at lunch like everybody else. On Sunday they are usually open for a few hours in the morning and sometimes in the late afternoon. Petrol is the same price all over the country except on Ouvea where it's quite a lot dearer. In general you'll pay 96F per litre for super or leadfree and 70F per litre for diesel. If the supply boat is delayed, the islands sometimes go onto petrol rationing and, occasionally, even run dry.

Hitching

Hitching is never entirely safe in any country in the world, and we don't recommend it. Travellers who decide to hitch should understand that they are taking a small but serious risk. However, many people do choose to hitch, and the advice that follows should help to make their journeys as fast and safe as possible.

Hitchhiking can be an effective way to travel around New Caledonia. Kanaks will usually pick you up if there is room amongst the eight or nine people already in the back of the pick-up truck, while the French enjoy the opportunity to air their opinions about the situation in New Caledonia. Only on the rare occasion will you be asked to pay for a lift.

That said, not all travellers have found hitching easy. Ian Diddams of England wrote saying that he had 'no luck whatsoever hitching in New Caledonia. I can only advocate it for those who are: (a) desperate (b) flush with time and inclination (c) mad (d) all of the above'.

On the Loyauté islands and Île des Pins, hitching, sometimes referred to as *faire le pouce* or 'doing the thumb', is practically the only way to get around other than hiring a car or bike or going on a tour.

SEA
Island Connections

While boats were once the mainstay of inter-island travel in New Caledonia, planes have now largely taken over these services, especially in the case of Île des Pins and the Loyauté islands. Any ships heading their way from Noumea are basically cargo vessels supplying the islands with food stocks and petrol. A few islanders still use the boats, but as schedules are irregular and prone to delays and cancellations, most Kanaks going to their home islands go by plane. Boats leaving for Île des Pins and the Loyauté islands depart from Quai des Caboteurs in Baie de la Moselle. For details on fares and schedules, see the Getting There & Away section in those two chapters.

As for the remote islands in the far north of Grande Terre, there are no organised, regular boat services. The Belep Islands are visited roughly twice a week by the *Tui II* departing from Poum while Île Pam, Île Baaba, Île Balabio and several other smaller islets are connected with the mainland only when someone from a local clan goes over.

No boats regularly visit any of New Caledonia's uninhabited dependencies.

Tourist Vessels

High-speed boats designed to get tourists out of Noumea and away to destinations closer to the reef leave from either the pier at Club Med in Anse Vata or from one of the gangways at the new Port Moselle. For details on boats to Amédée Islet and the Seahorse Pontoon, see the Water Excursion section in the Noumea chapter. Information on boats to Île Ouen is detailed in the Île Ouen section in the Southern Grande Terre chapter.

For information on ocean liners which offer cruises between Noumea, Île des Pins and Hienghene, see the Sea section in the Getting There & Away chapter.

Yacht & Speed Boat Charters

Four types of boats with varying degrees of size, comfort and price can be chartered from Noumea Yacht Charters (☎ 28.66.66; fax 28.74.82), BP 1068 Noumea, which has an office at Port Moselle. As an indication of price, you'll be looking at between 27,000F and 48,000F per day for a boat for five to 10 people. A skipper is an extra 10,000F per day and a security deposit of 100,000F is required.

This company also delivers boats to Île des Pins for A$650 or to the Loyauté islands for A$800, from where you can take over. The charter rates for daily rental in Australian dollars are A$490 for two days, A$390 for three to nine days and A$340 for 10 or more days. All-inclusive yachting package holidays are done in cooperation with Charter World (☎ (03) 521 0033) 579 Hampton St, Hampton, Melbourne, Victoria 3188, Australia.

Pacific Charter (☎ 26.10.55), 138 Route de l'Anse Vata, Noumea, has 200 to 400HP speed boats available for rent from 30,000F to 55,000F per day. It also has yachts such as a catamaran for 40,000F per day and a twin-mast ketch for six people for 33,000F per day.

You can also check charters by Vagabond Charter (☎ 26.14.93) and Alizés Voiles (☎ 27.50.43).

YACHTIE'S GUIDE

New Caledonia welcomes about a thousand yachties every year, mostly during the peak season between August and October. The lagoon's calm water offers excellent sailing while all the joys of the Pacific – reefs, atolls and deserted sandy cays – await. Sheltered anchorages can be found in the many protected bays and, for the most part, are deserted, with the exception of Amédée Islet and Île des Pins, which are popular sailing destinations for locals on weekends. The only place in the country with full facilities for yachties is Noumea; the approach to the capital is well marked.

Sailing There & Away

The most popular sailing route is from Australia's east coast, or New Zealand, to Noumea. From there, you can sail north to the Solomon Islands and across to Papua New Guinea; north-east to Vanuatu; due east to Fiji, Samoa, Tonga and Tahiti; or north across the Pacific Ocean to Hawaii.

When either arriving from the east or leaving in that direction, one popular route is to skirt the southern tip of Grande Terre with breaks on Île des Pins and Ouvea (though strictly speaking these stops are illegal if you haven't signed in or have already signed out – see Formalities below).

The trade winds predominantly blow in south-easterly to north-easterly directions. From November to April it's cyclone season, with often dramatic wind shifts and overcast days.

Many skippers are looking for crews, and do not always require people with sailing experience. If you're looking for a ride in any direction, you can try posting a message on the notice boards of yacht clubs or shops that supply yachting equipment.

Formalities Noumea is the only official port of call. Strictly speaking, you must arrive here first and go through immigration formalities before dropping anchor anywhere else. However, local authorities usually give the nod when, for example, you've sailed into Ouvea from Vanuatu and can't resist the temptation to anchor there before heading to Noumea. In the case of an emergency, you can call into any port although only Noumea has the facilities to get you out of whatever mess you're in.

Ahead of arrival in Noumea, use Noumea Radio (VHF Channel 16) to contact the *capitainerie* (harbour master's office) (☎ 27.71.97; fax 27.71.29), BP 2960 Noumea

(VHF Channel 67), who will guide you with entry procedures and warn customs and immigration authorities. You'll need to show a clearance certificate from the last visited port, and it's considerate to fly the international yellow quarantine flag. While import and export regulations are adapted somewhat to meet yachties' specific situations, visa requirements are the same for all international visitors (see the Visas & Embassies section in the Facts for the Visitor chapter for details). Firearms must be declared and will be confiscated. They are held in the army's safekeeping until you sign your departure declaration which, once again, theoretically means you must immediately leave New Caledonian waters. Yachties must also declare all pharmaceutical drugs including morphine.

Sailing Around

Generally there's a persistent good breeze from the south-east to east between five and 15 knots increasing to 25 knots, with winds in the lagoon picking up in the afternoon. Westerlies are often strong and can affect anchorages, while sudden gusts from the mountains can have surprising strength. A depression nearing from the Tasman Sea often gives two to three days of overcast weather with increasing rain from the north. A south-easterly swell prevails but is blocked on the south and east coasts. In general, the lagoon is good with some difficult passages. Navigation is easier along the west coast while the east coast has strong currents. Water temperature averages around 25°C, increasing to 29°C in summer and dropping to 20°C in winter. The tide is rather negligible, only around 1.2 metres.

Cyclones can occur from November to April with winds up to 200 km/h. Three hours before and after a cyclone has passed, winds average around 75 knots. Daily weather forecasts *(météo* in French) and, if necessary, regular cyclone warnings, are displayed at the capitainerie or broadcast over the radio.

Noumea is a two to three-days' voyage from the Loyauté islands. Coming from the east, you cross the strait to Grande Terre then follow the coast to meet the southern lagoon. The seas can be pretty rough along here as the tidal current bumps against the Pacific swell. At the very southern tip, the Havannah Passage can be difficult to navigate but it's dotted with lighthouses.

Another option from the Loyautés is to steer north-west to the Belep Islands and sail down along Grande Terre's calm western lagoon; from Moindou south take extra care. The Belep area is not well mapped and caution is demanded. At Grande Terre's northern tip, Boat-Pass is only two to five metres deep and, with a strong current, it's not recommended as a turning. You'd be better off going up and around Ile Baaba.

Dropping Anchor

Port Moselle This visitor's marina in Baie de la Moselle in Noumea has water and electrical facilities on the pontoons. At the corner of the marina is the capitainerie (for a contact address see the previous Formalities section). It also acts as a little tourist office with books and folders to browse through and there's a list of all the necessary addresses for repairs, gas refills, ice, fuel, engine problems etc. It has a poste restante mail service and showers, and displays daily updated weather bulletins and other nautical information, as well as crewing and other ads. It is open weekdays from 7.30 am to 12.30 pm and 2 to 5.30 pm, Saturday from 7.30 to 11.30 am and Sunday 8 to 10 am.

The first day's anchorage at Port Moselle is free. After that you'll pay 1200F per day for vessels up to nine metres and 1600F for those nine to 12 metres. The use of marina facilities for vessels anchored outside the marina costs 400F per day or 8400F per month. The shop at the far end of the jetty is open daily and has fuel (same price as in the petrol stations) and a washing machine (550F for a load).

The Cercle Nautique Calédonien This yacht club, known as the CNC (☎ 26.27.27; fax 26.28.38), BP 235 Noumea, is on Rue du Capitaine Desmier at Baie des Pêcheurs. It is the best place in Noumea to settle for a while. The CNC's visitor's wharf at the end of the marina has 15 berths for three week maximum stays. The first two days are free, after that the first week costs 200F per day and the second/third weeks are 400/600F per day. It has a bar and restaurant, charts for consultation, petrol, poste restante, a fax and telephone and a notice board in the corner outside the bar. The office and bar are normally open daily from 8 am to 12.30 pm and 4 to 8.30 pm (until 8 pm on weekends).

Suggested Anchorages All anchorages can be heaven one day and hell the next morning. Good sheltered east coast anchorages are (from south to north) Baie de Port Bouquet; at the end of the deep Nakety and Canala bays; Baie de Kouaoua (though muddy from mining); and the islets offshore from Ponerihouen to Hienghene. If the weather turns bad, there's a sheltered marina at Touho.

In Grande Terre's north, the bays and islands around Poum are beautiful, while in the south Baie de Prony is a popular spot with locals on weekends as is the western bay of Île Ouen. Ouvea's lagoon is one big draw card while the islets between Lifou and Mare are just as tempting, as are some of the bays on these two islands and on Île des Pins.

Information

The bars most frequented by yachties are those at the CNC, the Squash club, Relais de la Poste and Hôtel San Francisco.

Books Noumea Yacht Charters published a book entitled *Croisière en Nouvelle Calédonie: Guide des Mouillages* which gives an exhaustive list of the best anchorages around the islands. *Cruising New Caledonia & Vanuatu* (Universal, Melbourne, 1981), by Alan Lucas, gives details on many natural harbours and out-of-the-way anchorages.

Marine Maps Charts can be looked at in the CNC or the capitainerie or purchased in the Marine Corail shop. The Service Hydro-

graphique et Océanographique de la Marine (SHOM) produces excellent mariners' maps covering all New Caledonia's territorial waters. They're available from Marine Corail.

The well-known Admiralty Charts are also good for planning anchorages and routes. The following is a list of some of these local maps:

Nr 936 A & B – North & South New Caledonia
Nr 1384 – Anchorages in the Loyauté islands
Nrs 2906-09 – Several anchorages from Île des Pins to Bourail
Nr 339 – Canala
Nr 3033 – Vanuatu & New Caledonia with Walpole, Matthew and Hunter Islands
Nr 3445 – Ouvea & Beautemps-Beaupré
Nr 4602 – Tasman & Coral Seas
Nr 349 – Chesterfield Group

Useful Shops A few of the many shops in Noumea where yachties may find what they need are:

Marine Corail
    40 Rue de la République; well set out with charts and all general stocks (☎ 27.58.48)
Limousin Marine
    70 Route Port Despointes, Faubourg Blanchot (☎ 27.41.86)
La Boussolle
    33 Rue Jules Garnier (☎ 26.16.27)
Noumea Voiles
    3 Rue Edouard Glasser, Motor Pool; for sail repairs (☎ 26.22.55)

Yacht Races

Yacht races around Noumea are organised by individual enthusiasts, the CNC and various clubs and yacht charter companies. There are weekend races and, every Wednesday afternoon from September to March, an informal twilight race.

International races calling into Noumea include:

Sydney-Noumea-Gold Coast
    Every two years in May; organised by the Southport Yacht Club, Qld, Australia.
Sydney/Brisbane-Noumea
    Biannual (last one in August '93); organised by the Cruising Yacht Club, famous for the Sydney-Hobart challenge.

Auckland-Noumea
Every two years (next one May '94); organised by the Royal New Zealand Yacht Squadron.
Noumea-Port Vila
In the same year and month as the above race; organised by the CNC.
Solitary Around the World
This inaugural race starts in October '94 from Noumea; organised by the CNC.

ORGANISED TOURS

A host of tour operators in Noumea organise trips to get visitors out of the capital and into la brousse, for either one day or a few. Aerial adventures include helicopter rides over the reef, or air/land trips to the Rivière Bleue park, Baie de Prony and Île des Pins. The ultra-light plane school at Dumbea also plans to start reef flights in 1993. Popular day trips in either a conventional or 4WD minibus include the Yate/Waho region, the Monts Koghis, the west coast as far as Bourail or a southern east/west coast circuit taking in Bouloupari, Thio, Canala and Sarramea. In three days, tours skirt the whole of Grande Terre, from Noumea up along the east coast to Balade and back along the western flank. If you want to get out onto the water, boats sail to Île Ouen, Îlot Maître (otherwise known as Escapade Island Resort) and Amédée Islet, or you can cruise round a few bays on a yacht.

Outside Noumea, gîte and hotel owners on Île des Pins and the Loyauté islands run tours of their islands. Many of their counterparts on Grande Terre's northern coasts also run day tours of their local areas including reef excursions, visits to old mines or sites of natural beauty such as waterfalls. Weekends horse treks are organised at Kone and Bourail.

Noumea

Noumea is the nerve centre of New Caledonia. Most of the country's wealth is focused here and 40% of the population – some 65,000 people – have made it their home. It is also the top tourist destination, largely due to the fact that, as the capital, Noumea has long monopolised services and the attention of the outside world. So while the rest of New Caledonia is geographically diverse, culturally stimulating and often beautifully unspoilt, it is still true that many tourists will see only the capital during their holiday.

Sitting on a peninsula at a latitude of 22° in the south-western region of Grande Terre, Noumea is made up of hills and sloping valleys which have gradually been integrated into the growing metropolis. Bay after bay carves the coastline, giving it the charm of a city that opens out to the sea. It is said to have a thousand views and, after a few days wandering around here, you'll find that figure justifiable. Its name is believed to mean 'sunrise' in one Kanak language.

Noumea is home to the majority of the country's Europeans, as well as nearly the entire Wallisian, Indonesian, Tahitian, and Vietnamese populations. Europeans aside, many of these people originally came to New Caledonia to work in the mines and at the huge nickel smelter just north of the city centre, whose presence has made Noumea the South Pacific's most industrialised city. Those same jobs are largely taken these days by Kanaks who have come to the capital in search of employment. The result of all this is a dichotomous city, where low-paid workers live in slum conditions while well-off residents celebrate the city's Frenchness by awarding it sister city status to Nice, France.

For tourists, Noumea is an ideal starting point for exploring New Caledonia. It has all the facilities of a modern city minus the frenetic pace. Its restaurants offer some of the best gourmet cuisine in the South Pacific, while close to hand are long white beaches lined with coconut palms and lapped by aqua waters.

HISTORY

The English trader James Paddon was the first European to settle in the vicinity of present-day Noumea. In 1851 he set up a trading station on Île Nou, an island just west of the present city, where there was a deep, sheltered harbour providing excellent anchorage.

Three years later a French naval officer, Tardy de Montravel, also recognised the site's potential and, wanting to seal France's recent possession of New Caledonia, he chose Noumea as the site for the colony's administrative centre. Facilities in Balade on the far north-east coast were dismantled and Noumea became the capital. Montravel renamed it Port-de-France, but it was changed back to Noumea in 1866 as the French postal service continually mixed it up with Fort-de-France, the capital of one of France's colonies in the West Indies. While Melanesian clan groupings in this area were relatively sparse, the new capital occasionally found itself under attack, but such offensives were easily thwarted.

In the early 1860s, the French decided to use New Caledonia as a location for a convict prison, and Île Nou became the chosen site. James Paddon was paid 60,000F and given a large tract of land at Paita in exchange for the island. In 1864, the first convict ship, *Iphigénie*, arrived with 248 galley slaves from France's notorious Toulon prison.

From then on, convict labour slowly developed what was, until then, still a small military outpost. Hillocks were levelled and wetlands reclaimed. A couple of straight macadam streets were laid and named after military events of France's Second Empire (the time of Napoleon III). One of these, Rue de Sébastopol (named after Sevastopol in the Crimea where France had recently been in conflict), was to become Noumea's main street.

Within a decade, the peninsula of Ducos to the north had also been established as a

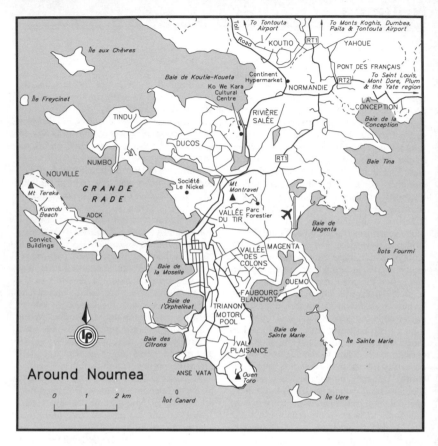

Around Noumea

convict penitentiary. It was reserved for so-called dangerous political prisoners such as the leaders of the Berber revolt in Algiers in 1871 and Communards like Henri de Roche-fort and Louise Michel. Later, Ducos became the home of the territory's leper colony.

The town's economy and life style were transformed from 1875, when gold and nickel started to be mined and Noumea's industrial revolution began. However, it was to be many years before the provincial atmosphere of a colonial town, complete with mules and horse-drawn buggies, was lost. Old folk still talk of a time when the colons

came into town on horseback and swaggered into Le Saint Hubert café for a drink just like cowboys from the American West. But not everyone had such romanticised images of the town. When Scottish author Robert Louis Stevenson visited in 1890, he described Noumea as an unimpressive place 'built from vermouth cases'. By this time, the town's population was 8000, including traders and clerks and, in the Latin Quarter, prostitutes and labourers.

In WW II the city was the US's military headquarters during Pacific operations. Soon after it became the permanent seat of the South Pacific Commission (SPC), an organisation involving all countries in the region, set up to promote research throughout the South Pacific. With the nickel boom of the late 1960s and early '70s, Noumea's population grew rapidly and the city began to resemble a sprawling metropolis. Apartment blocks were erected and the already vanishing colonial architecture was further neglected.

Then came the Events and an abrupt end to the tourist trade as violent confrontations erupted in Noumea, mainly between members of the right-wing RPCR and the pro-independence party, FLNKS. In one incident in May 1985, a young Kanak was killed when rioting broke out on Place des Cocotiers during the commemoration of the 40th anniversary of the end of WW II in Europe. In December of the same year, two bombs ripped through central Noumea in the space of 24 hours. In the rubble of the court complex, destroyed in the second explosion, police found a note calling for the release of the seven men temporarily jailed over the Hienghene massacre of 1984. A nightly 8 pm curfew was introduced and political graffiti sprayed the centre. One favoured site for slogan writing was the wall of the Catholic primary school on Rue de Sébastopol, which is these days innocently adorned with a mural of Baloo the bear and his *Jungle Book* mates.

Since the signing of the Matignon Accords, peace has returned to Noumea. Street marches are not uncommon, but nowadays they're staged to demand better standards for teachers and health workers and to protest over mass sackings rather than to fire up the independence issue. In recent years the city has been going through a building spree unparalleled since the nickel boom era.

ORIENTATION

Noumea stretches for some 15 km from the distant northern suburbs of Koutio and Yahoue to its most prestigious southern beach, Anse Vata. At the centre of this long peninsula is Mt Montravel.

The city centre is spread along Baie de la Moselle, a sheltered harbour where cruise liners, fishing boats and a fleet of private yachts dock. A grid of ruler-straight streets line the centre, the heart of which is Place des Cocotiers.

The main tourist area is about four km to the south at Anse Vata, connected to central Noumea by two main routes. The inland road, Route de l'Anse Vata, climbs a high ridge and passes through the suburbs of Trianon and Motor Pool, the latter named by US servicemen during WW II. The coastal route is more picturesque as it hugs the three large bays that carve the city's south-western reach.

The first of this trio is Baie de l'Orphelinat; attached to it, as if by afterthought, is the tiny Baie des Pêcheurs. Though it is not naturally beautiful, Baie de l'Orphelinat is the site of the city's newest yacht harbour, Les Marinas, which has brought the area new-found prestige.

Over the next rise is Baie des Citrons, a sheltered bay about 40 minutes' walk from Place des Cocotiers. Its one-km-long beach follows a gentle arch. On the ridge above it are the many villas and new units belonging to Noumea's well-to-do families. The bay ends abruptly at the rocky headland of Rocher à la Voile, the site of Noumea's most exclusive hotel, the Château Royal, and the country's only casino. From here, Anse Vata sweeps around in a two-km stretch of fine-sand beach backed by swaying palms and a busy four-lane boulevard known as Promenade Roger Laroque. From the beach you can see the small uninhabited Île aux Canards (Duck Island).

Anse Vata ends where Ouen Toro rises. This hill, designated a provincial park, affords spectacular views of the bay and nearby islands. Rounding the base of the hill, the boulevard changes name to Promenade Pierre Vernier and continues along the peninsula's relatively undeveloped eastern flank to the quiet, mixed neighbourhood of Faubourg Blanchot. The only suburb en route is Val Plaisance, nestled in part into the foot of Ouen Toro but also rising to give the

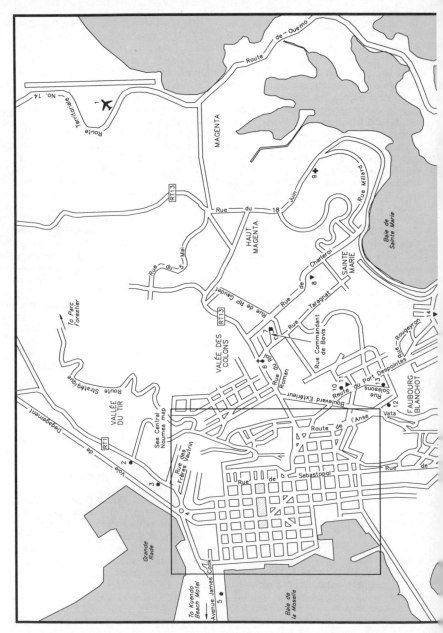

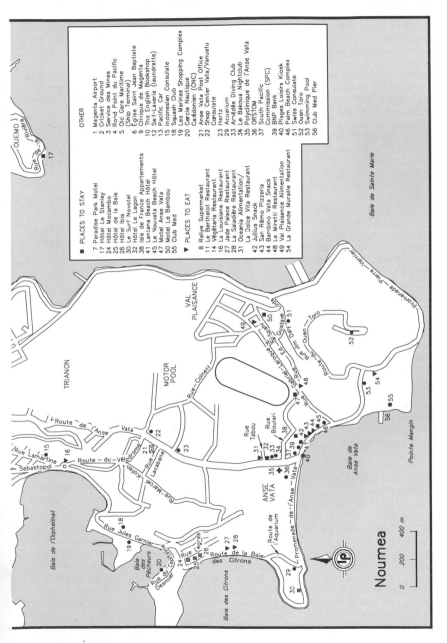

■ PLACES TO STAY

7   Paradise Park Motel
17 Hôtel Le Stanley
24 Hôtel Mocambo
25 Hôtel de la Baie
26 Hôtel Ibis
30 Le Surf Novotel
32 Hôtel Le Lagon
38 Isle de France Appartements
41 Lantana Beach Hôtel
45 Le Nouvata Beach Hôtel
47 Motel Anse Vata
50 Motel Le Bambou
55 Club Med

▼ PLACES TO EAT

8   Rallye Supermarket
11 Le Berthelot Restaurant
14 Végétaria Restaurant
16 La Louisiane Restaurant
27 Jade Palace Restaurant
28 La Saladière Restaurant
31 Oceania Alimentation/
    La Dolce Vita Restaurant
42 Julius Snack
43 San Rémo Pizzeria
44 Bambino Vata Snack
48 Le Miretti Restaurant
49 Val Plaisance Alimentation
54 La Grande Muraille Restaurant

OTHER

1   Magenta Airport
2   Cricket Ground
3   Service des Mines
4   Rond Point du Pacific
5   Old Gare Maritime
    (Ship Terminal)
6   Eglise Saint Jean Baptiste
9   Clinique de Magenta
10 The English Bookshop
13 Sel-Laverie (laundrette)
15 Indonesian Consulate
18 Pacific Car
19 Les Marinas Shopping Complex
20 Squash Club
20 Cercle Nautique
    Calédonien (CNC)
21 Anse Vata Post Office
22 Shop Center Vata/Vanuatu
    Consulate
23 Hertz
29 Aquarium
33 Arnédée Diving Club
34 Le Bakoua Nightclub
35 Polyclinique de l'Anse Vata
36 ORSTOM
37 South Pacific
    Commission (SPC)
39 BNP Bank
40 Plages Loisirs Kiosk
46 Palm Beach Complex
51 Swiss Consulate
52 Ouen Toro
53 Swimming Pool
56 Club Med Pier

Noumea

0   200   400 m

wealthier home owners wide views of the windswept Baie de Sainte Marie and the island of the same name.

Noumea's central district is bordered to the south by Ave de la Victoire, commonly called RT13. Heading east along this busy road you'll pass through the city's small Quartier Latin (Latin Quarter) which, with vivid use of your imagination, can feel like a small slice of the famous Parisian district. Follow RT13 up and over a crest and Vallée des Colons lies before you, eventually melding into Magenta and the well-off waterside suburbs of Ouemo and Sainte Marie.

West of the centre, the road leads to the peninsula of Nouville, a former island that housed the colony's first convict prison. En route is the Grande Rade, Noumea's cargo ship harbour and shelter in times of bad cyclones.

Immediately north of central Noumea, the land is mainly industrial. A large chunk of it is occupied by Société Le Nickel's smelter. Many of the Kanaks who work in SLN's factory live across the road in the overcrowded Vallée du Tir. Farther north is Ducos, an unimpressive residential and industrial suburb.

From Ducos, the RT1 and another highway continue north (by land, the only possible direction out of town), past the suburbs of Rivière Salée and Normandie. From here, seven km from the city centre, all roads lead north-west or east into la Brousse.

INFORMATION
Tourist Office

The Office Municipal de l'Animation et du Tourisme (OMAT) (☎ 28.75.80; fax 28.75.85) is Noumea's main tourist office. Housed in a small green office on Rue du Gouverneur Sautot, it's open weekdays from 8 am to 5.30 pm and Saturday from 9 am to noon. The friendly staff generally speak some English and have photo folders, covering all of New Caledonia, that you can browse through. In general, however, this place is not a mine of information and, if what you're looking for isn't in a pamphlet or brochure, it probably won't be of great assistance.

The people at American Express (see the following Money section) are noted for going out of their way to help travellers seeking information on anywhere in New Caledonia.

Other sources for information on destinations outside Noumea include the Maison de Lifou (see the following Things to See section) and the North Province Tourist Office (☎ 27.78.05; fax 27.48.87) in the Immeuble Manhattan, 39 Rue de Verdun.

Money

Most banks have their major branch on Ave de la Victoire. The exception is Westpac, which is on the corner of Ave du Maréchal Foch and Rue de l'Alma.

The Banque Nationale de Paris (BNP) has several useful branches dotted around Noumea. There is one at Anse Vata at 111 Promenade Roger Laroque, and the branch on Rue Anatole France is the closest bank to the new gare maritime. The BNP branch at the Rallye supermarket on Rue de Charleroi in Sainte Marie is the only bank in Noumea to open on a Saturday. It has slightly different hours from normal, opening Tuesday to Saturday from 7.50 am to 4.15 pm. Take bus No 2 to get there.

As all banks charge 500F for cashing travellers' cheques, the best place for foreign exchange is the American Express office (☎ 28.40.40/28.47.37) on the ground floor of Center Voyages at 27bis Ave du Maréchal Foch. They do not charge commission on any travellers' cheques or on cash, and their rate is equivalent to the banks'.

Post & Telecommunications

The main post office is at 9 Rue Eugène Porcheron, open weekdays from 7.45 to 11.15 am and 12.15 to 3.30 pm, and Saturday from 7.30 to 11 am. Poste restante is collected from here and international telephone calls and faxes can be made from counter 17.

The branch closest to Anse Vata is on the

corner of Route de l'Anse Vata and Rue Lacabane. It's open standard hours.

Foreign Embassies
The addresses of the foreign embassies and consulates in Noumea are listed in the Facts for the Visitor chapter.

Travel Agencies
Rue de Sébastopol is dotted with travel agencies. For the offices of Air France, Air Calédonie International and Qantas, see the Getting There & Away section in this chapter. Some of Noumea's travel agencies include:

Agence Jean Brock
    14 Rue Georges Clémenceau; general agent for Air New Zealand, Air India, British Airways, Singapore Airlines and TWA (☎ 28.34.39)
Axxcess Travel
    15 Rue de Verdun; specialises in Pacific destinations and is the agent for Air Vanuatu (☎ 28.66.77)
Center Voyages
    27bis Ave du Maréchal Foch (☎ 28.40.40)
Orchid Travel
    27 Ave du Maréchal Foch; agent for Malaysian Airlines (☎ 27.30.30)
Sofragence
    Immeuble Manhattan, 39 Rue de Verdun; agent for Thai International and SAS (☎ 28.27.27)

Bookshops
Thanks to the tenacity of an English woman, Phillida Stephens, there is now an English-language bookshop in Noumea. Simply called The English Bookshop (☎ 27.23.25), it is at 11bis Route du Port Despointes in Faubourg Blanchot.

The shop has an excellent assortment of British classics and modern literature, travel books including a huge range of Lonely Planet guides, literature on New Caledonia and the South Pacific, teach-yourself-French books and French dictionaries. Ms Stephens sells and swaps used books and, for those settled in Noumea, she rents videos. Strictly speaking, the shop is open Monday to Saturday from 9.30 am to noon and 3 to 6.30 pm but if you ring the doorbell outside these hours you probably won't be ignored. It's

about 20 minutes' walk from Place des Cocotiers or you can take bus No 4, which stops nearby.

An excellent source for information on Kanak culture is the Agence de Développement de la Culture Kanak (ADCK; ☎ 28.32.90), BP 378 Nouville, Noumea. While most of their books and publications are in French, some have been translated into English and are for sale at the reception. Bus No 13 passes here.

The French bookshops in Noumea include:

Librairie Pentecost
    34 Rue de l'Alma; small range of contemporary English-language novels and loads in French, good selection of international magazines and newspapers, and maps (☎ 26.40.35)
Librairie Montaigne
    27 Rue de Sébastopol; entire IGN map series on New Caledonia, some regional travel guides (☎ 27.34.88)
Librairie Hachette
    8 Ave du Maréchal Foch; big on French school books and a few classic English novels (☎ 28.28.81)
Librairie 4 Z'Arts
    21 Rue Jean Jaurès; dusty selection of English novels from romance to tales of adventure (☎ 27.38.11)

Laundry
The YHA hostel has a recently installed washing machine, top-end hotels have laundry services, and the city has one expensive do-it-yourself laundrette. Other than that, you'll have to rely on laundries where they wash and dry your five kg for a set charge, usually between 800 to 850F. Pressing Tourville at 4 Rue Tourville in the Latin Quarter and Lav' Services, 47 Rue Jean Jaurès in the centre, are two such options. Gluttons for punishment can do their own at the Self-Laverie, 13 Route de l'Anse Vata, at Trianon for 880F.

Medical Services
Hôpital Gaston Bourret (☎ 27.21.21) on Ave Paul Doumer is the city's main hospital, dating back to colonial days. Clinics in and around Noumea include:

Institut Pasteur
Ave Paul Doumer, next to the main hospital (☎ 27.26.66)
Clinique Mangin
1 Rue R P Roman, Vallée des Colons (☎ 27.27.84)
Clinique de Magenta
Rue du 18 Juin, Magenta (☎ 27.21.21)
Polyclinique de l'Anse Vata
Route de l'Anse Vata (☎ 26.14.22)
Clinique de Baie des Citrons
Rue Fernand Legras (☎ 26.18.66)

Emergency

The Commissariat Central (main police station; ☎ 27.22.53) is on Ave de la Victoire, and the gendarmerie (police headquarters; ☎ 27.28.22) is at Rue Frédéric Surleau. For lost or stolen passports you must go to the Bureau des Étrangers (☎ 27.28.22) at 18 Ave Paul Doumer.

For telephone numbers to call in an emergency see Emergency Telephone Numbers under Useful Organisations in the Facts for the Visitor chapter.

PLACE DES COCOTIERS

The natural starting point for exploring Noumea is Place des Cocotiers, the army's vegetable garden in the 19th century. Although the square is named after coconut palms, these trees are noticeably absent (though other palm species grow nearby). The square is instead fanned by flame trees which set the area on fire in December. Two schools of thought exist to explain the square's apparent misnomer. One is that the coconut palms were all chopped down long ago by order of the town council as falling coconuts posed too great a danger to passersby. The other is that there never were any coconut palms, and the name was simply given as it was the trend in all exotic French colonies of that time to have a square called Place des Cocotiers.

In the middle of the square is the Monumental Fountain erected in 1892. It marks the starting point for determining all road distances throughout the territory. To the east is a recently renovated bandstand dating back to the late 1800s. On the western side is a statue of Admiral Orly, the colony's governor between 1878 and 1880, while to the north is the old town hall, built in 1875 and these days one of the city's finest examples of colonial architecture.

MUSÉE NÉO-CALÉDONIEN

The New Caledonia museum (☎ 27.23.42), 42 Ave du Maréchal Foch, is an excellent base to start exploring Kanak culture.

The first room on the ground floor is devoted to a magnificent exhibition of sculptured wooden totems. Positioned as they are in the subtly lit room, they give the impression of a gathering of old spirits – some angry, some laughing, some pensive. Also on this floor are two traditional *cases* from Lifou – a round hut known as a living hut and a rectangular one used for cooking. Inside the latter *case* are three finely engraved bamboo sticks – the only examples of this ancient art on public display in New Caledonia.

Still on the ground floor are cases containing ceremonial axes and a variety of spectacular weapons, including the bec d'oiseau (bird's beak club) and the phallic-looking casse-têtes (head breaker). Nearby is an enormous pirogue, crafted by the old folk at Goro for the Melanesia 2000 festival in 1977. In the outside courtyard stands a beautiful replica of a grande case from the Canala region.

Archaeological finds such as petroglyphs – the carved rocks found around New Caledonia and believed to be from prehistoric times – and some ancient Lapita pottery are displayed in the rear section of the first floor. The remainder of the floor is taken over by fearsome masks with grotesquely alluring expressions from nearby Papua New Guinea and Vanuatu.

Unfortunately, all explanations are in French, though there is an English brochure called the *Museum Journal* (100F) that has good general explanations of Kanak culture. Entry to the museum is free and it's open from 9 to 11.30 am and 12.15 to 4.30 pm (closed Tuesday).

Mask with the hooked nose known as a *tidi*

BIBLIOTHÈQUE BERNHEIM

Bibliothèque Bernheim (☎ 27.23.43), on the corner of Rue de la Somme and Ave du Maréchal Foch, is the main library in Noumea. The original building on this site was constructed as the New Caledonian pavilion for the Paris Universal Exposition in 1900. The idea to turn it into a library came from Louis Bernheim, a mining mogul who made his fortune in New Caledonia. In 1901 he donated the money to set up the library; other buildings were added later.

The main colonial-style building has a lovely wooden interior with large fans and shuttered French windows, while the outside courtyard is pleasant and quiet amidst the noisy traffic. For those wanting to browse, the library stocks ORSTOM's monumental atlas of New Caledonia, in part translated into English, and copies of *Pacific Islands Monthly* magazine.

Opening hours are Tuesday to Friday from 9 to 11 am and 1.30 to 6 pm, and Saturday from 9 am to 4 pm.

CHURCHES

One of Noumea's landmarks is Saint Joseph's cathedral, which stands on a hill at the end of Rue de Verdun. It overlooks the city and is easily spotted from the sea at Baie de la Moselle. Built in 1888 by convict labour, it has beautiful stained-glass windows, illuminated every Wednesday evening. The main entrance is generally locked but side doors are open.

North of the cathedral, on Blvd Vauban, is a humble Protestant church built in 1893.

WAR MEMORIAL

Just east of the Latin Quarter on Place Bir Hakeim stand the original French army barracks, built in 1869 and still in use today. In front of the barracks is a large memorial to those New Caledonians who died in combat during WW I. Unjustly, the full names of all the Europeans are inscribed over three sides, whereas the 372 Kanak men who died for France are listed (on the back) by region only, their names not even rating a mention.

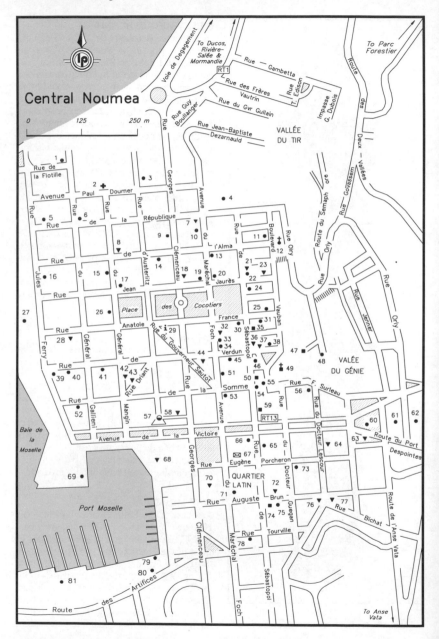

Central Noumea

0   125   250 m

KANAK CULTURAL CENTRES

The **Ko We Kara Cultural Centre** is a commanding piece of architecture. Its name means 'Welcome', and it does this handsomely if you enter the city along the toll road from Tontouta Airport. The centre is the venue for occasional exhibits of local or Polynesian art and is also used as a theatre. From central Noumea, it's about 5½ km north. No buses pass the front door, but bus No 9 will get you within walking distance. Get off just before the bus turns off the highway towards Rivière Salée.

In time, Ko We Kara will probably be surpassed by the **Jean-Marie Tjibaou Cultural Centre**. This yet-to-be-built complex is dedicated to the man many remember as New Caledonia's peacemaker. It is planned to be an exhibition, theatre, training and workshop complex. According to Tjibaou's widow, Marie-Claude, it is 'the first official gesture of recognition of Kanak culture by the French government and the French people'. The complex has been endorsed by President Mitterrand and, once completed, will go down in the history books as one of

■ PLACES TO STAY		OTHER		41	Axxcess Travel
				45	Qantas
35	Hôtel Lapérouse	1	Parc Provincial de la	46	Air France
47	Noumea Youth		Rivière Bleue Office	48	FOL
	Hostel	2	Hôpital Gaston Bourret	49	Saint Joseph
50	Hôtel Le Paris	3	Bureau des Étrangers		Cathedral
59	Hôtel San Francisco	4	High Commission of	51	Le Village Shopping
74	Hôtel Caledonia		the Republic		Complex
		5	SCEA (bus company)	52	Billard du Port
▼ PLACES TO EAT		6	Galérie Galéria	53	Bibliothèque
		9	Agence Jean Brock		Bernheim
7	Self Foch Restaurant	10	Librairie Hachette	54	City Cinema
8	Ballande	11	New Zealand Consulate	55	Air Calédonie
	Supermarket	12	Protestant Church		International
18	Café de la Paix	13	Westpac Bank	56	Gendarmerie
21	Tan Viet Restaurant	14	Librairie Pentecost	57	Gare Routière
23	La Palette	15	New Orléans Bar		(Bus Station)
	Restaurant	16	Belgian Consulate	60	Place Bir Hakeim
28	Johnston	17	Librairie 4 Z'Arts	61	War Memorial
	Supermarket	19	Old Town Hall	62	Army Barracks
32	Mogador Restaurant	20	Australian Consulate	65	Plaza Cinema
36	Café Le Flore	22	Lav' Services (Laundry)	66	Commissariat
37	Le Moustache Café	24	Librairie Montagne		Central (Main
42	Aux 3 Palmiers	25	Le Coin du Cuir and SEP		Police Station)
	Restaurant		(Artisan Shops)	67	Main Post Office
43	Snack	26	Hôtel de Ville	69	Quai des Caboteurs
44	Hameau II Snack		(City Hall)	71	Musée Néo-
50	Café de Paris	27	New Gare Maritime		Calédonien
58	Savah Supermarket		(Ship Terminal)	73	Relais de la Poste
63	La Cigogne	29	Tourist Office	75	Noumea Diving
	Alimentation	30	Le Saint Hubert Café	78	Pressing Tourville
64	Le Panda Restaurant	31	Maison de Lifou		(Laundry)
68	Market	33	Orchid Travel	79	Capitainerie
70	Food Vans	34	Center Voyages/American	80	South Province
72	Restaurante El		Express/Agence Orima		Headquarters
	Salvatore	38	Immeuble Manhattan/Air	81	Noumea Yacht
76	Maité Restaurant		Calédonie		Charters
77	El Cordobes	39	Le Santa Bar		
	Restaurant	40	Galérie Aquatine		

his 'major projects'. Building was due to commence at a site in Magenta in early 1993 but, at the time of updating, things had been put on hold.

PARC FORESTIER

Parc Forestier (☎ 27.89.51) on Route Stratégique, just below the summit of Mt Montravel, is a botanical garden and fauna park established in 1972. It is the only place in New Caledonia where you're guaranteed to see the national emblem, the cagou.

There are about 10 of these beautiful, flightless grey birds in the park, as attempts to raise the number with a breeding programme have been unsuccessful. Their reluctance to mate is understandable considering the treatment they put up with from some visitors. Sticks are poked at the birds or rattled along the sides of the cages while other intellectuals give their best dog impersonations – all in a fruitless attempt to get the cagou to hoist its wings, raise its crest and make its famous 'barking' cry. Needless to say, the management takes unkindly to visitors of this kind.

The cagou aside, the reserve boasts many species of birds endemic to either New Caledonia or other Pacific nations. Included in this list are the rare Ouvea crested parakeet and the little green and red-faced Pape de Noumea. Unfortunately, all are in cages that are quite small.

Down near the small lake is a cage of roussettes, while the entry foyer houses exhibits of butterflies, coral and what the management believes is the largest trocchus shell ever found. As well there's a run down on the country's ubiquitous *bulimes* or land snails.

Overall, the park is a peaceful respite from the bustle of Noumea below. It's about four km north-east of the city centre; organised tour buses arrive at the gate but no public buses pass this way. The closest that a blue bus (the No 12) will drop you off is at the low-cost, orange-and-white housing complex at Montravel. Wait until the driver has done his tour of the complex before getting off at the base of the road that winds up the

hill. Parc Forestier is 1¼ km up this road; there's not much traffic.

Alternatively, you can walk from the city centre to the start of Route Stratégique and try your luck at hitching. This road winds along the crest leading up to Mt Montravel and gives magnificent views of Noumea and its surrounding mountains, bays and islands. Once on Route Stratégique you shouldn't have too much trouble getting a ride for the remaining couple of km.

Between 1 May and 31 August the park is open Monday to Saturday from 1.30 to 4 pm; the rest of the year it stays open until 5 pm. On Sundays and public holidays it's open from 11 am to 5 pm. Admission is 300/100F for adults/children and it's accessible to wheelchairs.

VALLÉE DES COLONS & MAGENTA

Named after New Caledonia's first European settlers, Vallée des Colons is a lively suburb just east of central Noumea and these days is home to many Polynesian immigrants and Kanaks. The Vallée's most distinctive building is the **Église Saint Jean Baptiste**, a church built in 1901. Though the front door is often locked, the side doors are open until sunset and you can wander in to see the stained-glass windows and paintings depicting the Stations of the Cross. Masses are held on Saturday evening and Sunday morning. The church is on RT13, about 1¼ km from Place des Cocotiers. After a short tour of neighbouring streets, bus No 2 stops next to the church.

Magenta is the residential suburb farther east, about four km from Place des Cocotiers. It is home to the French University of the South Pacific and the domestic airport. Close to the airport is an Olympic-size stadium, built in 1966 for the second annual South Pacific Games. Magenta will also be the site of the future Jean-Marie Tjibaou Cultural Centre.

DONIAMBO NICKEL SMELTER

You cannot miss the huge 'furnace of Doniambo', the metallurgical factory owned by SLN, sitting just north of the city centre.

This eight-chimney eyesore has operated since 1910 (it was expanded in 1958) and employs some 1700 workers.

Nickel and cobalt extracted from mines around Grande Terre are processed here. The plant creates two end products called ferronickel and matte. Ferronickel is 75% iron and 25% nickel and is used to manufacture stainless steel. Matte is 75% nickel combined with cobalt and sold through SLN's plant in Le Havre, France, to make quality steel products.

SERVICE DES MINES

Probably only mineralogists will be interested in the exhibition at the Service des Mines (☎ 27.39.44) on RT1 in Vallée du Tir. Dusty display cabinets feature specimens of the many minerals found in New Caledonia – chrome, jasper, jade and of course nickel, to mention just a few. On the walls hang a couple of B&W photos taken early this century of the nearby Doniambo smelter and a picture of its Le Havre counterpart.

The Service des Mines is about 400 metres north-east of the Rond Point du Pacifique. It's a 15-minute walk from Place des Cocotiers or you can take bus No 10 or 12. Admission is free.

NOUMEA AQUARIUM

The aquarium (☎ 26.27.31) on Route de l'Aquarium at Anse Vata was created in 1956 by Dr and Mrs Catala who sold it to the city in 1977. These days it is the first stop on many tourists' agendas.

The display tanks contain rare and unusual species of marine life, including tropical fish, sea snakes, eels, shellfish, sharks and sponges, all in a natural coral environment. The tanks use mainly natural light and water pumped in directly from the sea at Baie des Citrons. All up it is probably one of the most natural aquariums in the Pacific, surpassed only by its outstanding counterpart in Townsville, Australia, which even goes to the extent of emulating wave motion.

One of the rooms is lit by ultraviolet light to show the striking beauty of living coral. Here is where you will find the species of nautilus that has remained unchanged since prehistoric times and is native to New Caledonia.

The aquarium is open from 1.30 to 4.30 pm (closed Monday). Admission costs 550/200/100F for adults/students/children. There are English, Japanese and French explanations; bus No 6 stops out the front.

SOUTH PACIFIC COMMISSION

The SPC or Commission du Pacifique Sud occupies the multi-winged building on the corner of Route de l'Anse Vata and Promenade Roger Laroque at Anse Vata. This place was built in 1942 as the command post for Admiral Halsey when the Americans entered the Pacific war, and has been the SPC's headquarters since the organisation's conception in 1947. Despite this, its days here are numbered as the Noumea fire brigade has warned that the termite-infested building is a fire hazard. It is due to relocate to a new beachfront building to be erected down the road past ORSTOM by late 1994.

At present, you can just wander into the SPC's spacious lobby where occasional temporary exhibitions, such as posters depicting International Women's Day in the Pacific, are held.

The SPC
The South Pacific Commission, or SPC as it's locally known, is the oldest organisation of its kind in the Pacific region. With its headquarters in Noumea, it was set up in 1947 by the region's six colonial powers of the time – Australia, France, the Netherlands, New Zealand, the UK and USA. Its mandate was to ensure the economic, social and military stability of the 22 island nations and territories within its fold.

These days its character has changed and it now plays the role of an information agency, providing technical assistance and advice and training in social, economic and cultural fields to all member countries. ■

MAISON DE LIFOU

The Maison de Lifou (☎ 27.47.81) at 48 Rue Anatole France promotes the culture, music and crafts of Lifou, the largest of the four Loyauté islands. Run by a very pleasant woman from Inagoj on Lifou's south-east coast, it's a welcoming place whether you're there to buy, browse, pick up information on the island or just chat about New Caledonia in general. It is open weekdays from 7.30 to 11.30 am and 1.30 to 5.30 pm, and Saturdays from 8 to 11 am.

ART GALLERIES

Noumea is sprinkled with small art galleries featuring and selling works by local artists. Though at present there is no national art gallery, the old gare maritime on Ave James Cook has been set aside as a future gallery and could one day fit the bill. Admission to all the galleries is free – to find out what's on, just look at the posters stuck up on shop windows, and particularly bookstores, around town.

One of the newest galleries is **Galerie Aquatine** (☎ 25.16.25) at 8 Rue de la Somme, specialising in watercolours and pastels. It's open Monday to Saturday from 7 am to 6 pm.

More unusual are the works found in **Le Caillou** on the ground floor of Le Village shopping complex on Ave du Maréchal Foch. This small but cavernous gallery features lapidary works as well as sand and bark paintings. The sand pieces are exquisite, generally depicting traditional aspects of Kanak culture such as a flèche faîtière or a grande case. The bark paintings use pieces of niaouli tree. A few shops away is **La Villa Gallery**, where resident artists make pottery and produce hand-painted silk.

Another gallery with more of the unusual is **Galérie Galéria** on the corner of Rue de la République and Rue du Général Gallieni, featuring art work as well as antiques and artefacts from all over the world. At the far end of the gallery is a small room where local painters often exhibit their works. The gallery is open weekdays from 9 am to noon and 1.30 to 6 pm, and Saturday mornings.

Temporary exhibits are also staged at **FOL** (Fédération des Œuvres Laïques) in the large building on the hill behind the cathedral. Also on the circuit is the gallery in the foyer of Le Surf Novotel hotel at Anse Vata and the old town hall just off Place des Cocotiers.

NOUVILLE

The quiet, hilly peninsula of Nouville rises to the west of central Noumea. It has some interesting reminders of convict days and is also the site of the territory's modern-day, beachfront prison, as well as the ADCK. Noumea's smallest and most picturesque beach is at Kuendu Bay. Originally, Nouville was an island called Île Nou, but it changed name when fill from the smelting factory was used to connect it to the mainland.

Several old **convict buildings** still stand, including the hospital, chapel, guards' quarters and prison workshops, located halfway along the peninsula's southern flank. Until the 1920s, the hospital was home to aged convicts who were serving life terms and were too old to care for themselves. It eventually became a psychiatric asylum, and continues to be one today. If you want to wander around the centre, just ask at reception.

About 1½ km past the asylum is the secluded **Kuendu Beach**, accessed either along the sealed road down the middle of the peninsula or from the dirt road which follows the coastline from the asylum. There's a top-end hotel here with restaurants and a bar overlooking the bay. The neatly arched beach resembles the Côte d'Azur in that topless sunbathing is almost *de rigueur* and, on busy days, sand is virtually allocated by the metre. It's a great place for swimming and the area around the headland is good for snorkelling. Over the hill from Kuendu is a small rocky beach, popular with gay men.

Kuendu Bay is sheltered by **Mt Tereka**, a 127-metre-high hill affording an exquisite view of the turquoise bay and a revolting vista of the port and SLN's factory. At the top are sunken stone walls, all that remain of a fort built in 1878, and four cannons mounted in the late 1890s to defend the colony. Mt

Tereka is reached by winding up the 1½-km-long dirt road that starts on the right just before the hotel.

To get to Nouville, bus No 13 goes to the old hospital every 45 minutes, but only four buses per day continue to Kuendu Beach. These leave the Noumea bus station at 7.45 and 10.45 am, 1.45 and 5.30 pm. Hitching from anywhere along Ave James Cook shouldn't pose too many problems, particularly on weekends, when many Noumeans are heading to their favourite beach.

WATER EXCURSIONS
Amédée Islet

This small coral islet, about 20 km south of Noumea, is noted for its clear water, its popularity as a day-trip destination and the 56-metre-high lighthouse that rises from its centre.

Visible as a speck on the horizon from Anse Vata, the lighthouse is an impressive testament to the ingenuity of 19th century engineering. The gleaming white tower was built in Paris in 1862 and then taken apart and shipped to the colony, where it was reassembled and erected on the little island in 1865. In good weather, the beam has a range of 60 km and guards the Passe de Boulari, a busy shipping passage for boats to and from Australia. You can normally climb the lighthouse's 231 steps; however, in early 1993 the public was indefinitely barred from entering while renovations were carried out – travel agents will know if it has reopened. Sitting remorsefully on the horizon to the west is the wreck of the *Ever Prosperity*, which ran aground in 1970.

Amédée is extremely popular with tourist and local day-trippers, the latter arriving on weekends in a drove of speed boats. Swimming, snorkelling and sunbathing are the lazy pastimes while the more energetic can walk around the islet in 20 minutes. Snorkelling is best near the reef to the west but be aware that you may have to face a strong tidal current when paddling back. There are occasional reef sharks, sea snakes, lots of fish and steep drop-offs.

Two companies run day trips to Amédée, both leaving from the Club Med wharf at Anse Vata. The largest operator is Mary D (☎ 26.31.31) with an office in the Palm Beach complex at Anse Vata. Tickets can be bought here or from many tour operators around town. Its plush vessel, *Princess*, reaches the island in 40 minutes, leaving at 9 am and returning by 4 pm. Tickets cost 7000/4500F for adults/children and should be purchased a day in advance. A smorgasbord lunch plus wine is included, along with a Polynesian floorshow. Snorkelling equipment can be rented for 1000F (plus 1000F deposit).

A much cheaper way to get to the islet is with the Amédée Diving Club (see the following Activities section), which runs a small dive boat daily except Tuesday. It's a rougher ride and takes 45 minutes, leaving at 7.30 am and returning by 4.45 pm. They charge 3000F for the return trip. You can have an excellent three-course lunch on Amédée with the divers for an extra 1500F but you must let the chef know on the voyage over. Alternatively, just pack a picnic plus drinking water.

Seahorse Pontoon

Anchored to the sea bed 25 km west of Noumea, the Seahorse Pontoon is Noumea's newest tourist attraction. Set up by an Australian man in January 1993, it's designed to give you a taste of the reef and all it has to offer without you even getting sand between your toes.

The pontoon sits in a crescent of the Récif de l'Annibal, part of the outer barrier reef. On average it's seven metres to the white sand floor, where enormous bommies (coral outcrops) are interspersed with forests of staghorn coral. A few metres from the pontoon is the wreck of the *Titania*, a British schooner which ran into the reef during a storm in 1903 while searching for the Dumbea Passage, some five km south. Rusted relics of the ship still pierce the water's surface.

Once at the pontoon, landlubbers can watch a slide show or view the reef from an underwater tube. Alternatively, glass-bottom boats await or you can dive straight in for some excellent snorkelling. Though there is plenty to see close to the pontoon, snorkelling is best on the inside of the barrier reef where there are deep passages, hovering reef sharks and giant trevally. Don't cross the reef and keep in mind that there may be a strong current when you're swimming back. There are showers, toilets and a snack bar on board.

The pontoon is reached in 45 minutes by the *Manta*, a 70-seat catamaran that leaves from wharf K6 at Port Moselle. Half-day excursions are run twice daily (except Tuesday) leaving at 7.30 am and 12.45 pm, and cost 4950/3200F for adults/children. On weekends there are also full day trips for 7800/5200F; they include a barbecue lunch and depart at 9.45 am. Tickets can be bought from Lagon Loisirs (☎ 26.24.40), 101 Route de l'Anse Vata, or from many travel agencies, including Center Voyages.

Other Islands & Islets

The Plages Loisirs kiosk at Anse Vata has a watertaxi for dropping off potential Robinson Crusoes at any one of the offshore islets in the morning and picking them up again in the afternoon. A return trip to Îlot Canard, just off Anse Vata beach costs 500F; to Îlot Maître farther south it's 2000F; to Îlot Larégnèze way out to the west the cost is 4000F.

Île Ouen, a lovely island at the southern tip of Grande Terre, is also reached from Noumea by boat. For details on the island and how to get there, see the Île Ouen section in the following chapter.

ACTIVITIES
Walks & Views

Whether at water level or on a mountain ridge, it's almost impossible to walk around Noumea without having a great view of something.

A good vantage point is **Ouen Toro** (128 metres) at Anse Vata. It's reached by a road that winds 1½ km to the summit where two cannons stand guard. These are leftovers from an Australian artillery unit, stationed on

Ouen Toro for seven months during WW II to install the six-inch cannons and train local servicemen. From the hill you can see all of Anse Vata, the nearby islands, a small red-and-white lighthouse and, farther to the south, its larger counterpart on Amédée Islet. Another easy climb is **Mt Tereka** – see the previous Nouville section for details.

The palm-lined **Promenade Pierre Vernier** is a waterside walkway popular with joggers and cyclists. It skirts the base of Ouen Toro then continues for three km to Faubourg Blanchot. It's good on fine days, but during bad weather gale-force winds batter this strip.

The most comprehensive picture you can get of Noumea is from **Mt Montravel** (167 metres). Though you can't climb to the top, the view from the road which runs along the crest, known as Route Stratégique, is good enough. You can see the twin peaks of the Monts Koghis to the north-east, while the bald Mont Dore broods directly east. This viewpoint is perhaps most interesting because it lays Noumea out like an open hand, with the opulence of the southern beach suburbs clashing sharply with the western shanty homes living under the dust of SLN's smelter.

Beaches

Anse Vata and **Baie des Citrons** are the two most popular tourist beaches. Baie des Citrons has a 'family' tag, due more than anything to its sheltered position and calm water. Anse Vata is the more chic of the pair, and the water here even breaks into white-capped waves in stormy weather.

Anse Vata's water quality has been a controversial issue in recent years. The beach was closed for several months from October 1992 as waste products being pumped into the western end of the bay were not being treated strongly enough and bathers were coming out of the water with itchy rashes. Apparently the problem has been rectified but you'll still find few locals swimming here. Instead they go to their weekend haunt, **Kuendu Beach** (see the previous Nouville section for details).

Snorkelling

Marine life and water visibility are obviously at their best as far away from humans and their rubbish as possible. For really good snorkelling you'll need to get to the outer reef or one of the offshore coral islets (see the previous Water Excursions section for local possibilities).

In Noumea itself, your best bet would be off Pointe Mangin just round from Club Med or, better still, near Kuendu Beach at Nouville. Kuendu's sheltered bay is itself a waste of time but if you snorkel out from the beach (or follow the foot track) and then swing to the left around the peninsula there are soft corals, the odd sea snake and plenty of colourful fish, including clown, trigger and parrot fish.

Snorkelling equipment can be hired from the Plages Loisirs kiosk at Anse Vata for 700F per day. If you're shopping for gear, ABC Marine at 28 Rue du Verdun in central Noumea has a good selection of brands and prices.

Scuba Diving

For general information on diving and dive sites, see the Activities section in the Facts for the Visitor chapter.

Noumea has some excellent offshore dive spots. There are two internationally recognised diving clubs based in the city which exploit these locations as well as run courses.

Amédée Diving Club (☎ 26.40.29; fax 28.57.55), BP 2675 Noumea, has an office at 138 Route de l'Anse Vata at Anse Vata. Bernard and his helpful staff speak English and the atmosphere is relaxed. The club organises day excursions to Amédée Islet where there's a club house complete with compressor, a small library of marine life books and a restaurant. From here you go by boat to your dive site – there are 10 on the surrounding reefs.

The club charges 11,800F for one day, which includes two dives, transport and all equipment. If you're staying at the Noumea YHA Hostel, there's a 1300F discount. Discounts also apply if you tee up 10 or more dives. The club's chef prepares an excellent three-course lunch for an extra 1500F.

Underwater cameras plus flash are for hire at 3500F per day. Novices can do a 30-minute 'baptismal' dive with introductory theory for 5000F. A four-day PADI open-water course costs 42,000F. Children between eight and 12 can do the course for 32,000F.

The Amédée Diving Club's boat, *Spanish Dancer*, leaves from the Club Med wharf to go to Amédée Islet daily, except Tuesday, at 7.45 am; it's back around 5 pm. You should book dives at least a day in advance.

The other option is Noumea Diving (☎ 25.16.88) at 12 Rue Auguste Brun in the Latin Quarter. It runs half-day trips with one/two dives for 6750/10,200F, or a full day with two dives for 11,750F. Sites visited are mainly within the marine reserve to the east and south of Noumea. The price includes transport and equipment; the boat leaves from Port Moselle.

For advanced divers, it also organises trips farther afield to sites like the Baie de Prony, with its magnificent underwater *aiguille* (needle-shaped formation), the nearby Canal de Woodin and Grotte Merlet, way to the south near the Passe de Uatio. There is time for two dives on each of these trips for the all-inclusive price of 10,000F.

Other Water Sports

The Plages Loisirs kiosk on the beachfront at Anse Vata hires equipment by the hour, half-day or day. Catamarans cost 2000F per hour, sailboards are 1000F, two-person canoes are 1500F and single kayaks cost 1000F. The kiosk is open daily from 8.30 am to 5.30 pm.

Windsurfing is good at Anse Vata, particularly off Pointe Mangin near Club Med, and is also popular on Baie de Magenta.

Swimming Pool Noumea's municipal swimming pool is behind Club Med on Promenade Roger Laroque at Anse Vata. It is an Olympic-size pool open to the public on weekdays from 7.30 am to 5 pm, Saturday from 1 to 5 pm and Sunday from 9.30 am to noon and 1 to 4.15 pm. Admission is 150F. Bus Nos 3 and 6 stop out front.

Squash

For squash freaks there's a good club (☎ 26. 22.18) at 21 Rue Jules Garnier, opposite Les Marinas shopping centre at Baie de l'Orphelinat (officially its address is Baie des Pêcheurs). It is open daily from 8 am to 10 pm (Sunday from 4 to 10 pm). A court costs 450F for half an hour. The club has an equally good bar, run by an Australian guy, where yachties hang out.

Organised Tours

Several operators run English-speaking minibus tours of Noumea, usually lasting three hours, with pick-ups from your hotel. The tours may not run every day – check with the agent. For details on organised day trips to Île des Pins, see the Getting There & Away section in the Île des Pins chapter. Many Noumean operators arrange tours onto the reef or, with an English-speaking guide, into la Brousse. You may need four to six (sometimes more) people; tours are generally run once a week or on request. A few companies include:

Agence ORIMA
    1st floor, 27bis Ave Maréchal Foch; this agency, run by Mrs Manoi Othis, organises tours covering much of southern Grande Terre. There are three city tours – to the aquarium (3000F), the Parc Forestier (3000F) and a four-hour evening tour, including dinner, for 5500F. Day trips by boat to Amédée or Escapade Island Resort cost 6500F per person, as does a drive up Grande Terre's west coast to Bouloupari. Lunch is included in all-day excursions. It also offers tours to the Yate/Waho region or to places closer to Noumea, such as Mont Dore, Plum and Dumbea. A four-hour tour to Monts Koghis and Nouville with lunch at Kuendu Beach costs 6500F. For details call ☎ 28.28.42.
Amac Tours
    In the Palm Beach complex at Anse Vata; this company has a city tour taking in the aquarium for 2950F. Around la Brousse it organises adventurous trips incorporating, where possible, 4WDs, ultra-light planes, sailing boats, canoes and horse treks. A full-day minivan tour of the southern east and west coasts costs 8500F per person; to the Rivière Bleue park it's 7000F. With sufficient people, they'll do a three-day, 1200-km tour of Grande Terre. By boat they can get you to Île Ouen, Amédée, out deep-sea fishing or on sunset

yacht trips. A half or full day's yachting will cost 2500/5000F. Their contact number is ☎ 26.38.38.
Pacific Raids
    9 Cité Bellevue, Haut Magenta; this company offers a good-value city tour which goes to both the aquarium and Parc Forestier for 2500F in 4¼ hours. Helicopter flights can take you over the reefs around Noumea with aerial views of Amédée Islet and the *Ever Prosperity* wreck. It also has a combined air/land trip for 18,000F per person to either Baie de Prony or the Rivière Bleue park whereby you fly there, have a picnic and drive back in a 4WD. The three-day Grande Terre tour for 46,000F per person includes overnight stops in hotels in Bourail, Koumac and Hienghene; a minimum of three is needed. For information call ☎ 28.23.25.

FESTIVALS

Fourteen July – or Bastille Day as it's better known – is a time of celebration for the French and there's always a military parade through the streets of Noumea and entertainment the night before (for details see the Cultural Events section in the Facts for the Visitors chapter).

During the warm months there are numerous water events in Noumea, including windsurfing and catamaran races, jet-ski competitions and the annual La Régate des Touques (barrel raft race) in mid-May.

PLACES TO STAY

Accommodation in Noumea ranges from spartan to luxurious. However, the scale is not balanced, and top-end abodes are heavily favoured, while campers are not – there are no facilities for them in the city. Some bottom-end and many mid-range hotels have rooms with adjoining kitchenettes, which saves you dining out every night. A room tax of 140F, 280F or 380F per night, depending on the cost of the room, is added to all bills unless you're staying at a hotel with less than 10 rooms.

Places to Stay – bottom end

Camping The city council will not give permits for camping grounds within a 20-km radius of Noumea. The closest place you can safely 'free camp' is off the road to the Dumbea dam, about 20 km north of Noumea.

YHA Hostel The cheapest place to stay in Noumea, as long as you don't mind climbing a hill, is the *Auberge de Jeunesse* or YHA Hostel (☎ 27.58.79) on Route Château d'Eau, BP 676 Noumea. It has a fantastic location, perched way up behind Saint Joseph's cathedral, and with a wide view of Baie de la Moselle.

The hostel is run by Jacky Sorin and Andrea Schaefer, both energetic individuals who keep the hostel in top condition and are mines of information about New Caledonia. The main accommodation block is a large, four-storey building, added to the original A-frame hostel in the early '90s. In total there are 90 beds, many taken by itinerant French workers in search of a job or long-term accommodation. In mid-1993 a new office and a washing machine were added. There is a large kitchen with excellent cooking facilities – and the rule is if you use something, you clean it. The atmosphere is very relaxed – alcohol is allowed, there is no

daytime lockup or nightly curfew. Luggage can be stored in the office if you're going away for a few days and mail can be sent here. Breakfast is not provided.

The hostel charges 900/1000F per member/non-member in a four-bunk room, or 2400/2600F for a double room with two single beds. Membership cards are available for 1500F. Most of the rooms have large, lockable metal wardrobes. Office hours are Monday to Saturday from 9 to 10 am and 6 to 7.30 pm, and Sunday evening. Outside these times you can drop off luggage but you can't check into a room. The office is also open to welcome those on late, incoming flights.

Direct transport to and from Tontouta Airport can be arranged with SCEA bus company (for details see the Getting Around section in this chapter). From the town centre, the easiest access is up the 102 stairs at the eastern end of Rue Jean Jaurès.

Hotels The choice here is rather lean as rooms in the cheapest hotels are pretty much solidly booked by workers.

City Centre Bikers and rock aficionados need go no farther than *H tel San Francisco* (☎ 28.26.25) at 55 Rue de Sébastopol, the most inexpensive hotel in central Noumea. Owned by an American, Emery, and his French partner, Dédé, this place is the rendezvous point for the city's many Harley Davidson riders and anyone else just seeking a cool hang-out. Formerly called H tel Mon Logis, it has 13 very basic studio rooms with kitchenette (a small refrigerator plus two-burner hot plate), a double and single bed, and toilet and shower. There are no TVs, air-con or telephones in the rooms and even lino or carpet is scarce. The rate is 4000F per night with no additional room tax; however, overnighters are rare as this place is popular for long-term rentals. The downstairs bar plays loud music until early morning.

Another cheapie (though opposite in character) is the *H tel Caledonia* (☎ 27.38.21; fax 27.81.45), on the corner of Rue de Sébastopol and Rue Auguste Brun in the

Saint Joseph's Cathedral

Latin Quarter. It is on a busy intersection and street-front rooms get direct traffic noise. When we visited, the management made it blatantly obvious that Kanaks are not welcome and neither are people speaking imperfect French. 'I'd rather talk in English than hear your bad French,' was one comment made. Room rates are the same whether you're overlooking the intersection or set back off the street. A double costs 4250F including tax. Six of the rooms have kitchenettes and cost 4750F. A continental breakfast is served for 350F. The downstairs corner bar resembles a Caldoche club for hard-drinking, middle-aged men.

The nicest and most central hotel in this bracket is *Hôtel Lapérouse* (☎ 27.22.51; fax 27.11.87) at 33 Rue de Sébastopol. It has 18 simple rooms, all adequate and clean but with nothing to rave about. They do not have kitchenettes, refrigerators or coffee/tea-making facilities. The hotel's pricing policy is similar to that of a theatre – the higher you go, the cheaper the room. A 4th-floor single/double with communal shower/toilet and no TV costs 3960/4460F. Rooms on all the lower floors have TVs. On the 3rd and 2nd floors, rooms cost 4760/5060F with private shower or 4960/5360F with shower and toilet. Second-floor rooms with private facilities and air-con cost 5460/5810F. There's a 140F room tax and petit déjeuner costs 600F. At street level there is a café, Pub Lapérouse, but it closes early.

Baie des Citrons The most inexpensive accommodation away from the centre is *Hôtel de la Baie* (☎ 26.21.33) at 5 Route de la Baie des Citrons next to Hôtel Ibis. This is a scruffy place, catering mainly for weekly (26,000F) or monthly (90,000F) rentals. If there's a vacancy, the proprietor, François, will give it to an overnighter and rates are cheap enough at 3000/4000F for a double room without/with kitchenette. The reception is at the counter of the downstairs Pizza Pino restaurant.

Anse Vata Area The *Motel Le Bambou* (☎ 26.12.90; fax 26.30.58) on 44 Rue Spahr

in Val Plaisance is the best option for budget accommodation after the YHA hostel. Set in a residential area, the motel is quiet, clean and run by a friendly Belgian family. There are 16 compact but homey studios. Each has a small balcony, fan and excellent cooking facilities but, unfortunately, no mosquito screens. Laundry can be done for 500F for five kg. Singles/doubles/triples cost 4500/4850/5500F with a room tax of 140F. The motel is one km from Anse Vata beach. Bus Nos 3 and 6 stop a block from the motel at the Val Plaisance Alimentation on Rue Gabriel Laroque.

The only other budget option is *Motel Anse Vata* (☎ 26.26.12; fax 28.44.53) on 19 Rue Gabriel Laroque. When we looked at it, the rooms were pretty grotty, with broken window locks and ripped mosquito screens. Singles/doubles are 5000/5500F and triples/quads cost 6000/6500F. All have air-con, TV and a kitchenette. If you're staying more than two weeks, a 10% discount applies. Bus Nos 3 and 6 stop out front.

Note that the SCEA buses connecting with Tontouta Airport will not pick up or drop off at these two motels, though the private minivans will.

Places to Stay – middle

City Centre The large, uninspiring *Hôtel Le Paris* (☎ 28.17.00; fax 27.60.80) on 47 Rue de Sébastopol has 48 rooms with all the creature comforts but little atmosphere. Singles/doubles/triples are 5500/6100/7100F with a room tax of 280F. Directly below the hotel, Café de Paris remains open until midnight and the noise from the many young soldiers who drink here can carry up to the rooms.

Vallée des Colons The *Paradise Park Motel* (☎ 27.25.41; fax 27.61.31) at the end of Rue Commandant de Bovis is a low-level complex covering a large, leafy block in a busy suburb. The 62 rooms are built in long rows around two swimming pools and well-tended gardens. The rooms are colourful and airy and have private shower/toilet and kitchens. This place is a favourite with

Top Left: Traditional hut at the Noumea museum (LF)
Top Right: Saint Louis mission church (LF)
Bottom: Waiting for the passing trade (GC)

Top: Yachts (DNC)
Top Right: Beach composition (GC)

workers and is often full. If there's a vacancy, the nightly single/double rate is 8000/8650F. There's a poolside bar open until 11 pm. Bus No 2 stops nearby – get off at the second stop on Rue Taragnat.

Baie des Citrons A friendly hotel popular with Australians and Japanese on package deals is *Hôtel Ibis* (☎ 26.20.55; fax 26.20.44) on 9 Route de la Baie des Citrons. Across from the beach, the front rooms are perfect for watching the sun set and you can hear the water gently lapping the shore at night. There are 60 rooms, all with modern furnishings, though the hotel itself looks a little tired. Facilities include a café and French restaurant where off-duty soldiers come to drink on Sunday afternoons, a Japanese restaurant and a small swimming pool. Bikes can be hired from the hotel. Standard singles/doubles are 8400/9400F; a triple is 10,900F. Rooms at the front with a view cost an extra 1100F. There's a 280F tax, coffee and tea are provided, and breakfast costs 700F.

Before rounding the last bend to Baie des Citrons is *Hôtel Mocambo* (☎ 26.27.01; fax 26.38.77), 49 Route Jules Garnier. Melanesian-style decor and timber carvings have produced an unfortunately dark and dreary-looking hotel. The 38 rooms, all with TV, refrigerator and coffee facilities, are good value at the flat rate of 5000F for a single or double. The room tax is 280F. Breakfast is a pricey 800F.

Anse Vata The *Lantana Beach Hôtel* (☎ 26.22.12; fax 26.26.12), 133 Promenade Roger Laroque, is in the heart of Anse Vata, across the street from the beach. The hotel has all the necessary amenities but it is slightly drab. There are 37 rooms, some with a balcony and view and some with coffee-making facilities. You should request both as neither costs extra. The price for a single/double/triple is 7000/8000/9000F; the room tax is 280F. Continental breakfast is available for 700F and an American breakfast for 1200F.

Close by is *Le Nouvata Beach Hôtel*

(☎ 26.22.00) at 123 Promenade Roger Laroque. In the past, this hotel was slightly more expensive than the Lantana but with the same run-down air. However, the hotel has recently been renovated and offers 75 rooms, all with air-con, and the usual facilities, including swimming pool. Rooms start at 7500F.

Places to Stay – top end
Anse Vata The *Hôtel Le Lagon* (☎ 26.12.55; fax 26.12.44) at 143 Route de l'Anse Vata is a favoured hotel for tour groups and many of the facilities cater to the Japanese. The five-storey hotel is serenely decorated, with orchids filling the lobby and rooms adorned with Gauguin-style paintings done by the hotel's owner. The hotel has 59 rooms – singles/doubles cost 9200/10,200F and all have coffee/tea-making facilities. It is possible to rent a studio room containing one double bed, a pull-out double sofa bed plus a kitchen for 13,200F. There are two-bedroom apartments plus kitchen and terrace, big enough for six people, which cost 17,200F. Room tax is 280F and breakfast costs 800F. The hotel has a bar but no swimming pool. It's about a two-minute walk to the beach; bus No 3 stops out the front.

The *Isle de France Appartements* (☎ 26.24.22; fax 26.17.20) on Rue Boulari, offers fully equipped units with a choice of a studio, one-bedroom or two-bedroom apartments. The complex is set back one block from the beach and includes a main building and a round tower, the highest structure in Anse Vata. Except for those on the first couple of floors, all rooms have a view. There's a swimming pool, private club, wine bar and boutiques. Room prices differ depending on whether you stay in the building or tower. In the building, the daily rate for a studio for two people is 12,800F. One-bedroom apartments for four people cost 16,000F; and two-bedroom apartments for six people are 19,300F. Their equivalent in the tower cost 14,900/18,100/22,900F. A room tax of 380F is added to the rates.

At the eastern end of Anse Vata beach,

near Pointe Mangin, is the 280-room, five-storey *Club Méditerranée* (☎ 26.12.00; fax 26.20.71) on Promenade Roger Laroque. Also known as Château Royal or, more commonly Club Med, it has all the facilities for a tropical holiday, including sailboards, squash and tennis courts, entertainment, restaurants, three bars, a bank, shop, medical clinic and special Club Med lounge chairs. Prices differ dramatically between walk-in rates and pre-arranged package deals. If you just come in off the street, you'll be looking at 6,500F for one night including breakfast or 12,000F for *pension complet*, which is accommodation plus three meals. There's a 380F room tax on top. Compare that with the cheapest seven-night package deal out of Brisbane, Sydney or Melbourne, which costs A$1300 and includes air fare, all meals and accommodation.

At the opposite end of Anse Vata is Noumea's most prestigious hotel, *Le Surf Novotel* (☎ 28.66.88; fax 28.52.23), 55 Promenade Roger Laroque. Perched high upon the Rocher à la Voile overlooking the sea, this hotel houses the Casino Royal, and many visiting officials, journalists and performers stay here. However, it is not five-star material; according to one traveller it's simply 'mutton dressed up as lamb'. Singles without/with a view are 13,750/16,250F, while double rooms start at 15,850F and increase in luxury and panoramas to 18,350F. A *grande suite* will cost 35,000F; a lesser suite is 27,000F. There is a room tax of 380F. Continental breakfast costs 1200F or for 250F extra you can have an entire American buffet breakfast. There is a French restaurant here as well as a piano bar, lounge, pool, casino and gift shop. The hotel also has art exhibits on display in the main hotel lobby.

Noumea's first five-star casino/resort, a US$90 million *Méridien* hotel, is being built on Pointe Mangin next to Club Med. It will have 253 rooms and is expected to open towards the end of 1994.

Other Areas Anse Vata does not have sole rights to luxury hotels so, for those not wanting to be on the tourist doorstep, there are several options around Noumea's outskirts.

Le Stanley (☎ 26.32.77; fax 25.26.56) is on Rue de la Rivière at Ouemo east of the city centre. It is a new hotel, sitting at the end of a small peninsula and with a view over Baie de Sainte Marie. There's a pool, bar, restaurant and pier. The rooms have modern furnishings and all have a terrace. Singles/doubles cost 12,000F; triples are 14,000F. The room tax costs 380F and an American buffet breakfast is 1200F. Bus No 7 passes by the front door.

About 4½ km offshore from Anse Vata is *Escapade Island Resort* (☎/fax 28.53.20), a luxury resort built on small Îlot Maître. The islet is beautiful, less than one km long, bordered by sandy beaches and surrounded by a coral reef. From Anse Vata you can see its outline on the horizon. With such a secluded position, the resort is of course pricey. It's owned and operated by Japanese and has facilities similar to Club Med. Package deals are offered from abroad (most of the Australian travel agents listed under Package Tours in the Getting There & Away chapter will have details). Once you're in New Caledonia, the only way you can stay at Escapade is on an accommodation-plus-meals arrangement. The cheapest deal is one night's accommodation and lunch, dinner, breakfast and lunch the next day for 15,300/23,000F for one/two people. Transportation is provided to and from the island, leaving from Port Moselle.

Finally there's *Le Kuendu Beach Motel* (☎ 27.89.89; fax 27.60.33), BP 404 Noumea, on Nouville, 6½ km west of central Noumea. Built in the late '80s, this is the only place in Noumea where you can stay in individual, Melanesian-style thatched bungalows. The huts are dotted around a jade-coloured bay. Facilities include a swimming pool, two restaurants, and water sports equipment for hire. The motel has 20 bungalows, all with a kitchen, TV and air-con. They feature one double bedroom and two single beds perched in the 'attic'. Bungalow prices vary depending on position. If you can be content with a hut in the garden amongst fruit trees you'll pay less than those living by the beach. A garden bungalow for one or two people costs 12,000F; for three/four it is 15,000/18,000F. The equivalent by the beach costs 14,000/17,000/20,000F. The hotel provides free transport for its guests to and from central Noumea three times a day.

PLACES TO EAT

At least 120 restaurants compete for the appetites of tourists and locals alike, offering Vietnamese, Indian and Japanese cuisines among others. Seafood and traditional French cuisine are, of course, abundant but they generally tend to be at the top of the price scale. Unless otherwise stated, all the cafés and restaurants mentioned here are closed on Sundays and public holidays.

Places to Eat – bottom end

City Centre Just about every small snack/café in the 'little Chinatown' area near the bus station is inexpensive. Some are cleaner than others, some are always full while others are forever empty, some are run by Polynesians or Vietnamese, others by Indians or Chinese.

A consistently popular choice with workers from around this area is *Hameau II* (☎ 28.48.32), 32 Rue de Verdun. Run by a friendly Vietnamese family, the quality is pretty good for the price – steak & chips with bread and salad will cost 750F. It is open weekdays from 6 am to 7.30 pm. On Saturday it closes at about 2 pm.

The little *snack* on Rue Driant is the only café in this area that operates on Sunday night. It has standard fare and is open until 8 pm. Those in need of an ultra-early breakfast can prop themselves up against the counter of the *café* inside the market. It is open daily from 5 am and serves croissants, coffee and freshly squeezed orange juice.

For a spacious, arty atmosphere there's *La Palette* (☎ 28.28.78) at 53 Rue Jean Jaurès. Undergoing renovations while we were updating, it previously had a good reputation, serving petit déjeuner for 350F and a

tasty lunch-time couscous or plat du jour for 950F. It does not open for dinner.

Café Le Flore (☎ 28.12.47), 39 Rue de Sébastopol, is one of more atmospheric cafés along this main drag. It acts as a late afternoon tearoom with locals coming here to play chess and listen to Western music. They have an 800F plat du jour at lunch time only.

Self Foch (☎ 28.37.77), 8 Avenue du Maréchal Foch, is a cafeteria-style place with good, cheap meals. The plat du jour is 750F, pre-made salads are 450F and soup of the day costs 350F. It's open from 6 am to 5.30 pm but it gets very crowded from 11.30 am to 1 pm when the office workers pour in.

Anse Vata The large hotels own and operate the snack bars along Anse Vata beach. At both *Jullius* and *Bambino Vata* on Promenade Roger Laroque you can get hamburgers for 450F, gaufres for 350F, a croque- monsieur (toasted cheese and ham sandwich) for 300F or a large plate of chips for 300F. Delicious ice creams and sorbets are available nearby from *La Sorbetière* or there are Mexican snacks in the Palm Beach complex.

The only relatively inexpensive restaurant is the new Italian place, *La Dolce Vita* (☎ 26.24.41) at 3 Rue Tabou. The food is good and the clientele a mixed bag of tourists and locals. Pasta dishes start at 800F and small/large pizzas from 450/800F. However, those with a hearty appetite for pizza would be better off round at San Rémo Pizzeria (see the following Anse Vata section).

Places to Eat – middle

City Centre One of the best value-for-money meals in town can be had at *La Moustache* (☎ 28.42.21), 37 Rue de Verdun, a tiny café which draws plenty of boozy office workers. It serves a three-course menu du jour including bread, a quarter-litre carafe of wine and an espresso for 1200F. The food is sound and filling and the menu du jour is available for lunch or dinner, daily except Sunday.

The *Café de la Paix* (☎ 28.11.55), 33 Rue Georges Clémenceau, is also OK for value if you're here at lunch time. It's a large, trendy café/bar frequented at midday by local business people who have come for the 1000F plat du jour plus dessert. In the evening it's more expensive, as it has à la carte only.

Le Saint Hubert (☎ 27.21.42) at 44 Rue Anatole France is where the locals of Noumea pass the time reading the newspaper or chatting over coffee. The café opens at 7.30 am for petit déjeuner and remains open until midnight.

The other Noumean institution is *Café de Paris* (☎ 28.20.00), 45 Rue de Sébastopol, a favourite spot for off-duty soldiers. It serves snacks and has a range of menus du jour for lunch and dinner starting at 1100F. This is one of the few places open on Sundays in Noumea but incidents are numerous and there are drunks in profusion.

For Indian cuisine, the *Mogador* (☎ 28.59.00) at 23 Ave Maréchal Foch is open for lunch and dinner. A full meal here will cost between 1500F and 2000F.

The *Tan Viet* (☎ 26.30.76), 15 Rue de Sébastopol, is a calm Vietnamese restaurant serving spring rolls, seafood, meat dishes and fresh salads. Dinner costs roughly 1100F. Another Vietnamese option is *Aux 3 Palmiers* (☎ 28.43.99) at 21 Rue du Général Mangin. The times we've been there, despite its occasionally doubling as a karaoke bar, it has been very dull. However, it is one of the few restaurants open for lunch and dinner on a Sunday. Main courses start at 850F.

In the Latin Quarter, *Maité* (☎ 27.45.74), 12 Rue du Docteur Lescour, in an enclosed square, is a classy little restaurant serving a good menu du jour for 1200F. Nearby, *Restaurante El Salvatore* (☎ 27.11.36) at 15 Rue Auguste Brun, has a plat du jour for 900F and pizzas from 1100F.

Still in this quarter, *Le Panda* (☎ 26.34.94) at 7bis Rue du Docteur Lescour is a cosy, pastel-toned Vietnamese restaurant with fine food. At lunch they serve a 1200F menu du jour; for dinner it's à la carte with main courses from 1100F. This is the only place in the Latin Quarter open on Sunday evenings.

Just out of central Noumea at Vallée des Colons, the *Paradise Park Motel* (see Places to Stay – middle) puts on a poolside barbecue every day except Monday. For 1100F you get steak (on Friday there's also grilled fish), salad, bread, a small carafe of wine and coffee. It runs from 11.30 am to 1 pm and is a big hit with local business people.

Nouville The *Kuendu Beach Motel* (see Places to Stay – top end) has two restaurants. The thatched restaurant attached to the motel is pricey, serving such à la carte items as baked Mai-Mai fillets with green pawpaw, chutney and manioc chips for 1800F. But the motel's second restaurant, just around the bay and also on the beachfront, is much less flash and serves a lunch-time menu du jour for 1550F including wine and coffee or a plat du jour for 800F. The only day these are not available is Sunday, when a 2900F buffet splurge is offered (lunch time only) complete with a Tahitian floorshow.

Baie des Citrons The *Jade Palace* (☎ 26.42.15), halfway along the bay, serves Chinese soup for 450F and mains for 800F. A hundred metres farther south is *La Saladière* (☎ 26.35.95) at 27 Route de la Baie des Citrons. Despite its name, it has an assortment of meals, including fish fresh from the lagoon for 1400F. The house specialities are crêpes, gaufres and liqueur sorbets, all of which are quite pricey.

For authentic Japanese cuisine try *Teppanyaki* (☎ 26.20.55) in the Hôtel Ibis. It has traditional seafood and chicken dishes from 1000F, or a menu du jour for 2200F.

Anse Vata One of the most popular eateries in Anse Vata is *San Rémo Pizzeria* (☎ 26.18.02) at 119 Promenade Roger Laroque. It is open daily and is highly recommended. Small pizzas start at 900F and large ones (ample for an average appetite) from 1350F.

Past the municipal pool on Promenade Pierre Vernier is *La Grande Muraille* (☎ 26.13.28), a Cantonese restaurant with excellent sea views. Most main courses cost 900F; the Imperial duck is very good. It's closed on Sunday and Monday.

Places to Eat – top end

Around the Centre One of the best restaurants in Noumea is *Le Berthelot* (☎ 28. 32.70), 13 Rue du Port Despointes in Faubourg Blanchot, upstairs in a small, beautifully restored colonial house. Seafood is the speciality but there are other delicacies such as an entrée of salade tiède de gésiers confits (warm salad of preserved gizzards) for 1250F, or a main course of crevettes flambées au pastis (Caledonian prawns flambéed in pastis) for 1550F. Half a rock lobster prepared Thermidor-style costs 2700F. It's closed Saturday lunch time and all day Sunday.

In the Latin Quarter, *El Cordobes* (☎ 27. 47.68) at 1 Rue Bichat also competes for highest honours. It is open for lunch and dinner, and serves gourmet French food with à la carte mains from 1700F to 2700F.

Halfway between the city centre and Baie de Citrons is *La Louisiane* (☎ 26.11.16) at 5 Route du Vélodrome. Occupying a huge colonial house, this restaurant is very popular with tourists and locals and has a good seafood selection. Entrées start at 900F and mains at 1400F. It's closed all day Sunday, and Monday at lunch time.

Anse Vata One of the newest restaurants in Anse Vata is *Le Miretti* (☎ 26.19.82), 24 Rue Gabriel Laroque, an intimate place with Impressionist reproductions adorning the apricot-toned walls. House specialities are seafood and cuisine from France's southwest Périgord region, such as confit de canard (duck preserved and cooked in its own fat) and foie gras (fattened goose liver). Main courses start at 2300F.

More chic is *La Coupole* (☎ 26.44.11) at Le Surf Novotel where a seafood menu du jour costs 7000F.

Vegetarian

Noumea's sole vegetarian eatery is *Végétaria* (☎ 28.10.65) at 78 Route du Port Despoints in Faubourg Blanchot. Opened in 1991 by Bertrand Bruyère, an enthusiastic man from the south of France, this small, laid-back restaurant has already attracted a sizeable clientele simply because the food is superb. The drawback is that it's a good hike out of the centre.

An entrée, such as a generous slice of asparagus tart served with salad, costs 450F and a large main plate of Indian curry or African couscous is 1100F. All meals come with his home-made bread – wholemeal, sesame or nut – which you can buy to take away. Végétaria is open weekdays from 11 am to 2 pm and from 7 to 9 pm. It's closed Saturday evening and all day Sunday.

Food Vans

A popular takeaway source is the contingent of old Citroën minivans which gather in the large car park on Rue Georges Clémenceau next to the market. Simply called 'the vans', these colourful vehicles line up every evening, including Sunday, at about 5 pm and serve an array of cold salads, drinks, cakes, nems and piping hot meals such as chicken or beef curry with rice and bread for 500F. The curry is one of the cheapest meals you'll get and, while it may not be fancy, it certainly is filling. The vans are individually numbered and very popular with locals. They operate until about 11 pm.

Self-Catering

Market Noumea's market is worth a look whether you're in need of food supplies or not. It's distinctively housed in half a dozen new blue-domed, hexagonal buildings opposite the bus station next to Port Moselle. There are four domes where vendors set up – one is solely the domain of fishmongers while the other three have a variety of stalls including fresh fruit and vegetables, croissants and pastries, Asian delicacies, meats and patés, bottled chillies, and shell jewellery.

The market starts daily at around 5 am. By 11 am, everything is packed up and closed. Friday, Saturday and Sunday are the busiest times while Monday is the quietest day with few traders and a scant selection of produce.

Supermarkets Noumea's main *super-marchés* and *alimentations* include:

SAVAH, 50 Rue Georges Clémenceau, opposite the bus station. Cluttered and shabby but with all the essentials; open Monday to Saturday from 6 am to 6.30 pm (until 5.30 pm on Saturday) and Sunday from 7 to 11 am.

Johnston, 6 Rue Anatole France, near the new gare maritime. New and well stocked; open Monday to Saturday from 7 am to 6.30 pm.

Ballande, corner of Rue de l'Alma and Rue du Général Mangin. Department store with fresh food section; open weekdays from 7.30 am to 6 pm and Saturday from 7.30 am to 5.30 pm.

La Cigogne, Place Bir Hakeim. Tiny alimentation with pricey wine, fruit, bread etc, but open every day until 9 pm.

Oceania, Route de l'Anse Vata. Small, expensive grocery store close to Anse Vata beach; open weekdays from 6 am to 7.30 pm and weekends from 6 am to 12.30 pm and 3 to 8 pm.

Rallye, 10 Rue Jules Garnier in Les Marinas shopping centre. It is the nearest large supermarket to Baie des Citrons; open Monday to Saturday from 7.30 am to 12.30 pm and 3 to 7.30 pm, Sunday from 7 am to noon and 4 to 7 pm.

Continent, north of central Noumea in the suburb of Normandie. To get there follow the RT1 out of town to the Tontouta Airport signs. Follow these signs until you see the complex on the right. Huge hypermarket with the cheapest prices in town; open Monday to Saturday from 8 am to 8 pm (until 9.30 pm on Friday) and Sunday from 8 am to 1 pm.

ENTERTAINMENT

Noumea's nightlife has picked up somewhat in recent times compared with the scene of 10 or even five years ago when the city used to shut down and lock up soon after sunset. However, it is still no raging metropolis and entertainment here is very tame in comparison with places like Papeete.

Casino

Casino Royal in the Surf Novotel hotel at Anse Vata is the country's only legal gambling venue, at least until the Méridien hotel and casino opens in 1994.

To enter the blackjack and roulette room you must show your passport, pay a 400F admission fee and be 'decently attired'. That means men should wear trousers (not jeans) and a shirt (it doesn't need a collar but it can't

be emblazoned with logos); a tie is not necessary. Thongs (flip-flops) are not suitable. Guests at many of Noumea's more expensive hotels receive a 1000F betting slip valid for this room.

There is no dress regulation or entry fee for the slot machines and dice (called *sic-bo*) den. In the afternoon this room is a sorry sight, packed with elderly Kanak women lined up feeding the machines 20, 50 and 100F coins.

The casino is open daily from 2 pm to 2 am. During the day, bus No 3 stops nearby – get off at the aquarium.

Bars & Cafés

Noumea's longest standing watering hole is *Le Saint Hubert* on Rue de Sébastopol. It's the sort of place where you just saunter in, sit back and sip drinks while being entertained by the occasional band or, more often than not, by the rest of the clientele – a mixed bag of locals, off-duty soldiers and tourists. Just down the road *Café de Paris* is the hang-out for lonely, bored soldiers.

Probably the coolest joint in town is the biker's bar at *Hôtel San Francisco*. This place reeks of American paraphernalia. Cowboy music drifts from the darkened bar while darts tournaments, barbecues and sushi parties are often staged. The bar is open every night until 1 am, later on Friday and Saturday nights when a band usually plays. On these nights, there's a 1000F cover charge entitling you to a drink.

A jazz ambience surrounds *New Orléans*, 12 Rue du Général Mangin, a very chic café featuring two hours of live jazz on Thursdays from 5 pm. This café closes each evening at about 7 pm.

An interesting pub is the *Relais de la Poste*, on the corner of Rue du Docteur Guegan and Rue Eugène Porcheron, where many of the more bohemian French and Kanaks hang out. Off-duty soldiers don't seem to like this pub, which doesn't bother the regulars much.

Down near the gare maritime, *Le Santa* at 29 Rue Jules Ferry is a spic, blue-and-white corner bar with adjoining nightclub, frequented by métros and tourists off the cruise ships. On Wednesday and Thursday until 1 am a Tahitian guitarist enlivens the scene, while on Friday and Saturday there's a full Polynesian floor show. Admission here is an outrageous 7000F.

Discos & Clubs
Anse Vata's most popular disco is *Le Bakoua* at 153 Route de l'Anse Vata next to Hôtel Le Lagon. The music is distinctly tropical, with reggae, rumba and African rhythm topping the disc jockey's list. It's open Thursday to Saturday from 10 pm; admission is 1000F. Café de Paris and Le Saint Hubert also have discos catering more to young Noumeans and soldiers.

Two private clubs in Anse Vata are *Black Jack* (☎ 26.42.86), 54 Route de l'Aquarium and *Le Privilège* (☎ 26.44.33) at 20 Rue Boulari.

Cinemas
There are four movie houses in central Noumea and, as is to be expected, most films are French, or American dubbed in French. On the odd occasion when one comes up with English subtitles, the posters will be marked *'avec sous titres'*.

The Plaza (☎ 28.66.60) at 65 Rue de Sébastopol and City (☎ 28.30.83), on the same street next to Café de Paris, screen current releases. The Rex (☎ 27.24.83) on Ave de la Victoire and Liberty (☎ 28.30.35) at 18 Rue de la Somme go in for violent action films. Admission costs from 600F to 650F. The Plaza has half-price entry on Tuesdays.

Billiard Halls
In the streets round the new gare maritime there are several large billiard halls. Billard du Port at 4 Rue de Verdun constantly attracts a young mixed crowd.

Spectator Sports
Pétanque Watching a game or two of pétanque is an easy and enjoyable way to spend an afternoon. It's played most days from around 3.30 or 4 pm between the bandstand and the fountain on Place des Cocotiers, and next to the Plages Loisirs kiosk at Anse Vata.

Cricket Women's cricket New Caledonian-style is played Saturday afternoon and all day Sunday (in season) at the cricket pitch on RT1 in Vallée du Tir, about 600 metres north of the Rond Point du Pacific. Bus Nos 9, 10 and 12 pass nearby.

THINGS TO BUY
Duty-free shops are dotted along Rue de Sébastopol and Rue de l'Alma but, with the possible exception of French perfumes, there are no outstanding bargains to be had. Curio shops are also abundant, particularly along Rue Anatole France and Ave du Maréchal Foch. The bulk of their stock is polished shells, pareos, nickel clocks and generally a lot of junk.

For more interesting souvenir sources try the art galleries (see the reference in this chapter) or some of the following artisan shops:

Le Coin du Cuir, 23 Rue Anatole France – has hand-made leather bags and sandals (☎ 28.26.58)
SEP, 23bis Rue Anatole France, next to Le Coin du Cuir – sells stone and mineral, particularly nickel, artefacts (☎ 27.60.53)
Michel Rocton, 1 Rue du R P Rougeyron, Faubourg Blanchot – has polished stones and sculptures and even hand-sculpted chess sets (☎ 28.11.74)
Marie France Buchy, 6 Rue du RP Gaudet, Vallée des Colons – designs and sells nautical shells made into necklaces, and jewellery made from Île Ouen's jade (☎ 27.13.59)
Caldoshell's Creation, 2 Ave James Cook in the Maison des Métiers – another artisan who does very fine work with black coral (☎ 28.73.08)
Maison de Lifou, 48 Rue Anatole France – has wooden sculptures and paintings from Lifou, reproductions of ancient bamboo engravings and other works by Kanak artists from all over New Caledonia. Pro-independence T-shirts are also sold here (☎ 27.47.81).

French goods – such as perfume, clothing, lingerie and shoes – are sold in many of the shops and boutiques along Rue de Sébastopol and Rue de l'Alma. They include:

Champs Élysées Boutique, 38 Rue de l'Alma – specialises in clothing and shoes
Reflets de Paris, 31 Rue Jean Jaurés – has perfumes, leather goods and lingerie

GETTING THERE & AWAY

Air

All international flights arrive at Tontouta Airport, where passengers must pass through customs and immigration. See the introductory Getting There & Away chapter for details on international flights to/from New Caledonia.

Within the country, the domestic carrier Air Calédonie flies daily to/from Île des Pins and three of the Loyauté islands – Mare, Lifou and Ouvea. The fourth island, Tiga, is serviced only twice a week. Three towns on Grande Terre – Kone, Touho and Koumac – are all connected by regular flights, while the isolated Belep Islands in the far north are serviced twice a week with flights to/from Koumac. The introductory Getting Around chapter has more information on air travel within New Caledonia.

Airline Offices There are at least five Air France offices within the small enclave of the business district, but the main one (☎ 25. 88.00) is at 41-43 Rue de Sébastopol. The staff have a long-standing reputation for being consistently cool with foreign backpackers. The office is open weekdays from 7.30 am to 4.10 pm and Saturday from 8.15 to 10.30 am.

Other airline offices in Noumea are Air Calédonie International (☎ 28.33.33; 27.61.62 for reservations) at 8 Rue Frédéric Surleau and Qantas (☎ 28.65.46) on Rue de Verdun. Several other airlines are represented by general travel agents – you'll find these listed in the Information section of this chapter.

Boat

Most cruising yachts arrive at Port Moselle where they must clear customs and immigration at the capitainerie (for all details see the Yachtie's Guide in the Getting Around chapter).

Ocean cruise liners dock at either the new gare maritime on Rue Jules Ferry or the old harbour on Ave James Cook (for more information see Cruise Ships under the Sea section of the Getting There & Away chapter).

Cargo boats connect Noumea with Île des Pins and the Loyauté islands – see the Getting There & Away sections in those chapters for details.

Bus

The gare routière is at the end of Rue d'Austerlitz. Buses bound for destinations around Grande Terre leave from the left of the main building as you're facing the market. There is a smaller kiosk where you can get bus schedules and buy tickets. See the introductory Getting Around chapter for more details on bus travel around Grande Terre.

Driving

Cars, camper vans and motorcycles can be hired from the various rental companies in Noumea. For more details, see the Car section of the introductory Getting Around chapter.

Hitching

You will need to get to Noumea's northern outskirts to pick up rides going anywhere into la Brousse. For those heading east towards Yate, take bus No 8 to Cité de Saint Quentin, which will drop you off near the highway overpass at Normandie. From there you can get onto the east-bound RT2.

To go north, you have two choices: either the RT1 via Dumbea and Paita or the express toll road which bypasses these two towns. The RT1 carries less traffic than the toll road and you could find that many of the cars using it are only going as far as Dumbea or Paita. In its favour, it is relatively easy to get to – just take bus No 8 to the northern side of the Normandie overpass and start hitching.

The toll road starts at Koutio and is the more direct of the two northern routes. However, no local buses pass the toll gate, so your best bet would be to take bus No 9 and get off before the bus turns off the main road into Rivière Salée. It is still another four km to the toll gate, but a large percentage of cars that pass by here will be using the express route.

GETTING AROUND
To/From Tontouta Airport
Tontouta International Airport is 45 km, or 40 minutes by car, north of Noumea. It is serviced by buses and minivan operators. When leaving Noumea, you can arrange to be picked up at your hotel, motel or YHA hostel but you must ring two days in advance to book the ride, and then double-check the day before to ensure that the driver will pick you up.

Minivan One particularly nice operator is Jean Claude Cronstaedt from Vanuatu. He runs an agency called Pacific Tourist Transport (☎ 27.53.23) and has a desk at Tontouta Airport. He will pick up and drop off passengers at any hotel or motel in Noumea. The one-way/return fare is 1500/2500F.

Agence ORIMA (☎ 28.28.42), 27bis Avenue du Maréchal Foch, also operates minivans. It is managed by Mrs Manoi Othis. She will send someone to pick you up at your hotel or YHA hostel on request. It's 1800F one way to the airport.

Private Bus SCEA is a large bus company that drops off and picks up passengers from all major hotels in Noumea. However, it does not service some motels. Its office (☎ 28.61.00) is at 3 Rue de la République. A one-way fare is 1800F.

The Noumea YHA Hostel has a special deal with SCEA for those staying at the hostel. The bus will pick you up at Tontouta and take you to the hostel for 1800F, which includes your first night's accommodation. When leaving, a bus picks up passengers from the hostel about two hours before departure time; the fare is 500F even though the price on the ticket is 1800F.

Blue Bus These little public buses are the cheapest way of getting to and from the airport. At Tontouta, they wait outside the arrival hall, to the left as you exit the building. In Noumea, they depart from the main bus station. They take a lengthy route, with the journey taking about an hour and 10

minutes either way. A one-way fare is 400F (420F on weekends).

Schedules are the same whether you're taking the bus from Tontouta or Noumea. On weekdays, they are hourly between 6.30 am and 5.30 pm, leaving on the half-hour. On Saturdays the buses are hourly from 6.30 to 11.30 am and there are additional buses at 1, 3 and 5 pm. On Sundays there is a bus every two hours (on the hour) between 7 am and 5 pm.

Although the schedules detailed here are supposedly official, it is wise not to rely too heavily on them as buses have been known not to turn up when they should. If this happens when you're leaving Noumea, remember that any bus bound for northern Grande Terre is a potential lift to the airport. Just check with the driver first to make sure he has no objections – if the bus is not full, there should be no problem. He will then drop you off on the main RT1 road, a 10-minute walk from the airport.

Taxi Because taxis are not guaranteed passengers once they reach the airport, they charge for a return trip even if you are going only one way. The fare is 8000F, which makes prices in Manhattan, New York, seem dirt cheap.

To/From Magenta Airport
Bus Noumea's domestic airport at Magenta is four km east of the city centre and is easily reached by public transport. Blue bus No 7 leaves every 15 minutes from the main bus station in Noumea and will drop you at the doorstep. The fare is 100/120F on weekdays/weekends. The ride to the airport takes 20 minutes; the return trip is about 10 minutes longer as the bus does a little tour of Ouemo peninsula before heading back to town.

Taxi Taxis to Magenta Airport from Place des Cocotiers charge about 800F.

Bus
Noumea's urban bus system, called *transports en commun*, is very efficient. All buses

leave from the gare routière at the southern end of Rue d'Austerlitz. As you're facing the market, local buses depart from the right-hand side of the main building.

The system is pretty straightforward. Each bus waits in line until it is its turn to leave, when it slowly shunts past the waiting passengers. You pay the driver as you get on. En route, buses stop at the blue-and-white *autobus arrêt* signs – if you want to get on at one of these stops you must flag it down. Buses are considered full when there's a bottom on every seat, including the slippery little seats which fold into the centre aisle. At this point, bus drivers will not take on more passengers.

On weekdays, buses run from about 5/5.30 am to 6.15/6.30 pm. On weekends and public holidays they start later, finish slightly earlier and are less frequent. Fares are 100/60F for adults/children except on Saturday afternoons, Sundays and public holidays, when an extra 20F is levied.

Following are some bus numbers, their destinations and weekday frequencies:

No	Destination	Frequency
2	Magenta via Vallée des Colons	every 15 mins
3	Anse Vata via Trianon	every 10 mins
4	Faubourg Blanchot	every 45 mins
6	Anse Vata via Baie des Citrons	every 15 mins
7	Magenta Airport & Ouemo	every 15 mins
8	Cité de Saint Quentin	every 15 mins
9	Rivière Salée	every 10 mins
10	Ducos	every 20 mins
11	Tindu & Numbo	every 15 mins
12	Montravel	every 10 mins
13	Nouville	every 45 mins

Taxi

The main taxi rank is under the flame trees at Place des Cocotiers, though you can also hail a cab from virtually anywhere around Noumea. Taxis operate 24 hours a day, seven days a week but on Sundays you might have to order one – telephone Radio Taxi de Noumea (☎ 28.35.12).

Fares increase slightly after 6 pm. As an example, from Place des Cocotiers to Anse Vata you'll be looking at 800F in the day, 900F in the evening.

Car, Camper Van & Motorbike

For information on renting a car, camper van or motorbike, see the introductory Getting Around chapter.

Bikes & Mopeds

Bicycles can be rented from four outlets around Noumea. The best rates are from Reviens, je t'aime ('Come back, I love you'; ☎ 27.88.65) inside the new gare maritime on Rue Jules Ferry. The friendly woman who runs this shop rents both 18-speed VTTs and Peugeot mopeds. A VTT bike costs 500/1200F for two/eight hours or 1500/2500/6500F per one/two/seven days. Mopeds are 2000/3000F for four/eight hours or 4000/7000/9500F per one/two/three days. To rent a moped, you must have a valid driving licence and pay a 7000F deposit.

This shop also operates a buy-back scheme that could be interesting in the long term. You buy the VTT/moped for 29,500/130,000F and, if you bring it back in good condition, the shop will buy it back from you. It will return 60% of the buying price for a VTT, 75% for a moped.

Alternatively, at Anse Vata, the Plages Loisirs kiosk rents bikes at 800F for two hours and 1000/1500F for half-day/10 hours. At Baie des Citrons, Hôtel Ibis has the same rates for half-day and day rentals and charges 500F per hour. Photo-Curios (☎ 26.23.78), also at Baie des Citrons, has bikes for 1200/1600F per half/full day.

Hitching

Every local will tell you how difficult it is to hitch in Noumea – and that's while they're giving you a lift! At certain times of the day – just before midday when everyone's racing home for lunch and at 5.30 pm when they've finished work – it can be fruitless. The rest of the time it's not too hard. To thumb a ride from the city to Anse Vata, you're best off standing at the start of Route de l'Anse Vata.

Yacht

The Cercle Nautique Calédonien (CNC) on Rue du Capitaine Desmier at Baie des Pêcheurs is a good place to check if anything is happening on the water. Noumea Yacht Charters (☎ 28.66.66; fax 28.74.82) at Port Moselle sporadically gets yachties together to do a half-day sail to Îlot Maître, the reefs around Noumea or a sunset cruise off Anse Vata. You may be able to hitch a ride.

Southern Grande Terre

Head out of Noumea in any direction on land and you'll enter la Brousse. First, though, land travellers must pass through the urban continuation known as Greater Noumea, which includes the satellite communities of Mont Dore to the east (incorporating La Conception, Saint Louis and Plum) and Dumbea and Paita to the north. After that, the mountains of la Brousse are before you.

Southern Grande Terre has very few roads,

which makes much of it inaccessible. Travel through here, by whatever means, offers a bit of outback adventure. There are three distinct regions – the rugged and diverse southern tip, the west coast plain dotted with Caldoche towns and cut by the only road heading north, and the east coast mining towns where, despite the disruptive mining activities, Kanak people have managed to maintain their culture and way of life.

GEOGRAPHY

The southern part of Grande Terre is dominated by the Massif du Humboldt, a mountainous chain with many peaks, including the highest, Mt Humboldt (1618 metres). Much of the region has been mined and, particularly along the east coast and in the south (north of Baie de Prony), the earth is scarred red, as if it is bleeding. Fires often sweep through the hillsides, leaving a contrasting charred vegetation. Covering an immense area in the south-east is the artificial Lac de Yate (Lake Yate) where, in some of the drowned valleys there are graveyards of white trees, their dead branches piercing upwards from the intensely blue waters.

The bulk of New Caledonia's protected nature sites are found in southern Grande Terre, many dotted along the Massif du Humboldt (see the Protected Nature Sites map in the Facts about the Country chapter). The most highly prized is the Réserve de la Montagne des Sources, on the western slopes of the mountain of the same name. Thick in rainforest and rich in maquis (serpentine scrub), the area protects Noumea's water supply; only dedicated hikers should attempt to explore this area. Bordering it farther east is the Parc Provincial de la Rivière Bleue, a recreational park where, in the early morning, you may hear cagous barking. South of Lake Yate is the weird, wide landscape of the Plaine des Lacs, with its somewhat naked but mineral-rich terrain, dotted by lakes and marshlands. Here is the Chutes de la Madeleine reserve, a favourite weekend waterfall and swimming hole, as well as seven other small botanical reserves rich in various species of plants.

The country's only marine reserves are also situated in the south, including the highly protected Réserve Yves Merlet, a complex of reefs between Canal de la Havannah and Passe de la Sarcelle.

The Southern Tip

The area south-east of Noumea is, except for a few coastal settlements, completely undeveloped. It's a diverse region, with Kanak villages dotting the eastern coastline, weekend retreats of Noumeans lining the shores of Baie de Boulari near Mont Dore, the vast Lac de Yate offering wide panoramas and some superb areas for nature lovers. Much of this region is quite accessible from Noumea and, if you have a day or more to spare, it can be easily explored.

Heading east from Noumea along the RT2, the first sights of interest are the missionary villages of La Conception and Saint Louis. Soon after is the turn-off to Mont Dore and Plum.

Leaving the coast behind, the road narrows and climbs steadily through a desolate landscape, where red hills have been sliced open to make way for the electricity lines that bring power to Noumea from

Lac de Yate (Lake Yate)

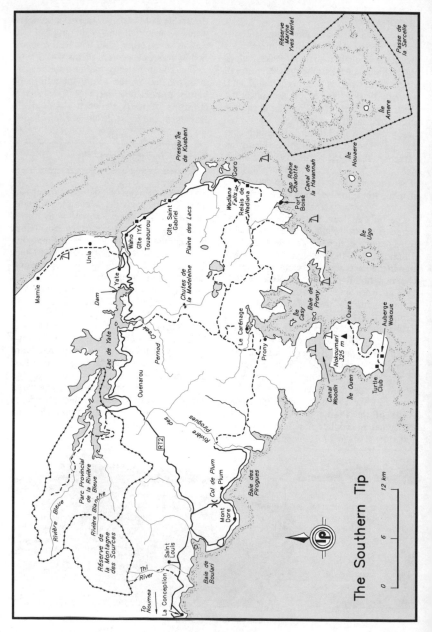

The Southern Tip

Yate's hydro-electric station. Yate Commune is home to about 1400 people and covers a large area – basically everything east of (and including) the Rivière Bleue park, to the villages of Yate, Unia, Mamie, Waho, Touaourou and Goro.

The 'real' southern tip, Baie de Prony and Île Ouen is accessible only by boat or, in the case of the former, by 4WD.

LA CONCEPTION

La Conception is a small village, a few km east of Noumea's northern suburbs, created by Marist missionaries at the end of last century. The village was the site of a large rally in 1975 at which several pro-independence parties made their first demand for an independent Kanaky.

La Conception's striking domed Catholic **church**, set 400 metres off the main road, is a landmark easily spotted as you fly in and out of Noumea's Magenta Airport. Built in 1874 and recently renovated, its extremities are painted a rich ochre that contrasts sharply with the unblemished white walls. The inside is rather austere except for the stained-glass windows and the windswept scene painted in the dome above the altar.

The nearby little **cemetery** at the junction of the RT2 and the road leading to Conception church is the burial place of two of the country's well-known indépendentistes – Pierre Declercq and the movement's *grand-père*, Roch Pidjot (see the aside on Roch Pidjot).

Pierre Declercq, the secretary-general of the Union Calédonienne (UC), was the first of the independence leaders to be killed. He was shot in his home in Noumea in 1981. His large, heavily flowered grave, easily visible from the road, is inscribed with the epitaph: *assassiné dans le combat pour la libération du peuple Kanak* – 'assassinated in the fight for the emancipation of the Kanak people'.

Any bus heading east from Noumea along the RT2 will stop at La Conception.

MISSION DE SAINT LOUIS

The Saint Louis mission is picturesquely perched on a small hill in the Thi River valley, 15 km east of Noumea. Its church, built in 1859, is supposedly the oldest in New Caledonia and, while slightly bigger than its counterpart at La Conception, it's even less decorative.

The mission is home to four fathers and nine sisters who have no objections to visitors' wandering around the property. Behind the mission loom the twin peaks of the Monts Koghis; walking trails through pasture land head up towards the mountains.

Saint Louis mission is easily reached by hopping on a Plum/Mont Dore bus at Noumea's bus station and getting off when the church steeple comes into view on the left (about a 20-minute ride; the fare is 200F).

Roch Pidjot
Roch Pidjot, or the 'old Pidjot' as he liked to be called, was the co-founder of the UC and the first Kanak to be elected to the French parliament. His ancestors lived at Pouebo on the north-east coast but Pidjot was born at La Conception in 1907. Up until the age of 39, he lived like all Kanaks under the indigénat code, carrying mail for the administration and working in the fields.

Following the demise of the indigénat system, Pidjot became increasingly involved with local politics. He was appointed UC president in 1956 and in 1964 was elected to the French National Assembly. In Paris he stubbornly lobbied for reforms leading to the liberation of Kanaks, putting forward proposals for self-government that were steadfastly ignored. He was to describe this time as 'preaching in the desert'.

In 1975, at a rally of pro-independence parties at La Conception, Pidjot was amongst those Kanak leaders to demand independence officially. A year later, he wrote a letter to a leading French newspaper, describing a country 'sinking into crisis', where some Whites were becoming scared of Blacks. 'They (the Whites) were forced to pack up 100 years ago. They are still standing with their suitcases in their hands. Twenty-four years before the year 2000, this is just astounding'. ■

MONT DORE

The community of Mont Dore, with a commune population of 16,000, is stretched along the foothills of the big, bald Mont Dore (772 metres). Coal traces were discovered here in 1853 and the mountain has since been scrubbed clean of practically all large vegetation. Weekend trekkers from Noumea climb to the peak but, if you've time for only one hike near Noumea, the landscape is more lush and the scenery grander around the Monts Koghis north of Noumea.

There's little to the actual 'town' of Mont Dore – a postal agency and a small grocery store are plonked on the main road while the waterfront is lined with houses of Noumean workers and those who like to get away here on weekends. Here too is the only restaurant, *Vallon d'Or*, an expensive place open Sundays only.

For details on buses to Mont Dore (300F one way) see the following Plum – Getting There & Away section.

PLUM

Like Mont Dore, Plum is the home of many Noumean workers and, except for weekends and school holidays, it's a rather deserted, lifeless place. Roughly 27 km from Noumea (if you drive over the Col de Plum; a bit farther via Mont Dore and the bay), it has a military camp and plenty of nearby beaches but not much else. Unfortunately, the water tends to be brown and murky from erosion and the beaches littered with flotsam.

Orientation & Information

From the Mont Dore turn-off on the RT2, Plum stretches for some 3½ km along the small Baie des Pirogues. The army barracks are set back from the road, halfway through town.

Things to See

The Col de Plum, four km north of Plum, offers a sea vista and a cold mountain *source* (spring) that supplies the country with bottled water. The water tastes so good that the Mont Dore bottling company complained of too many people arriving with jerry cans to tap the free water. It therefore decided to instal water meters at the spring whereby you have to pay 20/50/100F for every two/five/10 litres you take away. However, this hasn't yet been implemented.

Places to Stay & Eat

You can pitch a tent at the municipal campsite close to the beach (behind a stone and timber fence), 3½ km south of the Mont Dore turn-off. There are barbecues and a toilet block, though the latter is generally locked and the keys inconveniently kept at the Mobil petrol station, four km back on the road to Col de Plum.

There are two options, both on the road south of Plum. *Le Nukuhiva* (☎ 43.41.41), BP 323 Mont Dore, is the first hotel you come to, 4½ km from the Mont Dore turn-off. It's a new place, close to a black-sand beach, and it has eight bungalows with cooking facilities for 6000F per night for up to four people. During school holidays it is heavily booked. Le Nukuhiva's large restaurant is open for lunch daily, except Monday, and serves good-value menus du jour for between 1200F and 1400F.

Alternatively, there's *La Nouvelle Siesta* (☎ 43.39.10; fax 43.44.04), BP 83 Mont Dore, 1½ km farther on from Le Nukuhiva at the end of the bitumen road. It's quite secluded, situated 400 metres inland in a little valley over a hill from the beach. It has a swimming pool and 20 thatched bungalows, all with private shower and toilet. For one or two people they cost 3600/5300F without/with cooking facilities. The bungalows for four or five people cost 5300F but have no kitchens. The hotel's restaurant overlooks the swimming pool and serves simple meals for the few weekday passers-by. On weekends there's greater choice, including a 1600F menu du jour and homemade cakes.

The only other restaurant in Plum is *La Fontaine* (☎ 43.44.33) at the Mont Dore turn-off. Recently renovated, it serves only a weekday plat du jour for 650F (available lunch time only) and a whopping 2200F menu du jour on weekends.

Top Left: Conch shells – a traditional Kanak symbol (LF)
Top Right: Sorting sun-dried bêches-de-mer (GC)
Bottom: Beach at Hienghene (LF)

All photographs courtesy of DNC

Self-caterers have a grocery store at the entrance to town and a pâtisserie just before the army barracks.

Getting There & Away

On weekdays, Mont Dore/Plum buses leave from Noumea's bus terminal hourly between 6 am and 6 pm. On Saturday there are about nine buses per day and on Sunday four. It takes an hour to reach Plum and costs 350F.

To Noumea, buses run hourly from 5 am; the last bus leaves at about 4 pm. Hitching to/from Noumea is quite easy, particularly on weekends.

PARC PROVINCIAL DE LA RIVIÈRE BLEUE

This massive park is built around the Rivière Bleue (Blue River), at the western end of Lac de Yate. The park was created in 1980 and is a wildlife refuge and protected reserve of about 90 sq km – or 9045 hectares.

As part of the Upper Yate fauna reserve,
the Rivière Bleue park is primarily a place for nature lovers and bush walkers, with abundant waterfalls, swimming holes and hiking tracks. There are thick virgin forests of araucarias, houp and kauris, including the *Grand Kaori*, a giant kauri estimated to be somewhere between 800 and 1000 years old.

The park is home to many species of birds including the red-crowned parakeet, the black honeyeater and New Caledonia's national bird, the cagou. Park officials set up a cagou breeding programme in the 1980s when only 50 cagous remained in the area. By early 1993, they estimated there were 200.

Public interest in the park has grown at a similar rate over the last five years, largely due to promotion by the South Province. In 1989, just 7800 people visited the park. Four years later, the annual figure was 29,000. In 1993 the park received 30,623 visitors. The bulk of visitors are Noumeans seeking nature's solace, and therefore the busiest times are weekends and school holidays.

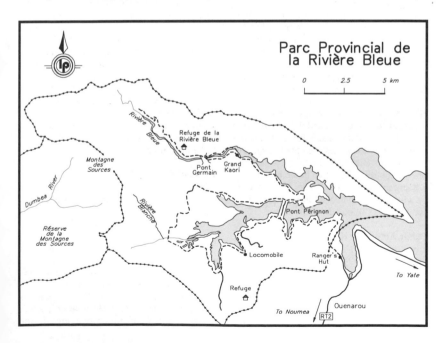

During the week you could easily have the park to yourself.

Information
The park's office (☎ 27.26.74) is at 4 Rue du Général Gallieni in Noumea (in the building marked Province Sud – Direction du Développement Rural). It publishes copies of an excellent park brochure (in English, French and Japanese) which includes a map plus detailed explanations of possible hikes, where you can stay and how to get there. The Noumea tourist office also stocks this free brochure.

The park is open daily except Monday from 7 am to 5.30 pm, with last cars allowed in at 4 pm. During heavy rains it is closed, as the rivers rise quickly. There's an entry fee of 300F per car, payable at the ranger's hut, three km from the RT2 turn-off.

All food supplies must be brought into the park as there are no shops.

Things to See & Do
Nature aside, the park's attractions include an antique locomotive, the **Locomobile**, that once carried valuable timber to Noumea along a now abandoned railway, and **Pont Pérignon**, a vast wooden bridge built in 1958 and resembling the bridge over the River Kwai.

Hiking The park office has specified five hikes, to suit all tastes, and detailed them in its brochure. They range from eight-hour tramps with views over the upper reaches of the Rivière Bleue, to half-day walks and one-hour strolls. The map in the brochure is not suitable for serious hikers – they would be wise to pick up IGN's 'Série Orange' map (scale 1:50,000) covering this area.

Other Activities Horse trekking, canoeing, kayaking and VTT bikes are planned to be introduced in 1994.

Places to Stay
Camping With your own tent, it's possible to camp at many points along the Rivière Bleue, mainly between Pont Germain and

the new *refuge* (hut). The campsites are equipped with a shelter, barbecue, drinking water, toilet and cold shower.

Refuges There are two *refuges* in the park where you can bed down overnight. Both are basic, containing a table and bunks. You must bring your own bedding or sleeping bag.

The newest is on the northern side of Pont Germain, built of native timber and with a fireplace out the back where you can boil a billy or have a barbecue. It's available to the public on weekdays only and it would be wise to book in advance at the park office in Noumea.

The other, rather dilapidated, refuge is in the park's southern section. Research teams often stay overnight here and in this area it's possible to hear the cagous barking before sunrise.

Getting There & Away
The park is off the RT2 to Yate. The turn-off, roughly halfway to Yate or 43 km from Noumea, is at Ouenarou (it's signposted). From here, it's three km to the ranger's office and another 15 km to the start of the park. The dirt road is accessible to conventional vehicles and 4WD. You can get to the turn-off on the bus to Yate, but there's no public transport down the 18 km to the park.

Once in the park, it is difficult to get around without a car; there are no buses travelling through it and hitching may prove to be difficult except on weekends.

PLAINE DES LACS
This 'Plain of the Lakes' encompasses the heart of Grande Terre's southern tip. As it's bedded by iron, water is unable to escape and a fascinating land of drowned trees, water holes and marshes has developed.

The main dirt road into this region leads off from the RT2 at Pernod Creek in the north, 20 km past the turn-off to the Rivière Bleue park. About 11 km into the journey you'll pass close by the area's most famous sight, the **Chutes de la Madeleine**, a small waterfall which cascades over a ridge of iron rock into a popular weekend swimming hole. Camping and picnicking here are possible as there's plenty of fresh water. The road up to the chutes is accessible (in dry weather) to conventional vehicles. After the falls, it's 4WD terrain.

YATE DAM

Built in 1959, this 45-metre-high *barrage* (dam), spanning about 200 metres, is part of a hydro-electric scheme that supplies all Noumea's power needs and some other areas of Grande Terre. The turn-off from the RT2 is a few km after the road leading off to Chutes de la Madeleine. From the turn-off it is then another two km. It's not possible to walk over the dam wall, though the view you get from the barricade is quite impressive.

After passing the dam turn-off and crossing the last col, the sea suddenly comes into view and the countryside becomes lush and tropical. The road descends sharply to the Yate bridge, where a turn-off to the left leads to Yate village and Unia, while the road over the bridge heads to Waho and Goro.

YATE

Yate village, often confused by visitors with the whole Yate Commune, climbs a valley at the end of a four-km, dead-end road from the Yate bridge. The road runs beside the waterway that leads down from Yate dam and out to the sea. Though tourist brochures say Yate is reminiscent of 'an Alpine village', in reality it's a tiny place overwhelmed by an enormous white power station generating so much electricity that the village is enveloped in a constant crackle and hum. There's a church, a little store with two petrol pumps, and a gendarmerie (☎ 46.41.17), but no accommodation.

There's a bus that passes through Yate from Noumea – see the following Waho & Touaourou section for details.

UNIA

Unia is a very small tribal settlement on the northern side of the waterway leading from Yate dam to the sea. It has no administrative buildings or facilities but there are many traditional houses and a few nicely cultivated rice fields.

To get to the village you must cross the waterway by *bac*, a generator-powered car ferry which uses a wire cable to pull it slowly across the water, making a lazy and enjoyable trip. Sadly, the days of this tiny ferry are numbered as, in early 1994, it is due to be replaced by a 75-metre-long bridge, custom-built in France and shipped out to New Caledonia. The road leading to Unia is very eroded and if there have been rains you may get stuck. From Unia, you can continue to the tribal village of Mamie.

WAHO & TOUAOUROU

Eighty km east of Noumea, Waho is the main centre of Yate Commune and the first village you'll come to after crossing the Yate bridge. Sitting just back from the sea, it has a school, mairie (town hall) and dispensaire but no gendarmerie or petrol station (they're at Yate village).

Waho is the first link in a series of sparsely populated coastal settlements which end at Goro, 20 km to the south. The next link in the chain is the mission of Touaourou, five km south of Waho, and then Saint Gabriel. There are traditional huts along the coast and the life style is laid-back. Most people live off the sea and from subsistence farming. The coast is rugged while the nearby interior is mountainous with fast-flowing rivers and waterfalls.

The road towards Goro runs about 300 metres inland which, combined with the lush vegetation, makes sea views rare. The exception is the crossing behind the beautiful Presqu'Île de Kuebeni, a peninsula with two nearby islands and fine stands of araucarias. The road is sealed as far as this peninsula, though major works were underway in mid-1993 and it shouldn't be long before the entire strip to Goro is bitumen.

The beach at Saint Gabriel is very good for exploring as there are various caves and shallow pools – bring snorkelling gear.

Orientation & Information

The region's sole post office and clinic are up behind the school, at the end of the first road to the right as you enter Waho from the Yate bridge. There are no banks in the region. The gendarmerie and the only petrol supplies are in Yate village (see that entry).

Places to Stay & Eat

On Tuesday and Saturday, a roving grocery van, which goes right the way to Goro, supplies the villagers with baguettes and the school kids with lollies.

The first place to stay along this road is *Gîte IYA* (☎ 46.42.32), which opened in 1993. It has three bungalows, each with a shower (and hot water!). The price for one or two people is 5000F per night; breakfast is 600F. Camping costs 1000F per night. Meals are also available – set menus cost between 1800 and 2000F and seafood menus are 2800F. It's a good idea to book early. The gîte is about four km south of Waho, down a track towards the beach. To locate it, look out for a bus shelter and three coconut palms on the right as you're heading south. The driveway at the coconut palms leads to an unmarked épicerie which stocks baguettes and canned goods but no fresh fruit or vegies.

Another km south and you'll come to Touaourou, with its waterfront mission. It's possible to camp for free here, using the ablutions block beside the football ground, but don't count on the showers working.

One km farther is a tiny épicerie set back into the trees and, opposite, a *snack bar* with very basic fare.

Next up is *Gîte Saint Gabriel* (☎ 46.42.77), four km past Touaourou, or nine km from Waho. It is run by a friendly Kanak family and has a superb beachfront location set amidst coconut palms. The bungalows overlook a protected beach, with the reef clearly visible and lullingly audible in the distance. There are five basic thatched bungalows, some newer than others, each with a toilet but no private shower or cooking corner. They cost 2500F for two people. A third person can be squeezed in for an extra 500F. Overnight camping will cost 1000F. If you're only here for the day to eat lunch under the palms and use the beach, there's a 500F 'picnicking charge'.

The family who runs Gîte Saint Gabriel specialises in seafood lunches and dinners. A standard plat du jour costs 1000F while a three-course meal, including a salad entrée, main course of fish or chicken, and fruit dessert, is 1600F. A crab/lobster meal will cost 1800/3500F but for these you'll have to ask a day or so in advance. Breakfast is 350F and a Number One beer costs 200F.

The only other place to stay along this coast is *Relais de Wadiana* at Goro (see the Goro section for details).

Getting There & Away

Bus The bus to Yate (500F), Waho (500F; 1¾ hours), Touaourou (600F), Gîte Saint Gabriel (700F) and Goro (900F; 2½ hours) leaves from the Noumea bus station Monday to Saturday at 11.30 am. You must let the driver know where you want to get off.

There's also only one bus back to Noumea, operating Monday to Saturday. It leaves from the Touaourou mission at 6 am, stopping at Waho and Yate en route. If you're staying farther south at Gîte Saint Gabriel or Relais de Wadiana, the owners of both these places will drive you to Touaourou in time to get the bus. They charge 200/300F respectively for this service.

Car & Hitching To drive to Yate Commune, take the RT1 out of Noumea to Normandie and then turn right onto the RT2.

Likewise, to hitch to the east, you have to get to the Normandie overpass. Bus No 8 to Cité de Saint Quentin will drop you near the overpass, from where you can get onto the RT2. You should have little trouble getting a lift; the same goes for the return journey. However, once on the east coast, hitching from Waho to Goro will take a very patient thumb.

GORO

Goro is 20 km south of Waho and is home to about 300 people, their houses stretched out for a km or so near the water. Four km before Goro, the road turns sharply inland and crosses a low wide causeway. This water comes down from the Plaine des Lacs and, after recent heavy rain, the bridge is sometimes flooded.

Things to See & Do

The **Wadiana Falls** are a km past Goro. The road passes right next to the falls, which cascade from a rocky cliff and form a natural pool at the bottom where you can swim.

The Relais de Wadiana (see Places to Stay) offers various half or full day **boat trips** out onto the lagoon and to nearby coral cays. You can visit the bay of Kuebeni to the north, Cap Reine Charlotte and the bay of Port Boisé to the south, or head out to the Havannah lighthouse.

The relais has a small dock with a ladder, from where you can take a swim. From the dock, a pair of huge, rusted cantilever loaders and a derelict pier are visible. They're what's left of the extensive mining that was carried out south of Goro during WW II. Iron and chrome ore were fed by conveyor belt into the waiting ships and taken to Noumea, where the rich minerals were sent to France and processed. The Goro mine is now a rusted relic that merely enhances the remote, forgotten atmosphere of southern Grande Terre.

Places to Stay & Eat

About one km after Wadiana Falls, the *Relais de Wadiana* (☎ 46.41.90), offers accommodation and meals in an idyllic spot overlooking the blue Pacific Ocean, with the Havannah lighthouse and cruising yachts in the distance.

It has two bungalows with showers and three without for 3000/2500F per couple. Each extra person is charged 600F; camping costs 1000F. However, until the road between Waho and Goro is finished, these bungalows will usually be rented out to a team of road workers, so phone before you go all the way down there.

The restaurant has waterfront views and serves two specialities – a seafood dinner for 3200F or a traditional bougna for 3500F (which will feed five people). You'd have to order a day in advance for both these meals. A normal salad and fish meal is 900F and petit déjeuner is 600F.

The relais' owner has plans to open a hotel/restaurant with camping at Port Boisé, halfway between Goro and Baie de Prony,

where many yachties drop anchor in favourable weather.

Getting There & Away

See the details in the previous Waho section.

LE CARÉNAGE & PRONY

Boat, 4WD and helicopter are the only ways to get to the small coastal communities of Le Carénage and Prony, at the very southern end of Grande Terre. The two abandoned mining villages offer spectacular views of the surrounding reef and Baie de Prony with its sole islet, Île Casy. The ocean cruiser, Club Med 2, anchors in the bay once a week so those on board can spend a day on Île Casy's beach.

Overland trips to this area are possible with 4WD tours from Noumea. They cover a good deal of mountainous terrain with no tribal villages to be seen en route. 4WD tracks lead in from three directions. From Plum, you cross Rivière des Pirogues into a scarred and desolate landscape of abandoned mines and forestry sites. The northern route comes down past the Chutes de la Madeleine while the eastern track leads up from Goro and contours the Plaine des Lacs.

Pacific Raids (☎ 28.23.25) in Noumea organises trips to the area for 18,000F, using 4WD one way and helicopter the other. Their main problem is that there's a good deal of erosion, so roads are often blocked; in the wet season, creek crossings are heavily flooded.

It's also possible to get to the bay via boat from Île Ouen (see the following section for details).

ÎLE OUEN

Île Ouen sits just off the tip of Grande Terre, 37 km south-east of Noumea. It is a large, sparsely vegetated, mountainous island, covering 116 sq km and home to the most southern 'mainland' clan, the Ouara. The 160 clan members live in an isolated community on the island's north-east coast. They have a primary school, clinic, wharf and a Catholic church. Once a month a priest from the mainland sails over to conduct a mass.

In 1847, a sandalwood trader aboard the ship *Eleonor* was the first White person to sight Île Ouen. The island has been left relatively natural and untouched since then except for the opencast mining of jade, evidence of which can be seen when you climb the southern slopes. There are two accommodation possibilities – the Turtle Club resort and a tribal gîte called Auberge Wokoue – but, even with these, very few people apart from weekend yachties from Noumea visit Île Ouen.

Things to See & Do

Should you happen to be on the island's highest point, Nokoumari (325 metres), in August and September, you might see whales pass by. Throughout the year, turtles and dugongs swim around the shallow waters of the lagoon immediately to the south-west.

Snorkelling equipment is available free from both the resort and the gîte. The Turtle Club also has surfboards with a clear plate for viewing fish and coral, and they can arrange water-skiing – two tours of the bay cost 1000F.

Excursions Baie de Prony and many deserted coral islets are a short boat trip from Île Ouen. The family running the gîte has a speedboat for trips to Île Mato (1500F per person) or to Prony (2000F).

Pierre, the man who operates the Turtle Club, owns the island's sole vehicle, a decrepit 4WD truck which still has the guts to get up the island's only road. With enough people, he'll organise an overland drive past the opencast jade mine on Nogoungoueto, the 258-metre-high hill behind the resort, and across to Ouara.

Bicycles can be hired from the gîte for 500F per hour or are free for those staying at the Turtle Club. It's debatable how useful they are, as the road is guttered with crevasses capable of swallowing bikes.

Places to Stay & Eat

Those living on the island use generators for power, while water comes from natural sources. The two accommodation choices are both good.

The older is the *Turtle Club* (☎ 28.53.62), a resort built 30 years ago around a sheltered palm-lined bay in the south-west corner. It is run by Pierre Gode, a pleasant chap from Brittany in France who secluded himself on the island seven years ago. In mid-1993 he was closing the resort for several months while 10 new beachfront bungalows were being built. The plan is to re-open around March 1994, in time for the arrival of a new boat which will link the island to Noumea on an almost daily basis.

The Turtle Club has an overnight package which includes the return boat trip, one night's accommodation, four meals and use of the non-motorised water equipment for 16,000F per person. Day-trippers have the option of buying a ticket for the return boat trip (4400F) and bringing their own picnic, or paying 6100F which includes the boat, a three-course lunch at the Club's casual restaurant and use of its water sports equipment.

Alternatively, there's the new *Auberge Wokoue* (☎ 28.57.67), a little waterfront gîte just five minutes' walk across the grass airstrip from the Turtle Club. It is run by the Tein family from Ouara and consists of three lovely bungalows, each of which sleeps four people and has a private shower/toilet. They cost 5000F for one or two people, and 500F for each extra person. The family will allow you to pitch a tent for 1000F, and have a shower and toilet available.

The auberge has an open-sided, Melanesian-style restaurant close to the water. At lunch time from Monday to Friday they serve a 1500F three-course meal (which rises to 1800F on weekends and in the evening). While lobster used to be profuse in the area, it's now quite scarce as a result of over-hunting. Breakfast is available for 450F.

To stay and/or eat here, you should make an advance booking by telephoning the auberge direct or through the Mary D at Anse Vata.

Getting There & Away

There are two tourist operators servicing Île Ouen: the Mary D (☎ 26.31.31) at the Palm Beach complex at Anse Vata, and the Turtle Club's new Australian-made boat, similar to the high-speed *Manta*, which runs to the Seahorse Pontoon. It operates from Wednesday to Sunday and leaves from the Club Med wharf. The voyage takes about an hour one way and hugs the coastline, providing excellent views of Mont Dore and the little-explored lands to the south. Boats dock at the small wooden wharf beside the Turtle Club.

The price of the return boat trip, excluding any meals or accommodation, costs the same for both boats; 4400F return or 6100F including lunch. With Mary D's present boat, *Hydroflight*, the trip takes about 1½ hours and leaves from Club Med's wharf on Saturday, Sunday and public holidays at 8.30 am, arriving back at 6 pm. Tickets can be booked through Mary D or Amac Tours (☎ 26.38.38).

The Road North

If you don't head east out of Noumea, then you must go north. Known as the Route Territoriale 1 (RT1) this road traverses the island's western coast all the way to Poum, a journey of 424 km, en route skirting the sometimes receding, and at other times threatening, mountain range. Occasionally the road passes through spectacular scenery. The interior is sparsely populated, with the occasional traditional Kanak village, like the serene Petit Couli near Sarramea. In places it is mined for nickel, while much of it is typically west-coast-style country of wide expanses, cattle stations and a Caldoche atmosphere.

More than anywhere else in New Caledonia, Grande Terre's west coast, particularly the central portion, was dramatically affected by colonisation. Convicts paved the roads and built the first settlements. Guarded by the army, which needed facilities, the convict penitentiaries developed into real settlements which in turn attracted many settlers. Together with freed convicts, they colonised the area. There were rebellions by the local Kanaks against this takeover, such

as the revolt lead by Chef Ataï in 1878, but the battles were very one-sided and the indigenous people had no way of winning. Most of their land was taken and made into cattle stations, while the local clans were deported to inland reservations.

Only two roads cut across the central mountain chain to the east coast. The first, the RT4, takes off just north of Bouloupari, leading to Thio. It's in better condition than its counterpart, the RT5bis, which breaks away just after La Foa. However the latter, which leads to Kouaoua and Canala, is unquestionably more scenic and exhilarating (and dirt for a good part of the way). If you're considering travelling between Canala and Thio, note that this road is sometimes impassable (see the following Canala – Getting There & Away section before you set off).

Two northbound roads lead out of Noumea. The more direct is the péage (toll) road, which starts at Koutio and runs for just 17 km (it costs 150F per car and is the one most often used by traffic to/from Tontouta Airport). In the meantime, the RT1 has wound past the Monts Koghis and Dumbea and through the heart of Paita, after which it connects with the toll road.

THE MONTS KOGHIS

When Noumea's sticky heat becomes too oppressive, the Monts Koghis is the place people head to. A chain of steep mountains whose peaks are often shrouded in clouds, it is clad in rainforest and rich in flora native to New Caledonia. On average, the air is 5°C cooler than in Noumea, just 14 km to the south. There is a restaurant halfway up the mountains, but no accommodation.

Just over Monts Koghis' ridge is the Réserve de Montagne des Sources, a protected nature reserve which is the source of the rivers feeding Dumbea dam, Noumea's water supply, as well as that of the Rivière Blanche, the second river to run through the Rivière Bleue park.

Hiking

At the restaurant you can pick up a free

The Central Ring Road

Approximate Scale

tourist map of the hiking trails that lead from here to the mountain's twin peaks, Mt Mone (1075 metres) and Mt Bouo (1059 metres). From these, in good weather, you can see Lac de Yate and many lower-altitude viewpoints and waterfalls.

Trails vary in length, ranging from 30 minutes to six hours, and of course in degree of difficulty. They are generally well marked but at times can be very steep and slippery. Some popular (under two-hour) walks include to the *Grand Kaori* tree or *la cascade*, a waterfall dropping into a two-metre-deep pool.

As the mountain is not a designated natural reserve or park, there are no rangers to assist hikers. Therefore, the unspoken rule is that if you get lost and a search party has to come out, you pay a *tournée générale* (a round) for everyone at the restaurant's bar when you get back.

Places to Stay & Eat

The *Auberge du Mont Koghi* (☎ 41.29.29) sits at 476 metres overlooking parts of Noumea, the Baie de la Dumbea, the Dumbea Plain and the shimmering barrier reef on the horizon. It has no accommodation but campers are welcome for free, providing they don't mind going without a shower.

The restaurant serves Savoyard lunches and dinners; that is, specialities from the Savoy region in the French Alps. Typical of this cuisine is raclette (a round of cheese which is grilled and then eaten with nibblies), and fondue. Either will cost 2400F per person, while a normal menu du jour is a pricey 3500F. At any time of the day you can stop in for a tea, coffee or ice cream, or something more fortifying such as an alcoholic apple cider from Brittany in France or one of Belgium's special (and very strong!) Trappist beers for 750F.

Getting There & Away

The Monts Koghis area is not easily reached without private transport. The turn-off to the auberge is 14 km north of central Noumea on the RT1 to Dumbea. From here, it's another five km through rainforest and then up steep bare slopes to the auberge.

Hitchhikers could take the Dumbea/Paita bus to the turn-off and try to hitch; however there is little traffic up this road except on weekends, when many vehicles will be full anyway.

If you're a group of four and intend eating at the auberge, the owner will pick you all up in Noumea for a transport fee of 3000F. Alternatively, Amac Tours and Agence Orima (see the Activities section in the Noumea chapter) run half-day tours to the mountains, but they're pricey.

DUMBEA

This sleepy town (population 10,000) is 18 km north of Noumea, lying quietly along the Dumbea estuary between the RT1 and the toll road north. Though actually part of Greater Noumea, it has a rural atmosphere distinct from the capital, making it a popular day trip for Noumean families wanting some outdoor fun. Hiking to the Dumbea dam, swimming in a nearby water hole, canoeing, kayaking, horse riding and ultra-light flights are all possible. Other than that, Dumbea's claim to fame is the annual Giant Omelette Festival. There is no accommodation in the town.

Things to See & Do

Barrage de la Dumbea The Dumbea dam, fed by rivers originating in the Montagne des Sources to the east, is Noumea's water supply (though water for the capital is also drawn up from the water table under the Dumbea Plain).

To get to the dam, turn right off the RT1 just before the Dumbea bridge at Parc Fayard and follow this road for seven km. En route, the track turns to dirt, the surrounding mountains become steep and the river cascades down a ravine past the Trou des Nurses, a popular swimming hole.

Ultra-Light Flights New Caledonia's only ultra-light plane club is based at Dumbea. For details on flights, see the Activities section in the Facts for the Visitor chapter.

Horse Trekking The Buffalo Ranch (☎ 41. 63.63), three km up the road to the dam, hires horses for 2000F for 1½ hours and 5000F for four hours. It is open daily except Tuesday.

Canoeing On weekends only, canoes and kayaks are hired from a team (☎ 41.61.19) which set up at Parc Fayard. A canoe costs 1500F per hour or 4500/6500F for a half/full day. You can paddle six km up to the Trou des Nurses water hole or 5½ km to the mouth of the Dumbea River.

Giant Omelette Festival

In 1993, 10 chefs used 10,000 eggs to cook a three-metre-wide omelette which was used to feed (for free) 10,000 onlookers. And the event gets bigger every year!

The festival is held on a weekend in late April or early May at Parc Fayard just off the RT1. Country & western bands play and the Miss Dumbea beauty queen is chosen from a troop of hopefuls.

Getting There & Away

Dumbea is easily reached by Noumea-Paita buses, leaving from Noumea's bus station every half-hour from early morning until 5.30 pm. The cost is 220F one way.

PAITA

Paita (population 6000), also part of Greater Noumea, is a small town 26 km north-west of Noumea on the RT1. It has a church built in 1876, a school, bank, post office, mairie and a gendarmerie. You will find as you travel throughout New Caledonia that most towns will have these six essential buildings. In addition, Paita has a bar and a Westpac bank.

Things to See

Petroglyphs About three km before Paita, coming from Dumbea on the RT1, there's a group of four petroglyphs on the rocks down by the creek to the right. It should be signposted.

Tomb of James Paddon The land around Paita was the eventual home of James Paddon, the influential English trader who greatly aided France's colonial administration by encouraging colonisation and agriculture.

He originally set up a trading station on Île Nou near Noumea in 1851 but released the land to the French so that they could make it into a convict prison. In exchange he was given property on the Gadji peninsula near Paita and 60,000F. Trading copra and sandalwood with the Chinese, he was credited with introducing the colony to cattle, horses and, according to some accounts, alcohol.

Paddon died in 1861. He has the tallest gravestone in a small family cemetery, hidden away in a paddock at the crossroad of the toll road from Noumea and the Gadji turn-off. No-one but the cows will mind if you wander in.

Places to Stay

Camping is the only possibility in this region. The closest campsite is at Enghoue beach, 21 km west of Paita, which looks towards the former nudist escape of Île Mba. It's a simple but calm place, right on the waterfront and popular with weekend and holiday campers. There is fresh water and a cold shower. The nightly fee is 200F per tent, payable to the warden who lives on site and who loves to tell a yarn or two. The road to Enghoue is almost deserted and the last seven km is dirt.

Getting There & Away

For details on buses to Paita (250F one way), see the previous Dumbea section.

MONT MOU

Mont Mou (1211 metres) dominates the scene between Paita and Tontouta Airport. Though part of the mountain is a designated botanical reserve, it is possible to climb to the peak from a track near the sanatorium, a health resort for the elderly, about one third of the way up the mountain slope.

The turn-off to the sanatorium from the RT1 is at Col de la Pirogue, 10 km north of Paita. A narrow tarred road, it winds for 2½ km through banana and fruit groves and lush vegetation where orchids hang from the trees. The sanatorium is marked by a red-and-white tower that is clearly visible on the way up. About 400 metres before arriving, there's a tiny wooden bridge from where a rough path starts up the slope. Information about this trek is nigh impossible to get but you'd be wise to allow a day.

Any northbound bus from Noumea will drop you off at the Col de la Pirogue turn-off.

TONTOUTA

Tontouta, or La Tontouta as it's formally known, is the site of New Caledonia's international airport and little else. Via the main toll road, it's 45 km north-west of Noumea; along the RT1 through Dumbea and Paita it's 54 km. The airport is 800 metres from the RT1 junction where there's a new Westpac bank, supermarket, snack bar and restaurant.

The scenery greeting you here is quite spectacular. The airport lies on a vast plain nestled between small hills which block the view of the sea, and the bulk of the Massif du Humboldt. To the north-east of Tontouta is the range's summit, Mt Humboldt, just 10 metres short of being New Caledonia's highest peak.

Places to Stay & Eat

Camping If you have just flown in or are

soon to fly out, the owner of the Relais des Ailes restaurant at the RT1 turn-off will let you set up camp on the grassy area out back. It's free but you'll have to forgo a shower.

Hotels The only nearby accommodation is the expensive *Hôtel Tontoutel* (☎ 35.11.11), BP 8 Tontouta, 1⅓ km north of the airport. It has a long stretch of 43 rooms built around a central pool. The rooms are comfortable, with (noisy) air-con and mosquito screens, but are hardly worth the top-end price. Singles/doubles/triples are 6500/8000/9000F and there is a 380F room tax. The hotel doubles as a hospitality school – those in the pink shirts are trainees.

To get there from the airport, head to the RT1 and then turn left. It's 500 metres on the right. Alternatively, the hotel picks up and drops off for a 300F per person fee.

Restaurants The expensive restaurant upstairs in the airport terminal maintains a lofty image and has few takers. The restaurant at *Hôtel Tontoutel* is open daily and offers a menu du jour for 2000F, a plat du jour for 1000F or à la carte. The *Relais des Ailes* (☎ 35.11.76) at the RT1 turn-off serves traditional French cuisine but, again, it's pricey (and closed on Tuesdays).

Getting There & Away
For details on transport options to/from Noumea, see the Getting Around section in the Noumea chapter. Hitchhikers should easily get a ride by waiting near the RT1 junction.

BOULOUPARI
Bouloupari (population 1500) sits on the plain several km from Mt Ouitchambo, an almost perfectly shaped conical mountain rising 587 metres to a fine tip, just north of the town. Except for some mines south at Tomo and oyster cultivation in the shallows of nearby Baie de Saint Vincent, the area is mainly rural and undeveloped. About one km north of the town centre is the junction for the RT4 to Thio (see the following Mining Towns section for details on Thio).

The town developed after the 1878 Kanak rebellion. Ten years earlier, a military post had been erected close to the nearby natural harbour of Bourake to assist in the arrival of convicts. However, during the rebellion many locals were killed, including workers at a rum distillery and a sawmill, and a local army brigade. The centre of activities was moved to the main road, a gendarmerie was installed, and Bouloupari gradually became a convenient stop on the route north.

More recently, there was a movement to change the town's name to 'Boulouparis', the addition of an 's' supposedly forging greater ties with France by bringing the famous capital a little closer to the colony. You'll see some of the movement's adherents have been unable to let it drop.

Orientation & Information
This one-horse type of town has a post office, school, gendarmerie (☎ 35.17.17), BCI bank (generally it does not handle foreign exchange) and four petrol stations, the latter testimony to its importance as a highway junction. It is the first place after Noumea that has a well-stocked grocery store, but accommodation choices are slim.

Places to Stay & Eat
It is possible to camp at Bourake beach, 16 km south of the town; however there is little shelter, no water and few cars on the road for hitching. Better is the campsite at Ouano Beach (see the following section).

The only accommodation is *Hôtel Les Paillottes de la Ouenghi* (☎ 35.17.35), BP 56 Bouloupari, a 'golf resort and country club', about 2½ km off the RT1, five km south of town. It has an 18-hole golf course, individual bungalows, spacious restaurant and swimming pool. The staff can organise horse riding or canoeing for 1500F per hour. Green fees are 2000F during the week and 3000F on weekends.

The six bungalows cost 5500F for a couple and 1000F for an extra person. A continental breakfast is a whopping 900F. The restaurant mainly serves à la carte, such as a good steak for 1000F. On Sunday only, several seafood menus du jour are offered, costing between 2600F and 3500F.

At the Thio turn-off there's a small shopping complex including a *supermarket* that's open until 7 pm, and a *pizzeria*.

Getting There & Away

Any bus heading from Noumea along the west coast or going up to the east coast will drop you in Bouloupari. The fare is 600F and it takes an hour. Hitching too is simple.

BOULOUPARI TO LA FOA

You're now entering real cattle country, where birds of prey soar over the plain and only an occasional niaouli stand breaks the wide open space.

Camp Brun

About 15 km north of Bouloupari, Camp Brun was the site of a double-walled prison reserved for the *incorrigibles* – those convicts who could not be corrected. They were used on the road gangs which paved the west coast.

Built in 1876 on land belonging to a colon named Brun, the prison soon earned a reputation for cruelty, and those sentenced here lived a life with little hope. Prisoners were chained and left in the burning sun, or put in cells resembling tiny cubes. Stories tell of men tearing out their eyes to escape the harsh treatment. The camp was closed in 1895, and today little remains.

Ouano Beach

While it's generally hard to rave about the southern west coast beaches, Ouano at least has some atmosphere. Sitting at the end of a hooked peninsula, it is home to a tiny settlement of bêche-de-mer divers who fish the surrounding waters of Baie Chambeyron.

Bêches-de-mer, also sometimes called trepang, are easy picking, lying harmlessly on the sea floor in shallow waters where they eat plankton or filter the sand like a natural vacuum cleaner. Once collected, they're gutted, boiled, washed and left out to dry on mesh tables, after which they're sold to Japan and China for about 1300F to 2000F per kg.

A small inland lagoon separates the divers' settlement – a row of five quaint houses each painted a different pastel colour – from the beach, where you can set up camp for free. A few picnic tables are dotted around but there is not much shade. Drinking water is available, and there are ablutions blocks, but they might be locked.

The turn-off from the RT1 to Ouano Beach is 22 km north of Bouloupari – it's signposted. From here, a dirt track leads through cattle country for another 10 km to the end of the peninsula. There are no homesteads en route but, because of the bêches-de-mer divers who come through, hitching would be difficult but not impossible.

LA FOA

La Foa (population 2150) is an historic settlement with some old New Caledonian homes that are still in good nick. About 110 km from Noumea, it is surrounded by lush cane fields and beautiful blackwood and araucaria trees. It has also been the scene of some bloody historical events.

After the construction of the nearby Fort Teremba, La Foa became another penal centre. While the men were incarcerated at the fort, the women's penitentiary was built at Ponwhary, six km north of La Foa on the road to Sarramea. The local authorities occasionally tried to pair off the convicts, seldom with success.

The Kanak revolt of 1878 ignited in La Foa when Kanaks attacked the gendarmerie and killed those inside. From here, the rebellion continued south to Bouloupari and as far north as Poya (see the History section in the Facts about the Country chapter for details on the revolt).

From 1880, 'Malabars' from Réunion, France's colony in the Indian Ocean, migrated here to work in the sugar cane fields and at a rum distillery. A hotel was built and the town grew. With the end of the convict era, the women's prison was turned into a girls' boarding school.

More recently, it was in a farmhouse near La Foa that one of the FLNKS leaders, Eloi Machoro, and his aid, Marcel Nonaro, were

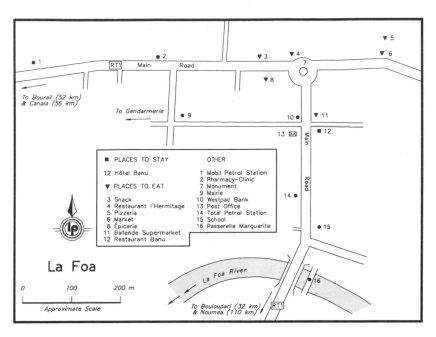

La Foa

PLACES TO STAY

12 Hôtel Banu

PLACES TO EAT

3 Snack
4 Restaurant l'Hermitage
5 Pizzeria
6 Market
8 Épicerie
11 Ballande Supermarket
12 Restaurant Banu

OTHER

1 Mobil Petrol Station
2 Pharmacy–Clinic
7 Monument
9 Mairie
10 Westpac Bank
13 Post Office
14 Total Petrol Station
15 School
16 Passerelle Marguerite

0   100   200 m

Approximate Scale

gunned down by French gendarmes on 12 January 1985.

Orientation & Information

The RT1 into town crosses the La Foa River before coming to a monument stuck in the middle of the road, indicating the centre of town. Just before the monument you'll pass the post office, with standard provincial hours, and next to it a Westpac bank, open weekdays from 7.45 am to 3.45 pm. Opposite is the town's only hotel and a busy Ballande supermarket.

On the main road heading to Bourail, there's a clinic and adjoining pharmacy while the gendarmerie (☎ 44.31.17) is one block off this road, to the left two streets before the Mobil petrol station.

Things to See

Passerelle Marguerite Named after the wife of a temporary governor of the colony, this bridge is a rare construction for New Caledonia, designed by two students of the famous engineer Gustave Eiffel. It was built in France in 1909 and weighs only four tonnes. During WW II, Passerelle Marguerite was superseded by a wider bridge erected alongside and, since then, only the odd admirer strolls across it.

Woodcarvings The tiny studio of Remy Weiss (☎ 44.31.26), an artist who does wood sculptures inspired by traditional Melanesian art, is about 1½ km from the monument, on the road towards Bourail. Some works are usually displayed in the front room of his studio/home, while Weiss can be found out back near the sawmill.

Places to Stay

Camping The closest coastal camping ground is at Ouano Beach (see the previous section for details). The turn-off is 15 km south of La Foa.

Hotel La Foa's only lodging is *Hôtel Banu* (☎ 44.31.19), BP 57 La Foa, opposite the post office on RT1. It has been around since about 1880 and, in 1940, was the temporary prison of Colonel Denis, the colony's deposed pro-Vichy governor. The tricolour flies proudly at the entrance, a none-too-subtle indication of how the owners feel about an independent Kanaky.

The hotel's main section is a well-preserved colonial building with a street-front bar, frequented by a mixture of travelling sales reps, military personnel and truckers. It boasts a collection of caps – there were 606 hanging from the ceiling when we last passed. Out the back is a separate, two-storey apricot-toned building with a spacious verandah and simple but soothing rooms. There are eight with private shower and toilet costing 4000/4800F for a single/double. The three rooms without such facilities cost 3000/3800F (there's a good ablutions block near by) and a third person can be squeezed in for an extra 800F. It is wise to book accommodation here as it's often full even during the week.

Places to Eat

Restaurants The tiny *pizzeria* at the social centre, to the right at the monument, is good for takeaways or a quick bite to eat at the counter. It is open from 10 am to 1 pm and 4.30 to 8.30 pm and has pizzas from 550F to 1400F.

Hôtel Banu's restaurant, behind the bar, is popular with local workers. A plat du jour costs 950F while menus du jour with traditional French fare range from 1650F to 2200F. Petit déjeuner is 500F and a cold Number One beer costs 250F. It's closed on Sunday evening.

An alternative is *Restaurant L'Hermitage* (☎ 43.36.20) directly behind the monument. A gracious colonial home built in the 1930s, it features a huge, cool terrace where traditional French lunches are served daily – the menu du jour costs 1300F. At dinner it's à la carte Chinese cuisine with entrées for 500F, main courses from 900F to 1800F, and desserts from 350F.

Self-Catering Many of the people living in Canala, Kouaoua and Sarramea come to La Foa for supplies picked up at the handful of small alimentations or the larger Ballande supermarket. The latter is open Monday to Saturday from 6.30 am to 12.30 pm and 2.30 to 7.30 pm, and Sunday from 7.30 to 11.30 am and 4.30 to 6.30 pm.

A small market operates at the social centre on Saturday morning. On weekdays, three Kanak women set up under a shady tree on the RT1 a couple of km south of town and sell their home-grown tomatoes, bananas, yams and cucumbers, and a range of bottled chillies.

Getting There & Away

Bus Buses pick up and drop off in front of the post office.

From Noumea to La Foa, there are buses, Monday to Saturday, at 4.05, 9.30 and 11.30 am. In addition to these regular services, from Monday to Thursday there are buses at 10 am, 12.30 and 3.30 pm (the latter does not run on Wednesday), on Wednesday at 8 am and 6.30 pm, on Friday at 5.30, 5.45, 6 and 6.30 pm, on Saturday at 11.45 am and on Sunday at 10, 11.30 am and 1 pm.

Heading from La Foa to Noumea, there are buses, Monday to Saturday, at 6, 8.55, 10.50 am and 3.40 pm (the latter also on Sunday). In addition to these, there's a daily bus (except Friday and Sunday) at 7.30 am and another (except Friday and Saturday) at 1.15 pm, while Monday to Thursday there's a bus at 11.45 am, on Friday at 9.30 pm and on Sunday at 2.45 and 3.45 pm.

Hitching Hitchhiking to or from La Foa is a viable option as there is a lot of traffic along this road.

LA FOA TO MOINDOU

Five km from La Foa is the turn-off to Farino and Sarramea (for details, see those two sections), this road eventually leading to Canala on the east coast.

Meanwhile, the RT1 meanders towards the western coastline and up to Bourail, passing Fort Teremba and the village of

Moindou en route. Closer to Bourail are two cemeteries – an Arab burial ground and the New Zealand Pacific War Cemetery. Both these sites are covered in the Bourail section of the North-West Coast chapter.

Fort Teremba

Perched above the plain overlooking Baie de Teremba, this fort housed convicts who were used to build the Canala-Bourail-Bouloupari roads. Over the years a small settlement, including a school, church, shop and wharf, sprouted around the prison and it became the headquarters of the local military.

In 1878, the fort was besieged by Kanaks during the great insurrection, but with soldiers, wardens and prisoners fighting alongside each other, the fort was never taken. It finally closed its doors in 1898 and is now used only for sound & light shows in late October/early November.

You can visit the fort at any time – a high stone wall still stands as does a guillotine. Generally there's not a soul in sight, with the exception (from February to April) of a million mosquitoes, who seem to be ferociously avenging the convicts who died here.

To get to the fort, you must turn off the RT1 to the left 10 km past La Foa and follow the dirt road for about two km.

Moindou

Moindou is a tiny hamlet built around a bend in the road. It is home to 450 people, a petrol station, a church and an épicerie. It kicked into existence in the late 1800s, when people from Alsace and Lorraine (France) emigrated here after the 1871 signing of the Treaty of Frankfurt, which saw the two regions handed over to Germany. In the 1920s Moindou became a coal centre, with up to 500 people working in the mines off the old Boghen road to the north-west. However, the coal was of poor grade and the centre declined.

LA FOA TO SARRAMEA

The road bound for the east coast, the RT5bis, turns off five km past La Foa. It's a spectacular route, passing Kanak villages with native huts intact, huge groves of bamboo and an ever-changing and unspoiled countryside. In bad weather, waterfalls drain the cloud-shrouded mountains.

The road is made of dirt (except after rain when it's mud) from the Col d'Amieu, just past the settlement of Grand Couli, to about 10 km before Canala. Mining trucks use the road so it's also heavily potholed, and in wet weather becomes a slippery quagmire that is positively uninviting. That said, it is passable by conventional vehicles going with care and without speed.

Farino

En route to Sarramea, Farino (population 200) is a tiny village at the top of a hill, three km from the main road turn-off. It has superb views over the valley back towards La Foa and out to sea. The tourist authorities promote the village as the venue for New Caledonia's 'smallest market', held on the second Sunday of each month outside the mairie. Other than the market and the view, the only thing in sight is a telephone box.

Petit Couli

Petit Couli is a small tribal village at the turn-off to Sarramea. It's famed for the beautiful, 80-year-old grande case, standing at the end of a double row of araucarias, on the main road just past the Sarramea turn-off. Customary gatherings are still held in the *case* – you should ask permission before photographing it. Just down the road is Grand Couli, the clan's larger settlement.

SARRAMEA

Sarramea is like a cool oasis after the open plains and dry country preceding it. Forests green the area, occasionally interrupted by meadows with tall blackwood trees, whose umbrella-like canopies fan out in a manner reminiscent of acacias on an African plain.

The three clans around Sarramea were, until their forced dispersal following the 1878 revolt, some of the largest and most important tribal communities on Grande Terre. These days, the area is home to about 480 people, a third of whom are Caldoches.

Orientation & Information

Sarramea has no real focal point and no facilities apart from a mairie and an adjoining postal agency (open two hours per day). It also has a very pleasant hotel. There is no signpost to the village – you just turn off before Petit Couli. The road winds for three km up a gently sloping valley beside a gushing creek before reaching the post office. One km farther on, the road ends at the hotel.

Things to See & Do

From the hotel, you can walk 300 metres through a cow paddock to **Trou Feuillet**, a five-metre-deep water hole fed by a mountain stream. It is deliciously cool for swimming.

For the more athletic, a track goes up to **Plateau de Dogny** (1050 metres) from where both coasts are visible. This is at least a two-hour walk.

Places To Stay & Eat

The *Évasion 130* (☎ 44.32.35) BP 56 Sarramea, is four km from the Petit Couli turn-off. Before the Events, this place was a popular weekend getaway for Noumeans and held a disco that attracted revellers from afar. Now it's quiet, more at peace with its environment and frequented only by occasional tourists and passing sales reps.

Surrounded by dense forest, it has 14 square bungalows, all with shower and toilet, but no cooking facilities. They're not flash but they are comfortable enough. In the evenings, geckoes come inside to feed on the smorgasbord of insects attracted by the lights. Rooms cost 3500/4000F for one/two people and extras are each charged 800F; there's a 380F room tax.

The hotel's restaurant is built around a huge rock, penetrating like a landslide into the dining room, which in turn seems to have been pushed out onto a poolside terrace close to the stream. Menus du jour are offered, varying in price from 2500 to 3000F. A fish or meat dish costs 1500F while a standard baguette, butter and coffee breakfast costs 500F.

Getting There & Away

Bus One of the bus drivers on the Noumea-La Foa route lives in Sarramea, giving the village one bus connection per day (weekdays only). This driver leaves Noumea at 3.30 pm, arriving at La Foa at 5.30 pm and Sarramea postal agency 15 minutes later. It's 750F one way from Noumea. The driver starts the return journey at 5 am the following day. Alternatively, the two buses (weekdays only) that go from Noumea to either Kouaoüa or Canala can drop you at the turn-off to Sarramea. For bus details, see the Kouaoua and Canala sections.

Hitching There won't be a bounty of rides if you're hitching from the RT5bis turn-off to Sarramea, but it shouldn't be impossible. If it turns out to be fruitless, it's a cool walk. If you're going over to the east coast, it's best to start out early in the day and you'll probably need some patience.

The Mining Towns

Hidden by the central mountain chain, southern Grande Terre's east coast mining region, which includes the towns of Kouaoua, Poro, Canala and Thio, tends to leave travellers in a mixed state of awe and unease. The mountains droop with the burden of mining and most peoples' lives are veiled by the sombre day-to-day routine of work. Here, too, many of the violent confrontations designed to disrupt elections during the Events took place and somehow, even these days, there's not the airy lightness characteristic of Grande Terre's northern east coast.

Nowadays, all is quiet throughout the region. Away from the areas of mining, the scenery can be stunning, with waterfalls dropping from the mountains and deep bays gouging out the coastline. Beaches are scarce or far from the road, except in the case of Ouroue near Thio. In all, it's a region few Noumeans, except those here to work, ever see. Travellers with a sense of adventure are likely to enjoy it.

KOUAOUA & PORO

Halfway from Sarramea to Canala is the turn-off to the coastal enclaves of Kouaoua (25 km) and the smaller Poro (83 km). They might be worth visiting if you are interested in seeing opencast mining techniques and the transportation of raw materials into waiting ships.

From the turn-off, the scenery en route isn't very appealing. Mining activity is all too evident in the red-scarred, decapitated hills and the 11-km-long conveyor belt which runs down the slope and along the Kouaoua Valley. The Kouaoua River is one long expanse of mud leading into an enormous bay that is so filled with slurry you could stand the proverbial spoon in it. From the pier at the end of town, the ore is poured straight into the hold of cargo ships bound for Noumea or Japan.

The Kouaoua mines were opened in 1977 by SLN and there is an estimated 20 million tons of nickel ore to be extracted from this mineral-rich region. At a rate of one million tonnes per year, one miner said they'll be there well into the next century.

Farther north, Poro offers more of the same. The mines started in 1964 and, in 1990, a mining and quarrying training centre was opened in the town in a bid to modernise industry practices.

Besides streets lined with brown cottages, both towns have a clinic, gendarmerie, post office and grocery store.

Places to Stay & Eat

The only place in either town to bunk down for the night is the hotel/restaurant *l'Oasis* (☎ 42.44.85) in Kouaoua, the meeting place of all kinds of workers. Its eight rooms, opposite the restaurant, each sleep three people and cost 3000F per person. You'd better book in advance as miners generally fill them up.

L'Oasis' large restaurant, with a cool fresh atmosphere fully justifying its name, serves a filling menu du jour for 1800F, including bread, a quarter litre of wine and bottomless cups of coffee. The owner is a talkative man who chats with the folk at each table. L'Oasis closes on weekends.

In Poro there's a Vietnamese-run restaurant which is a humble but good place to eat.

Getting There & Away

Bus On weekdays only, there is one bus to Kouaoua which leaves Noumea at 3 pm, arrives in La Foa at 5 pm and reaches Kouaoua by 6 pm. Only mine buses continue to Poro. The trip from La Foa costs 500F, from Noumea 1000F. The return bus leaves at 5 am the next day (except on Monday when it leaves at 3 am!).

Car From the RT5bis turn-off, the road to Kouaoua is asphalt except at creek crossings. From Kouaoua, a windy mountainous road continues to Poro. It's unsealed for the first 15 km and one creek crossing is prone to flood.

LA CROUEN

About 10 km before Canala are the thermal hot springs of La Crouen – Kouho in Xârâcùù, the local Kanak language. The waters here reach a maximum of 43°C; containing sodium and sulphur, they are believed to be beneficial for asthma and rheumatism sufferers.

The springs are set up as a traditional-style thermal bath house where one sits and bathes but, on no account, does one swim. It's an odd place, and is certainly not the Vichy of New Caledonia. It receives enthusiastic reports from some travellers but not so endearing ones from others. As one reader wrote: 'It's best not to dwell too much on what's floating in the water...hygiene freaks would be put off'.

Indeed, it's not somewhere to go out of your way to see. The bath house is open from 7.30 am to 10 pm; admission costs 300/150F per adult/child for a 30-minute dip. The people who run it will let you camp on the grass for 300F per night. The springs are 1½ km off the road – the turn-off is at the end of the dirt section before Canala.

CANALA

Canala sits at the end of a long, wide waterway, the Baie de Canala, which is surrounded by protective hills and provides excellent shelter for ships during cyclones. The town and surrounding area (population 4000) is backed by steep, scrubby mountains from which the mighty Ciu waterfalls cascade.

In the late 19th century, Canala was the country's mining centre and the second-oldest European settlement. It rivalled Noumea in importance but was soon outstripped. Later, as the independence movement gained momentum, Canala became one of its strongholds. Eloi Machoro, the FLNKS leader killed at La Foa, came from Nakety, the village 10 km to the east. An EPK school was set up in the town.

On election day in November 1984, 200 Kanaks stormed the Canala polling booth and tore up ballot papers in a violent clash with gendarmes. At the 1988 election, road-blocks were erected around the town and the gendarmerie was besieged. The attacks on it continued for two days, during which time 100 civilians were airlifted to Noumea.

These days all is quiet, but even so few Caldoches or métros from Noumea, 165 km away, venture out here.

Orientation & Information

Canala has the usual post office, clinic and gendarmerie (☎ 42.31.17). A new school, designed with Melanesian-style buildings, is under construction on the outskirts of town towards Thio.

Ciu Waterfalls

After a lot of rain, the Ciu waterfalls are spectacular. Situated in an inland valley, they offer wide views over the valley and the start of the deep bay. You can swim in a pool at the top. The falls can be reached along a dirt road to the right, about 1½ km from Canala on the road towards Thio. The turn-off is unmarked. From here it's about four km to the top of the falls, past thatched huts and a hillside richly clad in banana trees, coconut palms and bamboo. A black-and-white sign reading 'cascades' marks the path from the road to the falls. Don't count on there being any traffic on this road for hitching a lift.

Places to Stay & Eat

As you enter the town from La Crouen, you'll see on your right *Chez Jeanette* (☎ 42.31.51), a run-down colonial-style home that offers food, accommodation and camping. It is run by a friendly Arab man and, while scruffy, it's clean enough. Rooms cost 1250F per person, but are often taken by Vietnamese and ni-Vanuatu men working on new buildings at the nearby mines. Campers can stay for free providing they eat at the owner's so-called 'restaurant'. There's no menu du jour as such; instead the owner cooks one huge meal in the evening for everyone and charges diners 1000F. He'll fix lunch on request for about 700F; breakfast is 350F.

One km past Chez Jeanette, also on your right, there is a small *grocery store* and the *Relais de Canala*, a very basic *snack*/café offering a plat du jour for 1000F and Number One beers for 120F.

Getting There & Away

Bus A bus leaves Noumea on weekdays only at 2 pm and travels via La Foa to Canala. The trip takes 3½ hours and costs 900F. For the trip to Noumea, the bus leaves from outside the grocery store on the main road at 5 am, except on Monday, when it's the 2 am mail bus. There are no buses linking Canala and Thio.

Car The Canala-Thio road (sometimes called the Petchecara Road) is, in the words of one traveller, 'an experience not to be missed!'. True, it's also one of the most hair-raising roads in New Caledonia.

The 26-km road includes a 13-km single-lane dirt road, open to traffic from either direction at alternate hours, which snakes up and around a steep hill eventually to cross Col de Petchecara (435 metres). Rock slides, swollen creeks, quagmires and, in parts, missing road are all par for the course. In bad weather it is impassable in a conventional car and even for a 4WD it could be dangerous.

The one-way section starts 13 km south of Canala just past the village of Nakety. From Canala, the road is open during even-numbered hours starting from 6 am; from Thio it's open odd-numbered hours from 7 am. But just because it's one way, don't count on not meeting traffic coming the other direction. Drivers have been known not to bother waiting for their hour to roll round and, when this happens, it's a tight and pretty scary squeeze.

Hitching It would be possible to hitch the Canala-Thio road if you got to the start of the road before the beginning of each designated hour. Bear in mind that if you get to the start and no cars pass in that hour, it'll be another hour before the next car may come along.

In the direction of La Foa, hitching will also be an enterprising pastime and you'll have to consider yourself lucky to catch a ride.

THIO

Thio is the town which, perhaps more than any other, symbolises the Kanaks' fight for independence. A long-time nickel-mining centre, it was dramatically captured by Kanak militants during the Events and, at local elections the following year, came under the control of the FLNKS. Those loyal to France mourned Thio as a martyr.

Today, this gritty town with its colonial buildings and surrounding stripped mountains is a cheerless place where shop windows and homes are covered with a rusty hue. The whole commune is home to about 3000 people, 2500 of whom are Kanaks; according to the local mayor, there is 'almost no contact between races here at Thio'.

History

Nickel was discovered here in 1876, though it wasn't until 1889 that SLN founded the mines. By 1931 there were two fusion factories, one at Ouroue near the present-day town and the other at the mission across the river to the south. Two villages sprouted around the activity – an exclusive White person's

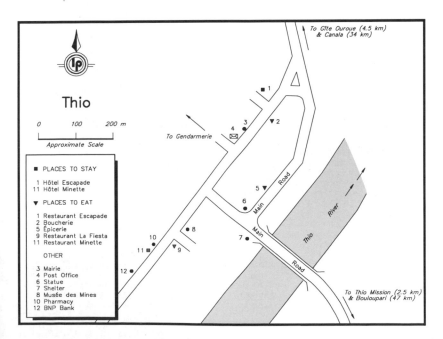

Thio

0   100   200 m
Approximate Scale

To Gîte Ouroue (4.5 km) & Canala (34 km)

To Gendarmerie

To Thio Mission (2.5 km) & Bouloupari (47 km)

Main Road

Thio River

■ PLACES TO STAY
1 Hôtel Escapade
11 Hôtel Minette

▼ PLACES TO EAT
1 Restaurant Escapade
2 Boucherie
5 Épicerie
9 Restaurant La Fiesta
11 Restaurant Minette

OTHER
3 Mairie
4 Post Office
6 Statue
7 Shelter
8 Musée des Mines
10 Pharmacy
12 BNP Bank

domain to the north and the mission, which acted as the home of everyone else. Miners came from Europe, Polynesia and Asia. About 1200 Japanese worked here until their forced expulsion from New Caledonia following the attack on Pearl Harbor in 1941.

In November 1984, two days after the territorial election, Eloi Machoro and 200 FLNKS militants seized the Thio gendarmerie and raised the Kanak flag. The whole town was held under siege for several weeks and mining halted. Machoro explained the action as 'psychological pressure' to get France to grant independence.

Orientation & Information

Thio has two parts – the town centre and Thio Mission – situated three km apart and separated by the Thio River. The latter is the industrial centre. A statue of the Madonna and child indicates your arrival in the town centre where everything lines two parallel streets. The main one rarely bustles to life these days except on pay day (generally the eighth day of the month).

The post office is in an old colonial building and has standard hours. The small BNP bank branch generally caters to miners but will also cash travellers' cheques if you happen to be here on the one day of the week that it's open – Tuesday from 9 am to 4.30 pm.

There's a clinic with a resident French doctor. The gendarmerie (☎ 44.51.23) is just off the main street.

Things to See & Do

Musée des Mines This mine museum (☎ 44.51.78; 44.52.33) on the main street is housed in a lovely restored colonial building with a minuscule old steam train out front. It displays local photographs from the early 1900s and a collection of minerals. It is open Thursdays and weekends from 9 am to noon; entry is free.

Thio Mission & Mines The Catholic mission at Thio was founded in 1913. Set back from the road is a little church whose steeple is visible long before you arrive. After the

---

Eloi Machoro

Eloi Machoro was given many names. To his supporters he was the *chef de guerre* or the leader of the war, while many Caldoches regarded him as a 'militant extremist' whom they targeted with 'Kill Him' graffiti. The media simply dubbed him the South Pacific's Che Guevara. He was a leader who wouldn't compromise, which, according to a friend, is what led to his being isolated from other FLNKS leaders and ultimately to his death.

A former school teacher, Machoro took over the role of UC secretary-general in 1981, after Pierre Declercq was assassinated. In 1984 the Kanak provisional government was formed and, as a tactical strategist, Machoro was appointed the government's security minister. His opponents soon dubbed him 'minister of insecurity', for Machoro was everywhere where there was tension and was intensely hated by the Caldoche community. At the same time, he became a model for Kanak youth who painted his portrait on bus stops and shop walls, depicting him with his characteristic cap, moustache, dark sunglasses and striped T-shirt.

During the boycott of the November 1984 election, Machoro led the 'disruption' of the east-coast mining town of Thio, and a controversial photograph of him smashing a ballot box with an axe appeared in newspapers. A fortnight later, he captured the same town and held it under siege for three weeks. 'We're a peaceful people, but we've been frustrated in our right for independence for too long,' he explained at the time.

One month later, Machoro, 38, was shot dead by paramilitary sharpshooters. The circumstances of his shooting have remained a controversy. The police version was that Machoro and 35 other Kanaks were in the farmhouse when gendarmes called on them to surrender. According to the official statement, Machoro came out firing, so police fired back twice, one shot killing Machoro and the other Nonaro. The FLNKS leadership rejected this version, saying the men came out of the house to parley when they were gunned down. Tjibaou, Machoro's partner in the struggle, described it as a 'barbarous act showing the violence of colonialism.' ∎

church, there's not much to see except for some mining houses, a few dilapidated sheds and, eventually, a messy beach.

From the beach you can see the nickel mines on the north-western plateau at Ouroue. To the south-east, ore is transported in buckets along a cable and then loaded into ships bound for Noumea (once a week) or Japan (five times a year) for processing.

The mission turn-off is one km south of Thio bridge. From here it's another 1½ km.

Places to Stay & Eat

The most pleasant place to stay around Thio is *Gîte Ouroue* (☎ 44.51.63), stretched along the beachfront 4½ km from town off the road to Canala. You can camp here for 500F – there's a cold shower – or stay in one of four bungalows which have views of coconut palms and the water. The family who runs the gîte lives in a haphazard array of sheds and lean-tos at the far end of the grounds. The bungalows, all lined and thatched with niaouli bark, cost 3000F for up to three people. Simple meals are available for 1200F, a fish dinner costs 1500F and a lobster feast is 2000F (the latter's available only if you warn them in advance). Breakfast is 300F.

The gîte is signposted but it's easily missed if you're coming from Canala; look out for a wooden bridge. From the turn-off, it's 1½ km to the beach.

In Thio itself, accommodation is very basic. The *Escapade* (☎ 44.53.10), just off the main street to the north and marked by a Heineken sign, has singles/doubles for 1200F. The building is about 100 years old and has wide porches, pointed roofs and shuttered windows. The Escapade's restaurant serves a set dinner including dessert for 1200F; petit déjeuner is 450F. It is closed Saturday evening and Sunday.

Restaurant Minette has some bungalows in a row out the back which cost 3500F for two people. Its lunch-time menu du jour is 1300F. The restaurant is closed on weekends.

La Fiesta (☎ 44.51.81) is a tiny but cosy room where Chinese lunches are dished up for 800F and meat or chicken meals for 900F. Both these last two restaurants may be open for dinner, depending on the number of clients available.

Getting There & Away

Bus Buses from Noumea travel the RT4 to Thio, leaving Monday to Saturday at 11.30 am. The trip takes 2½ hours and costs 800F. To Noumea, there is one bus a day leaving at 4.30 am. There are no buses from Thio to Canala.

Car Bouloupari is 47 km away, roughly an hour's drive, along the good but windy RT4 over the Col de Nassirah (350 metres). This road was constructed by Kanak labourers during the days of the indigénat system. For details on the road to Canala, see the previous Canala – Getting There & Away section.

Hitching It is easy to hitchhike to Bouloupari or even Noumea from Thio.

The North-West Coast

Much of the north-west coast has been cattle country since the early colonial days, when settlers claimed the land and the Kanaks were moved onto reservations. It is estimated that 93% of the land in this region belongs to Caldoche families of these original folk.

Everything here – the landscape, climate, people and atmosphere – is different from that across the mountain range to the east. The scenery can be quite monotonous, the rounded brown hills often begging for rain as they stretch down to grassy plains. These, in turn, are swallowed up by coastal mangrove swamps and shallow bays where the beaches are nothing to get excited about. Be warned: in season the beaches are favourite hunting grounds for mosquitoes. In the far north, beyond Koumac, is savane à niaoulis, while around Nepoui the hills have been sliced open for nickel mining.

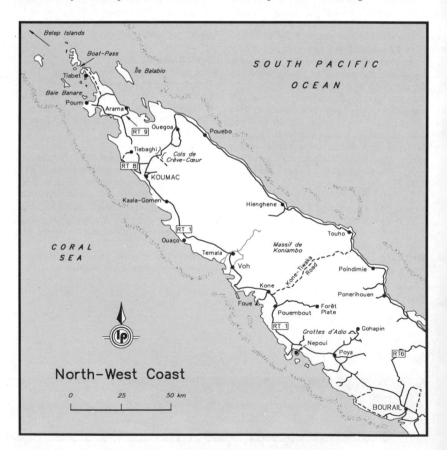

North–West Coast

Administratively, this coast is halved between the RPCR-controlled South Province and the FLNKS-ruled North Province, based at Kone. Poya is the border. This division is relatively new (since the Matignon Accords) and therefore the atmosphere of most towns along here is still distinctly 'Caldoche'. Particularly south of Poya, the towns maintain a well-ordered, middle-class aura that makes them rather bland and predictable. The RT1 acts as a divide, with Kanak settlements usually nestled at the end of a river valley on the eastern, inland, side. Rarely do they occupy land west of the road.

Many of the young Caldoches with inherited land can't make a living raising cattle in what has become a depressed industry. So the land is not used and has become overgrown. Meanwhile, Kanak communities are calling for the return of their tribal lands, an issue that has only started to be resolved.

GETTING THERE & AWAY

The RT1 is a good sealed road, skirting the mountains all the way from Noumea to Poum in the north, through flat or slightly hilly country. Only very rarely does it go near the sea. Until 1994, when the new Kone-Tiwaka road is due to open, there are just two roads (one from Bourail, the other from Koumac) leading off from the north-west across the mountains to the east.

Air

Air Calédonie has flights from Noumea's Magenta Airport to Kone and Koumac, and farther to the Belep Islands (see those sections for details). It's also possible to get a charter flight from Noumea to Malabou Beach Hôtel north of Koumac (see Koumac to Poum – Malabou Beach Hôtel).

Bus

Bourail and Koumac are the major north-west coast junctions. While many buses travel the entire distance from Noumea to Koumac, some go only as far as Bourail or Kone, hence services to these two towns (and all places en route) are slightly more frequent than to Koumac. From Bourail, a few buses head across the Col des Roussettes to Houailou and other places on the north-east coast. Only the occasional bus goes from Koumac north to Poum or to the east coast villages of Ouegoa and Pouebo (for details see Koumac – Getting There & Away).

The following timetable lists departure times of buses travelling the north-west coast from both Noumea and Koumac. These buses drop off and pick up passengers in every main town or large village (see the second table for destinations, journey times and fares).

	from Noumea	from Koumac
Monday	4.05 am	4.05 am
	10.00 am	7.30 am
	11.30 am	9.15 am
		11.45 am
Tuesday	4.05 am	4.05 am
	10.00 am	9.15 am
	11.30 am	11.45 am
Wednesday	4.05 am	4.05 am
	8.00 am	9.15 am
	10.00 am	11.45 am
	11.30 am	
Thursday	4.05 am	4.05 am
	10.00 am	7.30 am
	11.30 am	9.15 am
		11.45 am
Friday	4.05 am	4.05 am
	11.30 am	11.45 am
	5.45 pm	5.30 pm
	6.00 pm	
Saturday	4.05 am	4.05 am
	11.30 am	11.45 am
Sunday	10 am	9.15 am
	11.30 am	11.45 am

The table below lists the journey times from both Noumea and Koumac to various north-west coast destinations and the one-way fare from Noumea:

	Fare from Noumea	Time from Noumea	Time from Koumac
Bourail	900F	2½ hours	3 hours
Poya	1000F	3¼ hours	2¼ hours
Nepoui	1100F	3¾ hours	1¾ hours
Pouembout	1100F	4 hours	1½ hours
Kone	1100F	4¼ hours	1¼ hours
Voh	1200F	4½ hours	1 hour
Kaala-Gomen	1400F	5¼ hours	¼ hour
Koumac	1450F	5½ hours	

BOURAIL

Bourail (population 4100; pronounced 'boo-rai' as in 'Thai') is New Caledonia's second largest town, sitting on the plain 162 km from the capital.

It was founded in 1867 as a penitentiary and had the typical array of convict facilities – male and female cells, the commander's quarters, a storehouse and bakery and later a school and post office – nearly all built by the inmates. Connected to the sea by the wide Nera River, a port was built and sheds were erected as accommodation for freed convicts. Bourail grew to a large settlement of 400 families but in 1897, when the flow of convicts stopped, the town stagnated and became just like any other rural village. In the early 19th century, small enterprises such as an oil-pressing mill, a tannery and a *sucrerie* for making sugar kept the town alive, until WW II when many New Zealand troops were stationed here.

Bourail is still a strong Caldoche commu-nity with pastimes such as deer hunting and fishing. The nearby coast, with its famous landmark, La Roche Percée, and sandy beach, Plage de Poe, welcomes many visi-tors. Before arriving in the town from the south you'll pass Arab and New Zealand cemeteries.

Orientation & Information

You'd have to be totally devoid of a sense of direction to get lost in Bourail. There is just one main street – the RT1, locally known as Rue Simon Drémon – which is prone to intense flooding during cyclones. Every-thing is located along this street – the midway point is the humble white church with its French flag. From here, it's two km south to the turn-off at the Nera River bridge to Plage de Poe and La Roche Percée.

Post Bourail's little post office is opposite the old mairie. It has the standard provincial week-day opening hours – from 7.45 to 11.15 am

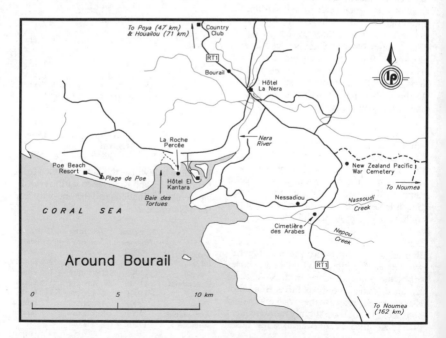

and 12.15 to 3.00 pm. On Saturday it's open from 7.45 to 11 am.

Money The Westpac bank is at the northern end of Rue Simon Drémon, open weekdays from 7.45 am to 3.30 pm.

Bookshop Librairie Charlemagne, halfway along Rue Simon Drémon, sells copies of two Australian magazines, *Women's Weekly* and *Women's Day*, but little else in English.

Emergency Bourail's hospital and the gendarmerie (☎ 44.12.70) are on a hill on the town's southern outskirts. There's also a large pharmacy on Rue Simon Drémon.

Things to See
Bourail Museum About 800 metres south from the town centre, the Bourail Museum (☎ 44.16.66) greets visitors with a large imprint on its stone wall: *'Ce que nous savons est peu de chose en regard de ce que nous ne savons pas'* – 'What we know is little compared with what we don't know'. It's an appropriate expression for this little museum, which crams as much as possible into its premises including, out the back, a grande case.

The main building was originally a store house where freed convicts received food and clothing for the first 30 months after release. It later functioned as a school and then a *fromagerie* (a place where cheese is made) until WW II, when the Americans arrived and preferred corned beef to cheese. It was renovated in 1984.

The museum integrates the different cultural and historic influences in New Caledonia, from a local point of view. It focuses on the early settlers of Bourail, recreating a typical kitchen and bedroom accompanied by a display of antique farming equipment. There are photographs of the stoic French settlers with their proud faces and peasant-like features. The museum displays a few artefacts used by the Kanaks from around Bourail, including baskets, war clubs and traditional ceremonial objects. There's a vast shell collection and a display of petroglyphs.

WW II is depicted by an extensive series of B&W photos of New Zealand troops. Original plans marking out the site of the New Zealand war cemetery and lists of the names of those buried there are pinned to the wall.

The museum is open Wednesday, Saturday and Sunday from 8 to 11 am and 1 to 5 pm. Outside these times, you can still see the *case* if you just wander around the back. Admission is free and there are some English explanations.

La Roche Percée Translated as 'the pierced rock', La Roche Percée is the north-west coast's only unusual rock formation and so it features on every tourist brochure and postcard of the region. It's seven km from the RT1 turn-off, en route to Plage de Poe.

Unlike most of Grande Terre, the coastline at this point is protected by neither barrier nor fringing reefs, giving the sea the chance to carve out a rugged coast with many sea caves. La Roche Percée's hard quartz was eroded by centuries of battering into its present statuesque form with a yawning hollow. Another name frequently used is *'Bonhomme'* – 'fellow', because it is shaped like a human face. At low tide it's possible to wander through the hollow or climb around the base of the rock to Baie des Tortues, a

La Roche Percée

quaint little beach which is hidden on the other side.

On top of La Roche Percée, the **Belvédère lookout** offers views enveloping the entire area – the Nera River, the beaches on either side of the rock, and the wide bay. A small statue of Notre Dame des Flots, erected in 1990 and draped with pieces of cloth, looks out to sea to the ships she's supposed to protect. The lookout can be reached via a steep track that begins on the beach next to La Roche Percée or, with a car, along a dirt road on the left, one km past the rock turn-off. Keep bearing to the left along this road until the end.

Baie des Tortues This pristine cove, towered over by araucaria pines, is now and then the morning haunt of turtles, hence its name (though you'll have to be lucky and very early to see them). The bay is accessible by vehicle from the road that leads to the Belvédère lookout. When you get to the fork, take the road to the right.

Plage de Poe Possibly the nicest beach on this stretch of the north-west coast, Plage de Poe (pronounced 'poh-weh') is an 18-km stretch of fine sand and lovely shells. The water is very shallow and warm, and snorkelling is OK once you pass the weed and meet the clownfish and triggerfish and the odd sea snake.

From the RT1 turn-off near Bourail, it's 15½ km to the start of the beach, where there's a casual camping ground and a seafood restaurant. About 1½ km farther is Poe Beach Resort.

New Zealand Pacific War Cemetery Flanking the RT1 about 9½ km south of Bourail, this cemetery is the resting place for 212 soldiers killed in the Pacific War. They were mainly men from the Royal NZ Army and Airforce, but some of those buried here were from local and Solomon Islands forces. In addition, the cemetery acts as a memorial to another 450 soldiers whose bodies were never found.

The majority of the NZ troops arrived in 1942 to train for jungle warfare against the Japanese. They were stationed in five camps in the Bourail region, between Camp du Cap in the north and the Boghen area south-east of the town. The cemetery is on land which belonged to a local farmer who had good relations with the soldiers. Four long rows of graves sweep down to a cross and a wall inscribed with the names of the dead, while inside the small brick shelter is a Commonwealth War Graves Commission register listing all the men commemorated here.

Cimetière des Arabes This Arab cemetery is between the Nepou and Nassoudi creeks, close to Nessadiou about 2½ km south of the New Zealand cemetery (or 12 km south of Bourail). It's easily seen from the road.

A crescent and star mark the gate, but many of the graves have no inscription. The origins of those buried here date back to the 1871 Berber insurrection in the former French colony of Algeria. These rebels were deported to Île des Pins where they raised goats and sold their cheese at the market. In 1880 a general amnesty for all political prisoners was given, but the Berbers were forgotten, achieving freedom only at the end of their prison terms. While some then worked to pay their passage back home, others chose to stay, settling around Nessadiou, where they had been allocated land. They kept their religion and traditions, and many of these original families are buried in this immaculately tended cemetery.

Activities
Horse Trekking You can spend a weekend, organised by Marcel Velayoudon, in the mountains around Bourail (☎ 44.14.90 between 7 and 8 pm). With a minimum of six riders he offers weekend treks of one/two/three days for 8000/12,000/19,000F per person, meals included. Accommodation is at Marcel's country hideaway where meals are prepared for you. A typical two-day excursion would involve riding into the mountains followed by deer hunting in the late afternoon, which of course is not obligatory. The route into his camp follows a mountain ridge

with spectacular views. On day two, the group drops in on a tribal community and follows a different route on horseback to Bourail.

Places to Stay

All of Bourail's coastal accommodation is heavily booked by Noumeans on long weekends and school holidays.

Camping Bourail's closest official *camping ground* (☎ 44.14.10) is at Plage de Poe, 15½ km from the Nera Bridge turn-off. It's a lovely spot, right on the beachfront and with plenty of shade. Camping costs 400F per tent and is payable to the guardian who lives on the spot. There are cold showers, toilets and an expensive restaurant nearby.

Otherwise, there are two places you can camp for free en route to Plage de Poe, though keep in mind there is no fresh water. The first is the long beach at La Roche Percée; however, this site is unprotected and sometimes mosquito-infested because of the slow-running Nera River. The adjacent Baie des Tortues is more endearing and secluded.

Hotels – middle The wise choice in this bracket is *Hôtel El Kantara* (☎ 44.13.22; fax

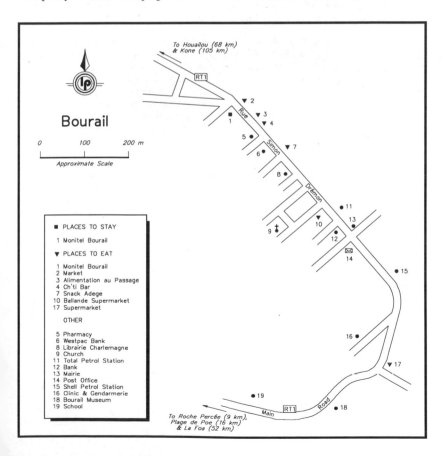

To Houailou (68 km)
& Kone (105 km)

RT1

Bourail

0   100   200 m

Approximate Scale

Rue Simon

Drémon

To Houailou (68 km)

■ PLACES TO STAY

1 Monitel Bourail

▼ PLACES TO EAT

1 Monitel Bourail
2 Market
3 Alimentation au Passage
4 Ch'ti Bar
7 Snack Adege
10 Ballande Supermarket
17 Supermarket

OTHER

5 Pharmacy
6 Westpac Bank
8 Librairie Charlemagne
9 Church
11 Total Petrol Station
12 Bank
13 Mairie
14 Post Office
15 Shell Petrol Station
16 Clinic & Gendarmerie
18 Bourail Museum
19 School

Main   RT1   Road

To Roche Percée (9 km),
Plage de Poe (16 km)
& La Foa (52 km)

44.20.33), BP 244 Bourail, situated along the Nera River near La Roche Percée. It has been highly recommended by several sources – one group of travellers even awarded the owner their 'most considerate host' title.

Set in bushy surroundings (mosquitoes can be bad), this slightly Moorish-style hotel, built by a nostalgic pied noir, has a swimming pool and restaurant. Its 20 rooms, all with private facilities, are set out in long blocks of adjoining units. Singles/doubles cost 4400F; an extra person is charged 800F. There's a 380F hotel tax and it's 800F extra if you want a key to make the air-conditioner work. Behind the hotel on the river bank is a monument where Japanese newly weds like to be photographed.

To get to the hotel, turn off to the left at La Roche Percée and follow this road for one km. It's well signposted. If you're stuck for transport, the manager will arrange a free lift from Bourail.

The new *Hôtel La Nera* (☎ 44.16.44; fax 44.18.31), on the RT1 at the turn-off to Plage de Poe, is next to the Nera River and offers lots of water activities. However it's also right on the highway and not too tranquil.

It has eight rooms, all with tea/coffee facilities, TV, private facilities and air-con. They cost 4800/5600F for one/two people or 6400F for three or four. There is one room known as the 'honeymoon suite' which has a bathroom *en suite* plus a salon in addition to the rest. It costs 7200F for any would-be bride or groom who's been stood up, 8000F if you've tied the knot, or 8800F if the two of you are there with a chaperon. The hotel has a package deal whereby you get dinner and a room plus breakfast for 8400/12,800/17,100F for one/two/three people.

Hôtel La Nera has a swimming pool and spa, rents canoes for 500F per hour and organises 10-minute jet-boat rides along the river for 1000F. At night, it does 4WD excursions to spot deer and, for those so inclined, expensive hunting can also be arranged.

Lastly there's the *Country Club* (☎ 44.11.50), four km north of Bourail. It's a bar/restaurant/disco/trucker's stop which, when we last visited, was run-down and

gloomy, with basic single rooms for 4600F. Each extra person is charged 800F and air-con is 800F on top.

Hotels – top end Bourail has two new hotels in this bracket. In town, the *Monitel Bourail* (☎ 44.17.77; fax 44.16.33), BP 499 Bourail, at the northern end of Rue Simon Drémon, opened in 1992 and is modern but slightly sterile. It has 18 rooms in a multi-level complex. Singles/doubles with bath are 5500F; if you'd prefer a shower instead these rooms cost 6500/7000F. Extra guests are charged 500F each.

Alternatively there's the *Poe Beach Resort* (☎ 44.18.50; fax 44.10.70), BP 481 Bourail, at the far end of Plage de Poe, 17 km from the RT1 turn-off. Tranquillity, a turquoise lagoon, the beach on your doorstep, and colourful sprays of bougainvillaea are all reminders that you're sojourning in the tropics. Of course, it's not everyone's cup of tea. One LP reader wrote to say he thought the place looked like 'a stack of army huts in the Libyan desert'. So much for the tropics!

Opened in early 1991, the resort has an assortment of attractive cabins, each made into either adjoining double rooms or single private bungalows. The 24 rooms have a fan, shower, TV, and refrigerator and cost 6100F for two people. The six bungalows have air-con, bath, TV and fridge and are rented for 8000F for two. An extra person is charged 500F.

The host of available activities (prices are listed for an hour's rental) include horse riding (2000F); glass-bottom boats (1000F); sailboards (1500F); and catamarans (2000F). A 20-minute flight in an ultra-light plane can be arranged for 4500F. Excursions around Bourail cost 1500F. Tennis, the swimming pool, pétanque, volleyball, darts and ping-pong are all free.

Places to Eat
Snacks Several operators have kiosks on Rue Simon Drémon. One of the most popular is *Snack Adege*, run by an Indonesian family, which has lunch and dinner for about 1000F.

Restaurants – In Town The *Monitel*'s elegant restaurant is probably the best value around, especially for those in need of a substantial meal. Its 1500F menu du jour includes coffee but is available only for weekday lunches. For the remainder, it's à la carte. A petit déjeuner costs 500F.

Across the road is the *Ch'ti Bar* (☎ 44. 13.94), a breezy pizzeria/bar popular with locals and passers-by for quick coffees, leisurely beers, pizzas starting at 1000F or other main dishes from 1100F.

The *Country Club* (see Places to Stay above) has an ordinary weekday lunch-time menu du jour for 2000F.

Restaurants – Outside Bourail The tidy restaurant at *Hôtel La Nera* serves traditional French cuisine with an emphasis on local game – that is, venison. It serves à la carte only, with main meals costing between 1200F and 1500F. Breakfast is 450F.

The *Hôtel El Kantara* has both à la carte and a variety of menus du jour, the latter starting at 1850F. Breakfast is served for 450F. This place is open daily.

The first place you come to at Plage de Poe is *L'Eden Roc* (☎ 44.10.65), a restaurant/bar with a large terrace and lovely timbered interior. It opened in 1990 and offers a mouthwatering selection of seafood as well as other dishes. Entrées such as a normal salad cost 800F or there is salade océan including seafood for 1100F. A main course crevettes à l'ail (garlic prawns) costs 1650F and meat dishes cost 1400F. This place is closed Sunday evening, all day Monday and Tuesday at lunch time.

Finally *Poe Beach Resort's* delightful restaurant, overlooking the pool and the water, serves expensive à la carte, a menu du jour for 1950F and continental breakfast for 600F.

Self-Catering The *Ballande* supermarket next to the church is open daily except Sunday and has all the essentials. For longer trading hours there's *Alimentation au Passage*, a busy épicerie at the northern end of town, open daily from 5.30 am to 8 pm. On Sunday it closes for a few hours at lunch time. Alter-natively, a handful of local Kanak women set up a *market* in the shelter opposite the Monitel hotel on Tuesday and Saturday mornings.

Getting There & Away
Bourail is the major junction for all vehicles travelling between Noumea and the east and west coasts of Grande Terre. Depending on your destination, either end of town is an excellent spot for hitching.

Bus All buses stop here for half an hour, usually outside either Snack Adege or Alimentation au Passage at the northern end of the main street. The 2½-hour trip between Noumea and Bourail costs 900F.

From Noumea to Bourail there are buses at 4.05, 9.30 and 11.30 am Monday to Satur-day. In addition to these regular services, from Monday to Thursday there are buses at 10 am and 12.30 pm; on Wednesday there's a bus a 8 am; on Friday there are buses at 5.30, 5.45 and 6 pm; and on Saturday there's one at 11.45 am. On Sunday buses leave at 10, 11.30 am and 1 pm.

Heading from Bourail to Noumea, there are buses Monday to Saturday at 8.15, 9.50 am and 2.55 pm (the latter also on Sunday). In addition, there's a daily bus (except on Friday and Sunday) at 6.30 am and another (except on Friday and Saturday) at 12.30 pm. On Monday and Thursday there's one at 11 am, on Friday at 8.45 pm and on Sunday at 2 and 3 pm.

Most buses arriving from Noumea will either continue along the north-west coast or cross to the north-east.

POYA TO POUEMBOUT
Poya
This rather nondescript town (population 1900) started out as a military post in the late 1800s. These days its main activities centre around the mining industry at nearby Nepoui. It has the standard administrative buildings stretched out along the RT1, including a gendarmerie (☎ 47.17.17), petrol station and general store. But there's little to offer tourists and no accommodation or places to eat.

Grottes d'Adio

Two km north of Poya is the turn-off to the Grottes d'Adio or Adio Caves. Situated 14 km inland along a dirt road which sees little traffic, it's a side trip feasible only for those with a car.

To get to the caves, turn right at the first fork, cross the river and continue straight through the valley, skirting the Massif du Boulinda on your left. There are a couple of creek crossings including one that would be impassable after heavy rain. The dirt road eventually winds up to a col where a rough track leads off to the left. There *might* be a signpost. The track is not fit for cars, so you'll have to walk the final km from here.

En route, you'll see a monolith of black rock in the distance – the cave is at the side of its base. When you get to an abandoned shelter, turn left (don't cross the creek) and continue for 50 metres to the rock wall. Here is the well-camouflaged narrow entrance to the grotte. You'll need a good torch and a strong sense of adventure to dare to go any farther.

Back on the road, if you continue beyond the cave turn-off towards the tribal village of Gohapin, you'll eventually pass a huge lime-stone nugget, the Roche d'Adio. Gohapin, 25 km from Poya, marks the geographical heart of the island. Just before the village, there's a foot/4WD track which leads up and over the 1000-metre-high mountain range with the Réserve de l'Aoupinie on its eastern slopes.

Nepoui

This little coastal enclave of brown bunga-lows and potholed streets is the north-west coast's main mining centre. Though ear-marked to be a future deep-water port and industrial centre, at present it's simply a small town perched on a hill above the sea and a nickel-loading wharf. The centre is an uninspiring grid of streets lined with num-bered miners' bungalows. There's a petrol station, Mag Co supermarket and gendar-merie (☎ 47.11.51).

The turn-off to Nepoui from the RT1 is on Col de Mueo, 19 km north of Poya. It's six km from there. North of the pass, the mining environment is immediately obvious. A con-veyor belt careers down the side of the Massif de Kopeto to the east. The tops of the mountains have been sliced open and mud and erosion streams scar the slopes.

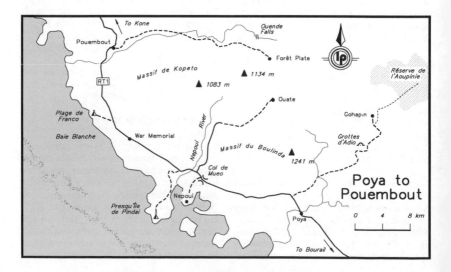

Places to Stay & Eat The sole place in town is the inappropriately named *Le Passage* (☎ 47.12.28). Its 12 basic rooms are occupied by well-entrenched regulars, but if there happens to be a vacancy, you'll get the room for 3000F per night. The restaurant has a 1500F menu du jour (weekdays only) and breakfast for 500F. To find the place, turn left after the supermarket on the main road into town and follow the road until the signpost.

Beaches

Between Nepoui and Pouembout are two quite desolate beaches where you can picnic or pitch your tent for free. Neither is really remarkable, as each is stony rather than sandy and home to plenty of mosquitoes.

The first is at the end of **Presqu'Île de Pindai**, the peninsula west of Nepoui. A dirt track five km past the Nepoui turn-off leads to the beach, which is nine km away. From here you'll see the occasional ship full of Nepoui nickel gliding by as it works its way out of the lagoon.

Otherwise, 11 km south of Pouembout is the turn-off for **Plage de Franco**. This beach, at the end of a three-km track, is lined with trees and has a few derelict timber picnic sheds and fresh water.

War Memorial

On top of a hill, halfway between Nepoui and Pouembout, is the Mémorial de la Plaine des Gaïacs, commemorating the Allied fighters who 'paid with their lives for the freedom of the Pacific' during WW II. This drab memorial consists of a wall of round bronze-coloured dots with a broken wooden carving at one end and wooden kangaroo, boomerang and kiwi sculptures at the other. A dirt road winds up to the plateau from where there's a view of the flat scrubby land leading to the turquoise Baie Blanche. Looking towards the sea you can make out the faint outline of what was a wartime airstrip.

POUEMBOUT

Pouembout (population 900) is one of Grande Terre's most expanding villages.

With the recent construction of the Hôtel de la Province du Nord (North Province administrative headquarters), just to the north on the road to Kone, and its position as a future gateway to the east coast, Pouembout has seen a building boom unparalleled for a New Caledonian village of its size. The new Kone-Tiwaka highway to the east coast starts at the huge roundabout in front of the province headquarters.

Orientation & Information

Coming in from the south, the RT1 does a sharp turn to the left at a new shopping complex before continuing towards Kone. The village's only hotel is before this junction, while the post office is just around from the turn.

The new cream-coloured shopping centre has a Crédit Lyonnais bank, open all day Tuesday to Friday and from 7 am to 1.45 pm on Saturday, where you can cash travellers' cheques. It also contains a bookshop, Nopa Nord, which stocks a couple of Lonely Planet guides to Pacific regions but no English magazines or newspapers.

Things to See

The village's prize possession is a beautiful, two-storey stone building called **Le Pigeonnier** (the pigeon house), standing alone near the post office on the road north to Kone. According to local legend it was built in 1898, from the ballast stones used in the convict ships. Restored in the early 1980s, it is now the municipal library.

Inland from Pouembout, the road past the *hippodrome* (race track) leads to the Kanak community of Forêt Plate, 25 km away. A few km before the settlement, a track to the left winds for 1½ km to the 100-metre-high **Ouende waterfall**.

Places to Stay & Eat

The new *Hôtel/Relais Le Bougainville* (☎ 35.52.55; fax 35.59.84) at the southern entry to Pouembout, has perhaps the largest and most impressive replica of a grande case (made for commercial purposes) to be found in New Caledonia. The restaurant and hotel reception occupy the entire *case* with a large wooden bar counter curling around the rear wall.

The hotel has six bungalows, somewhat haphazardly placed around the garden but nice enough, and a line of seven basic but clean rooms at the back of the complex. They sleep up to four, costing 4000F for one/two people plus 500F for each extra person. Optional air-con is 800F. The restaurant serves a good-value menu du jour including coffee for 1500F. It's available for lunch and dinner, weekdays only. French and Asian à la carte cuisine is also served; the restaurant is closed Sundays.

Self-caterers will find a small but modern *Uniprix* supermarket, with all the essentials, in the new shopping centre. It is open weekdays from 6.30 am to noon and 1 to 7 pm, and on Saturday morning. Opposite Hôtel Le Bougainville, *Comptoir de Pouembout* (the Counter of Pouembout) is a small épicerie open daily from 6 am to 8 pm and Sunday from 6 am to 1 pm and 5 to 8 pm.

Getting There & Away
All Noumea-Koumac buses stop at Pouembout (for details see the tables in the Getting There & Away section at the start of this chapter). In addition to those services, other buses leave Noumea, Monday to Saturday at 9.30 am and on Sunday at 1 pm. To Noumea, there's an extra bus from Monday to Saturday which passes through Pouembout at 8.15 am and another on Sunday at 12.25 pm.

KONE
Kone (population 3000; pronounced 'koh-nay') is a fairly large town, surrounded by the rolling hills of the Massif de Koniambo and flat cattle pastures. Like Pouembout to the south, it has grown significantly in recent times, evidenced by the number of hotels which have sprung up in the last five years. The development is due to Kone's preparations to become the capital of the North Province, whose Melanesian-style headquarters were erected several km south of the town in 1992.

Despite all this hubbub, Kone is still essentially a rustic settlement. Some old colonial buildings dot the town's small centre. They were left over from the late 1800s when it was founded as an important military post following the 1878 Kanak revolt. Mining on the nickel-rich Koniambo mountains started in 1904, employing about 200 people until its closure in 1928.

To the south-west of town is the Foue Plain where the geologist Pirouet uncovered finely decorated Lapita pottery in 1917. This pottery has been an essential part of dating and recording the earliest Melanesian settlers, and in trying to learn more about their way of life.

Orientation
Kone sits between two waterways, with the larger Kone River marking the southern border. The RT1 goes straight through town, skirting a roundabout with a WW II monument in the centre. Just off this roundabout is the mairie, where the FLNKS flag flies

---

Lapita Pottery
The pottery found at Lapita, as the site near Kone became known, formed the basis of the Lapita culture theory. Compared with other archaeological findings elsewhere in the Pacific, it allowed researchers to understand better the original Melanesian migration patterns.

Having its origins in the late Neolithic cultures of the Philippines and East Indonesia, the Lapita culture penetrated the West Pacific between 2000 BC and 1000 BC. The people were highly mobile Austronesian-speaking voyagers with an advanced maritime technology. They lived on fish, pigs and domestic fowl.

In New Caledonia the pottery styles differed in the north and south, varying from simply decorated objects to those showing a more elaborate approach using handles and glazes. Around 300 AD, Lapita pottery disappeared throughout Melanesia. ∎

Top: Thatching the roof after a cyclone (GC)
Bottom: The ubiquitous roadside stall (LL)

Top: The turquoise waters and towering araucarias of Île des Pins (LL)
Bottom Left: Fishing from coral rocks, Lifou (LL)
Bottom Right: Spectacular palms and pinnacles near Hienghene (GC)

alongside the French tricolour, an unusual sight for a town on this side of Grande Terre but essential for one with provincial capital status. Before the Kone River bridge to Foue a road turns off the RT1– it's six km down a flat dusty road to the beach and wharf.

Information

There are two banks where you can cash travellers' cheques and change money. The Westpac is open weekdays only from 7.45 am to 3.45 pm. The BNP has roughly the same hours except it has a lunch break from 11.15 am to 12.30 pm. The dispensaire and gendarmerie (☎ 35.51.17) are up the hill behind the post office, which is open normal hours.

Things to See & Do

Except for a wander past the few colonial buildings in town, there's little to see in Kone. Tuesday evening is movie night when a film, dubbed in French, is screened in the school opposite the post office.

Horse Trekking Kone is probably most noted for its excellent horse-riding terrain. Kone Rodéo (☎ 35.51.51), run by Patrick

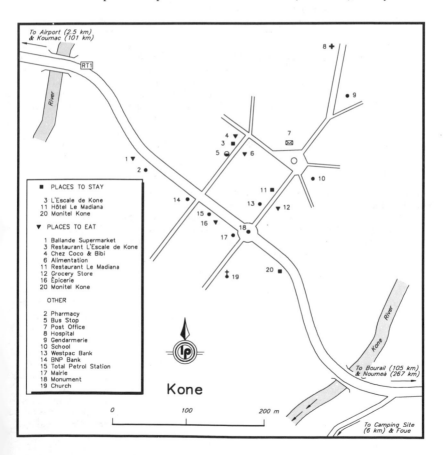

■	PLACES TO STAY
3	L'Escale de Kone
11	Hôtel Le Madiana
20	Monitel Kone

▼	PLACES TO EAT
1	Ballande Supermarket
3	Restaurant L'Escale de Kone
4	Chez Coco & Bibi
6	Alimentation
11	Restaurant Le Madiana
12	Grocery Store
16	Épicerie
20	Monitel Kone

OTHER

2	Pharmacy
5	Bus Stop
7	Post Office
8	Hospital
9	School
10	Gendarmerie
13	Westpac Bank
14	BNP Bank
15	Total Petrol Station
17	Mairie
18	Monument
19	Church

Kone

Ardimani, organises treks into the untamed regions around town. The stables are two km north of town, down a dirt road to the right, and should be signposted. With at least two riders, Patrick will organise two-hour treks for 2000F per person. He can also organise full-day rides with a bougna lunch *chez* the Pwanaki clan to the north and some afternoon cattle herding for 6000F. With a free long weekend, six riders and 22,000F each, he'll arrange a trek into Grande Terre's central mountain chain. Over the three days you'll fish for prawns, hunt deer (only if you want) and have a bougna with the Ateu, the Pwanaki's northern neighbour. All meals and accommodation are included.

Places to Stay

Camping Kone offers two free camping possibilities. The one closer to town is the spacious grounds of the *Hôtel Koniambo*; however a condition of camping is that you must have at least a lunch or dinner in the hotel's restaurant.

Alternatively there's the beach at Foue. It's quite a nice spot and slightly protected from the wind, though this could be bad news in mosquito season. A Melanesian-style thatched shelter provides shade and there are cement barbecues and tables. Cold showers are attached to the wall of a boat shed. A few locals who fish for a living dwell at the end of the beach. Except for weekends and school holidays, this place is rarely crowded. It's six km from Kone. At the fork towards the end of the dirt road, take the road to the left. The one to the right leads to a little wharf.

Hotels The cheapest rooms in town are at the *L'Escale de Kone* (☎ 35.51.09) across from the post office. Owned by a big friendly ni-Vanuatu guy, its appeal is its price and the crumbling colonial grandeur of the hotel's façade. There are two types of rooms – old or new. The seven old, basic rooms with cement floors, communal toilet and shower cost 3880F for one or two people. Adjacent is the new, double-storey block of eight small rooms, all with private facilities, which sleep four people and cost 4880F per night.

The next rung up the price ladder is the *Hôtel Le Madiana* (☎ 35.50.09), next to the Westpac bank. It has four rooms, situated motel-style at the back of the main building. All are pretty sparse – a table, beds and private shower and toilet. Prices start at 3200F for one person, rising by 1100F for each extra person. Supplementary air-con is 700F.

The best choice in Kone is the *Hôtel Koniambo* (☎ 35.51.86; fax 35.53.03), BP 35 Kone, opposite the airport on the RT1 about three km north of the centre. Run by the friendly, English-speaking Yannick Girard, the complex has, amongst other things, a swimming pool and a few tame deer. You have a choice in accommodation: either a row of motel rooms featuring private cooking facilities or individual cabins (minus kitchen) designed to make woodcutters from the Rocky Mountains feel very much at home. Prices for the rooms and cabins are the same – 5000F for one person and 500F for each extra person. Air-con is another 500F. The hotel offers a weekend package deal, particularly good value if you're solo, for 6000F per person including one night's accommodation, lunch, dinner and breakfast.

Kone's top-end abode is the *Monitel Kone* (☎ 35.52.61; fax 35.55.35), a modern hotel at the southern entry to town with single/double rooms for 6500/7000F. Like the one in Bourail, it's comfortable but radiates an impersonal atmosphere.

Places to Eat

Restaurants *L'Escale de Kone* has an unpretentious restaurant with a friendly small-town atmosphere. It offers a great-value menu du jour including entrée, main course, bread, dessert, a quarter-litre carafe of wine, and coffee for 1500F, available at lunch and dinner from Monday to Thursday. On Friday and Saturday à la carte only is served; on Sunday it is closed. The food is not exceptional but it'll fill you up. Snacks and sandwiches are available any time from 4.30 am (when it opens for a 400F breakfast) until 9.30 pm.

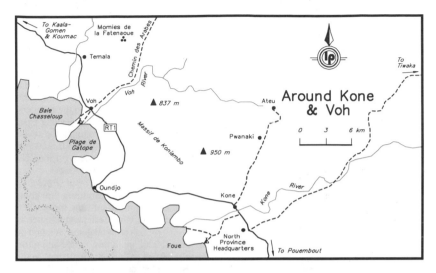

Around Kone & Voh

The *Hôtel Le Madiana* has a plain restaurant which serves breakfast for 400F, sandwiches for 300F, and a lunch-time menu du jour for 1750F. In the evening à la carte is featured. The restaurant is closed on Sunday and, if you happen to be here on a Saturday night, dining is by reservation only.

The restaurant at *Hôtel Koniambo* is popular with locals for a night out. It has a rustic decor of polished niaouli timber and a few sculptures by the late Charles Weiss, the woodcarver who made the works of art in the Koumac church. A menu du jour, coffee included, costs 1800F, while a normal plat du jour is 1500F. Breakfast is served for 500F.

The *Monitel Kone* has a very good value menu du jour for 1500F but it's available on weekdays at lunch time only.

Self-Catering Supplies can be picked up from the mural-coated *Chez Coco & Bibi*, a little épicerie attached to the L'Escale de Kone Hôtel. It is open weekdays from 5 am to 7.30 pm and weekends from 5 am to noon. There's another small alimentation across the road.

Getting There & Away

Air Kone's airport is 2½ km north of town along the main road. The Air Calédonie agent is Mme Charossay (☎ 35.51.13).

There is at least one flight Monday to Saturday both ways between Noumea and Kone (6240F one way), and on some days there are two flights. Direct flights take 45 minutes; however, the majority of the flights have a triangular-shaped route, going from Noumea to Kone then Touho and back to Noumea or vice versa. The Kone-Touho leg costs 3460F and takes 20 minutes, while the total journey time from Kone to Noumea via Touho is 1⅓ hours.

There are just two flights per week between Kone and Koumac (4090F; 25 minutes) and onto the Belep Islands (6240F; 1⅕ hours). Grande Terre air schedules change frequently so check with Air Calédonie for the current timetable.

Bus Kone's bus stop is in front of the *L'Escale de Kone* restaurant. All Noumea-Koumac buses stop here (for regular schedules and fare details see the tables in the Getting There & Away section at the start of this chapter). In addition to those services, a bus departs from Noumea to Kone, Monday to Saturday at 9.30 am and on Sunday at 1 pm. From Kone to Noumea, there's an additional bus, Monday to Saturday, at 8.15 am and on Sunday at 12.25 pm.

Car Rental cars are available at Hôtel Koniambo for 5000F per day plus 40F per km. A one-way rental to Noumea can be arranged with the owner.

KONE TO VOH
North of Kone, the RT1 skirts the 950-metre-high Massif de Koniambo, a mountain dotted with red lights at night to warn incoming planes of the bulk ahead. The road briefly touches on the coast near the tribal hamlet of Oundjo, a grouping of traditional conical Kanak houses which is a rare sight along the north-west RT1.

VOH
The original village of Voh was destroyed by a cyclone in 1893. These days, Voh (population 1700) stretches rather monotonously for three km along the RT1. There is no real town centre, just a few facilities like an épicerie, school or service station every few hundred metres or so. A monument halfway along the road marks the turn-off to Plage de Gatope, the closest beach. The post office, opposite the Total petrol station, and the gendarmerie (☎ 35.57.17) and dispensaire are at the northern tip of town.

Voh is at the western end of the Chemin des Arabes, a hiking trail across Grande Terre's central mountain chain that comes out near Hienghene on the east coast. It is a rarely used path but locals estimate the trip would take three days. Water is said to be plentiful en route.

Places to Stay & Eat
There's not much on offer in Voh. Those with a tent can make for Plage de Gatope, five km south-west, a free *camping* area with a cold water hose, toilets and barbecue facilities. It's pretty deserted, except for (you guessed it!) mosquitoes, and overlooks Baie Chasseloup, a rather shallow and murky bay.

To get there, take the road to the left at the central monument.

In Voh, there's a *gîte* with no name (or signpost) about 1½ km down the first road to the right that you come to when entering Voh from the south – turn off at the apricot-coloured Le Royal Bourbon restaurant. When the road veers sharply to the right, the gîte is just off to the left. This place is basic – cement floors, no table, communal showers and toilets, and rooms so small you can hardly swipe at the mosquitoes. At 1500F per person, you'd have to be desperate.

The restaurant, *Le Royal Bourbon* (☎ 35.57.49), is the first building you come to on entering from Kone. It's the poshest place in town, serving fresh produce such as family-caught fish or local game. A menu du jour costs 2200F including coffee and wine. If you're relying on this place for a meal, you'd be wise to telephone to make sure it's open.

Self-caterers will find several small *épiceries*. The small store and petrol station attached to Le Royal Bourbon is open daily including Saturday and Sunday mornings. A larger Ballande supermarket is located next to the Mobil petrol station just before the river. There's also a tiny épicerie next to the monument, run by an old, weathered Caldoche man, and another opposite the post office to the north.

Getting There & Away
Voh is 30 km north of Kone and 70 km south of Koumac. All the Noumea-Koumac buses stop here (see the tables in the Getting There & Away section at the start of this chapter for details).

VOH TO KOUMAC
The country between Voh and Koumac is a mix of scrubby plains and hilly grazing land. Rather uninspiring – most travellers will hardly be tempted to spend time on the few things to see in this vacant land.

Temala
Temala is a tiny community, next to a river of the same name, nine km north of Voh. It's little more than a large bridge with a store.

Momies de la Fatenaoue

North-east of Temala, in the steep slopes and caves of Fatenaoue, is a sacred burial ground of ancient chieftains. These century-old mummified remains, buried in foetal position, were until recently subject to tourist attention – so much so that it degenerated into stealing. Understandably, the local clans no longer give permission for strangers to enter.

Ouaco

A small community, halfway between Voh and Kaala Gomen, Ouaco sits on a plain where the RT1 comes within a few km of the sea. It is New Caledonia's closest point to Australia and so it was the takeoff point for two attempts in the '30s to reach Australia by plane. Close by, an underground telegraph cable once linked Grande Terre with Bundaberg, Australia.

Kaala-Gomen

This is the area where the niaouli tree essence, Gomenol, supposedly originated and was therefore named after the local Gomen clan. Kanaks chew the leaves of the niaouli tree, and lay them on wounds to aid healing (for more information on the niaouli see the aside in the Facts about the Country chapter).

The town of Kaala-Gomen (population 1600), the last stop on the road before Koumac, has a post office, gendarmerie, church, small store and petrol station. If you have time, there are side routes around Kaala-Gomen where various clans live, and the seashore is just three km to the southwest.

KOUMAC

Sitting on the edge of a sprawling plain, Koumac (population 2300) is the north-west coast's last major town, and has a real 'business-as-usual' atmosphere. A small suburban housing complex, located on the eastern outskirts of town, is home to many of the French families involved in the region's mining. Keep going inland from Koumac, towards the Koumac caves, and the country suddenly

opens up, stretching towards Mt Konio and Pic Yamboue. A few Kanak homes are nestled into the grasslands here, mostly tin-roofed shacks without doors and quite a contrast to the affluent mining neighbourhood a stone's throw away.

The town itself is quite sterile and not really geared for tourism; most of the hotels are filled with business people and sub-contractors. During summer Koumac takes the title of 'mosquito city', with vans driving around town at dusk, pumping clouds of pesticide onto the streets and anyone walking along them.

Orientation & Information

All roads leading into Koumac will deposit you at the town's hub – the roundabout – from where the two main streets, Ave Émile Frouin and Ave Georges Baudoux, lead off.

Money The Westpac bank on the roundabout is open weekdays from 7.45 am to 3.45 pm, while the BNP just off Ave Georges Baudoux is open weekdays from 7.20 to 11.30 am and 12.30 to 3.45 pm. Travellers' cheques can be cashed at either.

Post The post office, opposite the mairie, has standard weekday office hours but on Saturday is open from 8.15 to 10.15 am.

Bookshop Librairie Le Papyrus on Ave Georges Baudoux has a few magazines in English such as *Time*, the *Australian Women's Weekly*, *Island Business Pacific* and *Pacific Islands Monthly*.

Emergency There is a fairly large hospital (☎ 35.62.16) between the post office and Le Grand Cerf Hôtel, and a well-stocked pharmacy is located next to La Panthère Rose snack bar. The gendarmerie (☎ 35.61.17) is along the road to the camping ground.

Things to See & Do

Church The barrel-shaped Église Sainte Jeanne d'Arc was constructed in 1950 out of an aircraft hangar. The steeple is a simple design, with a bell that tolls every hour, and the church has beautiful stained-glass windows and woodcarvings.

Woodcarvings While Koumac's church is noteworthy simply for its strange design, the church's most impressive feature is its array of woodcarvings inspired by traditional Kanak art. A grande case, pirogue and cagou have been incorporated with Christian symbolism into works carved out of local wood such as gaïac.

The artist was Charles Weiss, better known as 'Charlie', a popular local sculptor, now deceased, who passed his knowledge

and love of woodwork onto his son, Léonce. Léonce still lives in Koumac and is well known in New Caledonia's art world. Together with the work of many of his contemporaries, his beautiful wooden sculptures featured in the recently released book on Kanak art, *Ko i Névâ*.

Léonce has a studio (☎ 35.65.32) across the road from the gendarmerie where his carvings are on display. He sells metre-long flèches faîtières for about 6000F, while grandes cases standing 30cm cost 18,000F. More of his work is found at the Malabou Beach Hôtel near Poum and in the Maison

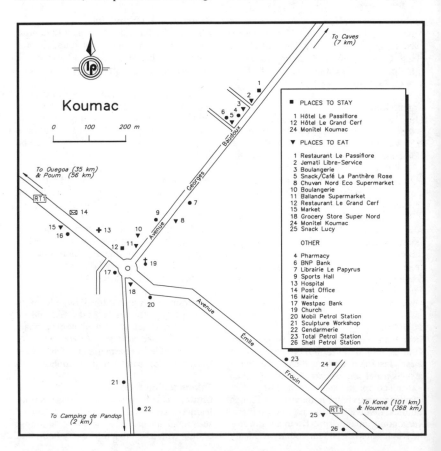

Koumac

0   100   200 m

To Caves (7 km)

To Ouegoa (35 km) & Poum (56 km)

RT1

To Kone (101 km) & Noumea (368 km)

To Camping de Pandop (2 km)

■ PLACES TO STAY

1 Hôtel Le Passiflore
12 Hôtel Le Grand Cerf
24 Monitel Koumac

▼ PLACES TO EAT

1 Restaurant Le Passiflore
2 Jemati Libre-Service
3 Boulangerie
5 Snack/Café La Panthère Rose
8 Chuvan Nord Eco Supermarket
10 Boulangerie
11 Ballande Supermarket
12 Restaurant Le Grand Cerf
15 Market
18 Grocery Store Super Nord
24 Monitel Koumac
25 Snack Lucy

OTHER

4 Pharmacy
6 BNP Bank
7 Librairie Le Papyrus
9 Sports Hall
13 Hospital
14 Post Office
16 Mairie
17 Westpac Bank
19 Church
20 Mobil Petrol Station
21 Sculpture Workshop
22 Gendarmerie
23 Total Petrol Station
26 Shell Petrol Station

des Métiers on Ave James Cook in Noumea. By mid-1994, Léonce's studio should be in Koumac's industrial zone, on the main road 2½ km south of town.

Maison Montagnat This modest little house, guarded by two sentinel-like palm trees, is a superb example of the colonial architecture that can still be found dotted around la Brousse. It's a little way out of town, on the right as you're leaving Koumac for the north.

Caves Koumac's seldom-visited limestone caves contain an array of stalactites and stalagmites. They are seven km east of town at the base of a large escarpment near a tributary of the Koumac River – very difficult to reach without your own transport.

To get there, go along Ave Georges Baudoux until the road veers sharply to the left – you go right. There should be rusted 'grotte' signs to follow from here, which will take you along a dirt road, with little or no traffic, in the direction of Pic Yamboue. You'll have to cross a river which floods after heavy rain before arriving at a small cave at the base of the escarpment. If you go farther to the right, then up some stairs, there's a bigger cave with better mineral formations that leads for more than three km into the hill. If you intend exploring, you'll need a good torch and some string to wind your way back.

Beaches The beaches around Koumac are quite barren and windswept and they do not have the variety of seashells found elsewhere in New Caledonia. The closest stretch of sand is about three km south of town, at the camping ground (see the following Places to Stay for details on how to get there). A few fishing skiffs dot this rather desolate beach while, on the other side of the peninsular hill, the odd pleasure boat docks at a small wharf.

Cinema A movie is screened every Monday at 7.30 pm at the mairie, dubbed into French of course. Photocopied posters on shop windows announce the next session.

Places to Stay
Koumac's hotels are heavily booked by companies, mainly from Monday to Thursday night, throughout most of the year. To be sure of somewhere to sleep, it's best to reserve in advance.

Camping The cheapest place to stay is the beachfront *Camping de Pandop*, three km south of town. To get there, take the first turn left after the gendarmerie and follow it to the water. This beach can be either very windy or covered in one big mosquito swarm. Security-wise it's well protected, as it is enclosed by a fence and has a live-in guard. There are large shady picnic shelters, showers and running water. It costs 1000F to pitch your tent; 500F if you're a day-tripper wanting to picnic here.

Hotels The most central place is *Hôtel Le Grand Cerf* (☎ 35.61.31; fax 35.60.16) just north of the roundabout. It has nine bungalows, a bar, restaurant and swimming pool. The hotel's main building and bungalows are skilfully built from stone found in the region, giving the place some local character. Each bungalow has a TV and private facilities and costs 5000F for one person plus 500F for each extra.

Alternatively, there's *Le Passiflore* (☎ 35. 62.10) on Ave Georges Baudoux. Simple single/double rooms in a row at the back of the hotel cost 3500F without a private shower, or 4500/5000F with shower. It is 500F per extra person and there's a small bar and restaurant.

The *Monitel Koumac* (☎ 35.61.05), south of the roundabout just off Ave Émile Frouin, is Koumac's most modern lodging – a low-set, ranch-style place with a bar that is very popular with young cowboy types. An assortment of psychedelic bungalows, all with the necessary private facilities plus a refrigerator, has been built around a large swimming pool out the back of the reception. A bungalow costs 6500F for two people. An extra person costs another 500F and there's a 380F room tax.

Places to Eat

Snacks The cheapest place to eat is *Snack Lucy* (☎ 35.69.32), past the Monitel on the road to Noumea. A plat du jour here costs 900F; it's open after 7 pm.

Alternatively, there's *Snack/Café La Panthère Rose* (☎ 35.63.47) on Ave Georges Baudoux. It's open weekdays only from 8 am to 5 pm and serves a croque-monsieur for 220F, steak-frites (steak & chips) for 1300F and a plat du jour for 1100F. Ice-creams are also available. Beer is plentiful and cold; a bottle of Number One costs 250F.

Restaurants All restaurants in Koumac are closed on Sundays.

The best-value meal in town is available at the large restaurant in the *Monitel Koumac*. The tone here is smart but casual and the bright floral decor is one of the most colourful sights in town. A menu du jour, available at lunch time, costs only 1500F. In the evenings it's à la carte. Breakfast is 700F.

Hôtel Le Grand Cerf's restaurant is a rather formal affair, serving only à la carte at both lunch and dinner. The food is very good, as you'd expect when facing a 3000F bill for a three-course meal. Petit déjeuner costs 500F.

Le Passiflore has a more casual restaurant that is popular with workers from around the area. It serves an ordinary plat du jour for 1100F and a menu du jour for 2000F. While breakfasting (500F) you can admire the shell collection.

Self-Catering Two boulangerie/pâtisseries and several well-stocked supermarkets make shopping a breeze in Koumac. There's also a communal *market*, next to the mairie on the road to Poum, where local farmers come to sell their limited array of produce on Wednesday and Saturday mornings.

The two *boulangeries* sell fresh croissants, pastries, baguettes and rolls. They are both on Ave Georges Baudoux, but the one with the better selection is between Le Passiflore hotel and the pharmacy. The other is near the roundabout.

The large, slightly chaotic *Chuvan Nord Eco* supermarket on Ave Georges Baudoux

has the town's longest trading hours. It is open weekdays from 6.45 am to noon and 1.30 to 7.30 pm; Saturday from 6.45 am to noon and 4 to 7 pm; and Sunday from 7.30 am to noon. Pierre, the manager, speaks English and enthusiastically welcomes travellers, whether they're customers or just after some local information.

Close to Le Passiflore hotel, the *Jemati libre-service* is small and clean, with fresh fruit, wine, beer etc, and is open weekdays from 7 am to noon and 2 to 7 pm.

The *Ballande* store on Ave Georges Baudoux is open through the week and Saturday mornings. On the roundabout, the *Super Nord* has trading hours similar to the Chuvan Nord Eco except that it's open from 6 am. It has a good supply of nems, cheese, yoghurt, bread and sliced ham, as well as mineral water and cold beer. The petrol station next door doubles as the town's bus stop.

Getting There & Away

Air Koumac's small airport (☎ 35.62.29) is 3½ km north of town, to the left off the road to Poum, then the first dirt track to the right. The Air Calédonie agent, where you can make or change bookings, is at Hôtel Le Grand Cerf (☎ 35.61.31).

There are only two flights per week between Koumac and Noumea (6960F; 1½ hours) via Kone (4090F; 25 minutes); or farther north to the Belep Islands (5200F; 25 minutes). Grande Terre schedules change frequently so check with Air Calédonie for the current timetable.

Bus The post office acts as Koumac's bus station for the mail bus. All other buses stop at the petrol station at the roundabout. For details on regular buses between Noumea and Koumac, see the tables in the Getting There & Away section at the start of this chapter.

North to Poum (180F; 1½ hours) via Arama (45 minutes), there's a regular bus leaving Koumac, Monday to Thursday, at 3.40 pm. Late Friday, there's a bus at 11.40 pm, and on Sunday one at 5.10 pm. Returning from Poum (via Arama) to Koumac and south to Noumea, there is one bus, Monday to Thursday and on Sunday, at 8 am; there is another on Friday at 4.15 pm. If you prefer to jump on a mail bus, there is one to Poum on Monday at 3.45 am; Wednesday at 1.15 pm; and Friday at 4.15pm (these buses return immediately after picking up the mail).

Heading east to Ouegoa (200F; one hour) and over to the east coast village of Pouebo (300F; two hours), there is one bus leaving Koumac on Wednesday at 1.35 pm and another on Friday at 11.20 pm. The Pouebo-bound mail bus leaves Monday and Thursday at 1.15 pm and Wednesday and Friday at 5.30 am. All services back to Koumac are just as infrequent (see Ouegoa & Pouebo in the North-East Coast chapter for details).

Car Noumea is 368 km away. If you are driving, Koumac is a good place to get petrol because the stations are few and far between in the top end of Grande Terre. The Mobil petrol station is open until 7.30 pm.

Hitching There are no problems when hitching south towards Noumea, but to Poum it might be more of an adventure.

KOUMAC TO POUM
On leaving Koumac, Grande Terre tapers into a narrow peninsula carved by many bays. The terrain becomes windswept and the soil dry, overtaken by savane à niaouli. Just north of town, a couple of beaches – Tangadiou and Baie de Sable – are popular weekend retreats for Koumac families. Both are along the RT8 which turns off to the left just after Koumac airport. About eight km north of Koumac, the RT7 turns eastwards off the RT8 and crosses the tip of Grande Terre through beautiful country over the Cols de Crève-Cœur, to Ouegoa and later the east coast.

Tiebaghi Mine
The Tiebaghi mine was once the largest and richest chrome mine in the world. It's now defunct and the village which rose around it is a ghost town, perched high on the scarred hills about 20 km north of Koumac and is easily visible from RT1.

In 1877, copper and chrome were discovered at Tiebaghi but it wasn't until 1902 that the mine kicked into operation. The site grew into a real village and, by the '50s, there were 1500 people living and working on the hilltop. A change of fortune forced the mine to close in 1964; however it was revived in the mid-'80s. Again it didn't last long. Within four years the reserves were exhausted and, in 1990, the mine folded.

Arama
Arama is a small coastal tribal settlement on the eastern side of this northern peninsula. There's a small church built in 1863 and a monument along the nearby coast commemorating the founding of the mission in 1860.

The turn-off to Arama is 35 km north of Koumac. From here it's another nine km, along the RT9 which winds up a small range and crosses a col. From Arama, you can follow the rough coastal road north along Baie d'Harcourt where, just before turning inland, you'll pass an old wharf used for loading copper from the now-abandoned Pilou mines in the nearby hills. Eventually you'll join up with the road to Gîte de Poingam and Boat-Pass, the two sitting at the farthermost end of Grande Terre.

Malabou Beach Hôtel
There is only one port of call along the lonely stretch between the turn-off to Arama and Poum, and that's the luxurious *Malabou Beach Hôtel* (☎ 35.60.60; fax 35.60.70), BP 4 Poum, built along the sandy Baie de Nehoue, about 15 km south of Poum. It's a brand new resort with everything you need for an away-from-it-all holiday.

A collection of 33 square bungalows and three luxury suites dot the peaceful grounds. All have terraces with views of the beach and the nearby artificial island, created as a platform for water sports enthusiasts. The bungalows have air-con, TV & video, a fridge and coffee facilities. Though quite plain from the outside, inside they are very tastefully decorated with bamboo furniture and wooden sculptures. Prices differ with the season; high seasons coincide with school

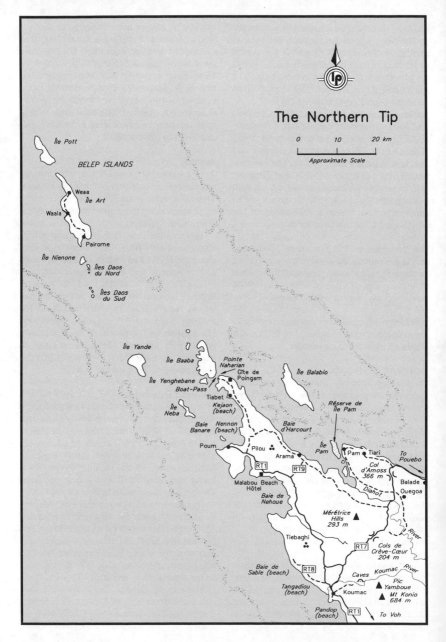

The Northern Tip

0   10   20 km

Approximate Scale

holidays and long weekends. A bungalow for up to three adults (or a couple plus two children under 12 years) costs 8200/9200F in low/high season. The suites, which have a separate salon and can sleep five adults, cost 14,500/16,500F. There's a 380F room tax.

Malabou Beach's restaurant offers a tantalising cuisine to complement the resort's tropical location. A menu du jour is available for 2000F or you can order à la carte specialities such as poulet façon Malabou (curry coconut chicken) for 1500F or perroquet aux courgettes (parrot fish with zucchini) for 1400F. For breakfast there's a choice of a standard buffet for 1000F or the American version (plus bacon and eggs) for 1300F.

All non-motorised activities – biking, tennis, windsurfing, snorkelling, canoeing – are free. Water-skiing costs 1000F for 15 minutes while reef excursions are 600F. The hotel arranges 4WD minibus tours to the Koumac Caves for 2500F, the old Pilou copper mine near Arama for 2000F and Boat-Pass in the far north for 1600F.

The **Pacific Diving Centre**, an internationally recognised scuba-diving club, operates out of Malabou Beach Hôtel. It organises reef trips for certified divers including one/two dives for 5000/9000F, all materials included. Baptismal dives cost 5000F or it can arrange a three-day FFESSM course for 30,000F.

Getting There & Away The hotel has a private airstrip serviced by Aviazur, a charter company based in Noumea. You'll be looking at 7,500F for a one-way flight to/from Noumea. For bookings contact Aviazur (☎ 25.37.09).

Avis works with Malabou to provide rental cars for those who want to explore the area or drive south. If you remain in the vicinity, a car costs 6900F per day plus 32F per km, with the first 100 km free. Alternatively, there's a one-way rental formula whereby you can drive the car to Tontouta Airport or Noumea for 10,200F per day with the bonus of unlimited km. Either way, you must book a week in advance to ensure that there's a car on site.

POUM

Poum (population 1100; pronounced 'poom') marks the end of the RT1. A windswept little community, it is the northernmost village on Grande Terre, sitting at the end of a plump peninsula, 56 km north of Koumac. Only a rough dirt road (five km before Poum) continues north, ending where a channel, known appropriately as Boat-Pass, separates Île Baaba from the mainland.

Well off the beaten track, Poum seldom draws visitors and in bad weather it is downright uninviting. The only strangers to stray into town are those who have missed the turn-off to Gîte de Poingam and Boat-Pass, or people heading for the Belep Islands by boat.

Orientation & Information

As soon as you enter Poum, a bitumen road goes off to the right at a small blue postal box, leading to the village's only store, petrol station, accommodation, restaurant and the wharf where boats leave for the Belep Islands. This road follows the waterfront before curling around and eventually rejoining the RT1 at an old church sitting on a small hill. From here it's straight into the village, past the post office, school and mairie. The gendarmerie (☎ 35.64.77) overlooks the water at the end of the road. The land beyond here to the south-west belongs to the Titch clan. Close to the gendarmerie is a small hospital.

Places to Stay & Eat

Campers can set up on the grass near the water just past the gendarmerie; however, there have been some reports of theft from this area.

The other option is *Chez Madame Froin* (☎ 35.64.70), Poum's only eatery and accommodation, overlooking the bay and islands on the road to the right before you get to the village. This little place, quiet but somewhat disorganised, has just three rooms, all with cooking facilities and facing the sea, costing 4500F. It doesn't take many people to make them *complet* (fully booked) so, if you want to be sure, reserve in advance.

Madame Froin's place also has the monopoly on the food scene and, for what it is, a meal here is pricey. You'll be looking at 2000F for an entrée, steak, bread and salad, served on terrace tables set up in a cool shady area behind her house. A simple breakfast costs 400F.

There's a small épicerie, *Chez Kenji*, just past Madame Froin towards the wharf and another, more run-down, shop across the road from it.

Getting There & Away

Bus For details on the infrequent bus connections between Koumac and Poum, see Getting There & Away in the Koumac section.

Hitching It's not easy to hitch to/from Poum, so whichever way you're going, start out early.

Boat About twice a week, the *Tui II* sails between Poum and Waala carrying passengers and supplies. Ask at the Poum post office or Madame Froin's to see if they know when the next boat is going.

BOAT-PASS

For those with their own transport or time, an adventurous trip from Poum or Koumac is to Pointe Naharian, the tip of Grande Terre. It's a hilly terrain exposed to the sea, with sandy beaches bordered by araucarias, palms and grassland and a gîte three km before the top. The road is rough and very slippery when wet, with some streams becoming impassable for conventional vehicles during rain. On the way, you pass some excellent desolate beaches, the two most popular being Nennon and Kejaon along Baie Banare.

The clan from Île Yenghebane, just west of Boat-Pass, fish the waters around this region and, being far away from the eyes of the law, don't hesitate to kill more than their legal share of protected wildlife. For a recent church fund-raising gathering in Poum, they provided the feast with eight dugongs and 25 turtles.

Places to Stay & Eat

There's one place along this secluded road where you can stop for a few meagre supplies, but don't count on its being open. It's about 10 km from Poum – look for a Coca-Cola sign outside a settler's home.

Near Boat-Pass is the family-owned *Gîte de Poingam* (☎ 35.63.40), an assortment of bungalows, clustered together on a 1¾-km-long private beach. The gîte is run by Denise and Claude Goulié together with their daughter and Australian son-in-law, who act as hostess and chef respectively. The Gouliés bought the land in 1961 and turned its isolation into a popular weekend and school holiday getaway for métros and Caldoches from the south.

At the time of updating there were eight bungalows, all capable of sleeping four people, except for a large hut that had room for seven (9000F). Each four-person bungalow costs 5000/5600F per night for one/two people and 600F for an extra person. The Gouliés are in the throes of expanding and by August 1994 they anticipate having 12 bungalows, some with cooking facilities, which they will rent for roughly the same price as the current bungalows. Electricity runs on a generator so lights go out after 10 pm. Be prepared for a few mosquitoes.

Campers are welcome and, once again, the site should have a private shower, toilet and barbecue facilities by 1994. The nightly charge is 500F per tent plus 250F per person.

It's possible to eat at the gîte's restaurant for lunch or dinner even if you're not staying overnight, but you should book a day or two ahead. All meals are based on local produce, with seafood bought from local fisherpeople. Set menus cost 1900F, and a meal with crab, fresh fish, salad, dessert and bread costs 2800F. If you want lobster it'll cost another 1000F. You can accompany this with a bottle of France's finest wine (at a price of course), or simply wash it down with a half-litre carafe of Aussie table wine for 600F. Breakfast is typically a platter of seasonal fruit for 700F.

As for things to do? Well, besides lolling on the beach, there are surf-skis for rent at

600F, or the Gouliés can take you on two-hour reef excursions for 1500F per person. At low tide you can walk to the little Watermelon islet, just east of the gîte. Snorkelling is not so good in these shallow waters.

Getting There & Away

To get to Boat-Pass and/or Gîte de Poingam, you must take the dirt road leading off the RT1 five km south of Poum. The gîte is 24 km down this road. In rainy weather take care at the creek crossings – they flood quickly, with the water sometimes rising a metre in 15 minutes. The only traffic you will encounter on this road will come from the Tiabet clan, who live on the coast six km before the gîte. A sign indicates the turn-off to their village.

With so little traffic, hitching along this road is almost a mission impossible.

BELEP ISLANDS

This remote archipelago sits 50 km north-west of the northern tip of Grande Terre. At its centre is Île Art, the group's largest island, stretching for 20 km. Just north is Île Pott which is also inhabited, while to the south are the small Île Nienone and the two Daos islets.

The Belep Islands (pronounced 'bay-lep') are home to 800 Kanaks who speak the Yâlayu language. They are rarely visited by tourists, as there are only a couple of flights and boats in and out per week, and no tourist accommodation. The best way to visit would be by invitation, though you'd have to be lucky to meet a Belep islander on the mainland.

In 1892, the islanders were evacuated by the colonial authorities and exiled to Balade on the north-east coast while their island was turned into a leper colony. The clan was forced to live at the Catholic mission in Balade until 1898 when the leper colony closed. Some of the Christian islanders never returned to Belep, while many of those who did took back with them a deep-seated resentment towards the French.

Information

The islands' main village, Waala, hugs a little bay on Île Art. There's a post office, store, clinic with a resident French doctor, a small airport, wharf and mission church. There is no accommodation nor established camp-sites; however, 'free' camping is possible if you first ask permission at the local chefferie. If you intend spending time on the islands, the IGN 'Série Orange' map (Nr 4801) could be useful.

Getting There & Away

There are two flights per week between the Belep Islands and Koumac (5200F one way; 25 minutes), Kone (6240F; 1¼ hour) and Noumea (9720F; 2¼ hours). Check with Air Calédonie for schedules. For details on the boat to the Belep Islands, see the Poum section.

The North-East Coast

Scenery, people and a spirit of independence make the north-east coast Grande Terre's most impressive region. As soon as you turn onto the RT6 (Grande Terre's central crossing), the dry landscape gives way to a region characterised by lush forests, streams, waterfalls and coastal coconut groves. Kingfishers watch the scene from their perches on powerlines or trees, and enormous frigate birds wing overhead. There are fascinating rock formations in the vicinity of Hienghene, and there's New Caledonia's highest peak, Mt Panie. North of Poindimie, the regional hub, are beaches awash with beautiful shells and unspoilt water filled with colourful fish, admired by snorkellers and scuba divers alike.

The north-east coast is home to numerous Kanak clans but few Europeans, most of whom left prior to or during the Events. The

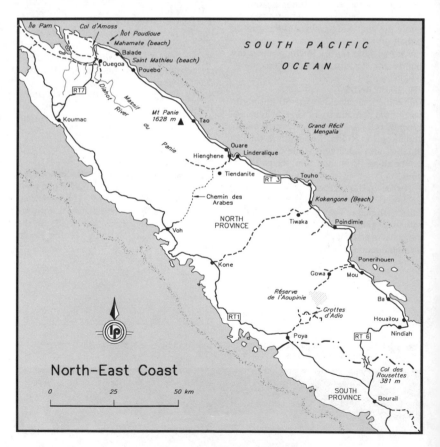

North-East Coast

independence movement has a strong foothold in some of these parts – this is where roadblocks were set up to disrupt elections in the 1980s, and FLNKS flags can be seen throughout the area. The flat walls of roadside bus stops are used by indépendantistes and artists as the perfect surface to paint large murals of Eloi Machoro or a colourful cagou. This entire coastline, as far south as Canala, is governed by the FLNKS-ruled North Province.

In the 1890s, coffee was an important crop in this region, usually cultivated by Kanak workers for European bosses. Some plantations are still worked, these days mainly planted with caffeine-rich Robusta coffee plants. Others have been abandoned, having been invaded by disease or tiny 'fire' ants, inadvertently imported with pines for plantations and which have a burning sting, making harvesting an unattractive job.

GETTING THERE & AWAY

Only two sealed roads span the central mountain chain – the RT6 between Bourail and Houailou and, in the far north, the RT7 linking Koumac-Ouegoa-Balade. However, sometime in 1994, the new Kone-Tiwaka road is supposed to open, providing faster access to the north-east coast.

Just one road, the RT3, winds along the entire north-east coast for some 210 km between Houailou and Pouebo. Unlike the RT1 on the west coast, this road tightly traces the shoreline, offering superb views en route. Indeed, north-east coast travel starts and ends with magnificent vistas, thanks to the high cols (mountain passes) which must be crossed to reach the area. Around the southern Col des Roussettes (381 metres), named after the fruit bats, the terrain is steep and rugged, overlooking valleys and abandoned taro terraces, while the view of the mountains and reefs seen from Col d'Amoss, right up in the north, is well worth the drive.

Air

Touho has the only regional airport. For details on flights see the Touho – Getting There & Away section.

Bus

Buses to this coastline are considerably less frequent than to destinations along the north-west coast. In general, there are two or three per day (fewer on Sunday) from Noumea. Most of them go only as far as Hienghene, stopping en route at all major villages and towns such as Houailou, Ponerihouen, Poindimie and Touho.

Buses depart from Noumea for Hienghene, from Monday to Saturday at 5.30 am (a mail bus) and 8 am; at 10.30 am there's an extra bus but it only goes to Touho. At noon there's a bus to Houailou only. On Sunday there's a bus at 10 am; and 11.30 am (to Touho only).

Departing from the north-east coast to Noumea, there's a mail bus which leaves Hienghene, from Monday to Saturday, at 5.30 am and another bus at 8 am (on Sunday at 10 am), stopping at all towns en route. Buses to Noumea, originating in Touho, leave at 5.45 am, 6.50 am and 9 am (on Sunday only at noon).

If you're heading north of Hienghene, only a mail bus goes to Pouebo and Balade and across the mountains to Ouegoa or Koumac. Pouebo, Balade and Ouegoa are infrequently serviced by buses from Koumac (see the Koumac Getting There & Away section in the North-West Coast chapter).

	Fare from Noumea	Time from Noumea	Time from Hienghene
Houailou	1050F	4 hours	2 hours
Ponerihouen	1200F	4½ hours	1½ hours
Poindimie	1250F	5 hours	1 hour
Touho	1350F	5½ hours	½ hour
Hienghene	1450F	6 hours	

Hitching

Hitching can be enjoyable or frustrating in this part of New Caledonia. Some people have no problems getting lifts, others wait for hours. In the far north, between Hienghene and Ouegoa, you will have to be patient. Make sure you pick a shady position with a good view.

HOUAILOU

Houailou (pronounced 'hoo-eye-ee-luh'), 68 km north-east of Bourail and 230 km from

Noumea, is the first coastal village you'll come to after descending from the mountains on the RT6. It's built along a river of the same name and is set in lush and beautiful surroundings. The eight tribal communities around here are very large, totalling 3650 people. The local language, Ajië, is the most widely spoken language on Grande Terre, used on a daily basis by the clans around Houailou as well as clans right across the mountain range to the west.

In the mid-1880s Protestant missionaries from the Loyauté islands set up here, followed in 1902 by Maurice Leenhardt, a much-respected French ethnologist. From his mission, Do Neva (My House), he pioneered the study of Kanak languages, spending many years there classifying them and putting some into written form. For a time, Ajië was used as a medium of instruction in secondary and pastor training schools. This ended in the mid-1940s when teaching in French was made compulsory.

In the more recent past, anti-French feelings have run high in Houailou, and Westerners have not been particularly welcome. Although it was one of the hot spots during the Events, these days, with little revolutionary action going on, there are no problems for visitors.

Orientation & Information

The village is one km off the main road – to get there continue straight when you get to the turn-off to the Houailou River bridge. Almost everything is on the main street – first up is the mairie and, opposite, a restaurant and épicerie. Several hundred metres on is the gendarmerie (☎ 42.51.17), while the post office is farther, just around the bend in the road. There is a rarely used airstrip north of the village, three km down a dirt road to the right after you've crossed the Houailou bridge.

Places to Stay & Eat

There are no hotels in Houailou. It is possible to camp near the beach at the airstrip but this is a desolate area, exposed to the wind. There have also been reports of occasional thefts.

The only restaurant is *Chez Néron* (☎ 40. 52.15) across from the mairie. When we were there, this place was very run down and, even around lunch time, pretty deserted. The only way you'd know it's a restaurant is the hand-painted sign saying so. It's closed on Sunday. The next-door grocery shop is open daily, but only until 11.45 am on Sundays.

Getting There & Away

For details on buses to Houailou, see the Getting There & Away section at the start of this chapter.

BA FALLS

The Ba Falls are 13½ km north of the Houailou bridge. The track leading to the falls is on the left directly after a large bridge – it is not signposted. There is often a chain blocking this track but it's quite OK to go up – the falls are about 1½ km farther on a mountain trail which travels upstream along the Ba River. You can climb to the top of the falls for a view of the area or swim at the base. Take note that in recent years there have been several reported incidents of cars being broken into and gear stolen while people are at these falls.

PONERIHOUEN

This small village, 46 km north-west of Houailou, and its surrounding coastal and interior lands are home to nine clans (population 2300). The village is a couple of km inland on a bend in the Nabai River. This large waterway empties into the sea to the north, soon after you cross the long steel cage-like bridge erected during WW II on the village's outskirts. Coffee is an important crop and is harvested and prepared for sale at a coffee station in town.

Just before you enter the village, a road leads off to the left and follows the river for 13 km to the tribal community of Gowa. From here, a foot/4WD track leads another five km into the fauna reserve of Mt Aoupinie. It's possible to follow this track all the way to the Grottes d'Adio and Poya on the west coast.

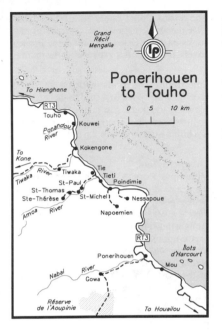

Ponerihouen to Touho

0   5   10 km

Grand Récif Mengalia

To Hienghene

RT3

Touho   Kouwei

Ponandou River

Kokengone

To Kone

Tiwaka River   Tiwaka   Tie   Tieti

St-Paul   Poindimie

St-Thomas   St-Michel   Nessapoue

Ste-Thérèse

Arnoa River   Napoemien

RT3

Îlots d'Harcourt

Ponerihouen   Mou

Nabai River

Gowa

Réserve de l'Aoupinie   To Houailou

Information
Unlike Houailou, the RT3 passes right through the middle of Ponerihouen, where you'll find the gendarmerie (☎ 42.85.17), a clinic, school, mairie and two tiny stores, one with petrol pumps.

Places to Stay & Eat
Camping It's possible to camp for free on the beach about 10 km south of Ponerihouen, just south of the settlement of Mou. However the sand here is black, the water is brown and there are no secluded spots.

Much better is the site seven km north of Ponerihouen where a local family has started a lovely beachfront camping ground set amidst a large palm grove. It's on the right-hand side, down a dirt track leading off the RT3, and is signposted. The family live just across the road. There's a traditional-style hut where you can eat a picnic lunch, though if you're not camping overnight you'll have to pay a 300F picnicking charge. To pitch

your tent for the night costs 700F. A toilet and a shower, supposedly with hot and cold water, are in the throes of being built.

Hotel/Restaurant The sole place to eat and stay in Ponerihouen is the hôtel/restaurant *Naha Shi* (☎ 42.85.16), on a residential street in the village centre. This place is not flash, with a basic room costing 3000F for three people plus a hefty 1500F charge if you want air-con. The restaurant serves a three-course meal for 1800F and breakfast for 300F.

To find it when coming in from Houailou, turn up the first street on the right immediately before a little shop plastered with advertising boards. Naha Shi is two houses along, on the right-hand side.

Getting There & Away
For bus fares and schedules, see the Getting There & Away section at the start of this chapter.

POINDIMIE
About 308 km from Noumea and with a local population of 3600, Poindimie (pronounced 'pwan-dim-ee-ay') is the administrative centre of the north-east coast and serves as an excellent point for exploring the region. It's a place with great atmosphere, stretched along a rocky coastline, and close to superb scuba diving sites. It has all the necessary services of a regional hub, such as inexpensive accommodation, good restaurants, and, perhaps most importantly, the north-east's only bakery.

The town was founded during WW II and retains one or two of the half-moon shaped, corrugated steel Quonset huts, built as supply sheds by the Americans during the war. Before the Events, Poindimie was largely a Caldoche settlement with most of the local Paicî-speaking Kanak population living on tribal lands along the coast or in the nearby valleys leading up to the mountains. But the upheaval of the mid-'80s saw about half of the 800 Caldoches leave. They were reimbursed by the French government and their properties handed over to the local clans.

Orientation
The town stretches for about 2½ km, from the first few buildings you pass coming in from Ponerihouen, to Tieti beach. The centre is over a large bridge which spans the Poindimie River, a sizeable waterway that comes straight from the mountains and can rapidly swell to twice its size during heavy rain.

Poindimie's centre is made up of a few parallel streets that climb round the foot of a small hill capped by a radio tower. From the large mairie, the RT3 follows the rise and curve of the land around a small headland and eventually comes to another bridge and then Tieti beach, 1½ km to the north. Another 3½ km north is Amoa bridge.

Information
Money There is a Société Générale bank across from the post office which cashes travellers' cheques and is open weekdays from 7.20 am to 3.45 pm. The BCI bank on the RT3 does not generally handle foreign exchange.

Post The post office, at the end of the second street past the mairie, is open standard provincial hours.

Bookstore Poindimie's small bookshop sells the daily national newspaper, glossy books on New Caledonia and some French novels. It's up the third street after the mairie.

Emergency The gendarmerie (☎ 42.71.69) is on the hill, up the first road to the left after rounding the point. Just before this road is a well-stocked pink pharmacy, behind which is a clinic that is open to the public.

Things to See
Municipal Pool & Vasarely Overlooking the ocean at the western end of town is the public pool. As you enter the pool area, there's a very fine mosaic made in 1961 by Hungarian-born artist Victor Vasarely. It was commissioned by the local council as Vasarely was a well-known artist in France at that time. He was one of the main figures of the post-WW II geometrism genre, his colourful work designed to brighten grey, urbanised areas and typically described as 'modern architectural integration art'. The pool is open (weekdays only) to visitors and is often used by school children; entry is 200/100F for adults/children.

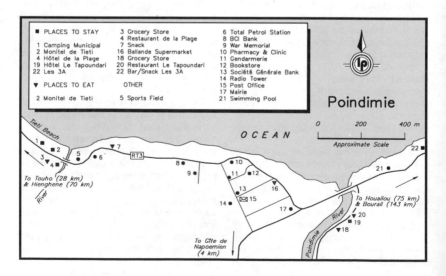

■ PLACES TO STAY		
1 Camping Municipal	3 Grocery Store	6 Total Petrol Station
2 Monitel de Tieti	4 Restaurant de la Plage	8 BCI Bank
4 Hôtel de la Plage	7 Snack	9 War Memorial
19 Hôtel Le Tapoundari	16 Ballande Supermarket	10 Pharmacy & Clinic
22 Les 3A	18 Grocery Store	11 Gendarmerie
	20 Restaurant Le Tapoundari	12 Bookstore
▼ PLACES TO EAT	22 Bar/Snack Les 3A	13 Société Générale Bank
		14 Radio Tower
2 Monitel de Tieti	OTHER	15 Post Office
		17 Mairie
	5 Sports Field	21 Swimming Pool

Poindimie

War Memorial A collection of WW II memorabilia has been erected on the hill before the BCI bank to commemorate the Americans' involvement in the Pacific during WW II. Included is the skeleton of a war plane, three propellers mounted onto a stone wall and two guns in firing position.

Tie Mission A few minutes' drive north of town along RT3 is the serene Tie Mission with a church built in 1866. Many of the missions along the north-east coast were home to displaced clans who lost their lands when the policy of resettlement began in the 1860s. Priests or ministers still live here, although for the most part, Melanesian men of the cloth have replaced the original Frenchmen.

The mission is on the left, 3½ km north of Tieti beach, just past the turn-off to the Amoa River valley.

Activities

Beaches The beaches around Poindimie are rough and somewhat rocky, but still excellent for swimming. One of the biggest sandy stretches is Tieti beach in front of the municipal camping ground. However, be careful of leaving your things lying on the beach, as campers have reported thefts.

Hiking Depending on your stamina, there is plenty of impromptu walking and hiking to be done around here. Above the radio tower looming over Poindimie, there is a hike to **Koyaboa hill**. Follow the 4WD track towards the radio tower, and proceed uphill from there.

Alternatively you can wander along any of the local valleys. Most convenient to town and quite picturesque is the deep valley leading to the clan of **Napoemien**, south of Poindimie. If you want to take time to really explore this valley, there's overnight accommodation at the clan's gîte (see the following Places to Stay section for details).

Just as you arrive in Poindimie from Ponerihouen, there's a track off to the left which winds inland over small creeks through **Nessapoue** tribal land. The terrain here is

much wider than around Napoemien, and before the Events this was Caldoche country. Cattle are still grazed but the coffee plantations are mostly abandoned.

About five km north of central Poindimie is the beginning of the **Amoa River valley**, with dirt roads leading into the valley along either river bank. The track on the southern flank meanders through sparsely populated terrain while the northern path passes the tribal villages of Saint Paul (5½ km), Saint Michel (7½ km), Saint Thomas (eight km) and Sainte Thérèse (8½ km).

Diving Poindimie overlooks distant islands and reefs that offer some of the best scuba diving on the north-east coast. This is mainly due to relatively little fishing or run-off from mined mountains, the two factors which have slowly killed the reefs farther south. There is no large dive club here but it is possible to arrange an excursion through Olivier Vilain at the Club Aqua Est (☎ 42. 71.23) in Poindimie.

Other Activities Bruno Masquelin, the owner of the Total petrol station (☎ 42.72.62), is a friendly Belgian who organises boat trips out to a small cay on the outer reef. He charges 2000F per person with a minimum of five people. He also rents VTT bikes for 2000F per day and has a canoe available for hire for 2500F per day.

Places to Stay – bottom end

Camping Two free camping options exist in Poindimie but both may appeal only to the adventurous. One is the *municipal camping ground* at Tieti beach next to the Monitel hotel. The site is quite lovely, with a grassy spot along the beach, and there is running water and shabby cold showers. However, reports of theft from this campsite are rife, so take all your gear with you when you leave each morning.

Alternatively, the manager of *Les 3A* (see the following Hotels section) will let you camp *gratuit* (no charge) on the rocky beach directly below the terrace of his place. However, there's not much beach (space for one small tent only) and it wouldn't be advisable at full moon when the tides are at their highest.

The final option is at *Gîte de Napoemien* (read on) where it costs 1000F to pitch your tent.

Gîte The *Gîte de Napoemien* (☎ 42.74.77) is in a beautiful valley in the tribal village of the same name. The village chief is Maurice Nenou, the RPCR deputy to the French National Assembly. The clan has two houses which it rents for 1500F per person per night. Both have kitchen facilities, though the local women may agree to making a bougna if you're without supplies.

The village is four km inland from Poindimie, along a dirt road that hugs a fast-flowing creek down which local kids ride rubber tubes. To stay at the gîte, you must ask at the A-frame house next to the Bienvenu (Welcome) sign just before a large bridge. The gîte is another 500 metres on.

Hotel About 400 metres before the bridge on RT3 is *Bar/Snack Les 3A* (☎ 42.74.03). Formerly Club des AAA, this place is something of an institution in Poindimie and promises to stay that way under the cordial new manager, Philippe Briand. He's given it a slight name change so that Les 3A now stands for *Accueil, Amitiés, Ambiance* (Welcome, Friendship, Atmosphere).

Though Philippe heartily welcomes travellers, it's stretching the limits to call his place a 'hotel' as it has only one, ultra-basic double room to rent. If you don't mind a cement floor and a bit of rubble, it's good value at 1500F per night. Other rooms are being renovated but he's in no rush so it could be some time before they're liveable. Les 3A is set low down and is hard to see from the road – look for the two Winfield cigarette signs.

Places to Stay – middle

Hôtel Le Tapoundari (☎ 42.71.11) is set beside the Poindimie River, just below the main bridge. While the hotel is a bit rough round the edges, its 10 rooms serve their

purpose and it has the drawcard of an enticing restaurant next door. Basic singles/doubles without air-con cost 3900/4200F, while recently renovated rooms with air-con and cooking facilities are 4500/4800F. An extra bed costs 800F. Theoretically, the reception desk is open daily, except Sundays, from 8 am to noon and from 1.30 to 8 pm but invariably there's no-one around for much of this time. If so, ask at the restaurant – they might be able to help.

The other option in this bracket is the large, multi-storey *Hôtel de la Plage* (☎ 42. 71.28) near Tieti beach to the north. The hotel has been run for many years by the same woman and it is a favourite overnight stop for business people and truck drivers. It has a restaurant and bar where guests sit around the small TV watching French films. The rooms are large and humble with shuttered windows that open to a view of the sea. A single or double with private amenities costs 4400F; a triple is 4700F.

Places to Stay – top end

Almost directly across the road from Hôtel de la Plage is the *Monitel de Tieti* (☎ 42.72. 73; fax 42.72.84), a luxury beachfront complex with private bungalows, rooms, a restaurant, swimming pool and bar. It has four modern bungalows, all with air-con, TV, a sea view and shower/toilet. They cost 7500/8000F for three/four people. Behind the bungalows runs a row of five rooms with tropical decor similar to that of the bungalows but lacking their spaciousness and beachfront view. They cost 6500/7000F for a single/double room.

Places to Eat

Snacks There's a popular *snack*, built in the circular fashion typical of a *case*, on the right-hand side of the main road on the way to Tieti beach. It is built down by the beach and serves snacks and Number One beer, as well as Kronenbourg, Heineken and Foster's. Depending on the tourist trade, it is also open for set lunches and dinners.

You can also get snacks all day at Le Tapoundari (see the next section).

Restaurants A favourite for travellers and locals alike is *Restaurant Le Tapoundari* (☎ 42.72.97), next to the hotel of the same name. Run by two young brothers from Normandy in France, its congenial atmosphere is quite unlike any other place on the north-east coast. According to Pascal, one of the brothers, 'Tapoundari' means 'I will return' in the local Kanak language and, with such a good omen, they decided to keep the name when they bought the restaurant a few years back. Open every day, it has a blackboard menu featuring mouthwaterers like prawns in curry or garlic for 1500F and seafood spaghetti for 1450F. Diners generally rave about the food. On weekdays, at lunch time only, there's a 1500F menu du jour. You can get snacks at any time including gourmet sandwiches made from half a baguette for 400F, or a vegetarian pizza for 750F.

If a view stimulates your appetite, you won't go better than *Bar/Snack Les 3A* (see Hotels). From outside it looks pretty run down, and even within it's not a palace, but it has a spacious dining terrace with a spectacular view of the sea and distant islands. Philippe serves an excellent seafood dish, with local vegetables, bread and water for 1200F at lunch time, 100F extra at dinner. A half carafe of wine is 500F; your basic petit déjeuner is 300F.

The restaurant downstairs at *Hôtel de la Plage* has had both rave reviews and others that are not so enthusiastic. Some travellers reported well-cooked French meals served in generous proportions, while one group complained that they were served 'a beef casserole which resembled boot leather – even the truck drivers were having difficulty chewing it'. A typical menu du jour is 1800F at lunch time, 2000F at dinner. Breakfast starts early and costs 500F.

The *Monitel de Tieti* has a large, elegant restaurant which opens to a poolside terrace where you can dine. A comprehensive à la carte menu is complemented by a similar wine list, but choosing from either will cost you. Better for the budget is the menu du jour for 1500F, available for lunch or dinner. The food is very good and portions are filling. A continental breakfast is served for 750F.

Self-Catering One of Poindimie's more remarkable shops is the chaotic little *alimentation* occupying a left-over WW II supply shed round the corner from Hôtel Le Tapoundari. It's a small-to-bursting shop, selling everything from clothing to tinned food, baguettes, beer and wine. Trading hours are weekdays from 6 am to noon and 2 to 7.30 pm; the same on Saturday except from 5 to 7.30 pm; and on Sunday it's open from 7.30 am to noon and 5 to 7.30 pm. Behind the shop is the north-east coast's sole bakery – it's not open to the public.

In the town centre, the *Ballande store* on RT3 has imported food, cheese, yoghurt and ham. Next door to Hôtel de la Plage is another *épicerie*. If you're heading farther north, you won't find such variety in food until you get to the large supply store north of Pouebo.

Entertainment

Things are pretty quiet on this scene. The bar at Restaurant Le Tapoundari is the most popular evening hang-out except on Saturday nights when Les 3A holds a disco from 10 pm to 3 am. The 1000F cover charge entitles you to one free drink.

Getting There & Away

Bus For details on Noumea-Poindimie bus times and the fare, see the Getting There & Away section at the start of this chapter. Buses heading north from Poindimie set out shortly after arriving in town, so between Monday and Saturday be ready by 10.30 am if you want to catch the mail bus heading north, or by 1 or 3.30 pm if you want to get either of the other two regular buses from Noumea.

Hitching It is relatively easy to hitch north to Touho, especially in the morning before the lunch break. Because Poindimie is the administrative centre of the north-east, office workers who work farther north often drive down for morning meetings or for grocery shopping. By 11 am, they are heading home towards Touho or Hienghene, and seem to welcome the company.

POINDIMIE TO TOUHO

Once you leave Poindimie, the scenery becomes more dramatic, with lush, mountainous countryside and distant waterfalls. The meandering coast looks out on the changing colours of a sea reminiscent of travel brochure photographs advertising paradise in the South Pacific.

The turn-off to the Amoa River valley is only a few minutes' drive out of town. Half a km farther is the Tie Mission. Eight km past the mission you'll cross the wide Tiwaka River and immediately come upon the turn-off for the new Kone-Tiwaka road. Just past this turn-off is Kokengone, a deserted and normally inviting beach where you can swim. After heavy rains the water is brown from run-off brought down by the Tiwaka River.

Five km south of Touho, just before the tribal community of Kouwei, is an even more tempting spot. Here, a track next to the Pon-andou River leads down to a waterfront coconut grove. There's not much beach but what sand it has is simply laden with beautiful shells including nautili (a pearly mollusc). It is possible to camp overnight here if you ask someone from the local clan, but keep in mind that there's no fresh water.

TOUHO

Touho is built on a bay which curls around to Cap Colnett and is protected from the sea by the Mengalia reef and nearby islands. All up it's an attractive coastal enclave. The community is small, with just under 2000 people, mainly from Cèmuhî-speaking clans who live in the village and surroundings. Touho has an active fishing fleet and a small protected marina, one of the few such harbours for yachties along the north-east coast. The reefs around Touho are excellent for diving but you'll need all your own equipment as there is no dive club or organiser here. Accommodation is pretty lean, but what is available is cheap enough that you could stay for days snorkelling, swimming and walking about. Unfortunately, there are no cheap places to eat. Just south of town is the north-east coast's only operational airport.

Orientation & Information

The RT3 runs through the heart of the village, which stretches for two km from the mairie, at the southern end, to the gendarmerie in the north. All administrative offices, restaurants and shops are along this road, with the hotel Relais Alison acting as the focal point. About 2¾ km south of Relais Alison is the airport, while the post office is about 300 metres north. There is no bank in Touho. On the northern outskirts of town, one km from Relais Alison, there is a small clinic staffed with a French doctor. Just opposite it is the gendarmerie (☎ 42.88.17). The town officially ends where you see the bleached-white mission church at the northern end of Touho Bay.

Things to See & Do

Marina The marina is 500 metres down the dirt road that leads towards the sea from Camping Aménagé Leveque. It's a pleasant walk, en route passing the homes of locals who fish for a living, with their nets and traps heaped in the front yards.

Touho Mission This mission was established by two Marists who came down the coast from Balade in 1853. Despite the local Kanaks' having had quite a bad experience with rough sandalwood traders, the Marists were allowed to settle without too many problems and the mission was founded a year later. The church was built in 1889, seven years after the setting up of a nearby military post.

It's a lovely spot as the mission is built close to the beach and surrounded by a coffee plantation, mandarin orchards and tall pines. A small donation is expected when you visit; however it is a question of finding someone to give it to. The church is always open and no-one seems to mind if you just wander through it or around the grounds.

The mission is about 2⅓ km north of Relais Alison. Simply continue past the gendarmerie until the first turn on your right which leads 800 metres down to the church.

Beaches There are many beaches in Touho

and on the outskirts, all featuring a staggering array of seashells and coral. Schools of small fish leap out of the water and, because of the protective reef, the sea is warm and calm. The beach off the town centre is popular with local children.

Hiking For a superb view over the reefs you can walk to the TV relay tower on top of the hill to the south of town. The road up starts at the new lycée (school) opposite the airport – from here it's roughly five km to the top.

Places to Stay – bottom end
The cheapest place to stay in Touho is *Camping Aménagé Leveque* (☎ 42.88.19), on the right-hand side of the road when arriving from the south. There are bungalows and open land for setting up tents, and the property leads directly to the beach.

The place is run by Yves Leveque, a Caldoche who has lived in Touho for many years. The adjacent épicerie, built on the property, is run by his sister-in-law. Leveque welcomes backpackers to his place and likes to air his views about the current situation in New Caledonia. The camping fee per night is only 300F. There are showers and toilets plus a few pits for making a fire. A bungalow with two beds and a table costs 1000F, however there are no sheets or blankets so it's handy to have a sleeping bag. Unfortunately for travellers, these bungalows are often rented out to long-term workers.

Alternatively you can camp for free at *Camping Gastaldi*, a calm spot dotted with coconut palms on the mouth of a small river north of Touho. It is about 3½ km from Touho's centre to the sign-posted turn-off (to the right off the RT3). The campsite is another km away, just beyond a small store (don't count on this place being open for food supplies). There's a cold shower and a toilet. If you continue along the track, you'll come to a large reception building, a troop of cement bungalows and a swimming pool – the remains of a defunct hotel. It's now used as a teacher training centre, though its semi-deserted atmosphere lends an odd aura.

Places to Stay – middle
Opposite the Leveque campsite is a small hotel/restaurant called *Relais Alison* (☎ 42. 88.12). It has three basic, air-conditioned rooms costing 4500F for one or two people; 5300F for three people.

Alternatively, you can head 13 km north of Touho to one of the north-east coast's newest abodes, *Gîte Mangalia* (☎ 42.87.60), BP 150 Touho. Overlooking the large Mengalia reef, it's a lovely place, located just off the RT3 and across the road from a strip of sand with some of the most beautiful shells the sea has to offer.

The gîte has eight pink bungalows, built in traditional style but with contemporary decor. Furnishing is spartan but there is an overhead fan and each room has its own toilet/shower. The bungalows' roofs are lined with niaouli tree bark and weighted down with stones. Each place has a little terrace from where bananas and pawpaws are almost in reach and, between the larger and smaller bungalows, there's a token swimming pool. The bar/restaurant is also designed in Melanesian style, with a low doorway which commands a bow from most adults.

Double/triple bungalows cost 4000/5000F. Despite the price, the gîte is not the sort of place to come to if you want to be waited on hand and foot as the Kanak women who run it are pretty blasé about tourists and their demands. If the women aren't in the bar area when you arrive, wander up to their house at the end of the track on the right.

Places to Eat
Restaurants *Relais Alison* has a menu du jour for a pricey 2000F, a fish dinner for 2500F, and a seafood dish that usually includes lobster and crab for 2800F. The restaurant is closed on weekends. Breakfast consists of the standard bread, jam and coffee and costs 500F.

A newer option, though again only for those with a healthy budget, is *Restaurant Adeline* (☎ 42.88.11), 500 metres north of the gendarmerie. It has a lunch-time menu du jour for 1950F; dinner is à la carte only. This place is closed on Sundays.

Gîte Mangalia's peaceful restaurant is open for lunch and dinner and serves either à la carte or menus du jour; however neither is cheap. A sumptuous seafood meal costs 3500F while a menu du jour with coffee is 2000F. Breakfast includes fresh locally grown fruit and costs 600F.

Self-Catering For the budget traveller, the best way to get around Touho's high-priced restaurants is to buy some bread, cheese and a bottle of Number One and dine under the stars on the beach. You won't be the first!

The *store* on the Leveque's property stocks freshly baked food from Poindimie's bakery, cold beer, tinned food, cheese, yoghurt, matches, batteries and towels but, like everything else, it's closed on Sunday. The village's only other *alimentation* is a few metres past the post office and, if anything, is slightly better stocked. It also has petrol but, once again, Sunday is the day off.

Getting There & Away
Air Touho's little aerodrome (☎ 42.88.01), with its two bright red-and-white buildings, is 2½ km south of the town centre. Air tickets can be bought in town from Relais Alison, which acts as the Air Calédonie agent.

There is at least one flight daily (except on Tuesday) from Noumea to Touho (6240F; 45 minutes) and back. On some days there are two flights. Not all the flights are direct; instead, many have a triangular-shaped route, going from Noumea to Touho then Kone and back to Noumea or vice versa. The Touho-Kone leg costs 3460F and takes 20 minutes, while the total journey time from Touho to Noumea via Kone is 1⅓ hours. On weekends, they tend to be direct Noumea-Touho-Noumea flights.

The charter company, Aviazur (see the Air section in the Getting Around chapter), flies to Touho almost exclusively for Club Med clients. If there's a spare seat, you may get on.

Bus Buses stop in front of the post office. For details on fares and the schedules between Noumea and Hienghene, see the

Getting There & Away section at the start of this chapter. In addition to the Hienghene-Noumea buses there are also a couple of extra services starting in Touho which go only as far south as Poindimie (400F) – on Monday and Friday they leave at 3.30 and 4.45 pm, Tuesday and Thursday at 4.30 pm and Wednesday at 2.30 pm.

If you are heading north to Hienghene, the mail bus passes through at about 11.30 am and the other bus at 1.30 pm.

Hitching It is relatively easy to hitchhike from Touho to either Poindimie or Hienghene but if you plan to hitch a ride back to Noumea, it would be wise to get an early start.

Getting Around
Touho has just one car available for rental. It's privately owned and costs 5000F per day plus 40F per km. You must phone ahead (☎ 42.88.38) to make sure it's not already taken.

TOUHO TO HIENGHENE
This is perhaps the most spectacular section of the north-east coast. From Touho, the RT3 closely hugs the water's edge all the way to

the Tipindje River crossing, passing sandy beaches seemingly littered with stunning sea shells. About nine km before Hienghene, the scenery dramatically changes to black cliffs towering over startling green water. Club Med's new village (see the following section for details) is located at the start of this scenic wonderland.

HIENGHENE

Hienghene (pronounced 'hee-yain-ghain') is known throughout New Caledonia for two main reasons. Firstly, its coastline is carved with the most fascinating rock formations that the country can offer. This scenery's attraction has lead to the construction of a new Club Med village south of Hienghene and, in season, weekly visits by the Club Med 2 cruise liner.

In a more sober vein, Hienghene was the scene in 1984 of one of the country's most brutal modern-day massacres. This event, coupled with the local population's long-standing zeal for independence, has made the village a symbol of the liberation struggle. Their spirit was personified by former Hienghene mayor and assassinated FLNKS leader, Jean-Marie Tjibaou, whose tribal community of Tiendanite (see the following section) lies about 20 km from Hienghene.

History

In the mid-19th century, the Hienghene valley clans were a close-knit, fiercely independent community of 8000 Fwâi-speaking people. Under the leadership of Bouarate, the tribal chief, they battled the French forces and colonialists until Bouarate was captured and deported to Tahiti. Missionaries tried to set up here as late as 1885, but with no success. The people's independent streak explains their more recent active role in the struggle for Kanaky. Although there are now about 2000 people in the whole Hienghene valley area, there are no French settlers living here. Their houses were burned and they were forced out after the bloody massacre of 10 Kanaks by mixed-race settlers in 1984.

The Hienghene Massacre

On 5 December 1984, a political meeting was held in Hienghene amongst militant FLNKS members. It was less than a month after the party had boycotted and severely disrupted the Territorial Assembly elections. Jean-Marie Tjibaou, the then FLNKS leader, was meant to attend but he was delayed in Noumea and never arrived.

Late in the evening 17 men, including two of Tjibaou's brothers, left the meeting to drive the 20 km back home to their village of Tiendanite. Eight km into the journey, a felled coconut palm stopped the two trucks in their tracks. The scene was lit by hunting spotlights and the attackers opened fire. Those who managed to escape the first volley tried to flee across the river, but spotlights and bullets tracked most of them down. Seven of them, however, managed to escape. The trucks and their dead occupants were set alight and the killers fled into the mountains.

When the police arrived many hours later, several bodies were still in the river. Some men had been shot 30 times, a few at point-blank range. The only evidence of arms amongst the Kanaks was a gun attached to the back seat of one of the vehicles. Though burnt in the blaze, it was clear that it had not been fired.

The 10 men were buried at Tiendanite, which in one foul swoop had lost many of its fathers, brothers and sons. Jean-Marie Tjibaou was unable to attend the mass funeral publicly as there were fears for his safety, given that those responsible for the ambush were still at large.

The killers eventually gave themselves up and seven men were charged and taken into custody. They were released in October 1987 after the magistrate investigating the event found the self-confessed killers had acted in 'self-defence' and therefore would not stand trial.

The New Caledonian chapter of the International League of Human Rights immediately made public that the magistrate had not included the testimony of the seven survivors in his report. The league accused him of bias and of causing a miscarriage of justice. The FLNKS has since maintained that the killings were a deadly premeditated ambush. In its 1988 annual report on human rights abuses, the human rights group Amnesty International cited the trial result. ∎

Orientation

The village stretches for some two km, from the Kanak Cultural Centre on the southern outskirts to the hilltop mairie where the FLNKS flag flies alongside the French tricolour.

Arriving from the south, the cultural centre is on your right just before a large bridge which spans the Hienghene River. Once across the bridge, there's a technical school on the left and, a few hundred metres farther, a wharf and modern ferry terminal. The latter are used only on Thursdays when the Club Med 2 anchors in the bay and small boats ferry the passengers ashore. Opposite is the run-down shop, Le Magasin. Another few hundred metres on the left is the post office and neighbouring clinic. From here the road rises to the mairie and, opposite, the gendarmerie. Below the gendarmerie is a primary school and the Base Nautique (Nautical Centre). The road past the gendarmerie leads north to Balade.

Information

The tourist office mooted to be installed inside the ferry terminal hasn't materialised. The hill-side post office has standard provincial hours.

There are no banks in Hienghene but, if desperate, you can change money and travellers' cheques at Club Med's village (see Places to Stay for details).

The clinic is just past the post office and is open to the public. There is one French doctor and one dentist. The gendarmerie (☎ 42.81.17) is perched on top of the hill and is complete with helicopter landing pad and barbed wire.

Things to See

Hienghene's sights are mainly outside the village. The following are listed in a south-to-north order.

Linderalique Cliffs These dramatic black limestone cliffs start about nine km south of Hienghene – basically where Club Med has set up – and continue to the bay of Hienghene. Rising abruptly out of nowhere, they are topped by jagged, razor-sharp edges, while jade-coloured waters lap their bases. The many caves and hidden coves are inhabited by swallows, flying foxes and human skeletons. The locals say that no native of Hienghene can marry outside the cliffs of Linderalique because their hearts are blocked by these walls of rock.

The most famous of the rock formations is la Poulet, or Brooding Hen, a high, rocky slab of exquisite sculpture that broke away from the pack at Linderalique to rise from the centre of Hienghene Bay. Slightly to the north-west is the Sphinx, another of nature's masterpieces. These two are best viewed from the lookout (see below).

Linderalique Cave The Linderalique cave is little more than a large cavern, hollowed out of a section of the cliffs, which has become a tourist attraction and source of revenue for the local Linderalique clan. It contains some interesting rock formations but many of the natural surfaces have been desecrated by graffiti and, in comparison, you can see more spectacular caves on the Loyauté islands. The locals have made a shrine to the Virgin Mary at the cave's entrance and charge an entry fee of 200/100F for adults/children. This is payable to the old man who waits in a large hut next to the handpainted sign announcing the grotte.

The turn-off to the cave from the RT3 is 2½ km south of Hienghene. If you're coming from the south, soon after the main slab of Linderalique cliffs there is a small road to the right in a thicket of trees and a few houses. It's not signposted. You have to follow this road for another km to reach the cave.

Lookout The best view you'll get of the Brooding Hen, the Sphinx and Hienghene's strange-coloured bay is from the lookout, 1½ km south of the Kanak Cultural Centre. No signpost marks the turn-off, but it's easily recognised by the well-worn dirt tracks which lead off the RT3 at the top of the hill. There's a new *snack* bar at the lookout, open only on Thursdays, when the Club Med 2 crowd are in town.

Beyond the Sphinx you can see the white steeple and tiny mission village of Ouare, nestled beneath coastal mountains on the main road north to Balade.

Kanak Cultural Centre This multi-faceted centre (☎ 42.81.50) is situated on the right just before the bridge into Hienghene. It contains a one-room museum (to which there is free admission) that exhibits wooden spears, weapons and woven baskets, a library that focuses on the Pacific, and a performance room used for the occasional theatrical, musical or legend-telling performance.

The centre is open Monday to Friday from 7.30 to 11.30 am and 12.30 to 4.30 pm. At the reception there are a few traditional and contemporary Kanak music cassettes on sale for about 1200F each.

Maringou-style hut

Activities

Hiking After crossing the bridge into Hienghene, there's a school and then a road off to the left which leads to Tiendanite. This is the start of a hiking path called the Chemin des Arabes, which crosses Grande Terre's central mountain chain before descending to the west coast near Voh. Few visitors, or locals, have done this walk but estimates are it would take three days and there is supposed to be plenty of water en route.

Base Nautique This nautical centre (☎ 42. 81.51), on the beach below the gendarmerie, is the place to come to for aquatic adventures, bike hire, and a new perspective on the Brooding Hen (from here it resembles the Towers of Notre Dame, its second name). The centre rents kayaks and sailboards, and can arrange scuba diving excursions to the outer reef. Day trips to the reef can also be organised for 2000F per person. VTT bikes are rented for 3000/5000F per half/full day.

Places to Stay

Hienghene has no hotels or gîtes. However, on either side of the village there is accommodation – a tribal gîte at Ouenpoues to the north or the new Club Med to the south.

Camping Ben, the guy in charge of the Base Nautique (☎ 42.81.51 weekdays only), has no objection to campers. He charges 350F per tent, there are shower and toilet facilities in the centre and you can store your gear there. The base is on the beach looking out over the bay – if you're coming from the south, take the dirt track to the right just past the gendarmerie. Providing it doesn't rain too much it is a pleasant place to stay.

The people at the Kanak Cultural Centre will let you camp for free in their grounds but there's no shower.

You can camp at Gîte Weouth (see following entry) for 800F per night or at two tribal sites north of Hienghene (see the following Hienghene to Pouebo section for details).

Gîte About 7½ km north-west of Hienghene is *Gîte Weouth* (☎ 42.81.42 weekdays only –

this is the Hienghene mairie's phone number as it takes bookings). Built by the local Ouenpoues clan, the gîte is in the heart of their calm, coastal community of about 40 people. It's just off the RT3 to the right – a hand-painted sign points the way.

The accommodation consists of two very basic cement bungalows which cost 1500F per person. Both sleep four and have single beds and a rough shower and toilet. Boat trips to a nearby island can be organised by the owners for 1500F per person or 2000F, including a picnic lunch.

Hotel Club Med's Koulnoue Village (☎ 42. 81.66; fax 42.81.75), BP 63 Hienghene, opened in mid-1992, is designed to be the perfect Melanesian village in one of the most picturesque parts of New Caledonia. The village is stretched along a beach in an area punctuated by coconut palms and over-looked by the Linderalique cliffs. There's a swimming pool, a massive bar and restaurant and a small shop selling sunscreen, choco-lates and pareos (sarongs). The reception has facilities for exchanging US, Australian and New Zealand dollars and Japanese yen, as well as all travellers' cheques.

The complex has 50 bungalows, all designed as thatched-roof Melanesian huts complete with an imitation flèche faîtière. Each has a private toilet and shower, ceiling fan, fridge, and coffee and tea making facili-ties. The walk-in rate for single/double rooms is 7000/8500F per night plus a 380F hotel tax. If you're planning to stay a while, you'd be wise to contact Club Med prior to arriving in New Caledonia and organise a package which will include accommodation, meals and use of all sporting facilities, but not local excursions.

The village runs three-hour minibus tours of Hienghene for 2000F per person or to Tao waterfalls farther north for 1800F. A 10-minute lagoon boat ride costs 800F while sailboards are 700F for an hour; VTT bikes cost 600F for two hours.

In season, the Club Med 2 anchors at Hien-ghene Bay and those on board are whisked to Koulnoue Village to partake in a buffet lunch along with the resident guests (mainly Japanese, Australians, New Zealanders and French).

The turn-off to Club Med is 8½ km south of Hienghene on the RT3. It's then another 1¼ km from the main road. The closest aerodrome is 34 km south at Touho, where Club Med can organise a minivan to pick up you up for a pricey 6000F.

Places to Eat
Restaurants The only place to eat in Hien-ghene itself is at *Snack Terminus* (☎ 42.81.27) at the wharf. It is supposedly open daily from 5.30 am to 10 pm though it's wise not to count on these times or even rely on its being open. If it's closed, there might be a little lunch-time *snack* place at the rear of the mairie – but once again, don't bet your lunch on it.

Meals at *Gîte Weouth* are prepared and eaten in a large, open-sided hut in front of the bungalows. Mostly it's local produce such as a manioc, taro, fish and salad for 1500F. A more extravagant seafood combination costs 2000F but you'd have to order this several days in advance. Breakfast is 400F; chilled Number One beers are available for 210F.

Club Med's restaurant is open to non-residents and serves a daily 2200F buffet lunch or dinner. The exceptions are Thursday lunch time and Saturday evening when the price goes up to 2500F to include wine and coffee. The restaurant also has an à la carte menu. An all-you-can-eat buffet breakfast is 1000F.

Self-Catering For basic supplies such as batteries, soap, bandages and a few nibblies, you can look around the dusty shelves of *Le Magasin* across the road from the wharf. The store, with its sloping porch, makeshift benches and bottle opener fastened to the wall, supplies cold beers, tinned food and baguettes, but generally it's very poorly stocked and expensive. It's open Monday to Saturday from 6.30 to 11.30 am and 2 to 6 pm (sometimes until 7 pm); Sunday from 9 to 11.30 am.

The only other store in town is the *Co-opératif*, down a dirt road to the right just past the post office as you're going up the hill. It's slightly better stocked than Le Magasin and is open weekdays from 7 to 11.30 am and 2.30 to 7 pm; Saturday from 7 am to noon.

Entertainment
Any temporary exhibitions or the like will be held at the Kanak Cultural Centre. The young men of Hienghene engage in football matches beneath the local school most afternoons at 4 pm. Otherwise there's always the bar at Club Med.

Getting There & Away
Bus Buses drop off and pick up from in front of Hienghene's post office. For details on services to and from Noumea, see the Getting There & Away section at the start of this chapter.

If you're heading north to Pouebo, you must rely entirely on mail buses. There's a bus from Hienghene to Pouebo (200F; 1¼ hours) on Monday, Tuesday and Thursday at 2 pm and Friday at 4 pm.

Hitching Heading north, there is very little traffic until you reach Ouegoa. Travellers have waited from three to six hours on this road for a car to pass.

TIENDANITE
Tiendanite was the tribal home of Jean-Marie Tjibaou, the FLNKS leader shot on Ouvea in 1989, and the 10 Kanaks murdered in the Hienghene massacre. They are all buried on a hill here, making Tiendanite a symbol to all Kanaks of how the struggle to be free from colonialism can be very painful.

A visit to the village, about 20 km south-west of Hienghene, will take you along a winding dirt road over streams and past waterfalls, through the lovely Hienghene River valley. Eight km out of Hienghene, you pass the memorial to the 10 Kanaks. It's simply the rusted wrecks of the two trucks they were travelling in when ambushed, draped in strips of faded cloth, and a gravestone inscribed with the names of the men. The site is marked by a torn FLNKS flag.

Four km farther on the road forks, with the left-hand track leading down to a causeway which crosses the river and continues for about seven km to the village, home to about 120 people. This causeway floods during heavy rain and can be impassable for several days. For this reason, we couldn't reach the village but an acquaintance, who knew Tjibaou well, described it as 'a sad place. There are no men in the village – only that row of graves'. She said travellers would feel welcome 'especially if they came to add a flower'.

HIENGHENE TO POUEBO
The road between Hienghene and Pouebo is best travelled during the day as it would be a pity to miss the splendid scenery along the way. For at least an hour, you cross numerous bridges between the incoming sea and fast-flowing rivers. Kanak huts and stalls dot the sides of the road and powerful waterfalls tumble down from the Massif du Panie. The sea is wild, the sand is bleached white and the road is rugged and sometimes treacherous.

Gradually, however, the scene becomes subdued. The land flattens out after the last waterfall and the earth becomes drier and more barren, dotted by niaouli trees and wild grass. This is more or less the scene as you approach Pouebo.

Ouaieme Bac
New Caledonia's last surviving river ferry (aside from the soon-to-be-superseded one at Yate) takes vehicles across the Ouaieme River, 17 km north-west of Hienghene. Called a bac in French, it runs from sunup to sundown and, from its greasy platform, you get powerful views of the surrounding mountains – the Roches d'Ouaieme rising from the river's southern bank and the start of the Massif du Panie to the north.

A bridge has never been built over Ouaieme River, supposedly because of a legend. It is a fact that the waters around Hienghene have sharks but it is said that a particular creature, which is part-giant and part-shark, lives at the source of this river. Because of its great size, it would not abide a bridge being built because it would obstruct its path to the ocean. This same giant is said to have left a huge footprint on the east bank, because it is so large that it takes only one 'giant' step to cross the river. Owing to this legend and the very real presence of sharks, the people of Hienghene never swim in the Ouaieme River.

Tao Waterfalls

The Tao waterfalls are in the mountainous Massif du Panie which dominates this section of the coast. The turn-off from the RT3 to the falls is about seven km north of the Ouaieme bac, and the path up starts on the left, opposite a cottage just after a bridge. The falls can easily be seen from the centre of this bridge.

Mt Panie

Mt Panie (1628 metres) is New Caledonia's highest peak and one of only two designated nature reserves along the north-east coast. With about five hours to spare, it is possible to climb the mountain from a trail starting near Tao falls. There is a refuge on the mountain at an altitude of 900 metres where hikers can stay overnight. The ideal time to climb is between August and September when the cooler days give clear skies and superb views over the reef and the hinterland.

Places to Stay & Eat

After Gîte Weouth (see Hienghene – Places to Stay), there are two tribal sites where you can pitch a tent and, farther on, a gîte which has both bungalows and camping space.

The first site is the home of Mr Théo Diakout at *Ouenguip*, 10½ km north of Hienghene. It should be signposted but, if a cyclone or heavy winds are brewing, Mr Diakout removes the sign and a few days can pass before it's back in place. In any case, just look for two huge palms and a letterbox on the right. From here, a rough track leads to their hut and then a beachfront coconut grove. You can pitch a tent here for 500F. They've dug a pit toilet and have one cold communal shower – an ingenious contraption using a system of pipes connected directly to a mountain water source. Electricity lines were in the process of being laid in mid-1993 but until they function there are no lights after sunset.

Another 8½ km farther north is land belonging to Mr Théo Thovet, where you can set up camp for 1000F per night. It's a lovely spot, with a stream running down one side of the grounds and the beach at the front. Palms shade the area and occasionally drop coconuts on Mr Thovet's nicely built, but brittle, bamboo picnic tables. A cold-water shower, stone fireplace and little storage shed com-

---

Roadside Stalls

In all of New Caledonia, roadside stalls are found only along Grande Terre's north-east coast and their uniqueness adds immensely to the joy of travelling through this region. Seasonal fruits, shells collected from the beach at sunrise, locally made woodcarvings and soapstone figurines are the standard wares. The stalls are generally humble affairs, consisting of a few lengths of bamboo strung together to form a sturdy lean-to and a thatched canopy for shelter from the rain. Very occasionally you'll pass a more robust construction resembling a proper little store complete with metal grill to lock out dishonest hands.

Supplies differ radically but the basic rule of thumb is that the farther north you go, the better the stocks. Some stalls will offer one bunch of green bananas and three shells while others are laden with seasonal fruits such as avocados, coconuts, pawpaw and lemons. Unfortunately for passers-by in search of an instant meal, the fruit is often sold unripe. Once past Hienghene, soapstone and woodcarvings are popular and sell for much less than in Noumea.

All the stalls have an honesty box, usually a little tin or clam shell, placed nearby for the money. The price might be marked on a scrap of paper tucked underneath an item or it might be written straight onto the fruit's skin. However, just because it's an honesty system, it doesn't mean nobody's watching. More often than not, the stall owner heard you arrive and is keeping an eye on things from behind the tropical foliage. ■

plete the scene. His place is on the right just before the first bridge you come to after the bac.

And finally there's *Gîte Galarino*, the last place on the north-east coast where you can stay in a bungalow overlooking the sea. It's 19 km north of Ouaieme (or 26 km south of Pouebo) in the clan of Colnett. The gîte is run by the extremely friendly Léon Foord, who makes staying here an absolute pleasure. Added to his charm is a picturesque location and serene atmosphere – in total the sort of place you just hate to leave.

Léon has built three cement bungalows with thatched roofs behind his own humble *case*. The bungalows have one double bedroom and a kitchen. They're not flash but they are sufficient. He charges 3500F per bungalow plus 500F for a car but if you stay a week he wipes the car fee. You can camp on the beachfront for 700F plus 500F for a car and there is a cold shower and toilet. He takes boat trips to the reef for 1000F per person.

For basic supplies (like bread), you have the choice of a tiny *magasin* about 10 km up the road or a grocery van which passes daily except Sunday. If you need something from the van, Léon will hang up a bag near the roadway so that the van's driver knows to stop. Alternatively, you can just ask Léon if he'd mind catching a few extra sardines when he takes his net out each day.

POUEBO

Pouebo, 63 km north-west of Hienghene, is the last village settled close to the sea on the north-east coast. It's about two km inland, and has five administrative buildings, plenty of mosquitoes and a bit of history. Much of the mangrove swamp around the village once belonged to a Frenchman, Maurice Janisel, who developed this land into a rice plantation. From the mission church, you can still see the vast plain of his former paddy fields.

History

The first Europeans to arrive in Pouebo were Catholic missionaries who had come down from Balade in the north in July 1847. They were not made to feel welcome and, within a week, they had to flee to *La Brillante*, a ship anchored offshore, after a local uprising.

The missionaries returned on 24 December 1852 and made a second, more successful, attempt to establish themselves. The first baptism ceremony took place the following year after Bishop Guillaume Douarre had converted 104 Kanaks. It was held in a thatched cottage, as construction of the present-day church did not commence until 1860. The year of the ceremony, Bishop Douarre died of the same epidemic that was wiping out the Kanaks. Somehow his death was fortuitous for the missionaries as it made them appear more 'human' to the Kanaks, who had become suspicious of the men of the cloth as they seemed impervious to disease.

In 1863 gold was discovered in the north. Gold seekers flooded the small mission, installing a gendarmerie and taking over Kanak land in their search for the precious metal. The land grabbing was protested by the Kanaks through a petition in 1866, but their chief, Hippolyte Bonou, one of the first Christian converts, was arrested and exiled to Île des Pins where he died the following year. Shortly after Bonou's deportation, violence erupted and Kanaks killed two gendarmes and several French settlers near Oubatche, about eight km south of Pouebo. In retaliation, the guillotine was installed at the mission and 10 Kanaks were executed. Eventually, some sort of order was restored and construction of the church resumed. It was completed in 1875, by which time the missionaries had successfully converted 800 Kanaks.

Orientation & Information

Pouebo is a quiet village. Its administrative offices stretch for 1½ km along the RT3; all of them are located on the left-hand side as you come in from the south.

There's no real centre and practically nothing is signposted, including one of the first buildings you'll pass, the new, blue-roofed mairie up a hill to the left opposite

Snack Canmen. Just past here is the post office and, 300 metres on, the gendarmerie (☎ 35.64.47). Half a km farther, up a bushy track to the left, is the clinic. Soon after, the school and mission church finally come into view. From here, the road turns slightly and crosses a small bridge, on the other side of which is a little épicerie. There are no banks or accommodation in Pouebo.

Things to See
Pouebo Mission Church The church still stands on the original mission site. Its interior is framed by splendid kauri timber beams reaching a height of 12 metres. The remains of Bishop Douarre are interred in the carved marble mausoleum brought from Sydney, Australia. The church has two columned pillars on each side of the entrance and stained-glass windows all the way around the sides.

La Salette This small chapel, two km north of Pouebo's small bridge, was constructed in 1876 by Brother Reboul. The site was named after La Salette, a village in Isère, France, where the Virgin Mary allegedly appeared before two children in 1846.

Places to Stay
Pouebo has no hotels or gîtes, the closest accommodation being *Gîte Galarino*, 26 km south (see the Hienghene to Pouebo section for details). Desperate campers could try the lonely Saint Mathieu beach to the north-east. From the Pouebo bridge, it's one km along the RT3 to the turn-off – look for a large rock on the right. This dirt track leads 1¼ km past the local rubbish tip and mangrove swamps to the beach, where there's a cement block housing a cold shower and an uninviting toilet. There are very few trees for shade.

Places to Eat
The village's sole eatery is *Snack Canmen* (☎ 35.61.81) on the main road at the southern entrance. Simple but filling meals cost 500F, steaks are 800F and sandwiches 300F. It's open daily from 6 am to 2 pm and 7 to 9.30 pm.

For supplies, there's a small *magasin* on the main road just over the bridge or, better still, a large, well-stocked shop on the left about three km north. It sells tinned goods, fresh fruit, baguettes, yoghurt, cold and frozen meats, drinks (but no beer or wine) plus petrol. Trading hours are weekdays from 7.30 to 11 am and 2.30 to 6 pm and weekends from 7.30 to 11 am. If you're heading farther north, this is *the* place to buy supplies as there are no shops until Ouegoa.

Getting There & Away
Bus As usual, the post office serves as the village bus stop. For details on buses from Hienghene, see the Hienghene – Getting There & Away section. To Koumac (300F; two hours) via Balade and Ouegoa (one hour) there's a bus on Monday and Thursday at 4 pm and on Wednesday and Friday at 8.25 am. From Koumac to Pouebo, see the Koumac section for details.

Hitching The traffic flow improves slightly between Pouebo and Ouegoa and, once you reach Ouegoa, there is a steady flow to Koumac and the west coast.

BALADE
Balade, 11 km north of Pouebo's mission church, is more an historical site than a village or community. Set amid dry hills, coastal mangrove plains and niaouli trees, this coastal enclave was the first place where European explorers set foot on New Caledonian soil. There are no administrative services, shops or accommodation in Balade. Only the sleepy mission with its church and girls' school offers any sign of life.

History
The Explorers Captain Cook sighted land here on 4 September 1774. He landed at Koulnoue M'Balan beach while his ship remained anchored in the cove of Balade. Cook and the astronomers and botanists who came with him were greeted by Chef Ti-Pouma and, after a cordial welcome, they set up an observatory on Îlot Poudioue off Mahamate beach (next to Koulnoue

M'Balan Beach) to witness the eclipse of the sun. The following week, they continued their voyage. In 1793, the French ships *Espérance* and *La Recherche* landed at Balade. Aware of Cook's favourable encounter with the natives, they were immediately surprised to find themselves amongst cannibalistic natives whom they deemed immodest and dishonest.

Historians have tried to piece together the reasons for the different perceptions of the English and French explorers. It has been put down to several possibilities – Cook's naivety, the harsher attitude of the French explorers, and the possibility that, in the two decades between the arrival of the two groups, new clans with different practices moved into the Balade area and these were the people the French met.

The Missionaries Catholic men of the cloth led by Bishop Douarre were the first missionaries to arrive on Grande Terre, landing at Mahamate beach on 21 December 1843. They were immediately given permission by Chef Paiama to construct a shelter for the Christmas Mass. Two years later, they moved inland.

In 1847, the mission was attacked by local clans who were dying from disease and starvation. The missionaries fled to the ship *La Brillante*, abandoning both the Balade and Pouebo missions. One of their brethren who didn't escape was Brother Blaise Marmoiton, the keeper of the mission's guard dogs. These dogs, used to prevent the Kanaks from taking food supplies during a time of great famine, were greatly feared by the Kanaks and were probably the reason Blaise became the victim of their anger. The Kanaks dragged his corpse across the river and beheaded it, hanging the head like a trophy at the chief's hut near Saint Denis for two years until, in 1849, the defeated natives returned it to the church.

Several years later, after the Kanaks had been punished by the gendarmes for their rebellion, the Balade mission was restarted, but it did not have a resident priest until 1892.

Things to See

Mission Church This stone church was built on the site of the mission's first chapel. Started only in 1918, it was finished nine years later and the result is a simple church with stained-glass windows depicting the historical events at Balade. The first Christmas Mass at Mahamate is featured, as well as the beheading of Brother Blaise, *La Brillante's* rescue of the missionaries and the return of Brother Blaise's skull.

Behind the church, the cemetery where Bishop Douarre was first buried is marked by a marble slab (he was later interred in a marble mausoleum in Pouebo church). Between the cemetery and the church, a small statue of the Virgin Mary marks the spot where Brother Blaise was killed. To the church, he was the first Catholic 'martyr' to die on New Caledonian soil.

Mahamate Beach This beautiful one-km-long beach (known locally as Maamaat) was the site of New Caledonia's first Catholic Mass, held under a banyan tree on Christmas Day 1843. The Mass was celebrated in a clay hut with a makeshift stone altar. These days, a small concrete altar standing near the banyan tree commemorates the event.

To get to Mahamate, and its neighbouring Koulnoue M'Balan beach, you must take the dirt road on your right at a solitary tree, which is 1½ km past the mission, before the 1913 monument. From this turn-off, it's another km to the beachfront where the road forks. The right-hand track leads to the banyan tree, 200 metres on. To the left, the track rejoins the main RT3.

1913 Monument You won't be able to miss the pyramid-shaped bronze monument that was erected in 1913 to commemorate France's occupation of New Caledonia 60 years earlier. About 2½ km north of the mission, it is engraved with the words:

Here, on 24th September 1853, Rear Admiral Febvrier-Despointes has taken over New Caledonia in the name of France.

The actual 1853 ceremony was held at Piwe, at the mouth of the Balade River. Here (as on Île des Pins), the raising of the French tricolour and the 21-gun salute was merely symbolic. About 150 Christian Kanaks were invited to the ceremony and were admitted into the stockade. Barred from it were several hundred hostile Kanaks and tribal chiefs. They watched the ceremony, which symbolised the end to their freedom and way of life, from a distance.

Places to Stay

If you have a tent, the only place to stay in Balade is at either Mahamate or Koulnoue-M'Balan beaches. There is no running water, but the locals may give you a jug of water for cooking. These beaches are very peaceful spots, with shady banyan trees and pure white sand. Young boys come to the beaches to spear fish, and the shoreline has flat, grassy land which is excellent for camping.

Getting There & Away

For details on the occasional buses coming north from Pouebo, see the previous Pouebo – Getting There & Away section. You can hitchhike from Balade to Ouegoa and, although you may have to wait a while for signs of traffic (or signs of life!), it's unlikely too many cars will leave you stranded.

BALADE TO OUEGOA

Upon leaving Balade, the region is desolate, dry and a bit disappointing after the spectacular countryside to the south. About nine km from Balade, the main road turns south and inland towards Col d'Amoss. At the turn, there is a rough, unsealed road which heads north, passing the communities of Tiari and Pam, before swinging round to meet the RT7 near Ouegoa.

Col d'Amoss (360 metres) is a great spot, affording wide views of the island of Pam and the larger, distant Île Balabio. It may be possible to get to Pam Island, a designated fauna reserve just west of the mainland community of Pam, by boat with the local clan. Unfortunately, much of the land on this north-eastern tip of Grande Terre is eroded from over-mining.

OUEGOA

Ouegoa is an outpost town and the only north-east community that is not settled close to the sea. The approach from Col d'Amoss is impressive as you make your way down through red-brown hills into the wide green valley of the Diahot River, the country's longest waterway which winds for 90 km from its source near the Massif du Panie. The town has a population of about 2000, including many administrators, French settlers and cattle ranchers. Though close to the north-east coast, it is a good introduction to the 'business as usual' attitude so prevalent along the west coast.

In the 1870s, Ouegoa was an important mining centre with various minerals – gold, zinc, manganese, blue malachite and lead – found in the Mérétrice hills to the south-west of town. Copper was discovered in the Pilou area to the west near Arama.

These days Ouegoa is a bit of a barren, one-horse town. There is little for visitors to do except perhaps join the local administrators who spend their leisure time fishing and boating along the Diahot River.

Orientation & Information

Ouegoa has two parts – the administrative centre and the southern junction. The main centre is two km inland from the main RT7 road, accessed by two roads leading off the RT7 – one from the direction of the north-east coast and the other from the south. The town's second stage is built around this southern junction, just north of the bridge over the Diahot River.

Ouegoa's centre has a single main street with the mairie and school on one side and a clinic, post office and petrol station on the other. Each side has an épicerie.

Places to Stay & Eat

The hotel/restaurant *Le Normandon* (☎ 35. 68.28), at the southern junction, is the only place in town where you can bed down for the night. It's an ordinary place, with a row of five basic rooms for 1500F a night which are often rented by local workers. The restaurant is also a humble affair and, as it's the only place to eat for miles around, the management charge what they like. A simple menu du jour costs a pricey 2000F – better value is a 400F sandwich.

There are three *épiceries* in town – a tiny one which doubles as a petrol station just down from the post office, and two more past the bend. The latter pair are stocked with the usual supplies of Coca-Cola, biscuits, tinned vegetables and baguettes and have similar trading hours – weekdays from 7 am to 11.30 am or noon and 2 to 7 pm, Saturday from 7 am to noon, and Sunday from 8 to 11 am.

Getting There & Away
Bus Buses stop at Le Normandon hotel and at the post office. For details on buses from either Pouebo or Koumac, see those sections.

To Koumac (200F; one hour), from where there are relatively frequent buses to Noumea, there is a bus on Monday and Thursday at 6.45 am and 4.55 pm, Wednesday and Friday at 9.45 am and Sunday at 11 am.

To Pouebo (one hour), there's a bus on Wednesday at 2.20 pm and another at midnight; and mail buses on Monday and Thursday at 2.10 pm; Wednesday and Friday at 6.30 am.

Hitching Once again, hitchhiking seems to be the most expedient way to travel over this far edge of the country. If you're heading to either Balade or Koumac, you should wait on the main road – the best place is probably at the hotel.

Île des Pins

This beautiful island, often called the 'Jewel of the Pacific', was given its contemporary name by English explorer Captain Cook. So inspired by the proud araucaria trees that line the island's shore, Cook called it the Isle of Pines. To its indigenous inhabitants, this little slice of the tropics is known as Kwênyii (pronounced 'koo-nee-yeh').

Fifty km south-east of Grande Terre, Île des Pins is the closest most tourists get to experiencing the New Caledonia that exists outside Noumea. The beaches and bays are sublime, the natural colours spectacular and the people hospitable and friendly. Most visitors go directly to the stunning Kuto and Kanumera beach area, while those interested in diving usually head to Baie de Ouameo, west of the airport. The latter is the starting point for dives off Kaaji, the northernmost point on the island.

HISTORY
First Arrivals

Pottery remains are evidence that the Lapita people passed by Île des Pins around 2000 BC, while tumuli show that another group of people visited even earlier, perhaps somewhere in the vicinity of 5000 BC. The island's original permanent settlers were the Kunies, people of Austro-Melanesian stock who lived peacefully on the island until the early 17th century, when they were conquered by a warring tribe from Lifou. This tribe, of mixed Polynesian and Melanesian blood, was led by Chef Katiouare. He soon gained the confidence of the locals and, over the generations, the clans merged to become a cohesive and powerful group of people.

The Europeans

In 1774, Captain Cook sighted and named Île des Pins but was not able to land because of the treacherous reefs surrounding the island. Not until the first half of the 1800s did the first Europeans, sandalwood traders, reach the island. They rushed from Sydney after hearing that the island abounded with the fragrant trees. Their legacy for the inhabitants was rough manners, alcohol and western diseases, all of which immediately took their toll on the local population.

The traders were soon followed by missionaries from the London Missionary Society who, in 1841, attempted to establish themselves on the island's northern tip. But they weren't successful as the Kunies' distrust of the sandalwood traders extended to the men of the cloth. Eventually, the Kunie leader, Chef Ti Touru Vendegou, drove the traders and missionaries away. Although both returned the following year, their ship, the *Star*, was attacked and everyone on board massacred.

Although the English first sighted Île des Pins, the French won the race to possess it. On 29 September 1853, five days after the rest of New Caledonia was proclaimed French territory, Admiral Febvrier Despointes annexed Île des Pins in a ceremony that was approved by Vendegou. By this time the Kunies' Catholic conversion was well underway, as French Marist missionaries had landed and been accepted into the community five years earlier.

Following Vendegou's death in 1855, tribal wars erupted, due in part to the issue of his succession by his daughter, Queen Hortense. Officially, Hortense's husband was the Grand Chef but Hortense had the stronger personality of the two and was regarded as the leader. Popular local legend has it that, between 1855 and 1856, Queen Hortense was forced to hide in a cave with her protectors while intertribal battles raged over the issue of her gender. Other factors leading to these wars were a breakdown in Kunie society, the growing authority of the missionaries and the ravages of disease and alcohol.

Queen Hortense worked side by side with the Marist priest Father Goujon and other

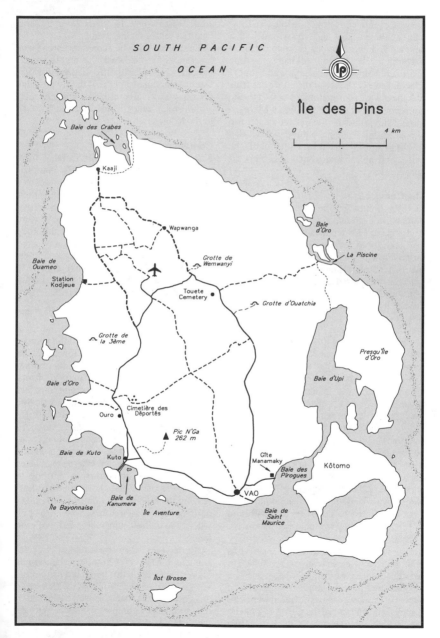

SOUTH   PACIFIC

OCEAN

Île des Pins

0   2   4 km

Baie des Crabes

Kaaji

Baie
d'Oro

Wapwanga

La Piscine

Grotte de
Wemwanyi

Baie de
Ouameo

Station
Kadjeue

Touete
Cemetery

Grotte d'Ouatchia

Grotte de
la 3ème

Presqu'Île
d'Oro

Baie d'Oro

Baie d'Upi

Cimetière des
Déportés

Ouro

Pic N'Ga
262 m

Baie de Kuto

Kuto

Gîte
Manamaky

Baie des
Pirogues

Kôtomo

Île Bayonnaise

Baie de
Kanumera

Île Aventure

VAO

Baie de
Saint
Maurice

Îlot Brosse

missionaries to convert her people to Christianity. She inspired their trust and had a devoted following among the population – as testimony, her portrait still hangs in some shops and homes on the island. The Kunies' adherence to Catholicism meant Île des Pins was the obvious destination for 900 Catholic converts who were exiled from Mare in 1870. This sudden population explosion almost caused a famine, but the locals aided the Mareans as best they could until the exiles were able to return home several years later.

The Convict Era

In 1872, Île des Pins became a convict settlement for Communards, political prisoners from the Paris Commune uprising in France. To make room for them, the Kunies were ordered to leave their island and set up on the mainland. The command was rejected by Queen Hortense and the colonial administration was forced to compromise. It divided the island in two, evicting tribes from the western side where the convict settlement was then established.

The first convicts arrived on the frigate *Danae*. During the next 25 years, over 3000 were held here, including the majority of the Communards. Many of these prisoners were young artisans and intellectuals who despised the work of the clergy and longed for the country from which they had been expelled. When amnesty came in 1879, most returned to France, though a few settled in Noumea. But not all of Île des Pins' convicts were Communards and not all received amnesty. The Berbers, deported to New Caledonia after the 1871 uprising in Algeria, were imprisoned on the island until they were transferred to Ducos on the mainland in 1881, where they saw out their sentences.

By this time, Île des Pins was an ordinary prison for 'preventive detainees', convicts who soon became known as 'wretches in paradise' as they were mainly petty thieves, beggars, tramps and alcoholics taken off the streets of France. Also incarcerated were 750 Kanaks who had staged the great 1878 uprising against colonial settlers in the La Foa

area. When freed 16 years later, several hundred settled on the island.

The policy of sending convicts abroad was re-evaluated in the late 1800s and the penal system in New Caledonia collapsed in 1897. But it wasn't until 1911 that the Île des Pins prison was finally closed. The colonial administration then handed the island back to the Kunies.

Contemporary Times

Kunies have remained quite isolated from politics throughout the ongoing independence issue. One reason for this is that, to a degree, they have been able to maintain their traditional way of life since the restrictive policies of the colonial government were loosened. As they own the island, they control what happens on it and unwanted European intervention is simply not tolerated. The last French National Assembly election in early 1993 showed the population marginally in favour of the FLNKS.

GEOGRAPHY

Île des Pins extends 17 km from north to south and is 14 km wide. The island is more or less circular in shape, with a low tableland sweeping around the 60-km coastal perimeter. This lowland was formed many millennia ago, when the surrounding reef rose, fusing itself to the original volcanic island, and so creating a coral platform where tropical vegetation took a stubborn hold. The lush flora of this coastal belt contrasts sharply with the arid terrain of the inland's high iron plateau, where small lakes act as freshwater reservoirs. According to local belief, one of these lakes is bottomless. Among the high bracken there's also plenty of life, as can be seen from October to March when wild orchids come out in a riot of pink tones.

Île des Pins' south-west region is dominated by Pic N'Ga (262 metres), the island's highest peak. From this perch is a panoramic view of the many beautiful bays which carve this corner of the island, as well as the rest of the terrain and a glimpse of Grande Terre on the distant horizon.

PEOPLE

Kunies make up about 92% of Île des Pins' current 1550 population. There are eight main clans: the Kere, Kaaji and Wapwanga tribes cover the island's north; the Touete and Ouatchia people the south-east; the Youwaty live mainly on the large island of Kôtomo in the south-east corner; members of the Vao tribe occupy the south; and the Comagna live in the area around Kuto. The main tribal dialect spoken is Nââ Kwênyii.

In early times, the Kunies were apparently the only people in New Caledonia who travelled by sea and could navigate by the stars. They sailed on pirogues, great double outrigger canoes which carried more than 40 people. Skilled at fishing and turtle hunting, they still prey on the latter; however the hunting season is now limited. During the Festival of the Yam, the Kunie chief traditionally ordered the killing of several turtles, and chunks of their meat were shared amongst those gathered. In 1993, no turtles were killed for this celebration.

The Kunies' maritime skills enabled them to dominate the southern half of New Caledonia, but the colonial government eventually forbade them to travel and trade by sea, and confined them to reservations and missions. With the end of the convict era and the repossession of their land, the island's Grand Chef restructured the tribal system into the eight tribal areas that exist today. He oversees the whole island, while each of the tribes has a Petit Chef (Little Chief). Decisions relating to land and la coutume are made by tribal elders.

Administratively, Île des Pins is part of New Caledonia's South Province, governed from Noumea. There is a locally elected mayor as well as a council which sits at the Melanesian-style mairie (town hall) in Vao, the island's only village. The council also takes part in provincial affairs. Tribal meetings are held in the chefferie not far from Vao's mission church. The small island's economy is based on the export of edible forest snails, sandalwood and some fruit.

RELIGION

Île des Pins' history explains why the Kunies are such fervent Christians. Although the island was a penal colony until the early 20th century, most of the administrative, economic and ideological work was carried out by the Marists at the Vao mission. Father Luquet, the successor of Father Goujon, was given the authority to govern the island. The mission had absolute control over trade and commerce and the daily life of Kunies. The French colonial leaders in Noumea rarely interfered or tried to wield authority over the mission and a cloistered, devoutly Catholic community evolved.

INFORMATION

The tiny tourist information booth at the airport is open when flights come and go but resources are minimal – you'd be better off picking up brochures from Air Calédonie's

---

A Gourmet's Snail

One of Île de Pins' few money spinners comes from the exportation of an edible snail. These large land molluscs are collected in their hundreds off the floor of the tropical forest by local women and then sent to Noumea to satisfy the appetite of a few gourmets. The snails are soaked in water for two days to induce them to defecate, after which they're cooked, in true French style, in butter and garlic.

Usually about six cm long, these edible snails are not to be confused with their common counterparts, the Giant African snail, which are found all over New Caledonia and considered an unwanted pest in neighbouring countries. The giant snails come out at dusk and feed until the heat of the day dries the last morning dew. They then disappear for the day under foliage or near cool rocks. You can tell the two snails apart firstly by their shells, as the edible version is very thick and bright orange inside, and secondly by the fact that, according to the island women, the common snails taste disgusting. ■

office in Noumea. One beautifully narrated and photographed book on the island is *Île des Pins – Where Nature Dreams* (for details see the Books section in the Facts for the Visitor chapter). Trekkers and keen hitchhikers should consider IGN's 'Série Orange' map (Nr 4838) detailing the island.

Île des Pins' only post office is in Vao. It also houses one of the island's two public telephones. The other is at the airport. At Kuto, Gîte Nataiwatch also has a telephone which the public may use. There are no banks on the island, however some of the gîtes accept credit cards.

DANGERS & REQUESTS

Along the rocky shores and pools you may encounter the venomous, striped jersey sea snake. These unaggressive snakes have a fatal bite so it's best just to leave them alone.

By request of the Grand Chef, topless and nude bathing is not permitted on any beaches on Île des Pins. Wearing only a swimsuit on roads and in the village of Vao is also not tolerated. Windsurfing is permitted only in Kuto and Kanumera bays.

THINGS TO DO

There are plenty of opportunities for water-based activities such as swimming, snorkelling and windsurfing. Excellent scuba diving sites can be reached off the north-western tip of Île des Pins. For details, see the Baie de Ouameo section.

Cycling and walking are great ways to get around the island.

ACCOMMODATION

Accommodation on Île des Pins consists of family-run gîtes. With the exception of Station Kodjeue, which is operated by a Swiss man, all the gîtes are run by locals on their tribal lands and most allow campers for a fee. As family establishments, they are well run, reasonably priced and the atmosphere is generally congenial.

FOOD & DRINK

The people of Île de Pins mainly live off locally grown and caught produce. Extra provisions arrive about once every three weeks when the *Boulari* from Noumea drops anchor. The few shops that exist are very poorly stocked in comparison with similar outlets on the Loyauté islands or around Grande Terre, and what they have is expensive. Similarly, eating in restaurants twice a day is pricey so, before leaving the mainland, it is advisable to bring some ingredients for a decent picnic.

The restaurants attached to the gîtes serve both lunch and dinner but you must give the staff a few hours' notice if you intend to dine. Seafood is a local speciality, the most common freshly caught fish being Spangled Emperor, reef tuna, whiting, mullet and sardines. Between April and June, crabs will feature. Lobster, turtle and edible snails are also on menus. Local fruits include banana, pawpaw, passionfruit, breadfruit, cinnamon apple, avocado and delicious mangoes.

Alcohol is available only over the bar or in restaurants at the gîtes. It's dear at 400F for a standard 250 ml can of beer. Luckily, fresh water is generally good and in abundance as it is stored in the small lakes on the plateau. That said, the island does occasionally experience times of drought, such as in the summer of 1992/93, when water restrictions were so bad the gîtes were temporarily closed.

THINGS TO BUY

Sandalwood can be bought in two forms – either as little carved *cases* or as fragrant wood shavings heaped into a plastic bag. Both are sold from the occasional roadside stall or maybe from the art shop in Vao.

During organised island tours, local women often sell handwoven hats made from coconut fronds and laden with colourful

Sandalwood

Sandalwood has been sought by traders in the Pacific for nearly two centuries and, arriving on Île des Pins in the early 1840s, they almost totally depleted the island's sources within two years. As it's a slow-growing tree, they then had to look for new sources and more of the same plundering took place on the Loyauté islands and later on the east coast of Grande Terre. The main market for sandalwood at that time was China. These days it's still in demand, especially in France, where its essential oil is used in perfumes.

The tree itself, *Santalum album*, is not very remarkable – it has a slim, lithe torso draped by small, shiny leaves. The roots and the adjoining yellowish heartwood, which grows up to about one metre high, contain the prized oil. Since the early 1980s, it has been the responsibility of Île des Pins' council to put an annual limit on the export of this precious wood. In 1990 they allowed the cutting and exportation of 100 tonnes which, on world markets at that time, reaped a sizeable profit. In 1992 and 1993, no cutting was permitted. ∎

hibiscus flowers. They also weave dried pandanus leaves into small bags. Hand-painted T-shirts and pareos are also an island speciality.

GETTING THERE & AWAY
Air

There are at least two flights per day to Île des Pins from Magenta Airport, and considerably more on weekends. The flight takes no longer than 20 minutes and costs 4740F one way (double for return). Though Air Calédonie mostly uses its larger ATR aircraft on this route, flights can still be fully booked by day-trippers so you'd be wise to make a reservation in advance.

Bookings are made in Noumea at Air Calédonie (☎ 25.21.77); you can also enquire about flights at Magenta Airport (☎ 25.21.77). Generally, when you reserve a flight to Île des Pins, the travel agent will book you into the gîte of your choice (and take payment for it on the spot), and arrange for the gîte owner to pick you up at the airport (for a fee payable once you're there). This is flexible however and, if you're camping, hitching or don't want to pre-book accommodation, just say so.

If you want to change your flight or if you have an open booking, you can rearrange your schedule at Air Calédonie's office (☎ 46.11.08) in Kuto. It is open weekdays from 7.15 to 11.15 am and 2 to 5 pm, and Saturday from 7.30 to 11.30 am.

The following flight schedules are from early 1993 and, of course, are subject to change.

	from Noumea	from Île des Pins
Monday	8.10 am	9.00 am
	4.25 pm	5.15 pm
Tuesday	8.10 am	9.00 am
	4.35 pm	5.25 pm
Wednesday	8.10 am	9.00 am
	4.25 pm	5.15 pm
Thursday	8.10 am	9.00 am
	8.55 am	9.35 am
	4.20 pm	5.00 pm
	4.35 pm	5.25 pm
Friday	8.10 am	9.00 am
	8.40 am	9.30 am
	3.25 pm	4.15 pm
	4.25 pm	5.15 pm
Saturday	7.35 am	8.15 am
	8.10 am	9.00 am
	8.40 am	9.30 am
	8.55 am	9.35 am
	4.25 pm	5.15 pm
	4.55 pm	5.45 pm
	5.10 pm	5.50 pm
Sunday	8.10 am	9.00 am
	8.40 am	9.30 am
	2.45 pm	3.25 pm
	3.25 pm	4.15 pm
	4.25 pm	5.15 pm

Boat

The *Boulari*, operated by Société Hanner (☎ 27.35.26), is a cargo ship that delivers supplies to Île des Pins from Noumea once every three weeks. It generally arrives on a

Friday, though its schedule depends greatly on the weather and tends to be pretty sporadic these days. It has been known to show up on Tuesdays instead.

Theoretically it should depart from Noumea's Quai des Caboteurs on Thursday at 10 pm, arriving at the Baie de Kuto wharf seven hours later. The one-way trip costs 2500F; there is room for about a dozen people. That said, there's no place to sleep and no seating area on board; however you are allowed to make yourself as comfortable as possible in the passageway between the captain's quarters and the operations room.

The return voyage to Noumea is probably more pleasant, not to mention scenic, as the *Boulari* sails in daylight hours, leaving Kuto wharf at about 11 am on the Friday. Again, it's better not to rely solely on this ship for a return ticket because, if the weather is bad or there is a labour dispute, you'll be stuck on Île des Pins for another three weeks.

Yacht

Yachties wanting supplies such as gas refills, batteries etc should try Chez Follenfant in Kuto. It's possible to have a chartered yacht delivered to Île des Pins, from where you can then sail it to your chosen destination. For details, refer to the Sea section in the introductory Getting Around chapter.

Organised Tours

Two Noumean tour agents organise day trips to Île des Pins which include return airfares, a minibus tour of the island and lunch at one of the gîtes. You should book at least a day ahead as these tours are very popular with package groups. Agence Orima (☎ 28.28.42), 1st floor, 27bis Ave Maréchal Foch charges 22,500F for its tour while with Amac Tours (☎ 26.38.38), in the Palm Beach complex at Anse Vata, it is 18,700F.

GETTING AROUND

There is no public transport on Île des Pins, but all the gîtes have minivans, in order to run tours and provide airport transfers.

To/From the Airport

Île des Pin's aerodrome is in the north of the island, laid out on the central tableland by US soldiers in 1942. Gîte owners do not automatically meet each incoming flight. They turn up only if you have pre-booked accommodation and the minivan transfer through the Air Calédonie office in Noumea. The gîtes at Kuto and Vao charge 600F for a one-way ride from the airport; 1200F for both ways (except Kuberka, which charges 1500F). Station Kodjeue, which is closer to the airport, charges 1000F return.

You must inform the family who run the gîte that you need airport transport for your Noumea-bound flight. They, in turn, inform the minivan driver and he arrives at the appropriate time to pick you up.

Car Rental

It is possible to rent cars on Île des Pins. With three or four people, plus a day to cover the island's 60 km of asphalt roads (there are plenty more that are unsealed), it is a viable alternative to a minibus tour.

Cars can be rented from Station Kodjeue for 4500F per day plus 45F per km, or from Gîte Nataiwatch for 5000F per day plus 50F per km. Alternatively, the Location de Voiture (Rent-a-Car) office is off the main street of Vao, at the entrance to the town coming in from Kuto. At most rental outlets you'll be looking at about a 20,000F deposit. Another option is to pre-book a car in Noumea through Tour des Îles (☎ 26.41.42) at 17 Rue Colnett. It charges 2800/4200F a half/full day plus 38F per km.

As the petrol station at Vao is defunct, the only place to buy fuel on the island is Chez Follenfant in Kuto. It's on a dirt road, just off the main road between Gîte Nataiwatch and Kuberka, but it's not signposted.

Bicycle

Cycling is a feasible and enjoyable way of getting round Île des Pins as, except for the high central plateau, there are no steep hills to contend with. Bikes can be rented from Gîte Nataiwatch for 700/1200F for a half/full day, or from Station Kodjeue for 1200/1700F.

Hitching

With very few vehicles on Île des Pins, traffic tends to be fairly infrequent, which means hitchhikers usually do more walking than riding. But it is a splendid island to explore in this manner and, in general, drivers will stop if they've got room. The exceptions are some of the minivan tour drivers – for them even to slow down you'll have to stand in front of their oncoming van. You'd need two or three days to do the island justice if you're travelling this way.

Tours

Tours of Île des Pins by minibus and/or pirogue are easily arranged, though for most you'll need a minimum of three or four people.

Bus Minibus tours cover the island's most important sights – Grotte de Wemwanyi, Wapwanga *case*, the Cimetière des Déportés, Baie de Saint Maurice and so on – in a space of two or three hours. On average they charge from 1300F to 1500F per person – ask at your gîte reception for details.

Pirogue Tours on one of Île des Pins' famous outrigger canoes can be arranged through any gîte, or by contacting the Outrigger Association (46.11.36) run by the Douepere family at Baie des Pirogues on the outskirts of Vao. All pirogue tours leave from this bay.

Destinations vary according to tides and the wind but the most popular is the full-day trip to the stunningly translucent waters which wash Baie d'Oro on the east coast. To get there, the pirogue sails to the northernmost point of Baie d'Upi, where you disembark. From here it's a 45-minute walk across the narrow neck of the Presqu'Île d'Oro. At the other end, you're greeted by the warm, shallow waters of Baie d'Oro where there's a large natural saltwater pool, often called *la piscine*, filled with fish and coral. From here you paddle through the water past towering araucarias to the mainland beach where a bougna lunch has been prepared by women from the local Touete tribe. In the afternoon a minibus takes you back to your gîte.

The price of this trip varies depending on the gîte through which you organise it. Gîte Manamaky charges 2000F per person plus a 1500F if you want to partake in the bougna. Gîte Nataiwatch and Oure charge 2500F plus 1700F for the bougna, while Station Kodjeue sets a flat 4400F per person.

Pirogues

Several decades ago, it was feared that the Kunies had lost the art of building pirogues. But in the '80s there was a revival in making these traditional outrigger canoes and, during a nationally celebrated event, many pirogues were constructed and a large flotilla sailed the more than 100 km to Noumea over a period of two days. The main difference between today's vessels and those of the ancestors is that the sails are made from fabric rather than plaited natural fibres. ∎

Another pirogue trip is the half-day trip which takes in Baie des Pirogues and Baie de Saint Maurice before turning south to Îlot Brosse. Again, this ranges in price from 1500F at Gîte Manamaky, to 2000F at Nataiwatch and Oure and 2800F at Station Kodjeue.

Around Île des Pins

Île des Pins sites have been listed in a clockwise direction, starting with Vao.

VAO
Vao, located on the island's southernmost tip, is the only real village on Île des Pins. It is home to the Grand Chef and has most of the administrative facilities, including a robust but attractive Melanesian-style mairie, built in the mid-'80s. The island's sole church dominates the village centre.

The people of Vao have long been known for their fishing prowess and, around this village, you'll see obvious signs of the clan's strong links with the sea. Nets and buoys hang from trees or are stretched out on the beach, though these days the fishers also use lines and spearguns. Pirogues bob on the water at the nearby Baie des Pirogues and Baie de Saint Maurice.

Orientation & Information
Coming in from Kuto, the mairie is the first main building you'll pass. Close by is the post office, which has standard hours, and then the dispensaire (clinic). From here, the road turns sharply to the left and the large cream church comes into view a few hundred metres on. On the other side of the church is a Catholic primary and intermediate school. There is no secondary school on the island – for this, young people must go to Noumea. In front of the church, the road twists sharply to the right and passes a tiny chapel before coming to an intersection. To head north, take the dog-leg to the left. If you continue straight on you will come to Baie des Pirogues.

Emergency
The clinic is open to the public but is closed on Thursday and Saturday afternoons and on Sunday (though there's always someone there to handle emergencies). The island's only gendarmerie is in Kuto.

Things to See & Do
Mission Church Vao's mission church was built in 1860, but has since been enlarged to accommodate the growing Kunie population. Church services are held daily and at least three are held on Sunday. The large church is simple in design, with wooden floors worn smooth with use. Every week, members of one of the island's clans clean the church. When visiting, it's polite to be suitably covered – a swimsuit and wrapped-around towel won't suffice.

The church was established by the Marist father Prosper Goujon, who managed to convert the entire island in just over 30 years from his arrival in 1848. His work was made easier by Queen Hortense, whose popularity and commitment to Christianity made the locals' conversion to Catholicism an easier task for the French missionaries.

Chapel Perched on a hill above the church is a small, hexagonal chapel. Built in 1875 but since restored, it shelters a statue of the Virgin Mary, her face covered as she cries for the sins of the world. It is a 10-minute climb up the path behind the church and worth the effort for the splendid views over the bays and the village below.

Lourdes Shrine About 100 metres directly in front of the church, there's a small replica of the famous holy shrine of Lourdes in France. It was erected to commemorate the island's 1940 dedication to Our Lady of Lourdes.

Chefferie With the gradual departure of the missionaries, many of the tribal decisions and disputes are now settled by the current Grand Chef of Île des Pins. He lives in Vao, in the village's largest house, on the right-hand side as you go down to Baie de Saint Maurice. His chefferie is nearby, as is a fertile garden where representatives of all the tribes participate in planting yams reserved for his consumption.

Baie de Saint Maurice This windswept little bay was the site of the first Catholic service held on Kwênyii. As a tribute, the locals have encircled a statue of Saint Maurice, who stands high upon a coral platform, with tree trunks carved as totems. Eagles, turtles, serpents and faces with poking tongues surround and guard the saint. The bay is about 500 metres from Vao church – to get there head back towards Kuto, take the first dirt track on the left and keep going until you reach the water.

Baie des Pirogues Named after the pirogues that are built and stored here, this lovely bay has a wide view often speckled with the silhouettes of outrigger canoes. The bay is sometimes also referred to as Baie de Saint Joseph, so called because of the saintly statue standing at the entry to the small community. Vao's only accommodation, Gîte Manamaky, is on the waterfront here, close to the departure point for pirogue tours to Baie d'Upi and the nearby islands.

Baie des Pirogues is two km from the mission church. For details on how to find it see the following section.

Places to Stay & Eat
Gîte Overlooking Baie des Pirogues is *Gîte Manamaky* (☎ 46.11.31), the only place where you can eat and sleep in the vicinity of Vao. It has four new and three old bungalows, all starting at 4000F for one person and going up by 500F for each extra person. The new bungalows are beautiful constructions, with high ceilings, wooden shutters, thatched walls using niaouli bark, and hand basins made from enormous clam shells imported from Bali. They have tea and coffee-making facilities. The older bungalows are also thatched but, standing next to their new rivals, they appear tired and worn out. All the rooms have private facilities but, as there is no public toilet or shower, campers aren't accepted.

The gîte's restaurant has a rather chaotic-looking kitchen but it still manages to dish up some great meals. A simple menu du jour costs 1400F, a seafood meal is 3300F and a lobster bougna big enough for four people is 4500F. A decent plate of forest snails costs 1800F; petit déjeuner is 400F.

Bus and pirogue tours and airport transport are all provided (for details see the Getting Around section in this chapter).

Gîte Manamaky is about two km from Vao's church; it's not signposted. To get there from the church, follow the main northbound road until it turns sharply to the left heading up to a sporting field. At this point, you continue straight on along the dirt road until, just before another sports ground, you see a turn-off to the right – this dirt road leads down to Baie des Pirogues and the gîte.

Self-Catering A *market* is held close to the church every Saturday from 6 to 9 am. It's a simple affair, with women bringing a basket of whatever produce they have. From April to October there's generally more choice than in the summer months, when high temperatures and water shortages make times more lean. For the remainder of the week, there's a large *shop* on the right just as you enter Vao from Kuto which has a few supplies.

Things to Buy
A new art shop has been set up in the village, selling wooden sculptures, polished shells and other local works. It is open on weekdays only. From the church, head straight along the road towards Baie des Pirogues – it's up the third street on the left.

KUTO & KANUMERA
This lovely area of white sand, coral sea and araucaria pines is Île des Pins' tourist hot spot. Here you'll find the bulk of gîtes and restaurants and the most stunning beaches that the island can offer. But even with all this, the area is quiet and unspoilt, a world away from the crowded beaches on Bali or the Côte d'Azur. One of the joys of this place

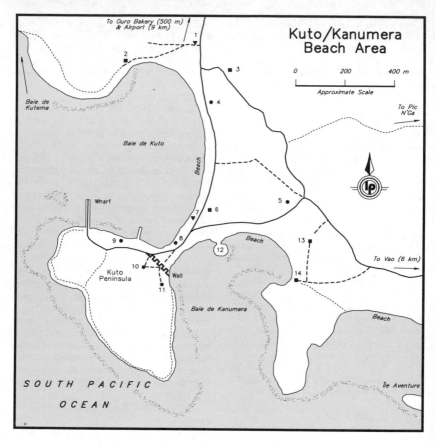

Kuto/Kanumera Beach Area

To Ouro Bakery (500 m) & Airport (9 km)

Baie de Kutema

Baie de Kuto

Beach

Wharf

Kuto Peninsula

Wall

Baie de Kanumera

Beach

Beach

To Pic N'Ga

To Vao (6 km)

Île Aventure

SOUTH PACIFIC OCEAN

can be just to walk along the powder-fine beach of Baie de Kanumera, past overhanging coconut palms, towards Baie de Kuto with its small wharf where folk from the local Comagna (also written Komwânya) tribe come at dusk to fish.

There's good snorkelling around Baie de Kanumera and swimming at Kuto is excellent. Once every few weeks, the *Club Med 2* or another luxury ocean cruiser drops anchor out from Kuto so that their passengers can loll on the beach for a day. Despite this burst of visitors, the Kuto/Kanumera area remains a serene paradise.

History

The area around Kuto was the island's focal point during the convict era. The small Kuto peninsula was barred from the rest of the island by a massive stone wall, behind which lived the colony's administration. Ouro, just a short walk north of Kuto, slowly developed into a small town based around the main prison. A hospital, sawmill and even a theatre were built there, though only the prison ruins remain today.

Orientation & Information

Kuto is six km from Vao. Although it is tribal

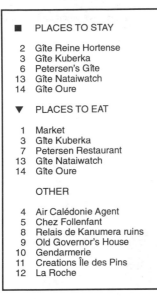

land, there are a few vestiges of European settlement. Midway along Kuto beach is an armed services holiday camp, while the peninsula's entrance is littered with the graffiti-covered ruins of the Relais de Kanumera, a hotel that was abandoned in 1979 after the Kunies forbade Club Med from taking it over and developing it into an exclusive village.

Emergency The gendarmerie (☎ 46.11.17) for Île des Pins is on Kuto peninsula, within the stone walls of the old penal administration area.

Warning A third of the way along Kanumera beach rises La Roche, an impressive coral outcrop connected to the beach by a sandy causeway. This coral rock which has a threadbare stick fence blocking its entrance, and the narrow strip of land between it and the main road, are off limits to tourists. Both are private property and their tribal owners do not like trespassers. There have been some ugly confrontations in the past, so if you're coming or going to Kuto Bay from

Nataiwatch and Oure gîtes, stick to either the beach or the road.

Things to See
An open-air exhibition, complete with a huge old dug-out canoe, has been set up in front of Kuto wharf by one of the island's few resident Europeans. It gives a glimpse of the island's history and culture.

Colonial Architecture Looking out from the southern end of Kuto Bay is an attractive, red-roofed colonial mansion – the former residence of the penal colony governor. Nowadays the building is owned by a European family, though the land belongs to the Kunies.

A street away stands the present-day gendarmerie, a cream-toned colonial house built in 1872 to accommodate the convicts' doctor. The building took on its current role in 1914 and is one of the most aesthetically pleasing gendarmeries you're ever likely to see.

Prison Ruins The ruins of the prison which held some of the deportees are just metres south of the Ouro bakery and easily visible from the road. The main building comprises two enormous cells with thick stone walls which, these days, sprout delicate pink-flowering vines. The latter's presence somehow lightens the aura of sadness around these ominous walls. To the rear stand the ruins of individual cells which were home to mentally unstable deportees. As one traveller put it: 'These cells must have been terrible places to be entombed, hardly conducive to improving the mental state of their internees'.

Opposite the bakery, along a gravel path off the main road, there are more ruins as well as an old waterworks building that is still in use.

In Kuto itself, the crumbling wall that blocked the soldiers and administration from the convicts is easily seen. It runs across the neck of Kuto peninsula, starting at the display near the wharf and ending almost in the water at Baie de Kanumera.

Cimetière des Déportés This cemetery contains the remains of some 260 deportees from the Paris Commune who died in exile on the island between 1871 and 1880. Twelve rows of graves line the ground; however only three tombs have headstones, the others are simply marked by rectangles of white-painted stones. The absence of headstones was the convicts' request as most were staunchly against the church and wanted no religious emblems fouling their final resting place. At the head of the graves, a white, pyramid-shaped monument contains a plaque listing the names of all those buried here, including five women and nine children.

The cemetery is about two km north of Kuto beach. To get there, walk 500 metres north from the Ouro bakery until you reach a well-travelled, unsealed road on the right. Go down this road for about 600 metres until you reach a fork; the track to the left leads to the nearby cemetery.

Pic N'Ga It is a 45-minute steady hike to the top of this 262-metre-high peak and the vista from the top is worth every minute of it. On a fine day you can see the entire island, with the colours radiating from Baie d'Oro in the north-east, right round to Baie d'Ouro in the west, simply defying superlatives.

At the summit stands a humble white cross from where there's a superb view of Kuto. On the ground behind the cross is the outline of a radar tracking station, set up by the Americans during WW II. Past this, a tiny track through the bushes leads over the crest of Pic N'Ga for views of the entire east coast.

The path to the summit begins between Gîte Nataiwatch and Kuberka, about 100 metres south of a house with four pine trees in front of it. It's not easy to find, hence some kindly soul has painted a red arrow on the road to indicate where it is. Unfortunately, this is now very faint and almost as hard to find. If there's been a lot of rain, you'll be up to your eyeballs in long grass for the first few hundred metres, but this abruptly clears at the forested area and the rest of the walk is easy.

Folk Dances On the days when cruise ships call in, pirogue rides, bougnas and folk dances are held on Kuto beach from about 10.30 or 11 am. The eight tribes take it in turn to do the dances and, strictly speaking, the whole beach scene is organised to entertain the cruise crowd exclusively. However no-one will notice an extra face or two, and if they do, it's unlikely they'll mind.

Preparing for a *pilou*

Things to Do

Walks There are plenty of lovely short walks to be had around this area. One of the nicest is a half-hour walk around Kuto peninsula's coral platform, starting from behind the old governor's mansion. An obvious track leads through the forest to a secluded bay with a steep beach. From here, a rougher path follows the platform edge around towards Baie de Kanumera, eventually joining the start of Kanumera beach.

From Gîte Reine Hortense you can walk over or around a windswept headland to Baie de Kutema, while behind Gîte Oure a footpath leads through a coconut grove to a windy beach overlooking Île Aventure. Of course Pic N'Ga (see above) is the ultimate recommendation.

Snorkelling The best places for viewing coral and fish are the eastern and western flanks of Baie de Kanumera. It's possible to see turtles and small sharks.

Places to Stay – bottom end

Camping Camping is at its most sublime at *Gîte Oure*. You can fall asleep listening to the waves lapping the beach and in the morning step from your tent onto the powdery white sand. On the down side, there are no amenities for campers but if a room is vacant you can use its shower (and facilities for campers are high on the owner's building plans). The nightly rate is 1000F per tent.

Campers at *Gîte Nataiwatch* have their own shady section which has nice touches like an open-sided, thatched hut for eating meals, a fire place and quality shower/toilet facilities. Camping rates are 750F for one person with a tent, 300F per extra person.

Gîtes The cheapest place to stay on Île des Pins is *Gîte Oure* (☎ 46.11.20), sometimes called Chez Christine. Ideally situated on the waterfront at the eastern end of Baie de Kanumera, it's known as the island's backpackers' haunt, though it has recently been spruced up with the construction of a lovely thatched restaurant-cum-reception and four new bungalows. These square bungalows, all with shower and toilet, can accommodate three people and cost 3000F for one person, 700F for each extra. The gîte also has four old studio rooms – nothing to rave about except that they're relatively cheap at 1500/2000/2500F for one/two/three people.

Places to Stay – middle

Gîte Nataiwatch (☎ 46.11.13) is the biggest and perhaps most sophisticated place to stay in this category. The gîte is about 150 metres from the water, set under coconut trees and tall ferns, towards the eastern end of Baie de Kanumera. It offers new, well-built bungalows, split in half to accommodate two lots of visitors. All have private shower and toilet and cost 4600F for one person and 600F per extra person (maximum of three). There are also two old bungalows, called 'traditionals',

which cost slightly less but don't have private facilities (the campers' amenities close by are excellent).

The gîte has a small shop selling postcards, hand-painted shorts and T-shirts and chunks of fragrant sandalwood. The owners will organise tours, airport transfers, rental cars and bicycles (see the Getting Around section earlier in this chapter for all details). They will also accept Visa cards.

New accommodation on the island includes *Gîte Kuberka* (☎ 46.11.18), on the main road through Kuto. Formerly just a restaurant, it now has a row of eight modern rooms out the back of the restaurant, all with immaculate private toilet/shower facilities and refrigerators. It's about a 350-metre walk to Kuto beach. Rooms cost 4800F per person and 600F for each extra. Camping is not allowed.

Also new is the gîte run by the owners of *Petersen Restaurant* (☎ 46.12.23) on the beachfront at Kuto. In 1993 this family were in the process of building 12 tourist bungalows which should be ready by the middle or the end of 1994. All the island's tribes participated in cutting the immense trunks used as pillars for the buildings, which are located across the road from the restaurant. Going by its perfect location and the restaurant's excellent reputation, the gîte should be worth checking out.

Another possibility is *Gîte Reine Hortense* (☎ 46.11.19), with perhaps the best location of all on the northern flank of Kuto beach. Many travellers have written to highly recommend this place; however it was deserted when we updated and looked run down. None of the locals knew if it would start up again.

Places to Eat

All Kuto's restaurants are attached to gîtes and all accept non-residents. Throughout Île des Pins, it is a good idea to place orders a few hours in advance to allow the staff time to plan the meal.

Restaurants The new restaurant at *Gîte Oure* has a friendly, relaxed atmosphere and good service. Sandwiches are available throughout the day or you can order a three-course chicken/lobster meal for 1300/2900F at lunch or dinner. The staff make excellent bougnas (even in wet weather when they prepare it in a large pot on the stove) with either fish or chicken for 1800F per person or lobster for 3200F/person. Their 500F petit déjeuner is an appetising platter of fresh seasonal fruit, fortified with bread and jam.

Neighbouring *Gîte Nataiwatch* has a more formal-style restaurant but with a similar menu. A basic three-course lunch or dinner costs 1700F, while a lobster meal is 3200F. They also serve the island's forest snails for 2500F. A dine-in bougna made from chicken/lobster costs 2200/3600F per person or they'll do a good-value takeaway one, which is big enough for two people, for 2800F. Breakfast is 500F. This restaurant is closed on Sunday.

Gîte Kuberka specialises in seafood, especially lobster. The lunch menu (1700F) is usually cheaper than the evening one (1900F). Breakfast costs 600F.

Petersen Restaurant (☎ 46.12.23), also known as Kou-Bugny, has long had a reputation for excellent food served in a beautiful beachfront setting. For 3500F, they'll prepare a virtual feast, including a pawpaw salad, bougna, curried chicken, fish, lobster, rice and dessert. If your appetite and budget can't cope with all that, they also serve smaller combinations for fewer francs.

Self-Catering Ouro Bakery, about 800 metres north of the Air Calédonie agency, acts as Kuto's *general store* but, even here, supplies are at a minimum. Baguettes are baked out the back of the store, then bought piping hot by the earliest customers. It's open Monday to Saturday from 6.30 to 10 am and 4.30 to 6 pm. No bread is baked on Thursday or Sunday (though the store still opens on Thursdays).

A small *market* where women sell locally grown fruit and vegetables is set up on Wednesday and Saturday mornings. Though the women are gathered until about 9 am, it's best to come early (around 7 am), if you want to be assured of a cup of steaming coffee and

a wedge of delicious home-made pineapple cake. The market shed is about 250 metres north of the Air Calédonie agency – look for the carved tree trunk out the front.

Things to Buy
Among the few people who speak English on the island are Albert and Cleo, the owners of the boutique/workshop, Creations Île des Pins, located beside the gendarmerie. Here they sew and handpaint T-shirts and pareos, as well as sell postcards and copies of Cleo's book (the author's real name is Hilary Roots) on Île des Pins. They will accept travellers' cheques and different currencies. While a wonderfully welcoming couple, they naturally enjoy time to themselves so, if you're dropping by (their boutique is also their home), try to avoid lunch times and Sunday afternoons. On the days when cruise ships are in, they have a colourful stall down by Kuto wharf.

GROTTE DE LA TROISIÈME
This freshwater cave has a name carried over from the penal era when the local district was known as the Third *(la troisième)* commune (you'll also see it written as Grotte de la 3ème). It's a cave where highly experienced scuba divers can dive amongst stalactites and stalagmites. If you're not a diver you can still visit but take care – the water is very clear and in the past the odd unsuspecting person has fallen in.

The cave is hard to find as there are no signposts but basically it's about six km north of Kuto, down a track to the left off the main dirt road towards Kaaji.

BAIE DE OUAMEO
Not quite as pristine as Kuto and Kanumera bays, this isolated westerly bay is the departure point for divers going to Kaaji, a 20-minute boat ride to the north.

Scuba Diving
All diving on Île des Pins is arranged through the Nauticlub (☎ 46.12.41/46.11.22), run by a jocular Swiss guy called Tony, and based at Station Kodjeue at Baie de Ouameo.

Divers are taken to the normally crystal-clear water around Kaaji, where underwater caves, coral gardens and varying reef drop-off levels have created what many divers call a paradise. In all there are 20 dive sites, either within the relatively calm lagoon, which is protected by a handful of islands, or on the nearby outer reef. There are no wrecks around here. The water temperature varies annually between 21°C and 26°C. In July and August whales can be seen and at any time it's possible to have dolphins competing with the dive boat on the voyage to and from Kaaji.

A minimum of three people are needed for trips to Kaaji. Tony charges certified divers 6000F for one dive with everything included. Two dives in a half-day cost 8000F; in a whole day 9000F (lunch is an extra 1700F). He also runs dive courses including a novice's half-day course plus a baptismal dive for 7000F. A four-day PADI open-water certification course costs 42,000F; to get an advanced level certificate it's 20,000F.

Places to Stay & Eat

The only place to stay in the north is *Station Kodjeue* (☎ 46.11.42), stretched along the calm waterfront of Baie de Ouameo. In mid-1993 it was in the process of changing from 'gîte' to 'relais' status, which means once it's approved you'll be hit with a nightly hotel tax.

The station has 15 square bungalows with corrugated iron roofs and rough interiors. They have a combined living/bedroom/kitchenette (the latter consisting of a single gas burner!) and private toilet/shower. The nightly rate is 5500F for one/two people and 550F for each extra person. You won't be able to do your own cooking once it becomes the Relais Kodjeue. Six older studio rooms, each with bathroom, cost 3900/3900/4500F for a single/double/triple. Depending on the season, mosquitoes are rampant, but you'll be given a mosquito coil to keep them at bay. It's also not unusual to find the odd crab in your room. Credit cards are accepted. Camping is free.

There's a swimming pool used for scuba training and a tennis court with grass growing in the cracks. To enable you to explore the wide bay, they hire snorkelling equipment for 2000/3000F per half/full day or you can take out a catamaran. Car and bicycle rental is also possible, and airport transfers and island tours can be arranged (see the Getting Around section earlier in this chapter for details).

The station has a good restaurant serving a simple meal of salad, main course, bread and dessert for 1700F, or a lobster meal for 3600F. Breakfast costs 550F and there's a tiny store where you can pick up a few supplies.

KAAJI

Kaaji (spelt Gadji in French), the northern-most community on the island, was formerly the capital of Kunie, where the Grands Chefs had their power base. From here, Chef Vendegou waged war on the tribes of Grande Terre; the Kunies would cross the waters in their pirogues and feast on their prisoners back at Kaaji.

Here too the first sandalwood traders and evangelists made landfall in New Caledonia, the latter led in 1841 by two young Samoan converts of the London Missionary Society. But the diseases which the traders had already introduced spread to epidemic proportions amongst the locals and Chef Vendegou expelled all the foreigners. When they returned the following year, their ship was besieged and everyone was killed.

From Kaaji you can easily visit Baie des Crabes, the island's northernmost bay; however you'll need a guide from the local tribe to help you locate the path.

WAPWANGA CASE

About halfway between Kaaji and the airport is Wapwanga *case*, built by the community at Wapwanga (also spelt Wapan) as an example of a traditional grande case, albeit a very low and squat one. Situated on the eastern dirt road from Kaaji, it is strictly a tourist attraction and gift shop, but the craftwork on the building itself is very impressive, as are the conch shells adorning the roof. It is one of only two places on Île des Pins that sells local indigenous crafts (the other is in Vao) and the island tours generally have it on their itinerary. It sells cowries, handmade replicas of a pirogue, woven baskets, tortoiseshell, jewellery, black coral and books on New Caledonia. The donation box at the entrance is a subtle but not obligatory hint.

GROTTE DE WEMWANYI

Grotte de Wemwanyi, also commonly called Grotte de la Reine Hortense, is Île des Pins' most famous and frequently visited cave. It was here that Queen Hortense supposedly hid for several months between 1855 and 1856 during the tribal wars. Entered from a cool forest with tall tree ferns, the cave contains a makeshift shrine featuring a statue of Mary draped in torn strips of cloth. This shrine marks the spot where Queen Hortense slept. The floor is flat with a high ceiling from which hang large moss-covered stalactites and roots. A little stream runs through the interior, disappearing, like the few tiny bats, into the depths of the cave.

The cave is about 40 minutes' walk east of the airport, or 2½ km south of Wapwanga *case*. Coming from Vao, it's about 13 km – you must take a dirt turn-off to the right just before the main road swings steeply up and around to continue to the airport. Follow the dirt road, which eventually leads to Wapwanga and Kaaji, for about 300 metres until you see a sign for the grotte. It's another 300 metres from the sign.

GROTTE D'OUATCHIA

Another cave worth exploring, though it's much less frequented by tourists, is Grotte d'Ouatchia (also written as Waacia) off the main Vao/airport road in the Touete region. The trail to this cave begins about one km south of the turn-off to Baie d'Oro, near a cross on top of a hill. It takes about 40 minutes to get there and may not be easy to reach without directions from the locals. The cave itself has a long, narrow passage that goes underground past splendid rock formations. Unless you have previous cave experience, it is better to have a guide. Guides can be found around the huts at the turn-off to Baie d'Oro.

BAIE D'ORO

Until 1988, this remote bay, halfway up the island's east coast, was rarely visited by tourists. At least five km from the nearest sealed road, it was accessible only from the sea or by a footpath which meandered through a butterfly-rich forest. But then came the road...and the delight of Baie d'Oro is now high on tourist itineraries (for details see Tours under the Getting Around section earlier in this chapter).

The bay is sheltered behind two islands, sitting just a hundred or so metres away, and a natural causeway. At high tide, the sea rushes in between the islands and the bay, covering the sandy causeway with water. Hours later, it empties, leaving just one pool of water, coloured the most exquisite turquoise imaginable. Towering over all this are proud araucarias.

No-one lives permanently at Baie d'Oro these days as there's no fresh water. In earlier times, the local Touete tribe survived there by carving hollows into the spine of coconut trees in order to collect rain water. This in turn led to plagues of mosquitoes and the practice was abandoned. However, you can still see a few hollowed-out trunks and the mosquitoes are also very much present.

The only way to get to Baie d'Oro other than on a tour is to walk or cycle along the white coral road which replaced the footpath. It starts opposite the Touete tribe's cemetery, about 11 km north of Vao, on the main road to the airport. If you're walking, don't expect to get a lift as only minivans on tours use this road.

The Loyauté Islands

The Loyauté islands consist of four raised coral atolls, about 100 km off the east coast of Grande Terre. From south to north they are Mare, Tiga, Lifou and Ouvea. Together they make up the Loyauté islands Province, the most sparsely populated of the country's three administrative regions established following the Matignon Accords.

In all of New Caledonia, traditional Kanak society has been best preserved on the Loyautés. Soon after the French annexation, it was decreed that only people indigenous to the islands could own land here. Although the islanders have been invaded, ravaged by disease, tribal and religious wars, and politicised by the independence movement, the clans and their customs have withstood change and adversity to remain an integral part of life on the islands today.

While nature is not as diverse here as on Grande Terre, the Loyauté islands' eroded limestone coastlines are very impressive. Towering araucarias and clinging pandanus look down on the most sublime beaches that New Caledonia can offer, awash with shells that could replace any crown jewels.

HISTORY

Melanesians inhabited the Loyauté islands for millennia, though it is speculated that other people lived on the islands even before them and that there were contacts with other islands, such as Vanuatu. Hundreds of years ago, seafaring Polynesians arrived, dominating and ultimately mingling with the Melanesians.

First European Contacts

While some historians claim that La Pérouse, in 1788, was the first European to sight the Loyauté islands, more evidence gives the honour of the initial discovery to Bruny d'Entrecasteaux, who spotted Ouvea before landing on Grande Terre in April 1793. In November of the same year, the English ship *Britannia* passed by Mare. Nothing more happened then until 1827, when Dumont d'Urville was officially sent to chart the islands.

Whalers and sandalwood traders were the next arrivals, the latter making their way to the Loyautés once Île des Pins' supplies ran dry. As elsewhere, this trade caused havoc to the native flora and brought disaster to the local communities, who were helpless against introduced Western diseases and alcohol.

The Men of God

An essentially deeper and more profound contact with Western culture occurred when evangelising Tongan teachers from the London Missionary Society established themselves on Mare in 1841, on Lifou the following year and lastly on Ouvea in 1856. The English missionaries were particularly active on the islands, translating the Bible into each island's Melanesian language while *Pilgrim's Progress* was translated into Drehu.

As news of the success of the Protestants reached the French Catholics (who were busy converting the natives on Grande Terre and Île des Pins), they too decided to have their say in the spreading of the Word of God on the Loyautés. France's 1953 annexation of New Caledonia (which did not take in the Loyautés) made it easy for the Catholic missionaries to impose themselves with military protection. They set up their own missions on northern Ouvea in 1856, Lifou in 1858 and Mare in 1866. However, the Protestants' headstart of 10 to 15 years on Lifou and Mare meant the Catholics were unable to convert all of the islanders, and many people on these two islands remained staunchly Protestant and anti-French for years. Caught between the two factions, the social structures of the clans on the three islands broke down and, on Lifou and Ouvea, wars in the name of God broke out. They raged until 1864, when the colony's Governor Guillian stepped in with the French military and officially took possession of Lifou and Mare. Ouvea followed the next year.

The Population Drain

In the second half of the 1800s, islanders from Mare and Ouvea were taken to Australian sugar cane plantations to work in much the same circumstances as Africans in the American cotton fields. This labour supply was called blackbirding.

After blackbirding came to an end, the two world wars and the appeal of the lucrative mining industry saw many more islanders leave their homes. In more recent decades they have been followed by students needing to gain a secondary or tertiary education and people in search of a job. This population drain has been rectified somewhat since the signing of the Matignon Accords, as new secondary and technical schools have been built on the islands and attempts are being made to promote local agricultural industries.

GEOGRAPHY

The Loyauté islands are geologically younger than Grande Terre. Separated by a 2000-metre-deep strait, the islands were not part of the mainland when it broke away from Gondwanaland millions of years ago. Instead, they were created when old volcanoes sank and coral reefs gradually built on their submerged slopes, forming perfect coral atolls. Minimal evidence of this volcanic era exists, and only on Mare. In the next stage, each atoll was uplifted, forming coral cliffs which rise to a central plateau, the former lagoon. On Mare this occurred in five stages, on Lifou in four, as is evidenced by the various layers making up their inland coral cliffs. Ouvea is the exception, never being totally pushed up but, instead, inclining only slightly to one side.

Totalling 1980 sq km, the Loyautés are roughly 50 km apart and have their highest point (140 metres) on Mare. There are no rivers, though fresh water is found in numerous deep caverns and *trous* (holes) in or

---

Blackbirding

As the traffic in South Pacific sandalwood declined, another form of trade took its place. Blackbirding – labour recruiting or kidnapping are other ways of describing it – became a major activity from 1863 right into the early 20th century. It involved the rounding up of large numbers of indentured Melanesian labourers from Vanuatu, the Solomon Islands and, to a lesser degree, New Caledonia's Loyauté islands. Recruits were used in work gangs in the sugar cane fields of Fiji, Queensland in north-east Australia, and the coconut plantations of Western Samoa. In the late 1860s, some 60 Kanaks per year were taken from the Loyautés.

Although some of the prospective labourers were eager to taste the European way of life, most were reluctant or even kidnapped. The crews of blackbirding ships would entice whole villages on board to trade, and then set sail. Some blackbirders even dressed up in clerical garb, held a religious service on the beach and then kidnapped the congregation. Recruits were deceived into thinking they would be away for three months when in fact it was at least three years and often much longer. The ships made huge profits and many vessels made several return trips a year. As in all slave ships, conditions were far from hygienic and many Melanesians died at sea and, later, from the exhausting 14-hour days that were demanded in the fields.

The British and Australian colonial authorities initially regulated the traffic but did not stop it. With Australian public opinion strongly on the blackbirders' side, it wasn't until 1904 that it was finally banned in Queensland. Fiji and Western Samoa followed less than 10 years later.

There are now some 20,000 descendants of the original 'Kanakas' (the name they were given by Australians), living in Australia. Preferring to be known as 'South Sea Islanders', these descendants are at present campaigning for recognition as a race. Their cause received backing from an Australian Human Rights Commission report released in 1993 which states that these people had 'suffered a century of racial discrimination and harsh treatment' comparable to that received by Australian Aborigines, yet, because they are not 'indigenous' Australians, they have not been able to claim government benefits. ■

under the coral platform which, like a sponge, allows liquid to seep through and be captured. The interiors of the islands are covered by dense undergrowth and tropical vegetation capable of growing on dry, thin soil collected in the pores of the rocks.

CLIMATE

With no mountains to catch the clouds, the islands receive 200 mm less rain per year than Grande Terre's average, while the days and nights are fresher because of a constant sea breeze. Ouvea is generally four degrees warmer than Mare, which has an average temperature of 22°C. On winter nights, it can drop to around six or eight degrees on the inland plateaux.

PEOPLE & CULTURE

The population, totalling about 24,000, is 98% Kanak with only a handful of French. However, a large proportion of these people live in Noumea, giving the islands a density of only 7.5 people per sq km and a young population (18 is the average age). Those working in Noumea financially support their island families but can rarely afford to visit.

Though customs and tribal life have been somewhat eroded in the last 150 years, ancient traditions remain strong and lifestyles centre around community concerns. The racial mixing and integration of Polynesians is evident in the Polynesian features of some islanders, in language (on Ouvea, the Faga Uvea language is a Polynesian derivative), in architecture and even in social organisation, as the Grand Chef has more power than in pure Kanak communities. On Mare, many elderly men wear pareos, another Polynesian practice.

Besides churches and modern stone homes, there is no typically Western architecture such as old colonial houses. Two types of tribal dwellings exist – the essentially Melanesian conical *case* and the rectangular thatched hut that is distinctly Polynesian. Many families, particularly on Lifou, use both types of huts.

Lifou and Mare are predominantly Protestant, and local languages (Drehu and Nengone respectively) contain English words from the times of the British missionaries. However Kanak coutume integrates with the Western religion to create a culture with mixed rituals. There is a Kanak pastor in almost every village while, in caves and niches in the coral cliffs, dead chiefs are laid out in a canoe or mounted into a sacred burial site, as ancient Kanak custom dictates.

DANGERS & ANNOYANCES

The deadly striped jersey sea snakes live in the water and around the rocky shores of the islands. They're not aggressive, but can be curious. Also, when walking through undergrowth, watch out for yellow-and-brown wasps which have a mighty sting that lasts a couple of hours.

ACTIVITIES
Sports

Soccer and cricket, the latter played by men and women, are enormously popular on the islands, particularly on Mare and Lifou. On Ouvea, volleyball competes in popularity. Matches are held on Saturday and Sunday afternoons and entire villages turn out to watch. Just ask around to find out which tribal community is hosting the main match of the day. You should have no trouble getting to it or back, as there'll be plenty of pick-up trucks with supporters and team members heading in the same direction.

Scuba Diving & Snorkelling

Snorkelling and diving are superb around all the islands but there are no organised diving clubs or companies – only the occasional European teacher or dentist might have all the necessary equipment. If you're lucky enough to tee something up you'll find 60 to 80-metre drop offs, unpolluted sites, tiger sharks, manta rays and the usual profusion of smaller fish and colourful corals.

GETTING THERE & AWAY
Air

All the Loyauté islands, except Tiga, are serviced by direct daily flights with Air

Calédonie from Noumea's Magenta Airport. Frequencies vary from island to island – for details see the following Getting There & Away sections at the start of each island. Flights are usually on the larger ATR planes and are rarely full. From the air, the islands' most obvious landmarks are the long coral roads which cross the green plateaux like unravelled white ribbons.

The only way to fly between the islands, other than by going back to Noumea and starting all over again, is with the inter-island flights which operate on Monday and Friday *only*. These flights are also the only means of getting to Tiga. There are two inter-island flights on both days, hopping between all four islands and back to Noumea in a clockwise or anti-clockwise direction. Small, twin-propeller Dornier planes are used and, with an average flying height of 1000 metres, they generally stick below the cloud cover. This means if you're flying between Noumea and one of the islands on a Monday or Friday, you can choose between the direct flight with the larger plane or the smaller island hopper. In cloudy weather, the latter will be your best chance for a good view of the islands and reefs.

Note that gîte bookings and airport transfers can be made at the Air Calédonie office in Noumea when you buy your air ticket. Theoretically, you should check in an hour before the flight departs.

For the price of each leg, see the Air Routes map in the Getting Around chapter. Timetables for the four inter-island flights from Magenta Airport are as follows:

Monday

anti-clockwise		clockwise	
dep Magenta	6.45 am	dep Magenta	2.00 pm
arr Tiga	7.25 am	arr Ouvea	2.40 pm
dep Tiga	7.40 am	dep Ouvea	2.55 pm
arr Mare	7.55 am	arr Lifou	3.15 pm
dep Mare	8.10 am	dep Lifou	3.40 pm
arr Tiga	8.25 am	arr Tiga	4.00 pm
dep Tiga	8.40 am	dep Tiga	4.15 pm
arr Lifou	9.00 am	arr Mare	4.30 pm
dep Lifou	9.25 am	dep Mare	4.45 pm
arr Ouvea	9.45 am	arr Tiga	5.00 pm
dep Ouvea	10.00 am	dep Tiga	5.15 pm
arr Magenta	10.40 am	arr Magenta	5.55 pm

Friday

anti-clockwise		clockwise	
dep Magenta	6.45 am	dep Magenta	2.30 pm
arr Ouvea	7.25 am	arr Mare	3.10 pm
dep Ouvea	7.40 am	dep Mare	3.25 pm
arr Lifou	8.00 am	arr Tiga	3.40 pm
dep Lifou	8.25 am	dep Tiga	3.55 pm
arr Tiga	8.45 am	arr Lifou	4.15 pm
dep Tiga	9.00 am	dep Lifou	4.40 pm
arr Mare	9.15 am	arr Ouvea	5.00 pm
dep Mare	9.30 am	dep Ouvea	5.15 pm
arr Magenta	10.10 am	arr Magenta	5.55 pm

Boat

Getting to, from or around the Loyauté islands by boat takes time and perseverance. Schedules for the few supply/passenger boats that connect the islands with Noumea change constantly, depending on weather conditions and unforeseen delays. Voyages are sometimes even cancelled and the islands left to their own meagre reserves for another week or two.

Société Hanner (☎ 27.35.26) has a 400-tonne cargo ship, *Boulari*, sailing from Noumea's Quai des Caboteurs roughly once every three weeks to take supplies to the three large Loyauté islands. To Mare it's a 14-hour trip, to Lifou 17 hours and to Ouvea 20 hours. It can take 12 passengers in rustic conditions, that is, there is no cabin or saloon and no seating, just a gangway between the captain's quarters and the bridge. Schedules are plagued by hiccups so enquire at the shipping company as to when it's meant to leave and then, the day before, ask again. You'll be looking at between 2500F and 3000F for a one-way trip to any of the islands.

Two other supply vessels, the *Cap Wabao* and the new *Lady Geraldine*, also make the run to the three islands with petrol and other supplies, but they do not accept passengers.

The Compagnie des Chargeurs Calédoniens (☎ 27.32.46) operates the *Ulima*, which departs roughly every two weeks from Noumea's Quai des Caboteurs, usually on a Monday at 7 pm, for Lifou. The trip costs 4000F. From Lifou, it goes to Mare, arriving there on Wednesday; Ouvea is not generally on its itinerary. It's a more comfortable vessel than the *Boulari* as it has an air-conditioned cabin with seats. Once again, you'll need to contact the company regarding precise schedules and fares.

Some time in the future, the *Président Yeiwene* should start a regular passenger/vehicle service between the islands and Noumea. This ship has been bought by the Loyauté islands Province as part of a big investment to improve sea links with Grande Terre. In turn, this has also meant the upgrading of harbour infrastructure at each island. In mid-1993 however, no date was set for the ship's arrival.

GETTING AROUND

No frequent public transport services the islands, although both Lifou and Ouvea do have a bus running up and down the island once or twice a day.

Car rental is available on all of the islands (except Tiga) and can be pre-arranged through the Tour des Îles company (☎ 26. 41.42) at 17 Rue Colnett in Noumea. It charges the same price for each island – 2800/4200F a half/full day plus 38F per km. Alternatively, you can keep your fingers crossed and just tee it up with the gîte or hotel when you get there. One day in a car would be sufficient for a quick tour of each island. Bikes and scooters are sometimes available for rent from the gîtes.

Hitching is the other, highly accepted alternative, with locals often getting rides before they've even raised their hands (don't you wait for the same thing to happen!). Many drivers of the almost omnipresent white Peugeot pick-up trucks even instal self-made wooden benches for the comfort of all those thumbing free rides. Where possible, try to suss out the local traffic and you can sometimes shorten the time you spend waiting or walking. For example, if you plan your visit to a particular off-beat site or village to coincide when the few locals may be returning home for, say, lunch, you may get the one lift of the day. When everyone in the village is going to the neighbouring soccer match, then is the time to go to that village.

Mare

Mare is a lush island with a magnificent, steep coastline dropping into the big blue. It is the second largest (650 sq km) of the Loyauté islands and its coral cliffs are the group's highest, rising abruptly to 140 metres. The middle of the flat central plateau contains pockets of basalt thought to be volcanic leftovers from the Miocene Age. While only a few beaches interrupt the clifflines, those that do are intensely beautiful.

There are no rivers on the island but caves, caverns and water holes, used as wells or swimming pools, abound. Legend says they were home to mythical sharks who came in from the ocean and were transformed into beautiful young people with plaited hair.

The island's agriculture is essentially for local consumption,though yams and taro are exported to Noumea, as are a few more commercial crops like oranges, avocados and lychees. Donkeys can be seen on the island, descendants of the ones brought in by the missionaries, and speckled pigs are common.

HISTORY

When the first whale and sandalwood hunters came to north Mare in 1840, they found a friendly and honest people. This peace lasted throughout the setting up of the LMS's first missions, although tribal structures were undermined by the missionaries' appointment of one chief as 'king' of Mare.

Then in 1866, the Marists missionaries took over the area between La Roche and Medu. Both visions were uncompromising and the clans were soon divided by their faiths leading, in 1870, to a shipload of 900 Catholic Mareans being exiled from the island. They fled, with their French missionaries, to Vao on Île des Pins where they were taken in and remained for many years before returning home.

In both world wars, Marean men fought and died because, as one returned soldier said years later: 'Our Grand Chef, Henri

Naisseline, said we should go to war...so we went'. Later they challenged the fact that, while they had acted for the liberty of France, France was not respecting their right to the same. Chef Naisseline became one of the loudest voices in the Kanaks' demand for French citizenship.

PEOPLE & CULTURE

The original Mareans were the Eletoks, a tribe who called themselves 'the sons of lizards'. They were possibly the builders of a stone wall at Hnaenedr which still puzzles today's archaeologists (see the section on La

Roche). In the 18th century, the Eletoks were overcome by stronger Polynesian races.

These days, Mare's population of 5600 encompasses about 20 clans. Only 1% of the population is French, made up of a handful of teachers, doctors, a dentist and the odd researcher. The clans all speak Nengone but are divided into three chiefdoms. The Grand Chef is Nidoish Naisseline, the son of the wartime chief. In the late 1960s, Nidoish Naisseline returned from university in Paris to help found the Kanak nationalist movement. Later, the charismatic Naisseline turned from radical to moderate social democrat,

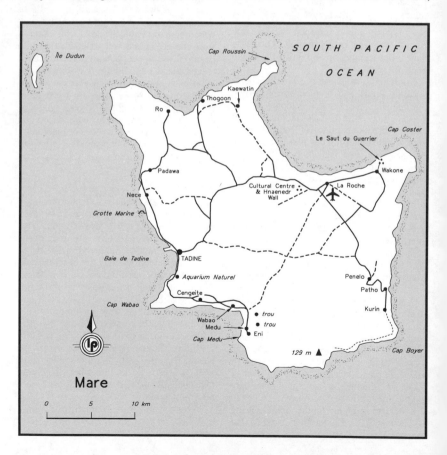

forming his own pro-independence Kanak Socialist Liberation party which is heavily supported on Mare. Nowadays 80% of the population is pro-independence.

The Mareans are extremely friendly and relaxed people. Everyone knows every one else and handshakes, non-verbal greetings, suppressed laughter and smiles are all part of their hospitality. Passengers in passing vehicles and even fellow walkers acknowledge cach other in a one-handed salute and you'll quickly feel the stranger you are if you don't return the greeting.

Legend-telling is still alive and well amongst older Mareans who speak to their children about the *Moyaac*, very old spirits, half-thing and half-animal, who existed before humans came to the island, and of the *Washongoshongo*, a spirit that brought fire from Vanuatu to Mare.

INFORMATION

The west-coast port town of Tadine is the island's administrative centre and port. The airport is near La Roche, a village 22 km north-east of Tadine. There are clinics at both La Roche and Tadine as well as a gendarmerie at the latter. See those village sections for details.

The IGN 'Série Orange' map (Nr 4845) covers both Mare and the nearby island of Tiga, as well as the three islets between Mare and Lifou.

ACTIVITIES
Diving

No club organises dives; however, with your own equipment you may be able to arrange a dive through the dentist at Wabao, who has an air compressor.

PLACES TO STAY & EAT

With the permission of the local villagers you can pitch your tent practically anywhere. Otherwise, only the west coast villages of Tadine, Cengeite and Nece have a gîte or a restaurant with a couple of basic rooms.

Except for the little snack bar opposite the airport, restaurants are attached only to accommodation. Mare is expensive for supplies in comparison with Noumea. A baguette costs 70F and a small tin of sardines is 100F. A Number One beer is 150F. The island's only bakery is at Nece. Baguettes, croissants and pastries are cooked daily (except Saturday) and distributed to the small shops around the island. On Saturday these shops usually sell *pain de marmite*, a heavy round bread baked in huge cooking pots by local women and sold by the *tranche* (slice) for about 100F.

GETTING THERE & AWAY
Air

Flying into Mare you can see the entire island – for the best view, sit on the right-hand side of the plane.

The small airport at La Roche, two km from the village, has an Air Calédonie counter (☎ 45.42.55) which opens shortly before and after flights.

Direct daily flights between Mare and Magenta Airport take 35 minutes and cost 7060F one way. As of early 1993, the timetable is as follows:

	from Magenta	from Mare
Monday	6.30 am	7.35 am
	3.30 pm	4.35 pm
Tuesday	6.30 am	7.35 am
	3.30 pm	4.35 pm
Wednesday	9.55 am	11.00 am
Thursday	6.30 am	7.35 am
	2.25 pm	3.30 pm
Friday	6.30 am	7.35 am
	1.45 pm	2.45 pm
	6.10 pm	7.15 pm
Saturday	6.30 am	7.35 am
Sunday	2.00 pm	3.00 pm
	6.10 pm	7.15 pm

For details on inter-island flights, see the Getting There & Away section at the start of this chapter.

Boat

Cargo/passenger boats dock at the wharf at Tadine. See the introductory Getting There & Away section of this chapter for details.

GETTING AROUND

Mare has no public transport so you must rely on your thumb, feet or wallet to get you around.

To/From the Airport

Transfers to and from the airport are organised only by Gîte Si-Hmed at Cengeite. It's best to arrange it when you book your accommodation for the gîte through the Air Calédonie office in Noumea. The return transfer costs 2400F. Once Restau Hnala at Tadine has finished its rooms, it too will offer transfers.

Cars, Bikes & Tours

All these can be arranged through Gîte Si-Hmed at Cengeite. Cars are available for 7000F per day but take note, petrol supplies can be rationed or even run out at times when the *Cap Wabao* is delayed.

Cycling around Mare is wonderful and, except for the climb up to the plateau, the terrain is pretty flat. Bikes are rented for 700/1200F per half/full day.

The gîte's owner organises three-hour, round-island tours costing 2500F per person.

Hitching

Everybody hitches on Mare. However, patience is required to get to some of the villages on the island's extremes, such as Ro and Patho.

Around Mare

TADINE

This gentle seaside town hit the national headlines in May 1989 as it was the hometown of Yeiwene Yeiwene, the second in command of the FLNKS, who was assassinated on Ouvea. He is buried here by the sea.

Tadine is the administrative centre of Mare, home to some 300 people and extending along the wide calm Baie de Tadine. There's no beach; instead the palm-lined shore is made up of sharp limestone rocks, pocked with craters and holes, beneath which the sea washes in. Boys and men fish from these rocks and, on warm afternoons, children dive bomb into the water.

A big new wharf is being built to accommodate the inter-island ferry and should be finished by February or March '94.

Orientation & Information

Tadine is made up of two roads. The one from La Roche comes down from the plateau to meet the main waterfront road at a T-intersection, marked by a war memorial.

Entering from La Roche, the first thing you'll pass is a large new secondary school. Next is the clinic, which is to the left on a sharp bend in the road, about 500 metres before the water. It is open to the public and there are two French doctors in residence.

Just before the war memorial is the town's co-op épicerie and, next to it, a large Protestant church built in the 1930s.

At the water, the road north heads to Nece past the new wharf, the mairie and a primary school. To the left is a new BCI bank (only good for exchanging French francs), a restaurant, the post office (open standard hours and has a public phone box) and, finally, the gendarmerie (☎ 45.41.17). This road continues to Cengeite.

Things to See

Sadly, Tadine's only 'sights' are memorials to the dead. At the T-junction there are two monuments. The one closer to the sea is dedicated to the people who drowned on an inter-island trader, *Monique*, in 1953. At least 126 people were on board, and no trace of the ship, which disappeared between Mare and Lifou, was ever found.

In front of it is a memorial to the 45 Mareans who fought and died on European soil in WW I.

Two km past the gendarmerie, on the road south to Cengeite, is the grave of Yeiwene. Draped in a mass of floral tributes and pieces of material, it sits on a small rocky outcrop in a lovely coconut grove next to the sea. You must ask permission at the nearby house before approaching the grave or taking photos.

Places to Stay & Eat

Tadine's sole accommodation and eatery is the new *Restau Hnala* (☎ 45.43.96) next to the post office. In mid-1993, the lodging section was still being built. It should be finished by early 1994. There will be five adjoining rooms which will cost about 3000F for one or two people, and 1500F for each extra person. The open-sided, thatched-roof restaurant is open daily for breakfast, lunch and dinner. It's very relaxing, with a few chickens pecking about under the tables and views of the palms. It serves a decent menu du jour for 1200F. Special meals like lobster or coconut crab cost 2000F and must be ordered a day or so in advance.

For self-caterers, the co-op store has a supply of bread, beer, biscuits and tinned sardines, but little fresh fruit or vegies. It is open daily from 7 to 11.30 am and 2 to 7 pm (afternoon trading on Saturday is from 3 to 7 pm and on Sunday from 6 to 7 pm).

AQUARIUM NATUREL

Between Tadine and Cengeite there is a rock pool known locally as the *aquarium naturel*. This round, naturally carved pool is fed from underground, and its clear translucent water is home to a variety of fish, bêches-de-mer and coral.

The aquarium is on the right-hand side, roughly three km from the Tadine gendarmerie, just before a slight rise in the road and the start of small cliffs to the left. It is unmarked. You must look for two telephone poles leaning together and, close by, some well-worn tyre tracks leading into heavy shrubs. The aquarium is just through this undergrowth.

CENGEITE

In all of New Caledonia, Cengeite (pronounced 'chen-gct-ay') perhaps best epitomises a slice of Pacific paradise. A tribal village with a bounty of fat squat huts that bristle with well-trimmed thatch, this grassy community is sprinkled with coconut palms and, nearby, has the purest of beaches. It is a must to visit for anyone coming to Mare.

About 10 km south of Tadine, the Cengeite clan lives between the main road and a smaller coastal road which leads off to the right as you arrive from Tadine. This latter route weaves through the village, past a épicerie and nearby church, to Gîte Si-Hmed, the only other real place for tourists to stay on Mare. Its location is sublime, overlooking a pristine beach of bleached white sand backed by an azure lagoon and a distant reef. In the evening, you can stroll through the village which is illuminated by fires and the stars, or simply make a campfire on the beach and watch the underwater spotlights of the lobster fishers.

Things to See & Do

If you can drag yourself away from combing the beach for nautilus shells, the area is perfect for just leisurely exploring either on foot or bike.

On Sundays, soccer and women's cricket are played side by side on a large field near the sea. It's a huge event, with up to eight cricket teams playing and plenty of spectators. To get to the field, take either the white coral road to the right off the main road (about 200 metres before the Cengeite turnoff when arriving from Tadine), or the coral road to the left before the church when coming from the gîte.

Places to Stay & Eat

Gîte The beachfront *Gîte Si-Hmed* (☎ 45. 41.51), one km from Cengeite village, is run by Mr Wadrobert and his friendly family. They have five basic bungalows, rented for 4500F for one person plus 500F for each extra. They're not flash, and sometimes not all that clean (and No 2 is known to leak) but all have a private shower/toilet and a table, though no cooking facilities.

Alternatively, there are a couple of ultrabasic studio rooms for 1500/3000F a single/double, or you can pitch your tent right on the beachfront for 1000F a night. There's a hot shower next to the gîte's restaurant (but you must ask one of the staff to turn on the gas). Bookings are generally made through Air Calédonie in Noumea, though of course you can ring direct or just turn up.

The gîte's large, thatched restaurant is open to non-guests for lunch and dinner, and the family does an excellent job at catering (but you must order at least a few hours in advance). There's usually a choice of coconut crab or lobster for 2500F or fish, chicken or pork for 1500F. The meal includes salad, a generous main dish, bread, dessert of seasonal fruit, and coffee. For several people, a traditional bougna can be prepared. The petit déjeuner costs 350F.

Self-Catering Cengeite's new *magasin* is the best stocked store on the island. It's a km from the gîte, down a dirt road which leads off to the left just before the village church. The store has a prominent blue roof. Supplies include yoghurt, cheeses, cold meats, fruit and ice creams, as well as the usual tinned sardines, beer and baguettes. It also has a good selection of cassettes by local bands, including Ynesse and Nodi Ak (The Earth, The Land), two of Mare's better known groups. The shop is open Monday to Saturday from 6 to 11.30 am and 2.30 to 7.30 pm, and Sunday from 6 to 11 am and 3 to 7 pm.

MEDU & ENI

These adjoining villages, stretched along the coastal road, are at the south-western end of the island, about nine km from Cengeite and past the village of Wabao.

Medu has a large Catholic church, set well back from the road, which was built as part of a mission in 1886. A few hundred metres down the road, Eni's small Protestant church is full every Sunday morning for the 9.30 am service. In front of it, a small sandy cove, looking out towards the distant Cap Wabao, is a popular playground for the local kids.

Before arriving at the villages there are two **trous** to the left just off the main road. The first one is about 100 metres past the junction of the coastal track from Waboa and the main road. The only landmark is a small palm. A footpath leads from here for 150 metres through the undergrowth to the chasm.

The second trou is more spectacular. It's about 500 metres before Medu on the road's final curve. A well-camouflaged foot track winds over the limestone floor for 100 metres to a deep cavern where stalactites drip into cool, green water.

NECE

Eight km north of Tadine, Nece (pronounced 'netchay') is the residence of the Grand Chef of Mare, Nidoish Naisseline. The chief's home is across the street from the mission church; there are several monuments close by in honour of the early Protestant missionaries.

The road between Tadine and Nece winds along a spectacular coastline of limestone rock, carved out by the deep blue sea. Rock ledges are seen on both sides of the road – along the water's edge and on the nearby cliffs which rise to Mare's central plateau. The curious inland columns of limestone are overgrown with banyan roots and birds fly in and out of the depressions in the rock. En route is one small beach but it's poor in comparison with Cengeite.

When you arrive in Nece, a road turns off to the left leading to the church while the main road continues north.

Things to See & Do

A few km south of Nece is a **grotte marine** or sea cave. There are actually two 'caves', one in the limestone platform before you reach the sea, and the other in the water itself. It's believed the two are joined. The first is more like a large, water-filled hollow than a cave. It's taboo to swim in it as someone once died there. All that's obvious of the cave in the sea are streaky lines where fresh and salt water meet. To see the grottes, you should ask at the ranch-style house just before the two traditional huts on the left as you're heading to Nece.

Places to Stay & Eat

Restaurant La Fourmi (☎ 45.42.96) is on the left-hand side of the main road, about one km past the turn-off to the church. It is run by M and Mme Cawa Kuanene, who rent out a couple of basic rooms for 3000F. They do not always welcome backpackers but, if there is a room available (rooms are often rented by workers) and they like your attitude, you can probably stay. It is also possible to camp here but there is no shower and you won't be on the beach's doorstep. Their restaurant has reasonable food, with a menu du jour costing 2000F and a lobster meal for 2800F.

Alternatively for food, 100 metres before La Fourmi and opposite a school, is Mare's only *bakery* selling croissants for 80F and little banana tarts for 120F. It doubles as a general store and is open daily from 5.30 to 11.30 am and 3.30 to 7.30 pm.

PADAWA & RO

After Nece, the road continues close to the base of the limestone cliffs before climbing steeply up the plateau to the village of Padawa. A tranquil place, it's totally dominated by a white church and matching separate bell 'tower' which face the sea and the distant Île Dudun.

From Padawa, it's about 10 km to the fishing community of Ro, Mare's northernmost village which looks straight out to the island of Tiga, not more than 30 km away. A very sleepy village, it somehow seems to be at the end of the world. It was here that the LMS's Samoan converts, Tataio and Tanielo, set up in 1841. A white pyramid-shaped monument commemorates their arrival, as does a huge pastel-coloured, dilapidated Protestant church. Whalers also had a base here.

Ro's 10 families share six cars. This, coupled with the fact that Ro sits at the end of a dead-end road, means hitching to/from here can be pretty tough.

LA ROCHE

La Roche, simply meaning 'the rock', is a spacious village built around the base of a limestone cliff, known locally as *Titi*, that is marked by a cross. Much development is going on in the vicinity of La Roche. A new technical school and the prestigious Yeiwene Yeiwene Cultural Centre have both recently been built about two km west on the main road to Tadine.

The village's focal point is the Catholic church and mission, founded in 1866, located about two km from the airport. The modern clinic at the start of the road heading east to Wakone has one doctor.

Things to See & Do
The Rock This steep limestone cliff can be climbed for a panoramic view of the village and sea. The path is slightly north of the church.

Mission Church La Roche's most noticeable structure after the rock is the impressive pink-toned church which sits at its base. Well-maintained and boasting the only stained-glass windows on the island, it is partly enclosed by thick stone walls seemingly capable of withstanding an army. Indeed, the religious wars which raged on Mare in 1869, 1880 and 1890 were fought around La Roche and the Catholics sought protection here.

Cultural Centre The Yeiwene Yeiwene Cultural Centre is about two km out of La Roche on the road to Tadine. A large, traditional Melanesian-style complex, it was finished in early 1993 and, in due course, will have an exhibition room, museum, library and reception hall for visiting dignitaries.

Hnaenedr Wall The stone wall of Hnaenedr is one of the most important historic structures of its kind in the Pacific. It dates back to 500 BC, and similar walls have been found on the Marquesas and other western Polynesian islands but are still historical enigmas.

Archaeologists believe there were originally four sides, each wall one to two-metres high and one metre wide, with a perimeter totalling 600 metres. At either end was an entrance where the rock walls were eight to 12 metres wide and about four metres high.

According to local legend, it was built by dwarfs who all agreed to construct walls at a certain time. Some cheated and started early; that is why La Roche's rock is so high while at Hnaenedr the rock wall is only just started.

What's remaining of the wall stands on

its original site, just behind the Yeiwene Yeiwene Cultural Centre. It's a little overgrown but the large rocks and a 'doorway' are obvious enough. The locals are considering setting up a circuit to lead visitors around the site but, for the time being, you're free just to wander around.

Places to Stay & Eat

La Roche has no accommodation but if you have a tent the sisters at the mission (to the right as you're facing the church), will let you set up camp at the back of their run-down building.

As for food, the main place is the *Snack Aréo* (☎ 45.40.02), across from the airport, open weekdays from 6.30 am to 5.30 pm. It's a popular meeting spot and serves sandwiches for 250F, slices of cake for 100F, a plat du jour for 800F and cups or bowls of coffee and tea.

The only other option is the professional school (☎ 45.41.44) just before the cultural centre. Students here prepare a good-value menu du jour for 800F on Tuesdays and Thursdays at lunch time only. However to dine here you must ring and reserve a day before.

For supplies, there's a *market* on Wednesday and Friday in the large, orange-and-red building across the road from the airport. It's supposed to run all day but you'd be best to arrive early. Otherwise, the only shop is at the petrol station several km out of town en route to Tadine.

LE SAUT DU GUERRIER

Seven km east of La Roche is the small settlement of Wakone. Just beyond this is *le Saut du Guerrier* or the 'Warrior's Leap'. Known as *Hna Didi Ni Hnor* in Nengone, it is a gap in the cliffs, five metres wide and 30 metres above the pounding surf, where Hnor from the Hnathege clan escaped his enemies by leaping across the abyss. The entire area around Wakone is rugged, with splendid rock formations and crevasses.

From the rocky ledge you have a view to the north-west of Cap Roussin, Mare's northernmost peninsula, while the smallest Loyauté island of Tiga, 45 km from here, is barely visible in the haze.

PATHO

The remote, coastal village of Patho (pronounced with a lisp) is 18 km south-east of La Roche, just past neighbouring Penelo. This corner of the island is rarely visited by tourists as there is no accommodation and little traffic. These two villages are the last on Mare's list to get electricity – it should have arrived by the end of 1993. There's little to see in Penelo besides the large Catholic church, noticeable to everyone passing through.

Patho is five km farther; the road into the village winds down from the plateau before rising to meet the dunes at the beach. Just before the dunes, a small road off to the left leads to the church, school and soccer field. There's a small unmarked shop on the right just before this road.

Things to See

Patho's beach is a long windswept stretch of white sand sloping to meet a stunning blue lagoon. About 150 metres out, a reef collides with the Pacific's unstoppable swell, creating a constant, lulling roar. The lagoon is superb for snorkelling, though there is a perceptible current, while the beach is laden with special shells, including, after recent storms, many nautili.

Close to where the road meets the dunes is Patho's weathered beachfront cemetery, the graves marked by chunks of coral and decorated with nautilus shells.

Places to Stay

There is nowhere to stay unless you're on an adventurous weekend retreat organised by Alex Wamedjio from Penelo and George Gope at La Roche. These weekends include a long walk down the coast and round Cap Boyer to a deserted beach belonging to the Kurin tribe. A camp is built and traps for coconut crabs set. At 12,000/15,000F per person, two/three days of living Robinson Crusoe-style doesn't come cheap. You'll need a few takers and must book in advance through the mairie at La Roche (☎ 45.42.18).

Tiga

The tiny island of Tiga, just six km by two km, sits midway between Mare and Lifou, roughly 30 km from the closest point of both. Like its neighbours, Tiga is a raised coral atoll, 76 metres at its highest point and encircled by a fringing reef.

The 350-strong Tokanod clan inhabit the north-west corner where Tiga is least exposed and the reef most accessible. The only product to come from the island is copra. Alcohol must not be brought in as, by tribal agreement, it's a 'dry' island.

Administratively, the island is part of the Lifou Commune, although traditionally the people are more akin to Mare. There's a post office, church, clinic and small supply store, but no accommodation. Tourists rarely stay as the island is serviced only twice a week by inter-island flights which means you must stay at least three nights. If you do, it's possible to camp at the airport or, with the owner's permission, on most private property.

On the protected leeward side of Tiga, there are underwater cliffs which abound with fish and coral, and some lovely, desolate beaches.

Tiga's Tale
The legend of Tiga refers to a rat who wanted to get between Lifou and Mare, so he hopped onto the back of a sea turtle to take him there. The turtle grew tired of his extra burden and threw the rat off his back between the two islands. And that is how the island of Tiga came to be. ■

GETTING THERE & AWAY
Tiga's grass airstrip is just south of the village. The inter-island flight from Mare (2670F one way) takes 15 minutes; from Lifou (3360F) it's a few minutes longer. The stopover is just 15 minutes – long enough to take supplies off and load the odd passenger on. Should you want to fly directly from Noumea to Tiga (7060F one way), Monday's inter-island flight has direct links. For the schedule of inter-island flights to Tiga see the Getting There & Away section at the start of this chapter.

Flying in from Mare, the left-hand side of the plane is best if you want to view Lifou in the distance. As Tiga is so small, you'll get a good look at it from either side.

Tiga-style hut

Lifou

Lifou is the largest of the four Loyauté islands, covering 1196 sq km, which makes it bigger than Tahiti or Martinique. A peculiar shape, some say reminiscent of the extinct Dodo bird, this raised coral atoll is geographically diverse with wonderful limestone caves, bleached white sand and rich sea life amidst the coral reefs. The capital, We, is Lifou's administrative centre as well as the headquarters of the Loyauté islands Province.

HISTORY
Long before Europeans arrived, Polynesians migrated to Lifou and overpowered the original Austro-Melanesians. The tribespeople became strong and warlike, and during the 17th century they conquered Île des Pins and parts of southern Grande Terre.

Whalers set up a processing plant on the island in the early 1800s and later, as had

Lifou

0   5   10 km

SOUTH PACIFIC

OCEAN

been the fate of its counterparts, Lifou was stripped of its sandalwood. The first missionaries, recent LMS converts from Rarotonga and Samoa, landed at Mu in the south in 1842 and proceeded to convert the local Grand Chef Boula to Protestantism. After New Caledonia's annexation, the Catholics began their concerted effort on the island. They were aided by the fact that Grand Chef Ukneneso from the north openly embraced them, as he'd been angered by the attention his southern rival gained by cooperating with the British. By 1859, the clans were embroiled in a religious war that raged until

a French military expedition established order and claimed the still-independent island as part of New Caledonia.

In 1947, a leper colony was founded at a place called Cila in the island's centre. Lepers from all over Lifou, as well as from the other Loyauté islands, were brought here to live together, ostracized to isolate the disease. The colony was disbanded when the penitentiary at Ducos near Noumea was turned into a leper settlement. A cemetery and a ruined church are about all that still exist of the island's colony, though there are about 10 lepers living in Ducos.

PEOPLE & CULTURE

Lifou is the most populated Loyauté Island, with some 15,000 people. However, only three-fifths of the population actually live on the island; the other 6000 reside, because of work or education reasons, in Noumea. The island has three chiefdoms – the northern Wetr (Wet in French), central Gaica (Gaïtcha) and, in the south, Losi (Loessi). The Grand Chef of each chiefdom resides in the villages of Hnathalo, Drueulu and Mu respectively.

The local language, Drehu (pronounced 'day-hoo'), is actually the indigenous name for Lifou. Drehu is the most widely spoken language among Kanaks after French, with even people from elsewhere in New Caledonia knowing some words. It benefited early on from the support of the English missionaries, who mastered it and then taught a few generations of children in their mother tongue. The Lifouans also adopted English words from the missionaries and, these days, a sprinkling of the words commonly used in Drehu are of Anglo-Saxon origin.

While Protestantism still dominates on Lifou, the people are not fervently religious. Every village has a church but the people's daily lives are influenced more by tribal rules and la coutume than by religion.

Most families have a traditional round *case* for sleeping plus a second 'living hut', either designed as a rectangular thatched hut or as a more contemporary-style house made from sheets of corrugated iron or cement. Many villages also have a *fare* (pronounced 'far-reh'), a large thatched, open-sided hut which acts as a communal meeting place for any sort of gathering or reunion. The word 'fare' occurs in various forms in Polynesian languages, always meaning 'house'.

While many young and middle-aged Lifouans are politically conscious and active, the island has never hit the limelight like neighbouring Ouvea. Its people, however, still have a reputation amongst the French in Noumea for being 'difficult' and they are decidedly pro-independence.

The Lifouans are very musical and the majority of modern Kanak bands hail from here. The island's ancient songs are being revived by local groups whose music can often be heard on home-made tapes throughout Lifou and also on Grande Terre. A few of the more popular current bands are Drui, Bwanjep and Pedro.

INFORMATION

We is Lifou's largest town, home to the provincial headquarters, the island's only bank and clinic, as well as the main gendarmerie and post office (there are smaller branches of these at Xepenehe). Located mid-way along the east coast, We holds a 'neutral' position at the junction of the three chiefdoms.

If you're spending any time on the island, IGN's 'Série Orange' maps cover Lifou in two sections – No 4840 for the north and No 4842 the south.

PLACES TO STAY

Unlike the other Loyauté islands, Lifou has quite a diverse range of accommodation, conveniently spread over the island. There's a resort at Jozip, a motel and a hotel at We, and tribal gîtes at Luengoni Beach, Jokin and Wedrumel. Some, but not all of these places, allow campers. With the permission of the locals, you can camp for free on any beach, such as Easo and the delightful Peng.

FOOD

Each of the previous accommodation options has some sort of attached restaurant. Again, they range from top-end dining with napkins, silverware and long-stemmed wine glasses at the resort, to more humble outings with often equally delicious meals at the tribal gîtes. Quite a few *snacks* operate around the island.

We has several well-stocked magasins with everything you'll need for a good picnic. Prices are higher than in Noumea, but not over the top as on Ouvea. Once you get away from the capital, supplies are quite limited, with some shops in small villages not even getting regular bread deliveries.

GETTING THERE & AWAY
Air

Lifou's new Wanaham airport terminal, finished in 1993, is 20 km north of We, close to the village of Hnathalo. Air Calédonie has a desk at the airport (☎ 45.11.18) as well as a modern main office (☎ 45.11.11) on the main road in We. Both offices are open weekdays from 7.30 to 11.15 am and 2 to 5.30 pm and Saturday morning. Outside the airport is a new pink eatery, *Aero Snack*, open Monday to Saturday from 6 am to 7 pm and Sunday from noon to 7 pm.

For the best views when flying into Lifou, you should be on the right-hand side of the plane coming from Noumea or on the left if you're arriving from Mare or Tiga.

At least three direct flights each day connect Lifou and Noumea's Magenta Airport. The trip takes 35 minutes and costs 7060F one way. In 1993, the schedules were:

	from Magenta	from Lifou
Monday	6.00 am	7.05 am
	8.40 am	9.45 am
	2.15 pm	3.20 pm
	5.40 pm	6.45 pm
Tuesday	6.00 am	7.05 am
	12.15 pm	1.20 pm
	5.40 pm	6.45 pm
Wednesday	6.00 am	7.05 am
	2.15 pm	3.20 pm
	6.10 pm	7.15 pm
Thursday	6.00 am	7.05 am
	12.15 pm	1.20 pm
	5.40 pm	6.45 pm
Friday	6.00 am	7.05 am
	8.55 am	9.55 am
	1.15 pm	2.20 pm
	5.10 pm	6.15 pm
	6.25 pm	7.20 pm
Saturday	6.00 am	7.05 am
	9.55 am	11.00 am
	2.15 pm	3.20 pm
Sunday	1.15 pm	2.20 pm
	2.15 pm	3.20 pm
	5.10 pm	6.15 pm
	6.25 pm	7.20 pm

For details on flying from Lifou to Ouvea, Tiga or Mare, see the inter-island flight timetables in the Getting There & Away section at the start of this chapter. For prices, see the Air Routes map in the Getting Around chapter.

Boat
Lifou is in the process of building a big new wharf at We. It is expected to be finished by February or March 1994, in time, it's hoped, to welcome the *President Yeiwene* when it starts making regular inter-island trips. Until then, all ships dock near Xepenehe in Baie du Santal on the western side of the island. For details on visiting vessels, see the Getting There & Away section at the start of this chapter.

GETTING AROUND
To/From the Airport
There is one public bus on the island which may connect with your flight but it's unlikely. Otherwise all the gîtes and hotels can arrange airport transfers, generally charging between 1600F and 2000F return (see the Places to Stay section in each town/village for exact prices).

The airport is 2½ km from the intersection of the Xepenehe-We road. Once there, it's an easy hitch in either direction.

Bus
The few school buses on the island will pick up passengers provided there are no kids already on the bus. Otherwise there's only one bus reserved for the public. It travels from Mu via We to the airport twice a day – once via the coastal road and once along the inland route – leaving Mu at 7 am and again at 1 pm. From Mu, it's 150F to We and 300F to the airport.

Car
Rental cars are available from several outlets in We including the Avenod-Peugeot garage (☎ 45.11.42), which has cars for 8000F per day, everything included. Otherwise, the Noumean-based company Tour des Îles works in conjunction with Hôtel Lifou Plaisance at Jozip (for price details see the Getting Around section at the start of this chapter). Gîte Neibash at Luengoni can organise a car for 5000F per day. All places will need some advance warning.

Bicycle & Scooter
Motel Chez Rachel at We rents bikes for 2500/4000F for one/two days and scooters

for 4500/6000F. Hôtel Lifou Plaisance at Jozip has free bikes for its guests. Gîte Neibash at Luengoni has bikes for 1500F a day.

Hitching

As Lifou has more cars and pick-up trucks than the other Loyauté islands, it should be the easiest for hitching. For some reason, however, drivers are not as ready to stop for travellers as are those on Mare, though you still shouldn't have too much trouble. The exception is the road across the southern inland plateau, particularly the stretch between Kedeigne and Hmelek, which is a very difficult hitch as vehicles from either end usually turn up one of the central plateau roads towards We rather than continuing straight across.

Organised Tours

Most of the accommodation places offer guided tours of the island, usually covering either the south or the north or both. Motel Chez Rachel at We has three-hour, half-island tours for 1800F. The gîtes at Jokin and Luengoni do the whole lot for 2000F, while Hôtel Lifou Plaisance at Jozip has half/full tours costing 1250/2500F.

Around Lifou

WE

We (pronounced 'way') is the administrative seat of the Loyauté islands. It is curled around the rather pompously named Baie de Châteaubriand, a wide sandy bay cut by a reef and dotted with rocky outcrops. The bay takes this name from the famous French writer of the pre-Romantic era; in Drehu it's called Opegejë Ne We. The area around We is divided into seven clans (from north to south): Luecila, Hnapalu, Qanono, Hnasse, Wailu, Huse and Qasa.

Orientation

We stretches for just over two km along a main waterfront road. It has no real centre, although the new, Melanesian-style Hôtel de la Province des Îles Loyauté (the administra-tive headquarters of the Loyauté Islands Province), is decidedly the focus of attention. Next door is the small mairie with its dilapidated waterfront WW I monument.

From the old colonial church on the bay, you can see the northernmost clan settlement of Luecila with its mission church and new traditional-style *fare*. The large new wharf for cargo ships is under construction on the southern end of the bay.

Information

Money The BNP bank on the main road changes travellers' cheques and will do cash advances for major credit cards. It is open weekdays from 7.20 am to 3.45 pm.

Post The post office, with a public phone booth out the front, is behind the province headquarters. Standard office hours apply – weekdays from 7.45 to 11.15 am and 12.15 to 3.00 pm, and Saturday from 7.30 to 11 am.

Emergency The new, large clinic, next to the province building, has two resident French doctors. The adjoining dispensaire is generally well-stocked with the essential medicines. The gendarmerie (☎ 45.12.17) is a few hundred metres down the road to the south-east.

Things to See & Do

Churches We's two churches stand side by side at the start of the beach. The more northern is a Catholic church, built in 1897 but recently spruced up to resemble a Disneyesque-castle. From the front it looks like a mini-fortress, though inside it's modest, with just four rows of seats. Next door is the modern Protestant temple. The two are separated by a monument that commemorates the founding of the Protestant mission.

Beach & Water Sports We's beach starts near the Catholic church and winds north around to Luecila. It's long and wide, but unfortunately often littered with driftwood and plastic bottles and cans.

Baie de Châteaubriand is OK for snorkelling as the reef is not far offshore. Sailboards and other water-sports equipment can be hired from the Base Nautique on the beach behind the Catholic church.

Other Sports The big sports stadium, built in 1991 behind Hôtel Le Cocotier, is the venue for volley, basket and hand ball. The adjacent playing fields are devoted to women's and men's cricket and soccer on weekends.

Caves North of town, well hidden in the thick vegetation that sprouts from Lifou's limestone ground, are two caves.

The more impressive is **Grotte d'Avio**, a huge cavern with four-metre-long stalactites and a pool of jade water where the locals sometimes swim. It's behind the ALEP technical school – to get to it you must find the faint path between the palms directly behind the school's volleyball court. From here it's about a 15-minute walk through the bush.

The other cave is **Grotte Bordo**, which is

100 metres along a track across the road from Magasin Anéka. Again, the start of the path is well camouflaged by long grass. Please don't swim here as this pool is connected to the fresh water table and therefore the drinking supply.

Places to Stay

For the time being, We has just two options, located at opposite ends of town.

The cheaper is *Hôtel Le Cocotier* (☎ 45. 11.36), just off the main road to the south and a 15-minute walk from the beach. It has six square bungalows, all painted creamy white with red tin roofs, with private toilet/shower facilities but no kitchenette. They're quite ordinary and cost 4000F for one person plus 1000F per extra person. As there is no communal ablutions block, they don't accept campers. Airport transfers cost 1600F return.

Alternatively, there's *Motel Chez Rachel* (☎ 45.12.43), set back off the beach to the north near the settlement of Luecila, and

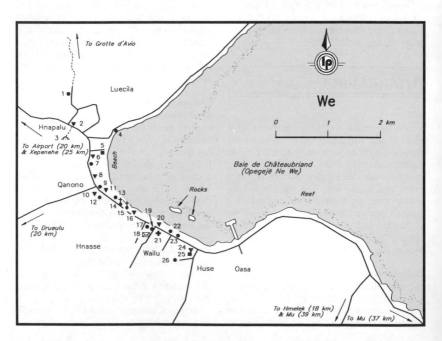

formerly known as Gîte de Luecila. It's an easy 10-minute stroll into We's centre, either along a sandy track which runs parallel to the beach or along the beach itself. The motel underwent major building and renovations in early 1993 and now has eight large bungalows with iron roofs, cooking facilities, refrigerator and private bathroom with solar-powered hot water. They cost 6500F for one person and 500F more for each extra guest. In addition there are three small studio rooms with kitchenette and private facilities costing 5500/6000/6500F for one/two/three people. Camping is possible but it's pricey at 1000F per person per night. A cooking/shower block is planned for campers but, until built, there are cold showers only. Motel Chez Rachel charges 1800F for a lift to and from the airport.

Lastly, plans have been drawn up for a hotel complex with at least 18 bungalows at Qanono, just south of Luecila. Building was due to start in 1992 but has been indefinitely delayed because of financial problems and landownership disputes, as the proposed site is an old, sacred burial ground.

Places to Eat

Restaurants *Motel Chez Rachel* has good food, charging 1800F for a standard menu du jour. Specialities include seafood meals for 3400F or a traditional chicken and vegetable bougna for 2800F. Breakfast costs 500F. The restaurant is closed to non-guests on Sundays.

The *Hôtel Le Cocotier* has a large popular restaurant with outdoor seating where you can tuck into a basic menu du jour for 1500F. A seafood meal of lobster or crab costs 4000F and a chicken bougna is 2500F per person (you'll need a minimum of three people). Petit déjeuner costs 350F.

Both restaurants are open to non-residents but it's wise to let them know you're coming.

Snacks There are several little eateries around town where you can get a decent meal.

Snack Le Champignon, also known as Snack Wenehua, is immensely popular with office workers from the province headquarters. It has tables inside as well as a tiny terrace out the back where you can dine with a view of the bay. The lunch-time menu du jour costs 1200F, or there's a *plat résistance* (main dish) for 650F. The food is filling though nothing to rave about, with typical French dishes like rôti de porc (roasted pork) or chicken in a white sauce. The front counter is covered in an array of snack foods (and a few flies) like nems for 150F, baguette sandwiches for 250F and boulets (deep-fried potato and meat balls) for 150F. It is open weekdays only from 6 am to 5 pm and serves breakfast for 220F.

The bright red-and-yellow *Snack Stanley*, attached to Chez Pauline épicerie, is a tiny eatery with four tables catering for breakfast and lunch diners. It's open weekdays only from 6.30 am to 2.30 pm.

Lastly there's *Chez Kalimane* out the back of the Kooperatif store on the main road. A rough place with corrugated iron walls, it's popular with local workmen tucking into the 1500F lunch-time menu du jour. It sells good-priced baguette sandwiches, boiled eggs, slices of pineapple or chocolate cake and big bowls of coffee; trading hours are weekdays only from 11 am to 3 pm.

Self-Catering We has a handful of épiceries but only one sells alcohol.

The *Impac* supermarket is the largest store in town with the biggest variety of produce, including snorkelling gear. There's a small fresh vegetable section, a cheese counter and plenty of tinned and cold goods. It is open Monday to Saturday from 6.30 am to noon and 2.30 to 6.30 pm, and Sunday from 7 to 11 am.

Just up the road, *Lifou Center* has few groceries but is the only store that sells beer and bottles of French wine. Trading hours are weekdays from 6.30 am to noon and 1.30 to 7 pm, and weekends from 6.30 to 11 am. Nearby, the *Kooperatif Ne Drehu* is slightly cheaper than Impac but has no fresh fruit. It is open from 6 to 11.30 am and 2 to 7 pm.

Chez Pauline near the churches has tinned goods, frozen meat and fish, baguettes, cold sodas and hot nems. There's little fresh fruit or cheese. It's open weekdays from 6.30 am to 8 pm, weekends from 6.30 am to noon and 4 to 8 pm (on Sunday it closes at 9 am instead of noon because of church).

HNATHALO

Three km south of the airport, Hnathalo (or Nathalo in French) is the home of the Grand Chef of Wetr; Wetr being Lifou's northern region. There is a **grande case** surrounded by a wooden palisade and set in a garden behind the chief's concrete house, next to the Catholic church. The *case* is massive inside with the usual central open fireplace, woven palm mats and an ironwood centre pole.

Next door, the huge Gothic-style **church**, built in 1881, seems very garish and out of place in this quiet, rural village. Its forbidding exterior seems to act as a reminder of the powerful struggles between Catholics and Protestants as they raced to convert the so-called heathens. The interior is very simple and spartan with stained-glass windows.

Round the corner from the church is a tiny magasin called Sama Wahiobe.

GROTTE DU DIABLE

This most spectacular 'Devil's Cave', called Hneope i Qanopeu in Drehu, is close to the northern village of Tingeting. It comprises three large, inter-connected rock caverns guarded by an almost Gothic-looking rock entrance hall with walls 30 metres high. Past this is the second cave, darker than the first, and for the third you'll need a lamp.

The cave can be visited only with a guide, Albert Trohmae (☎ 45.16.64), who acts as the cave's custodian. He lives in Tingeting. To find him, go 150 metres past the recently renovated church to a red sign pointing down a track to the right. This path leads to a blue building with psychedelic wall paintings. Here you must pay Mr Trohmae 700F per person to visit the cave, which is a 30-minute walk to the north (if you're in a car, you can drive the first two km and walk the last one). As you near the cave there's a little easy cliff-climbing involved.

Tingeting is only a tiny place at the end of a dead-end road six km north-east of the airport. It can be a difficult hitch and, if you're making the trip, you'd be well advised to ring Mr Trohmae before turning up on the doorstep, to ensure that he's there.

JOKIN

Jokin (Doking in French) is Lifou's northernmost village. It's a sublime spot, sitting high on the cliffs overlooking a magnificent bay and has one of the most attractive *cases* in all New Caledonia (unfortunately, you're not allowed to photograph it). The bay is superb for snorkelling and diving, with numerous huge fish, the occasional sea snake, and an underwater cave rich in multi-coloured fragile gorgonian coral.

Orientation & Information

Jokin is a tiny place with one tourist gîte sitting at the end of the main road (round the church to the right) before you tumble over the cliffs. The gîte is owned by the village's Petit Chef, Georges Kahlemu, a mine of information on the local area which he'll happily divulge in English.

Things to See & Do

The very beautiful *case* is between the gîte and the church. Outside the latter stands one of Lifou's ubiquitous 1992 **monuments** commemorating the arrival of the 'Word of God' on the island 150 years earlier.

Between the monument and the *case* is a footpath leading down to a little **limestone cove** from where you can dive into the turquoise waters. Enormous parrot fish and great drop offs are part of the scene. Georges (from the gîte) hires snorkelling gear for 500F and can organise raft excursions from here for 1000F per person.

Another **cove** is accessible via a track to the left, about 20 metres past the village's water tower. A few poles are kept here for making fishing rafts.

Places to Stay & Eat

Jokin's gîte (☎ 45.16.48) is called *Fare Falaise* meaning 'the meeting hut on the cliff'. It is run by the Kahlemu family and, staying here, you quickly feel part of the family. There is a *case* in the centre of the compact grounds where Georges' four kids sit and chat around a fire in the evenings.

At the time of updating, the gîte boasted just one bungalow, but what a bungalow it is. Built on the very edge of the cliff, it opens out to a view of the sea and the setting sun that is unrivalled in New Caledonia. Inside, it's pretty ordinary but cheap enough at 1500/3000/3750F for one/two/three people. You can pitch your tent anywhere that a chicken is not scratching for 1000F a night. The

gîte has a communal ablutions block – blue for men, pink for women, and cold showers for all. Airport transfers cost 1000F.

Fare Falaise has a nicely decorated restaurant run by Mrs Kahlemu, an excellent cook. If you're eating here, you should let her know a few hours beforehand. Lunch costs 1500F, dinner is 1800F. For that you'll get fresh oven-baked fish served with rice cooked in coconut cream, a basket of pain de marmite (bread cooked by local women that is much heavier than a baguette), a grated green pawpaw and carrot salad, and fresh fruit salad for dessert. Other dishes are available such as lobster (3500F), coconut crab (2800F), roussette (2000F) and bougna (1500F) but for these you must order a day or two in advance. Breakfast is 400F.

The only *shop* in Jokin is in the tiny square stone house on the left before the church as you enter the village. It's not well stocked.

Getting There & Away

Each weekday at 7 am, Georges acts as the local bus driver, driving his minivan to We, via Easo and Xepenehe, picking up folk en route. He leaves We at about 11 am to return to Jokin. He'll gladly give you a lift either way; the fare is a few hundred francs. Hitching to Jokin along the road from the airport through the village of Hnacaom isn't too hard. Alternatively there is another road just past Xepenehe but it can be quieter with less traffic.

EASO

This small coastal village, whose name means 'the fire that smokes', sits peacefully on a cliff above the wide Baie du Santal. Easo (written Eacho in French) is basically an extension of its slightly larger neighbour, Xepenehe. It has an interesting site or two, as well as a beach where you can camp. From Easo, the road continues to the westernmost communities of Siloam and Hunete.

The village's focal point is the heavy cement cross erected in the middle of the road at the junction of the Xepenehe-Siloam roads. The road to Jokin leads north about 600 metres east of the cross.

Things to See

Church Easo has one of Lifou's most unusual
Catholic churches. About 150 metres past the
cross, it was built in 1898 of a greyish stucco
and, with its domed tower, somehow resembles a mosque more than a church.

Beach Lifou's first Catholic missionaries
landed at Easo beach, about one km west of
the church. Here too, whalers once had a
station where whale blubber was transformed into oil.

The beach is accessible by road or, more
picturesquely, along the footpath that leads
down just past the ruined stone house opposite the church. It's not one of the most
enticing beaches, with a lot of weed and only
a thin strip of sand. More remarkable is the
large thatched *fare* on the grassy slope before
the sand.

Chapelle Notre Dame The road west of
Easo church leads to the Chapelle Notre
Dame de Lourdes, a small chapel topped by
a large statue, perched on a hill above the sea
at the end of Easo peninsula. It is the destination of some 200 pilgrims who gather
annually from around Lifou. While the door
appears to be padlocked, it's often left open,
revealing an austere chapel devoid even of
seating.

The chapel's setting provides a panoramic
view of Baie du Santal and both capes –
Pointe Aimé Martin to the west and Pointe
Lefèvre to the south-west. From Easo
church, it's a 20-minute walk, the road
ending at a car park from where a small path
on the left winds up for 200 metres to the
chapel. Just before the car park, a coral road
to the right leads down to a superb little bay.

Places to Stay & Eat

Camping You can camp for free on the
beach but you must first ask permission from
the Petit Chef who also holds the key to the
toilet. He lives 50 metres east of the big
cement cross, on the right as you're heading
to Xepenehe.

The beach is about one km past the church.
You can camp anywhere under the trees on
the grassy slope and there's a water tap next
to one of the workers' bungalows. For a bit
more privacy, there are two much smaller
beaches back towards Xepenehe but you'd
have to fetch drinking water from the tap.

Restaurant Easo's only eatery is *Chez
Simone* (☎ 45.13.59), also called La Baie du
Santal. It sits about 150 metres on the right
after the cement cross on the road to
Xepenehe. It's not signposted – just look out
for the property with the sturdy metal fence.
Although a bit run down, it has a great setting
on the edge of a cliff overlooking the bay,
and is in the hands of the very friendly
Simone. She'll prepare a three-course meal,
including chicken or fish for 1500F, or roussette, coconut crab or lobster for 2000F.
You'll have to give her some warning if you
want to eat here; Simone closes on Sunday.

Self-Catering *Chez Louise*, a tiny blue shop
with the bare minimum of supplies, is opposite the Petit Chef's house (see Camping for
details). Don't rely on it for your dinner as it
often doesn't even have bread. It's open daily
from 6.30 to 11 am and 2.30 to 5 pm (except
Sunday, when it closes at 9 am to allow the
woman who runs it time to attend church).

XEPENEHE

Written Chépénéhé in French and pronounced 'chay-pay-nay-hay', Xepenehe is
another coastal village, five km east of Easo,
overlooking Baie du Santal. Halfway between
the two is a wharf where ships between
Noumea, the other Loyauté islands and
Lifou dock. The village has a post office and
gendarmerie on the road towards Easo.
They're about one km past the village's central
point, the T-junction where the Hnathalo-
Easo roads meet. From here, you can see the
Protestant church on the slope towards the
bay. Xepenehe has no accommodation.

Things to See

On Friday afternoon, a little **market** is set up
on the left, about 600 metres out of town
going towards Hnathalo. The all-female
traders play bingo while awaiting customers.

At the nearby crossroad, a well-camouflaged cut in the ground leads to a **cave** with a cool underwater pool. You'll need a torch to explore the cave.

Places to Eat

The only place to eat is *Snack Marie* (☎ 45. 13.05), 400 metres after the T-junction in the direction of Hnathalo. It has a simple plat du jour for 800F and is open weekdays only from 11 am to 2 pm. At the junction is *Chez Tapé*, the village's biggest store. It is open weekdays from 6.30 am to noon and 2 to 7 pm, and Saturday morning and Sunday from 6.30 to 8.30 am. If you continue past the church towards the bay, *Chez Tane* is a smaller magasin open similar hours.

PENG

Peng is a blissful, secluded sandy beach on Baie du Santal. Before 1925 a tribe lived here but, with the outbreak of leprosy, the whole village packed up and moved four km south-east to Hapetra. They believed the less humid, inland climate would inhibit the disease's spread. The tribe never came back and today many people from Hapetra are deeply superstitious about Peng.

Only two people live here – a French man and a Kanak woman. A handful of fishers come daily to cast lines from their motor boats or, more traditionally, from hollowed-out wooden canoes. The shells of abandoned houses still stand, and at night roussettes wing their way through the palm trees. The beach is mesmerisingly calm and a fantastic spot for shell collectors.

You can camp for free on the beach or under the palms nearby, but you must first get permission from the Petit Chef in Hapetra. He lives about 200 metres before the turn-off on the left as you come in from We. If he's not around, ask at the house on the left at the turn-off. There's no drinking water at Peng but if you ask the friendly couple who live there they'll probably give you some of their limited supply. A few food items are available in Hapetra from two small épiceries.

It's a good 40-minute walk along a dirt road to the beach and there won't be any traffic. When coming from We, the turn-off is at the end of Hapetra, just where the road veers off in a westerly direction.

DRUEULU

Twenty km west of We, Drueulu (Drouéoulou in French) is the home of the Grand Chef of Gaica. The village lines the small Baie de Drueulu, part of the larger Baie du Santal, and is home to about 400 people, half of whom work in Noumea. There's a lovely beach and a sacred cave where the ancestors of the tribe were once buried (visitors aren't permitted).

From Drueulu you can take the long southern road through several tribal communities, including Wedrumel, Kedeigne, Hmelek and Huiwatrul, to Mu and Xodre in the south-east of the island. Hitching on this road can be time-consuming and virtually impossible along the eight km stretch between Kedeigne and Hmelek.

As you enter Drueulu from We, there is a shop on the right, a Catholic mission and school, and then a large cement cross. Farther along is a grande case and a Protestant church.

Things to See

The Grand Chef of Gaica, currently Pierre Zeula, lives in a large white house behind the beachfront grande case, about 200 metres from the shop. The grande case is enclosed by a stone and wood palisade against which rests a small cemetery. Bobbing on the nearby water is a little dinghy belonging to the chief. Visitors are welcome in the grande case but must ask first at the white house.

Places to Eat

No *snacks* or restaurants operate in Drueulu – the only supplies come from the red iron shop on the right as you enter from We. It's open daily and has tinned goods but no cold or fresh produce. However, the owner can whip you up a milk shake and also sells cold waffles.

WEDRUMEL

Wedrumel (Wédoumel in French) is the northernmost of the settlements dotting the vast southern plateau. It's very small but has an ultra-basic tourist gîte (no grocery shop) and some interesting, if overgrown, hiking paths. The road to Wedrumel climbs up the plateau about 100 metres before the shop in Drueulu, nine km away.

Things to See & Do

A path starts from Gîte Hnaxulu and winds west to the coast (1½ hours), from where you can pick your way farther south along the coral cliffs, little coves and sheltered bays (four hours). You can then take another track and come back through the forest, passing a cave which is linked to Kedeigne, 12 km south-east. This underground passageway was supposedly used by the ancestors during tribal wars. If you're going in, you'll need a torch and a fishing line to retrace your tracks. In all, this rather wild walk is best done with a local guide; ask at Gîte Hnaxulu.

Place to Stay & Eat

Gîte Hnaxulu (☎ 45.16.42), whose name appropriately means 'in the middle of the forest', is on the main road. It has seven, totally thatched bungalows, all closely set and costing 1500F per person. The gîte is powered by a noisy generator (though lines are being laid for electricity) and has a rough, communal toilet and cold shower. There's also a *case* where you can lie on the ground and watch TV with the family's kids, though the whole concept of TV in a *case* seems somewhat odd. The *snack*-cum-restaurant serves guests only – a meal costs 1500F and breakfast is 500F. Camping is permitted for 700F and airport transfers cost 1600F return. All in all, the gîte is relaxed and friendly but is not Lifou's pick of accommodation if you like your creature comforts.

JOZIP

The road south of We, all the way to Xodre, skirts coral cliffs which rise to the inland plateau. There are a few freshwater caves on the plateau but you'll need to ask at a local tribe for permission to enter, and you'll probably need a guide.

Jozip is 10 km from We, a quiet coastal settlement with a co-op store, a wooden sculpture workshop and nearby top-end accommodation.

Places to Stay & Eat

The *Hôtel Lifou Plaisance* (☎ 45.14.44; fax 45.13.33) is one km south of the Jozip co-op. It is a luxurious resort, opened in 1990 and caters mainly to Japanese groups who drop in for the weekend. Well laid-out on an eight-hectare coconut plantation, it has two delightful little sandy bays just across the road, and the reef is only 100 metres offshore.

The complex has four bulky, pastel-toned cabins each divided into three. All 12 rooms are subtly decorated with little extras like pareo bedspreads and a fridge (but no cooking facilities). They cost 5500/8000/9600F for one/two/three people plus a 280F room tax. Included in the price is the use of the tennis court, gym, sauna, token swimming pool, bikes and snorkelling gear. Airport transfers cost 1650F return.

The colourful terrace restaurant has good food and serves a menu du jour for 1400F on weekdays only, at lunch and dinner. À la carte meals range between 2400F and 4500F, and a continental breakfast is 900F.

LUENGONI

Mention Luengoni to any Lifouan and they'll sigh and tell you it is *the* most beautiful beach in New Caledonia. While they are perhaps a little biased, there's no denying that Luengoni, 26 km south of We, deserves only superlatives. Protected by a barrier reef, the turquoise lagoon is idyllic for swimming but is not all that great for snorkelling because it has a sandy bottom with little coral. Right on the beachfront is a tranquil tourist gîte, while stunning stands of araucarias rise from the nearby cape.

Four km south of Luengoni, a side road winds for two km to Lifou's only lighthouse on Cap des Pins, from where there's a view over three atolls, Tiga and, on the horizon, Mare.

Places to Stay & Eat

Named after one of the island's favourite bands, *Gîte Neibash* (☎ 45.15.68) has perhaps the most idyllic setting – for beach lovers anyway – of any gîte on Lifou. Shaded by palms and pines, you can step from your bungalow straight onto the powder-fine sand, and at night be lulled to sleep by the lapping of gentle waves.

The road to Gîte Neibash leads off to the left (coming from Wc) at Lucngoni's church – look for the sign nailed to a tree. The gîte is very new and comprises a cluster of just three square bungalows, all with bright-blue iron roofs. They're modern and comfortable, and cost 4500/6000/6500F for a single/double/triple. Beachfront camping costs 1000F per tent. If the gîte is closed, as it sporadically is, you can still camp if you ask at the adjoining shop. The gîte organises transport to and from the airport for 2000F.

The gîte's restaurant serves a menu du jour for 1800F and the chef can prepare a bougna for 2000F per person or a coconut crab meal costing 3000F. You'll have to give at least a few hours' notice.

Behind the gîte is a most convenient, newly built *shop*, open daily from 6 to 11.30 am and 2.30 to 7 pm but closed Sunday afternoon.

MU

Eleven km south of Luengoni is Lifou's southernmost village, Mu (Mou in French). It is home to some 300 people, the Grand Chef of Losi and, since early 1993, a crocodile named Hector. Mu has many traditional houses and vast groves of coconut palms along the coast. Some of these trees have been attacked by a disease, spread by insects, which is slowly killing the palms.

Coming into Mu, you'll pass the small oval-shaped Baie de Mu where fishers cast nets in the late afternoon. Here too is a new restaurant and telephone booth. The road continues past a Total petrol station and a shop to an almost identical cove, where the Grand Chef kept turtles until the enclosure's barrier was destroyed in a cyclone. Just past this cove is a cemetery, opposite which a road leads up to the inland plateau. Mu has no accommodation.

The inland road crosses the green central plateau, past a few quiet villages and turns off to We, to join up eventually with Drueulu. Few cars head off along this road. Meanwhile the entire southern coastline, carved by rugged cliffs, is quite inaccessible.

Places to Eat

A brand new restaurant named *Thipeze Avenir* and overlooking Baie de Mu may be up and running by the time you visit Mu. The *Kirikitr* shop farther south has baguettes and some fresh fruit and vegies but no beer or cheese. It sells snacks like a half a baguette sandwich with ham or chicken for 350F, and is open from 6.15 to 11.15 am and 3.15 to 6.15 pm.

XODRE

Lifou's southern road comes to a final halt at the settlement of Xodre (Xodé in French), a desolate spot close to the rugged coastline. There are no shops or services.

From the cemetery at the road's end, a footpath follows the jagged coral platform past pandanus thickets and limestone cliffs

---

A Croc Called Hector

Hector is a salt-water croc who turned up on the beach at Mu following a summer storm in April 1993. He is believed to have come from the Solomons and, as New Caledonia's only crocodile, immediately became the media event of the month. His photo was plastered on the front page of *Les Nouvelles Calédoniennes* and, later, full-page features were dedicated to him. The villagers adopted the croc, installing him in a bathroom in a local house, despite attempts by ORSTOM, the scientific research organisation in Noumea, to relieve the villagers of their charge. Unfortunately, Hector will probably never make it back to the Solomons. ∎

dotted with caves (one supposedly containing a sacred ancestral burial site) towards Cap de Flotte, Lifou's southernmost point. Offshore are three shimmering islets – Leliogat, Huo and Nie – all uninhabited except for huge coconut crabs weighing up to four kg and some wild goats.

The track peters out after about half an hour when the thick carpet of palm fronds covering the limestone floor becomes so dense that any trace of a path is totally concealed. By now though, you're in the last coconut grove, standing on a wind and wave-swept ledge where the seashore is utterly inaccessible. This is perhaps lucky as the water here is home to tiger sharks. Better company are the grove's free-roaming residents – Pinkie, Dirty, Spottie and Hungry – a family of porkers who'll happily trail you, snorting every now and then for some coconut or whatever else you've got in your bag.

Ouvea

Ouvea is the most unusual of the four Loyauté islands. A coral atoll, it comprises two large masses of limestone joined by a thin, natural causeway only 400 metres wide at its narrowest point. On one side of this sliver of land is a 14-km-long strip of unbroken white beach lapped by the tranquil, aqua-coloured waters of an enormous lagoon. On the other side, a fringing reef and coral cliffs break the Pacific's mighty swell.

Ouvea gets its name from the Wallisian word *uvea*, meaning 'island far away'. Historically, it has seen many turbulent times, divided between Melanesian and Polynesian cultures and, of course, by religion. In the late '80s, violent political events shook this little island and the tremors were felt all over New Caledonia.

The island's northern forests are home to the last surviving Ouvea parakeets, stunning birds protected by law but sadly almost extinct as smugglers continue to sell them to unscrupulous collectors.

HISTORY
The 18th Century

In the second half of this century, Polynesians from Wallis Island discovered Ouvea. Locals still point to the little Île Unyee (also called Île Ounes) in the north where legend says the first big canoe came ashore.

The first European to spot the island was the Frenchman Bruny d'Entrecasteaux in 1793. Thanks to the navigational skills of his engineer, Beautemps-Beaupré, he missed hitting a coral atoll just before sighting Ouvea, and instantly named that atoll after his colleague.

The 19th Century

Chef Wenegei from Canala on Grande Terre arrived at Fayaoue, in the island's southern portion, in the early 1800s with members of his clan. Tensions broke out, however, and he was killed by the Polynesian Chef Bazit from Weneki in the north. As legend has it, Wenegei tried to escape in a canoe but it sank. He swam ashore at Nieguinie but was immediately captured and cooked in the traditional way. That is why, they say, coconut trees refuse to grow at Nieguinie.

In 1856, two Protestant missionaries arrived from Mare to begin converting the islanders at Fayaoue. The French Catholics turned up the same year and started work in the north. The normal rivalry between the two faiths was intensified on Ouvea because of the long-standing tension between Polynesians and Melanesians. Tribal wars waged back and forth for a decade, with the majority of Polynesians embracing Catholicism and the Melanesians adopting Protestant beliefs. The battles did not stop until 1865 when Governor Guillian in Noumea asked the French military to suppress the locals. That done, Ouvea became the final Loyauté island to be officially annexed to New Caledonia.

During the late 1800s, a few Ouveans were blackbirded to work on the sugar plantations in Queensland, Australia. They never returned to Ouvea.

Recent Times

While the Events of 1984/85 were largely

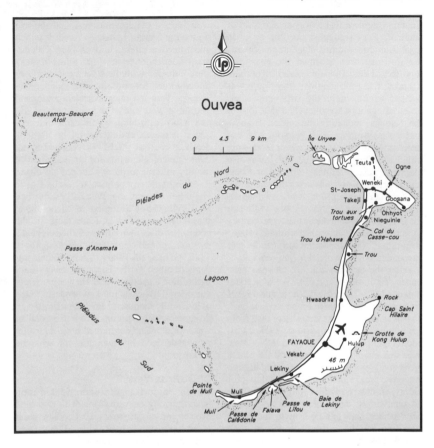

centred on Grande Terre, Ouveans were, and still are, an active component of the independence movement. However, since the violent climax to the struggle in the late '80s, the island has been calm.

The Hostage Crisis On 22 April 1988, just days before the French presidential election, a commando of Kanaks captured the gendarmerie at Fayaoue, Ouvea's capital, and killed four gendarmes. They took 27 hostages, 11 of whom were soon released, while the others were transported to a cave near Goosana in the far north.

Ouvea was declared a *zone militaire* and all communication and transport was cut. More than 300 soldiers were flown to the island to locate the cave; they found it unassailable. Captain Philippe Legorjus, head of France's elite anti-terrorist squad, then began negotiations with the hostage takers but, during attempts to secure the hostages' release, he too was captured. He was freed after coming to an agreement with the captors' young leader, Alphonse Dianou, on a date of release for the hostages, set for after the presidential election.

On May 4, three days before the election,

Captain Legorjus had two guns and a set of handcuff keys smuggled into the cave. In what was code-named 'Opération Victor', the military then stormed the cave and reported 'at least 16' people dead, all of them Kanaks. The following day, the figure was revised to 21, including two gendarmes. Later, allegations were levelled that four of the Kanaks, including the leader, Dianou, and Waina Amossa, a 19-year-old who had been sent into the cave to deliver food, were killed after they had surrendered. It was also claimed that the military tortured and beat civilians from Goosana during the operation. The human rights group Amnesty International took up the case, and France's Minister for Defence later announced that 'acts contrary to military duty have unfortunately been committed'. One gendarme commander was suspended but no judicial action was taken.

After the cave assault, 32 Ouvean prisoners, including Djubelly Wea, a local independence movement leader and FULK supporter, were flown to France to face trial. This was despite a previous assurance from the French High Commissioner in New Caledonia that trials would be held in Noumea. Wea was eventually released and the others were given amnesty as part of the Matignon Accords. Wea returned home to find that his elderly father had died shortly after the hostage crisis. His father had apparently been beaten and left tied up in the fierce sunshine by the military and was soon regarded as the '20th victim' of the Ouvea massacre.

The Assassinations Exactly a year to the day after the cave assault, Jean-Marie Tjibaou and Yeiwene Yeiwene were assassinated on Ouvea. They had come for a ceremony to end the 12 months of mourning for the 19 Kanaks killed at Goosana and were about to address the gathering when Djubelly Wea fatally shot Tjibaou. Yeiwene was killed by another gunman. One of Tjibaou's bodyguards then shot Wea. All three were buried in their tribal villages – Tjibaou, 53, at Tiendanite, Yeiwene, 44, at Tadine on Mare, and Wea, 44, at Goosana.

In June of the previous year, Tjibaou had signed the famous Matignon Accords which guaranteed a referendum on New Caledonian independence in 1998. Some Kanaks were unhappy with the agreement, and continued to call for an immediate independent Kanaky. Wea, a former Protestant pastor and journalist, was one of the discontented. He had a no-compromise policy on independence and was embittered by his father's death, as well as the FLNKS' failure to act over Ouvean demands for an international inquiry into the military's alleged atrocities.

A long-standing political leader on Ouvea and chief of Goosana, Wea had established an EPK school designed to 'decolonise' young Kanaks and educate them in the context of their own culture. When elected a regional councillor for the Loyauté islands in 1985, he used his salary to send Kanak students to other Pacific Island nations to learn agriculture and other skills. He was generally considered to be 'an unlikely assassin'. One of his family members said: 'Even those who disagree with his action cannot deny that he was a sincere and committed political leader who sacrificed his own life for what he believed in'.

GEOGRAPHY

Ouvea comprises the main 35-km-long island, a long curved island with two land masses converging to its most narrow point at Hahawa (also spelt Anawa), plus two smaller inhabited islands to the south. Together they curl around in an arc, commonly depicted as 'croissant-shaped', and all up cover 132 sq km. The main coral island is raised only on the eastern side, where limestone cliffs rise to just 46 metres. The 35-km-wide lagoon to the west is encircled by a string of 21 islets, known as the North and South Pléiades, which are split in the middle by the Passe d'Anamata.

Within the lagoon, sea life is abundant and, fortunately for the ecology, there is no organised fishing industry disrupting it. The Baie de Lekiny is a fishing reserve restricted by custom to the Lekiny tribe.

Ouvea has no rivers or reservoirs except

for a few water holes. The water coming out of taps and showers is generally saline and not recommended for drinking. Drinking water *(eau potable)* is pumped up from one point only on the water table and two trucks then deliver it to tanks at homes etc. In mid-1993, a project was underway to start a desalinisation station.

PEOPLE & CULTURE

About 3600 people live on Ouvea, divided amongst 17 clans. Many of the inhabitants are of Polynesian origin, with the Wallisian language Faga Uvea being spoken at both ends of the island, around Saint Joseph and Muli. The Melanesian language Iaai is used by tribes in the centre, between Hwaadrila and Fayaoue. Pockets of Iaai speakers also exist elsewhere, such as at Goosana. Many parents and teachers admit that the tribal structure is having a hard time surviving on Ouvea, with families split up by the need to go to Noumea for work or education.

INFORMATION

Fayaoue is the island's 'capital', though in reality it's little more than a very long village. There is no bank on Ouvea. A helpful reference may be IGN's 'Série Orange' map (Nr 4839).

DANGERS & REQUESTS

While the events of 1988 and 1989 are over, they have not been forgotten and have led to a few isolated incidents of anti-White hostility. More than anywhere this is true around Goosana, but stone-throwing and verbal abuse have occasionally been reported elsewhere on the island. This is not to say that it's dangerous or that Whites shouldn't go to Ouvea – on the contrary, many islanders warmly welcome all travellers – but do bear in mind that the wounds of the past are still healing.

ACCOMMODATION & FOOD

The only accommodation and eateries on Ouvea are at Fayaoue. Theoretically, the two gîtes can be booked through the Air Calédonie office in Noumea; however, you may find them reluctant to do it. If so, just arrange it yourself.

There are a few grocery shops but their stocks are expensive and limited, especially when the supply boat has been delayed. It may be wise to bring a few picnic supplies from Noumea.

Ouvea produces 80% of New Caledonia's copra, so coconut palms and, of course, coconuts are plentiful. Some traditional food sources, though not eaten as much these days, include coconut crabs, *anguilles* (eels) and tortues (turtles). The latter two are still found in water holes.

GETTING THERE & AWAY
Air

Ouvea's small airport at Hulup (also spelt Houloup) is five km north-east of Fayaoue. It has an Air Calédonie desk (☎ 45.71.42) that is open when flights arrive and leave.

Direct daily flights between Ouvea and Noumea's Magenta Airport take 35 minutes and cost 7060F one way. The timetable is:

	from Magenta	from Ouvea
Monday	9.55 am	11.00 am
Tuesday	2.25 pm	3.30 pm
Wednesday	12.05 pm	1.10 pm
Thursday	8.40 am	9.45 am
	3.30 pm	4.35 pm
Friday	2.15 pm	3.20 pm
Saturday	10.25 am	11.30 am
Sunday	3.55 pm	4.55 pm
	4.10 pm	5.10 pm

For details on inter-island flight schedules, see the Getting There & Away section at the beginning of this chapter. For prices, consult the Air Routes map in the Getting Around chapter.

Sea

Boat Ouvea's wharf, at the centre of the island and six km north of Hwaadrila, has recently been upgraded and now comfortably accommodates supply and passenger ships. However, vessels need a high tide to get across the wide lagoon, and are therefore often seen sitting idly out on the horizon waiting for the tide to turn. For details on passing ships, see the Getting There & Away section at the beginning of this chapter.

Yacht Protected by the encircling reef, Ouvea's lagoon is truly the idyllic spot to drop anchor. What's more, though it isn't the official port-of-call, it's a welcome stop after, or before, the crossing to Vanuatu. For more yachting details, see the Yachtie's Guide in the introductory Getting Around chapter.

GETTING AROUND
To/From the Airport
A blue bus is supposed to meet incoming flights and then head to Fayaoue, a 10-minute ride that costs 50F. However, the bus often doesn't turn up, so don't wait around for it. Your best move is to try to hitch a ride into Fayaoue from a fellow passenger on your flight.

Both gîtes will pick you up and take you back to the airport for 800F but you should arrange this when you reserve your room.

Bus
The island's one bus does a run from Saint Joseph to Muli and back once a day (not on Sunday) in the morning. It leaves Saint Joseph at 7 am, picking up passengers en route, and departs from Muli at 9 am. On this return trip it passes through Fayaoue at about 9.15 am (just flag him down anywhere). The bus is the best way to get to the north of the island, as then your only worry is getting a hitch back. From Fayaoue to Saint Joseph it's 150F; to Muli it costs 100F.

Car
It is possible to rent a car on Ouvea, but only if you tee it up before you arrive. The company to go through is Tour des Îles (see the Getting Around section at the start of this chapter for price details) which will arrange for the car to meet you at the airport. Keep in mind that, as with all the Loyautés, petrol supplies have a habit of running out. Petrol

is also considerably more expensive here than on Grande Terre – 115F per litre – but you won't use much anyway.

Bicycles
The island is excellent for cycling as there is only one tiny bump that even slightly resembles a hill, and the view from the road is always scenic. Unfortunately, finding a bike is not easy. If you persist, the manager of Gîte Beautemps-Beaupré may be able to line one up with someone from the nearby clan.

Hitching
Hitching on Ouvea involves an in-depth study of 'island time'. You must work out the hours when there's the most likelihood of traffic, such as the early morning when people come into Fayaoue to shop, before and after sports events or the Sunday Mass and, most importantly, the arrival and departure of planes. And even then, there's no guarantee of a ride. For unlike on Mare, drivers on Ouvea will not automatically stop to pick you up, so be prepared for some long, hot walks. Luckily, the sea is never far away for a quick dip between cars.

Yacht
As yachties regularly drop anchor in the lagoon, it may be possible to hitch a ride with one of them to explore the chain of Pléiade Islands.

Diodon

Around Ouvea

FAYAOUE
Ouvea's largest village, Fayaoue, offers essential services, food, accommodation and a seemingly never-ending beach.

Orientation & Information
Languidly stretched for three km along the lagoon, the village has no 'centre'. For want of a focal point, the two épiceries on opposite sides of the road are basically the village's heart.

Coming in from the north, you'll first pass Gîte Hwattau and the abandoned hotel complex. Then there's a Biarritz shop (with a public telephone inside) and, opposite, a snack bar and future restaurant. Fayaoue's school and the two facing magasins follow, as does the Protestant church and its larger, twin-towered Catholic neighbour. Next up is the post office, where there's another public telephone and, finally, the gendarmerie (☎ 45.71.17) which has four officers plus about 15 *gardes mobiles* (riot squad police). Only on Ouvea will you see the officer on guard with a machine gun in his hands. The clinic is on the road to the airport. There are no banks on Ouvea.

Places to Stay
Ouvea formerly had four gîtes along the shores of Fayaoue but only two now operate.

The well-maintained *Gîte Beautemps-Beaupré* (☎ 45.71.32) is a family-run gîte about a 15-minute walk north of Fayaoue's two central épiceries. The proprietor is from Bora Bora (Society Islands) but his wife is a local Kanak. The place is relatively modern and there are few complaints from people staying here. A bungalow for one adult costs 4000F, 5000F for two and 5800F for three. Studio rooms cost 3000/3500F for one/two people. There are no cooking facilities but all have private toilet/shower, though you can get hot water only in the evening. It is possible to camp on the property for 1000F per night.

Gîte Hwattau (☎ 45.71.25) *(hwattau* meaning 'frigate bird'), is a much smaller, laid-back gîte run by a friendly mixed family. It's the sort of place where you rapidly become part of the family – everyone eats in the same big dining room (forever lorded over by a TV) and the lovely kids are happy to guide you around. There are only two bungalows, built in traditional-style using only organic materials like thatch, reeds and wooden poles; there may be the odd leak during a downpour. They contain two beds, a table and a light bulb, and cost 3800F for one person and 500F for each extra person (maximum three). Unfortunately, they're often full on weekdays, booked up by construction companies. The communal ablutions block is quite grotty with only cold semi-saline water coming from the shower. Camping is free.

The multi-bungalow relais/hotel next door has been deserted since early 1980. It was recently bought by the Loyauté islands Province and is now owned collectively by all the Ouvean chiefs. Plans are in hand to restore it.

Places to Eat
Restaurants *Gîte Beautemps-Beaupré* prepares a simple but generous meal including fresh lagoon fish, salad, bread and native vegetables plus a piece of fruit for 1500F. Lobster and coconut crab dinners cost 3000F but you'll need to give them at least a day's warning of this desire. A standard petit déjeuner is 450F.

The story is much the same at *Gîte Hwattau*. The man who runs the gîte is a good cook and serves enormous meals of grilled chicken or fish fritters with chips, salad and bread and a slice of pawpaw for 1600F. Breakfast is 400F. Let them know half a day in advance if you want to dine.

Alternatively, *Snack de la Koop Iaai*, opposite the Biarritz shop, serves coffee and sandwiches. It is open from 6.30 to 11.30 am and 2.30 to 6.30 pm. The owners were also in the process of building a larger restaurant next door. It is to be named Ouvea Village and should be finished sometime in 1994.

Self-Catering The *Biarritz* shop, 150 metres south of Gîte Hwattau, is the best stocked store on the island. It sells slices of pain de marmite or baguettes (sold out by noon), beer, a few wilted vegies and bruised fruit. There's no cold produce like cheese, yoghurt or salami and, at times, it doesn't even have the ubiquitous Scotch Finger and Marie biscuits. In the side room are a few locally made wooden sculptures. It is open daily from 6.30 to 11.30 am and 1.30 to 6.30 pm, and Sunday from 7.30 am to noon.

Alternatively there's *Magasin Tropicale*, one of the few buildings on the beach side of the road, with a map of Ouvea painted on the outside wall and, opposite, a nameless, low-set yellow shop.

GROTTE DE KONG HULUP

This cave (also written Kong Houloup or, in French, Cong-Ouloup) is about five km east of Fayaoue. Together with a few other caves, it's directly aligned with the airstrip, and is set in a high cliff wall that obstructs the ocean view.

To go to the cave you need to ask permission from No-No, the owner of the area, who lives in the house by the football field just east of the airport. He has a lantern and other equipment and will guide you in return for some cigarettes or a 'gift'. This doesn't imply that he wants money, it is just a part of la coutume that should be respected. If No-No is having a siesta and his sons prefer to play football rather than to act as guides, they'll probably give you permission to go alone.

En route to the limestone cliffs there are a few interesting sights. Halfway there stands a banyan tree with a deep hole filled with water. Legend says this tree houses the gods from Canala on Grande Terre who arrived with Chef Wenegei. The banyan's roots are meant to connect with a similar tree at Canala, forming the 'way of the spirits'.

A few metres before the coral cliff, in an old sunken quarry, there's a slit in the rock allowing a glimpse of the lacework of stalactites dropping down in a seemingly endless curtain before disappearing into the darkness.

Grotte de Kong Hulup itself is to the left of the cliffs at the end of a well-camouflaged track. After a short climb, you'll pass a sacred burial site where the bones and skulls of the ancestors and the old chiefs have been laid in a little pirogue and mounted onto a ledge. This is a taboo place, and you should respect the traditions and beliefs by not climbing onto the ledge or touching the staring skulls.

Finally you'll reach the chaotic cave, swarming with swallows and shrieking bats in a rather lugubrious environment. Unexpectedly, at the end is the weird sight of a white statue of Saint Joseph, which in the semi-dark rather resembles a stalactite.

BAIE DE LEKINY

About nine km south of Fayaoue along the coastal road is Baie de Lekiny (also spelt Lékine), where a 100-metre-wide channel separates Ouvea's main island from the nearby tiny island of Faiava (also called Fayawa) and the southern island of Muli, home to the people of Muli.

Before 1982, a bac assured the connection between the main island and Muli, but now there's a bridge spanning the strong tidal currents. The view around here is almost surreal, with the white sand contrasting sharply against the different shades of brilliant blue water. Occasionally a turtle swims by.

The bay is protected by coral cliffs, formed long ago when the atoll was uplifted, and since undercut by years of wave action. Between the cliffs and Faiava is the Passe de Lifou, surrounded by fringing reef which is battered by waves.

Faiava is separated from Muli by the Passe de la Calédonie. The few dinghies moored on the island's beach act as the lifeline of the five families who live in the cluster of thatched huts. A priest is ferried over once a week to hold Mass in the red-roofed chapel.

At low tide, Baie de Lekiny's northern flank is almost dry, making it the right time to explore the **cliffs** and the coral cave round the corner. The cliffs are easily reached by following the beach around to a channel that leads farther inland, becoming a creek and finally marshland. At low tide, this channel is only shin-deep and easy to wade across. Once across, follow the beach under the cliffs towards the Passe de Lifou. You'll soon see a set of rickety wooden stairs which look like a prop for an Indiana Jones movie. Once up these, you can scramble around the cliffs to the somewhat disappointing coral cave with its chunky cement altar. With nerves of steel you may be able to scale your way to the sea-side of the cliffs, but it's not recommended.

MULI

Ouvea's southernmost village, Muli (also written Mouli or, in French, Mouly), is six km south-west of the Lekiny bridge, along a road with little sign of life. The village has scattered huts amidst the coconut groves and an FLNKS flag waving proudly. Dogs and people mill around, and on the seashore are large white plastic wells holding the brackish water used for washing people and clothes.

After Muli, the beach gives way to coral rocks, while a road meanders along the peninsula's last three km of road to **Pointe de Muli**. Here two rocky outcrops are separated by a small beach from where, in ultra-clear weather, Grande Terre is just visible on the horizon. The reef is very close to land along this coast, with waves spectacularly crashing close to shore. Underwater, there's plenty to fascinate snorkellers but you must beware of a strong cross current.

There's little to see en route to Pointe de Muli – two houses, a few goats, a large wooden cross facing three distant islands and a small stone shrine hidden in a bushy alcove. More spectacular are the abundant butterflies, including the striking black-and-blue *Papillon Montrouzieri*, as well as the endless fan of coconut palms which act as a cool roof-top awning. It's a 35-minute walk both to and from the point; don't expect any vehicles.

Places to Eat

There is one small shop in the village, behind the church, where you may be able to buy a drink or some bread while the *snack* is 'under construction'. The family at the beginning of the village, 300 metres before the church, is normally the local beer-only outlet but, in times of desperation, they'll also bail you out of hunger by whipping up superb ham, egg and lettuce sandwiches served on the front lawn with a big, icy-cold beer.

HWAADRILA

Hwaadrila (Wadrilla in French) is the first real village north of Fayaoue, though, being just seven km away, it has no shop or *snack*. Its proud church, the first Protestant temple to be built on the island in 1887, has an unusual façade which was given a new lease of life in 1992.

Hwaadrila has the unfortunate distinction of being the site where Jean-Marie Tjibaou and Yeiwene Yeiwene were killed, as well as being the memorial for the 19 Kanaks who died during the hostage crisis. All this combines to make it one sad little village.

The **memorial**, which contains the graves of the 19, is just off the main road, north of the church. Because the men were from different tribes, Hwaadrila was chosen as the burial site because it is the island's most central village. However, as none of the men was from here, some relatives later asked to exhume their sons for burial in their own village in order for their spirits to rest and find peace. The memorial's oval shape represents the cave where the men were killed. Each man is remembered by a photograph and the inscription of his name and date of birth, though these are usually hidden behind the many plastic flowers.

About six km east of Hwaadrila is **Cap Saint Hilaire**, a desolate rocky protrusion with a separate 40-metre-high coral rock. It's eloquently named the Grandes Roches de l'Eau du Crabe, which translates to 'the big rocks of the water of the crab'. The rock contains a cave strewn with fish bones which, according to legend, were the leftovers of a meal of an ancient bird. The cape is difficult to reach even on foot (which is the only possibility), as it's a six to seven-km walk from Hwaadrila, sticking as much as possible to the coastal track.

HWAADRILA TO SAINT JOSEPH

The thin long neck of land joining Ouvea's two land masses starts just after Hwaadrila and continues for 15 km almost to Saint Joseph. Its western coastline is not one long stretch of beach as is commonly described but, instead, small pockets of sand broken by large tracts of rock. The water is shallow but not that ideal for snorkelling as it's too sandy. The batch of rocks sitting on the horizon are some of the northern Pléiades.

Heading north from Hwaadrila, the road winds for six km to Ouvea's only **wharf** and neighbouring copra factory where oil is extracted for soap making. One and a half km farther, on the right and visible from the road, is a small **trou**, or sink hole, home to about 30 turtles who were caught and released here. Occasionally, one pops its head up.

Another 1½ km farther on is a second hole, the **Trou d'Hahawa**. This one is quite different – it is a large round hole with the most amazing royal-blue water. Surrounded by palms and shrub, it's thought to be about 40 metres deep and, if you throw a white rock in, you'll see it slowly disappear into the depths. To find the trou, take the dirt track off to the left when the road curves abruptly to the right. Follow this track for 100 metres to a clearing where an overgrown footpath to the right leads through the bush to the hole.

From here, the main road briefly skirts the rough, windswept eastern coast where there's one lovely **beach**. Promising waters lead to deceptive snorkelling here because of a strong current and wave-broken coral. However, the beach offers a good vista south-east towards Cap Saint Hilaire.

Continuing into the region of Hahawa, the road winds up to the little **Col du Casse-Cou** (in English, 'the reckless pass') marking Ouvea's narrowest point. Only 400 metres separate the two coasts here. Once over the col, the road retires to the west coast as far as Saint Joseph.

SAINT JOSEPH

Saint Joseph is Ouvea's northern hub. Several tribes, the Eo, Weneki and Takeji, live in the vicinity and their language is of Wallisian origin. Saint Joseph is spread along the palm-lined waterfront facing the lagoon. As you enter, there's a blue shop on the left and a chefferie surrounded by a wooden palisade. One km on is the Catholic mission church founded in 1857 and a small clinic.

From Saint Joseph, the road veers east, through the tribal settlement of Weneki. The Grand Chef of Weneki has his chefferie here while, down a bush track just past the settlement, there is a natural sink hole where he keeps turtles.

Ouvea's northernmost clan, the Teuta (Teouta), live five km north of Weneki. To the east, the main road continues through neighbouring Goosana to Ohhyot (also written Ognat), seven km from Weneki. Ohhyot, together with Ogne (Hony in French) north of Goosana, was a leper colony until 1947 when the colonial government rounded up all the island's lepers and transferred them to Cila on Lifou.

GOOSANA

Like Hwaadrila, Goosana (also spelt Gossanat or Gossanah) has an unhappy place in New Caledonia's history. In a cave close to here the 1988 hostage crisis unfolded, while the man who murdered Tjibaou, Djubelly Wea, is buried here in his home village.

As you enter the village, 2½ km east of Saint Joseph, there's a house on the left with a large white **tomb** in front of it. Draped in flowers and strips of material, it's Wea's grave. Just past the grave are broken buildings where the FLNKS flag has been hand-painted on the walls.

It is possible to visit the **hostage cave**, inside of which is a small memorial, but you must ask permission and go with a local guide. Each year, one month before the May 4 anniversary of the killing of the 19 Kanaks, a large banner is strung across the road where you enter Goosana and makeshift roadblocks are set up at either end of the village to commemorate their deaths.

At the time of the hostage taking, Goosana

and all of Ouvea's northern tip was off-limits to everyone but the military. These days the village is not *interdit*, but very few strangers come up this way and locals in Fayaoue will probably discourage you from visiting the north. At Goosana, the reception may range from a blunt, hostile statement like 'Whites are forbidden here' to a curious welcome.

THE PLÉIADES ISLANDS

The Pléiades Islands are a chain of 21 tiny, uninhabited coral islets surrounding Ouvea to the west like a necklace. The last testimony of a submerged crater, they are divided into northern and southern groups which come together at the central Passe d'Anemata, 40 km west of Ouvea.

The waters around the islands are specifically recommended for divers (though there's no diving club on Ouvea) and underwater visibility is very good. There are numerous submerged caves and coral inlets, and sharks and manta rays swim in the channels. Ouveans sometimes spear fish in this area, stuffing the fish into their belts – which

has led to a few people being killed by sharks. Turtles come onto Île Unyee during the egg-laying season.

BEAUTEMPS-BEAUPRÉ ATOLL

The unspoilt but very dangerous Beautemps-Beaupré atoll is 15 km north of the Passe d'Anemata. These low-lying islets are surrounded by waters which are rich in marine life and great for diving. Of course, getting there is going to be the hard part.

It wasn't until 1793 that the islets were discovered by the Entrecasteaux expedition. At that time the biggest islet was inhabited by the Eo clan. But then the elders told the people to move to Ouvea's mainland because the island's resources were too limited for the growing tribe. They abandoned their coconut trees, fields and water holes and sailed off to set up at Saint Joseph, 50 km away.

Another undisturbed patch of wonderful reefs is the Récifs de l'Astrolabe. These last remains of old volcanoes sit 80 km northwest of Beautemps-Beaupré.

Dependencies of New Caledonia

New Caledonia's four groups of dependencies are scattered around the perimeter of the territorial waters, hundreds of km from Grande Terre. They range from reefs with barely emerged coral cays and islets like the Chesterfield and Entrecasteaux groups to larger outcrops such as Walpole Island and the volcanic Matthew and Hunter islands. All are uninhabited by humans but have enormous ecological importance because of their rich variety of bird and marine life.

CHESTERFIELD ISLETS

Situated some 600 km west of the northern tip of Grande Terre, this group of islets and coral cays rises above the Coral Sea while the surrounding reef is anchored to the underwater Bellona plateau. In all it includes the Sable and Chesterfield islet groups, Caie de l'Observatoire and Bellona reefs. The land surface totals just one sq km. These scraps of land are essential sea bird rookeries and turtle nesting areas.

The largest group, the Chesterfield islets, was discovered in 1793 by Captain Matthew B Alt on the *Chesterfield*. It includes eight islets – the biggest being Long Island which is two km long and 140 metres wide – which form a semi-sheltered lagoon. The lagoon's protection was first exploited nearly two centuries ago when whaling ships found a safe anchorage here, though some also ended up shipwrecked off the reefs to the west of

the archipelago. The Chesterfields' isolation and rich coral make them an exquisite place for divers to explore amidst the wrecks.

RÉCIFS D'ENTRECASTEAUX

The Récifs d'Entrecasteaux are aligned with the Belep Islands and Grande Terre's mountain axis. They sit about 220 km to the north-west, separated by the Grand Passage, and are made up of a few atolls with a surface area of 65 hectares.

In the reef's southern region, just north of the Grand Passage, is a 30-km-long atoll enclosing a sheltered lagoon and dotted by the Fabre, Leizour and Surprise islets. A 10-km strait of deep water separates this atoll from another of similar size to the north-west. It has just one islet, Huon, overlooking a protected lagoon which lacks coral variety but makes up for it with a teeming array of fish. All the islets are nesting sites for birds and turtles.

Surprise Islet

This islet (called Bwano in one Kanak language, meaning 'bird manure') measures 600 by 400 metres and is covered in an abundance of flora, and fauna such as lizards, spiders, crickets, butterflies, geckos, rats and mosquitoes. Much of the lagoon is invaded by a black algae and therefore offers poor diving or snorkelling, but there are many fish and reef sharks. It's also noted for its many crabs and green turtles.

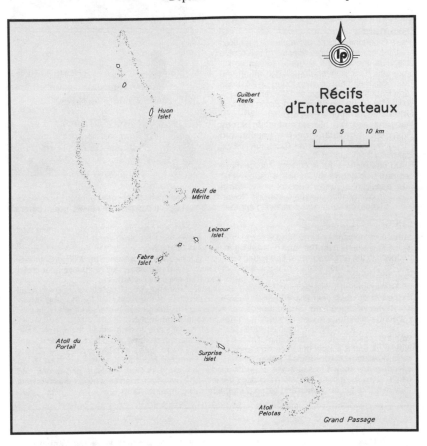

The islet is renowned as a haven for huge colonies of sea birds. At least three booby species nest here – the red-legged, the white-bellied and the blue-faced booby – as do small and large frigate birds.

Fabre & Leizour Islets

These twin islets, each of which is about the same size as Surprise, are the most important places in the area for turtles. Up to 300 of them lumber ashore each night during the egg-laying season. Both islets have tree cover, indicating that they are older than Surprise Islet.

Huon Islet

Huon Islet, one km long by 150 metres wide, is the only islet on another beautifully formed atoll. Its highest point is a mere four metres. There are no trees, only a covering of guano and grassy vegetation. Insects, sterns, boobies and turtles are all found here.

WALPOLE ISLAND

Walpole Island is a raised island three km long and 400 metres wide, located 150 km east of Île des Pins. It is exposed and inhospitable as it is not protected by reefs and has raised limestone cliffs some 70 metres

Sea Turtles

New Caledonia's territorial waters are a noted habitat for turtles. Three species of this reptile frequent these parts – green turtles which average 100 cm in length and can weigh 150 kg; loggerhead turtles, also found off Australia and Papua New Guinea; and the rarer hawksbill turtle, found too around the Solomons and PNG. They feed on algae, sponges and crustaceans and the females nest on sandy beaches, particularly on the uninhabited dependencies of the Récifs d'Entrecasteaux, far away from human life.

Hawksbill Turtle

In one night, a turtle can lay 100 or more eggs of ping-pong ball size with a texture a bit like paper, in a burrow dug out of the warm sand. In one nesting season (generally November to March), she may come back to shore six or seven times, on each occasion laying another clutch of eggs. It can then be several years before she returns to land again.

The eggs take about two months to hatch. The five-cm-long hatchlings instinctively make their way out of the sandy pit and into the sea as quickly as possible. Predators are abundant – hovering in the sky, sidling over the sand or awaiting in the sea – and the youngsters' numbers are greatly reduced in the first few hours. The young female hatchlings will not return to terra firma until they are ready to lay their first lot of eggs, and it can take 50 years before they're mature enough for that. When they do, they'll return to the same beach where they were born.

Turtle numbers are greatly endangered as a result of hunting. An estimated 100,000 are killed in the Pacific each year either for their flesh or, in the case of the hawksbill, for the shell. Many countries, including New Caledonia and neighbouring Australia, have protected them by law so that only indigenous people can hunt them for personal consumption.

Turtles have traditionally been a protein source for Kanaks and, in older times, their prized flesh was the preserve of the clan's chief. On the Loyauté islands, cavities in the coral coastline were closed off and a supply of turtles was traditionally kept there, close at hand to the chief. These days, Kanaks still hunt turtles, either for their own use or to meet tourists' desires. The Belep islanders are known to sail to the outer dependencies, such as Surprise Islet, and in one raid catch 30 turtles, if possible before the eggs are laid. The turtles are then kept alive for weeks until they're cooked in their shell and eaten during a festive gathering. ∎

high. During 1910 to 1936, guano was exported from this lonely spot, which is still popularly inhabited by sea birds.

MATTHEW & HUNTER ISLANDS

Closer to the most southern island of Vanuatu than to Grande Terre, these two tiny volcanic islets have been the issue of an ownership dispute between Vanuatu and New Caledonia (ie France) since 1929. At that time, the French authorities in New Caledonia included the pair in newly drawn maps of the territory despite customary claims to the islands by the people from Anatom, Vanuatu's most southern isle. A plaque was erected by the French on Hunter Island in 1975, only to be removed by the newly elected Vanuatu government after independence in 1980 and replaced by its flag. In turn, France pulled down the Vanuatu flag and raised the tricolour. It was then guarded by a French military contingent for seven years until, almost mad with boredom, the personnel was permanently withdrawn.

What exactly is the fight all about? Basically it's to have more territorial waters and two islands thrown in as well. Hunter and Matthew islands are of little interest to New Caledonians, sitting 450 km and 525 km respectively east of the southern tip of Grande Terre and home to many birds. The triangular-shaped Matthew Island, 500 metres long, is nothing more than the top of a huge volcano sticking 142 metres above the sea. Hunter Island has a few smoking volcanic vents and is more compact, though it also is only half a sq km in size. The only people really interested in them are the Anatom Islanders and the odd yachtie, en route to Fiji or Tonga, looking for a shelter for the night.

Alternative Place Names

The following abbreviations are used:
(E) English
(F) French
(K) Kanak Languages

GRANDE TERRE
Maamaat (K) – Mahamate (F)

ÎLE DES PINS
Isle of Pines (E) – Kwênyii (K)

Kaaji (K) – Gadji (F)
Kôtomo (K) – Koutomo (F)
Wapwanya (K) – Wapan (F)

LIFOU
Drueulu (K) – Droueoulou (F)
Easo (K) – Eacho (F)
Gaica (K) – Gaïtcha (F)
Hnaase (K) – Hnasse (F)
Hnathalo (K) – Nathalo (F)
Huiwatrul (K) – Wiwatoul (F)
Jokin (K) – Doking (F)
Losi (K) – Loessi (F)

Mu (K) – Mou (F)
Qanono (K) – Quahono (F)
Wedrumel (K) – Wédoumel (F)
Wetr (K) – Wet (F)
Xepenehe (K) – Chépénéhé (F)
Xodre (K) – Xodé (F)

MARE
Kurin (K) – Kurine (F)
Thogoon (K) – Thogone (F)

OUVEA
Faiava (K) – Fayawa (F)
Goosana (K) – Gossanat or Gossanah (F)
Hahawa (K) – Anawa (F)
Hulup (K) – Ouloup (F)
Hwaadrila (K) – Wadrilla (F)
Lekiny (K) – Lékine (F)
Muli (K) – Mouly (F)
Nieguinie (K) – Nenguine (F)
Ohhyot (K) – Ognat (F)
Takeji (K) – Takedji (F)
Unyee (K) – Ounes (F)
Vekatr (K) – Wakat (F)

Glossary

À la carte – French term meaning 'from the menu'. It distinguishes (usually) expensive restaurants from those specialising in cheaper dishes or meals of the day.

Araucaria – a coniferous, evergreen family of tree occurring almost solely in the southern hemisphere. The *Araucaria columnaris*, a columnar pine growing to 60 metres, is found along New Caledonia's coast.

Atoll – low-lying coral islets and reef which enclose a lagoon. The classic atoll is oval-shaped and made from coral growths that have built up around the edges of a submerged volcanic peak. The sand and coral islets build up on the higher points of the reef.

Bagayou – a penis covering worn in traditional times.

Bami – spicy Chinese or Indonesian dish based on noodles with chicken, pork or shrimps and vegetables.

Banyan – huge tree from the fig/rubber family with a wide canopy and big aerial roots.

Barrier reef – a long, narrow coral reef lying offshore from an island or coastline. The reef is separated from the land by a lagoon of deep water which shelters the land from the sea. See 'fringing reef'.

Bêche-de-mer – another term for a sea cucumber (also called trepang). A member of the echinoderm group, this harmless, lethargic bottom-dwelling sea creature has an elongated body, soft, leathery skin and a cluster of tentacles around its mouth. When alarmed, some varieties expel sticky, stinging threads from their anus as a defence. They are gathered, gutted, boiled and then dried or smoked to be sold to China where they are prized as a delicacy and aphrodisiac.

Biodiversity – the existence of a diverse range of plant and animal species in their natural environments.

Blackbirding – a labour recruitment system operating in the late 19th century when Melanesians were taken to work in sugar cane fields in Australia and Fiji and coconut plantations in Western Samoa. The term comes from 'blackbirds' *(merles)*, a common European songbird.

Bommie – large coral outcrop.

Booby – an intelligent-looking tropical sea bird, sometimes called a rock pelican *(Sulidae)*, with a strong beak. They live in colonies on tall sea-girthed rocks or islands.

Bougna – traditional Kanak meal of yam, taro and sweet potatoes with chicken, fish or crustaceans, wrapped in banana leaves and cooked in coconut milk in an earth oven.

Boulangerie – French for bakery.

Breadfruit – a huge fruit with a coarse green skin found on many Pacific islands. Its flesh is starchy and when cooked has a breadlike texture.

la Brousse – French term for the bush or outback. It is used in New Caledonia to encompass everything outside Noumea. People from la Brousse are sometimes called Broussards.

Cagou – New Caledonia's national bird.

Caldoche – white people born in New Caledonia whose ancestral ties go back to the convicts or the early French settlers.

Canaque – French for Kanak.

Case – the French word commonly used for traditional Kanak houses, either conical or rectangular. See also Grande Case.

Cassava – from the Haïtian *casavi*; also called yuca or manioc. It is one of the most popular, staple root foods used in tropical countries. With sweet and bitter varieties, it contains up to 40% starch but few nutrients. The plant's young leaves, however, are rich in protein. After grating and sifting, it can be used as flour. The starch, often called tapioca, is used as a thickener.

Casse croûte – a French term literally meaning 'break a crust' but used as an informal expression for a snack.

Cay – tiny, low island or large sandbank

composed of coral debris and sand where vegetation has sprouted. They can be unstable and threatened by weather and sea conditions.

Cephalopod – from the Greek *kephalè* meaning 'head' and *podos* 'foot'; class of molluscs, including octopus, cuttlefish, squid and nautilus.

Chef – French word for the customary leader of Melanesian and Polynesian clans.

Ciguatera – a type of poisoning caused by eating infected tropical fish.

Chefferie – French word for the chief's contemporary house.

Clan – another term for tribe, a clan is a grouping of people with a real or reputed descent from a common ancestor. Clans often derive their names from totems.

Coconut crab – a huge edible land crab.

Colon – French for a colonialist. These people were the original French settlers in New Caledonia.

Communard – a person who participated in the Paris Commune uprising of 1871.

Copra – dried coconut flesh from which oil is extracted. It is used in soap and margarine.

Coral – a marine polyp of soft or hard varieties. Hard coral has a lime skeleton which eventually forms reefs.

Coutume – French for custom. In New Caledonia, la coutume is a vital element of social and cultural life, giving rise to rules that must be followed. As a contemporary tourist, *la coutume* means that you must ask the chief's permission to visit a site and that you give a small gift if you stay in a village.

Cowrie – a gently rounded sea shell.

Croque-monsieur – French for a toasted cheese and ham sandwich.

Cyclone – a severe tropical storm, also called a hurricane or typhoon.

Dugong – fully protected but endangered sea mammal of tropical seas. Gentle and slow-moving, they live on sea grass. They bear only one young every three to seven years, and the calf suckles for two years on its mother's breast. Nets, traditional hunting and motorboat propellers cause a heavy toll on their numbers.

Épicerie – French for a grocery store.

Faire du cinq cinq – French expression meaning 'to make a lot of money'. Cinq Cinq (literally, five five) refers to the official rate between the CFP and the French franc (1 CFP = 0.055FFr).

Fare – Polynesian word used by Kanaks to mean a large, often open-sided, meeting house.

Ferronickel – metal alloy comprising iron and a minimum of 25% nickel.

Flèche Faîtière – French term used for the ornamental wooden spear seen on top of every grande case.

Frigate bird – large marine bird with a huge wing span found in tropical and sub-tropical climates.

Fringing reef – reef found along the shore of an island or mainland coast without enclosing a lagoon. See 'barrier reef'.

Gaïac – *Acacia spirorbis*, a little tree in the upper level of low altitude sclerophyll forest. Its heart wood is very hard and often used for making fence poles.

Gîte – French for a refuge. In New Caledonia it represents a group of bungalows, usually run by Kanaks, and used for tourist accommodation.

Gomenol – essence extracted from the leaves of niaouli trees.

Gondwanaland – the ancient continent that encompassed present-day Africa, Antarctica, India, Australia and New Zealand.

Grande Case – French term for the 'big house' where the tribal chief lives.

Guano – sea bird manure and dead bird bodies, rich in phosphates and nitrates. Once used as fertilisers but now replaced by artificial varieties.

Houp – *Montrouziera cauliflora*; one of the kings of Caledonian forests, this tree is highly sought for its beautiful yellowish wood. Its flowers are bright red.

Indépendantiste – French term for a person who is pro-independence.

Indigénat – Derived from the French word

indigène meaning 'indigenous', this word was used to describe the colonial authority's repressive system which forced Kanaks into reservations and obliged them to work for the authorities.

Jacaranda – pale-purple flowering tree, originating from South America.
Jade – dark-green semi-precious stone.

Kanaky – The name given to New Caledonia by those who are pro-independence. The French version is *Kanaké*.
Kanya – Kanak term for the maternal uncle.
Kauri – *Agathis lanceolata* from the Araucaria group; a conifer heavily forested for its good quality wood which is supple, light and without knots. Also one of the giants of the forest, it is called *kaori* in French.

Lagoon – area of water between the land and the ocean sealed off by a network of reefs or sandbars. Usually shallow, they have a depth of between five and 40 metres.
Lapita – site close to Kone on Grande Terre where old pottery was found. It gave its name to the Lapita people who inhabited much of Melanesia, including areas of New Caledonia, before 1000 BC.

Manioc – See Cassava.
Marist – Person from the religious society, Société de la Propagation de la Foi, founded in 1836 in Lyon. Its missionaries set up many missions in the Pacific.
Matte – an alloy resulting from refining ferronickel, matte contains cobalt and 75% nickel. It is prime material for nickel manufacture.
Melanesian – people of the west Pacific with curlier hair and darker skin than their Polynesian neighbours to the east. Melanesian countries include Papua New Guinea, the Solomon Islands, Vanuatu, Fiji and New Caledonia.
Menu du jour – the French equivalent of a three-course restaurant meal offered at a set price and sometimes including wine and coffee. It's often simply written as *menu*.
Métro – abbreviation of the French word

métropolitain; in New Caledonia it is used to describe someone from France.
Micronesian – people of the north-west Pacific, of Malay-Polynesian origin.
Moara – the Kanak term for a clan.

Nautilus – chambered sea creature with a beautiful red-brown and ivory-striped shell. Its form has remained unchanged for millions of years and therefore it's considered to be a living fossil.
Niaouli – these trees occupy a large portion of the dry east coast, forming a niaouli savannah, though they also grow elsewhere.
Nickel – silvery-white metal, harder than iron and more corrosion resistant than steel. Used for coins, wires and batteries or, as an alloy for example with chrome, as cooking plates, turbo jet engines and rockets.
Ni-Vanuatu – a person from Vanuatu.
Notou – a pigeon indigenous to New Caledonia.

Orohau – the Kanak term for a clan chief.

Pain de Marmite – French term for a big, heavy bread baked in a large round pot.
Pandanus – from the Malay word *pandan*, this tree is mostly found along the seashore and on rocky cliffs. Some species have edible nuts. Its leaves are used for weaving hats, mats and baskets.
Pareo – from the Tahitian *pareu*, this sarong-like wrap is made from a piece of light, hand-dyed material about three metres in length.
Pastis – Alcoholic aniseed-flavoured drink popular with the French.
Pétanque – a type of lawn bowls game that is played on a hard surface and is much loved in France and New Caledonia.
Petroglyphs – designs such as circles and spirals carved in stone and found throughout the Pacific, from the Torres Islands to Easter Island. The age and meaning of the petroglyphs' designs remain a mystery.
Pied noir – literally meaning 'black feet', this expression refers to French colonialists who left Algeria in 1961 after the fall of Algiers.

Pilou – a supreme Kanak dance, performed for important ceremonies or events.

Pirogue – a traditional outrigger canoe.

Plat du jour – French term literally meaning 'dish of the day'. Restaurant meals such as these are often cheaper than ordering à la carte.

Polynesian – the group of people from the central and south Pacific such as Hawaii, Tahiti, Samoa, Cook Islands and New Zealand.

Quonset – a half-moon-shaped shed made from sheets of corrugated steel built by the American troops in WW II.

Roussette – French for a flying fox.

Sandalwood – *Santalum album*, perfumed yellow-brown wood rich in aromatic essence. It was sought throughout the Pacific in the early to mid-19th century.

Sclerophyll – from the Greek *scleros*, meaning 'dry' and *phullon* 'leaf'; well-adapted plants typically found in dry areas.

Sweet potato – a tuberous root food which originated in South America.

Taboo – from the Polynesian word *tapu*, meaning 'that which must be avoided'.

Takata – the Kanak word for a medicine man.

Taro – staple root plant found all over the Pacific. The roots and leaves are eaten.

Totemism – the belief in a special relationship between a certain animal, plant or thing and a clan or person.

Trench – term used in oceanography for a long, narrow and very deep depression in the sea bed. The greatest depths are found in the Marianes Trench (11,200 metres) and Philippines Trench (11,524 metres), both north of Papua New Guinea.

Tribe – an autochthonous homogenous group, see 'clan'.

Trocchus – *Trocchus niloticus*; or *troca*, as it's written in French, is a coiled, pink-and-white shell. They're plentiful on Caledonian beaches and the snail-like sea creature inside is eaten.

Tumulus – believed to be a burial mound, found mainly on Île des Pins and Grande Terre.

Yam – a starchy tuber (*igname* in French) which is a staple food of Melanesians and can grow up to a metre long. It is highly respected in Kanak society and has important cultural significance.

Zoreille – a rather derogatory name used as an alternative to métro. This name, derived from the French *les oreilles* meaning 'the ears', originated in convict times when, so the story goes, the guards use to cup their hand behind their ear in order to eavesdrop on the convicts.

ACRONYMS

ADCK – Agence de Développement de la Culture Kanak, an agency to promote Kanak culture in New Caledonia and around the world.

ADRAF – Land & Rural Development Agency.

BCI – Banque Calédonienne d'Investissement.

BNP – Banque Nationale de Paris.

CFP – Communauté Française du Pacifique (local franc).

CNC – Cercle Nautique Calédonien (yacht club).

EPK – Écoles Populaires Kanaks, rebel schools set up to teach Kanak children their own culture in their mother tongue.

FFESSM – Fédération Française d'Études et Sports Sous-Marines.

FLNKS – Front de Libération National Kanak Socialiste, the main pro-independence political party.

FOL – Fédération des Œuvres Laïques.

FULK – Front Uni de Libération Kanak.

IGN – Institut Géographique National.

LMS – London Missionary Society, the first group of missionaries to arrive in New Caledonia.

OMAT – Office Municipal de l'Animation et du Tourisme.

ORSTOM – Organisation de Recherche Scientifique du Territoire Outre-Mer; the overseas French office for scientific research on the South Pacific.

PADI – Professional Association of Diving Instructors.

PALIKA – Parti de Libération Kanak.

RFO – Radio et Télédiffusion Française d'Outre Mer, the overseas arm of the French broadcasting service.

RPCR – Rassemblement pour Calédonie dans la République; New Caledonia's main right-wing, anti-independence political party.

RPR – Rassemblement pour la République.

RRB – Radio Rythme Bleu.

SAMU – emergency medical aid.

SLN – Société Le Nickel.

SMSP – Société Minière du Sud Pacifique.

SPC – South Pacific Commission; established in 1947 as an organisation to control the stability of the Pacific region.

UC – Union Calédonienne, the first New Caledonian political party involving Kanaks.

UMNC – Caledonian Multi-Racial Union.

VTT – *Vélo tout-terrain*; French for a mountain bike.

Index

TEXT

Map references are in **bold** type.

1878 Revolt 17, 151, 156
1917 Revolt 18

Accommodation 84-85
Adio Caves, *see* Grottes d'Adio
ADRAF Scandal 24
Air Travel
　To New Caledonia 92-93
　To/From Asia 96
　To/From Australia 93
　To/From Europe 95
　To/From Île des Pins 217
　To/From Japan 96
　To/From Lifou 243-244
　To/From Loyauté Islands 231-232
　To/From Mare 235
　To/From New Zealand 94
　To/From Ouvea 257
　To/From South America 96
　To/From the Pacific 94-95
　To/From the USA & Canada 95-96
　Within New Caledonia 100-101
Alt, Captain Matthew 264
Amédée Islet 123
Amoa River Valley 195
Anse Vata 124, 128, 129-133

Aquarium Naturel (Mare) 237
Arama 185

Ba Falls 192
Baie d'Oro 219, 228-229
Baie de Canala 161
Baie de Kanumera 225
Baie de Lekiny 260-261
Baie de Mu 253
Baie de Ouameo 227
Baie de Prony 150
Baie de Saint Joseph,
　see Baie des Pirogues
Baie de Saint Maurice 221
Baie de Tadine 236
Baie des Citrons 124, 128, 129, 132
Baie des Crabes 228
Baie des Pirogues 219, 221
Baie des Tortues 170, 171
Baie du Santal 251
Balade 208-210
Bamboo Engraving 51
Banks, *see* Money
Bargaining, *see* Money
Barrage de la Dumbea 153
Beaches
　Bourake 155
　Easo 250
　Enghoue 154
　Kokengone 198

Koulnoue M'balan 208
Koumac 183
Kuendu 122-123
Kuto 225
Mahamate 209
Nepoui to Pouembout 175
Ouano 156, 157
Poindimie 195
Saint Mathieu 208
Tieti 195
Touho 198-199
Bead Money 52
Beautemps-Beaupré Atoll 263
Belep Islands 189
Berbers 214
Bicycle Rental 103, 138
Bishop Douarre 209
Blackbirding 230
Boating
　Speed Boat Charters 105
　Tourist Vessels 104-105
Boat-pass 188-189
Bonou, Hippolyte 207
Books 67-71
　Yachting Books 107
Bouarate 201
Bouloupari 155-156
Bourail 168-173, **168**, **171**
Bourake Beach 155
Bus Travel 102
Bush Safaris 83

274

278 Index

Keep in touch!

We love hearing from you and think you'd like to hear from us.

The Lonely Planet Newsletter covers the when, where, how and what of travel (AND it's free!).

When...is the right time to see reindeer in Finland?
Where...can you hear the best palm-wine music in Ghana?
How...do you get from Asunción to Areguá by steam train?
What...should you leave behind to avoid hassles with customs in Iran?

To join our mailing list just contact us at any of our offices (details below).

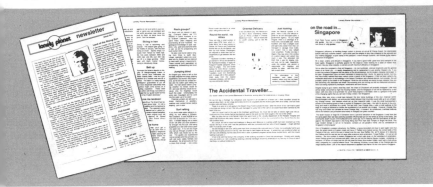

Every issue includes:

- *a letter from Lonely Planet founders Tony and Maureen Wheeler*
- *travel diary from a Lonely Planet author - find out what it's really like out on the road*
- *feature article on an important and topical travel issue*
- *a selection of recent letters from our readers*
- *the latest travel news from all over the world*
- *details on Lonely Planet's new and forthcoming releases*

Also available: Lonely Planet T-shirts. 100% heavyweight cotton (S, M, L, XL)

LONELY PLANET PUBLICATIONS

Australia: PO Box 617, Hawthorn 3122, Victoria (tel: 03-819 1877)
USA: Embarcadero West, 155 Filbert St, Suite 251, Oakland, CA 94607 (tel: 510-893 8555)
UK: Devonshire House, 12 Barley Mow Passage, Chiswick, London W4 4PH (tel: 081-742 3161)
France: 71 bis rue du Cardinal Lemoine – 75005 Paris (tel: 46 34 00 58)

Guides to the Pacific

Australia – a travel survival kit
The complete low-down on Down Under – home of Ayers Rock, the Great Barrier Reef, extraordinary animals, cosmopolitan cities, rainforests, beaches ... and Lonely Planet!

Bushwalking in Australia
Two experienced and respected walkers give details of the best walks in every state, covering many different terrains and climates.

Bushwalking in Papua New Guinea
The best way to get to know Papua New Guinea is from the ground up – and bushwalking is the best way to travel around the rugged and varied landscape of this island.

Islands of Australia's Great Barrier Reef – a travel survival kit
The Great Barrier Reef is one of the wonders of the world – and one of the great travel destinations! Whether you're looking for the best snorkelling, the liveliest nightlife or a secluded island hideaway, this guide has all the facts you'll need.

Melbourne – city guide
From historic houses to fascinating churches and from glorious parks to tapas bars, cafés and bistros, Melbourne is a dream for gourmets and a paradise for sightseers.

Sydney – city guide
From the Opera House to the surf; all you need to know in a handy pocket-sized format.

Victoria – Australia guide
From old gold rush towns to cosmopolitan Melbourne and from remote mountains to the most popular surf beaches, Victoria is packed with attractions and activities for everyone.

Fiji – a travel survival kit
Whether you prefer to stay in camping grounds, international hotels, or something in-between, this comprehensive guide will help you to enjoy the beautiful Fijian archipelago.

Hawaii – a travel survival kit
Share in the delights of this island paradise – and avoid some of its high prices – with this practical guide. It covers all of Hawaii's well-known attractions, plus plenty of uncrowded sights and activities.

Micronesia – a travel survival kit
The glorious beaches, lagoons and reefs of these 2100 islands would dazzle even the most jaded traveller. This guide has all the details on island-hopping across the Micronesian archipelago.

New Zealand – a travel survival kit
This practical guide will help you discover the very best New Zealand has to offer: Maori dances and feasts, some of the most spectacular scenery in the world, and every outdoor activity imaginable.

Tramping in New Zealand
Call it tramping, hiking, walking, bushwalking or trekking – travelling by foot is the best way to explore New Zealand's natural beauty. Detailed descriptions of over 40 walks of varying length and difficulty.

Papua New Guinea – a travel survival kit
With its coastal cities, villages perched beside mighty rivers, palm-fringed beaches and rushing mountain streams, Papua New Guinea promises memorable travel.

Rarotonga & the Cook Islands – a travel survival kit
Rarotonga and the Cook Islands have history, beauty and magic to rival the better-known islands of Hawaii and Tahiti, but the world has virtually passed them by.

Samoa – a travel survival kit
Two remarkably different countries, Western Samoa and American Samoa offer some wonderful island escapes, and Polynesian culture at its best.

Solomon Islands – a travel survival kit
The Solomon Islands are the best-kept secret of the Pacific. Discover remote tropical islands, jungle-covered volcanoes and traditional Melanesian villages with this detailed guide.

Tahiti & French Polynesia – a travel survival kit
Tahiti's idyllic beauty has seduced sailors, artists and travellers for generations. The latest edition of this book provides full details on the main island of Tahiti, the Tuamotos, Marquesas and other island groups. Invaluable information for independent travellers and package tourists alike.

Tonga – a travel survival kit
The only South Pacific country never to be colonised by Europeans, Tonga has also been ignored by tourists. The people of this far-flung island group offer some of the most sincere and unconditional hospitality in the world.

Vanuatu – a travel survival kit
Discover superb beaches, lush rainforests, dazzling coral reefs and traditional Melanesian customs in this glorious Pacific Ocean archipelago.

Also available:
Pidgin phrasebook.

Lonely Planet Guidebooks

Lonely Planet guidebooks cover every accessible part of Asia as well as Australia, the Pacific, South America, Africa, the Middle East, Europe and parts of North America. There are five series: *travel survival kits*, covering a country for a range of budgets; *shoestring guides* with compact information for low-budget travel in a major region; *walking guides*; *city guides* and *phrasebooks*.

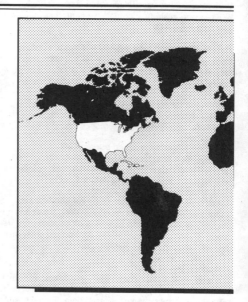

Mail Order

Lonely Planet guidebooks are distributed worldwide. They are also available by mail order from Lonely Planet, so if you have difficulty finding a title please write to us. US and Canadian residents should write to Embarcadero West, 155 Filbert St, Suite 251, Oakland CA 94607, USA; European residents should write to Devonshire House, 12 Barley Mow Passage, Chiswick, London W4 4PH; and residents of other countries to PO Box 617, Hawthorn, Victoria 3122, Australia.

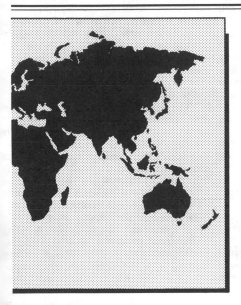

Indian Subcontinent
Bangladesh
India
Hindi/Urdu phrasebook
Trekking in the Indian Himalaya
Karakoram Highway
Kashmir, Ladakh & Zanskar
Nepal
Trekking in the Nepal Himalaya
Nepali phrasebook
Pakistan
Sri Lanka
Sri Lanka phrasebook

Africa
Africa on a shoestring
Central Africa
East Africa
Trekking in East Africa
Kenya
Swahili phrasebook
Morocco, Algeria & Tunisia
Arabic (Moroccan) phrasebook
South Africa, Lesotho & Swaziland
Zimbabwe, Botswana & Namibia
West Africa

Central America
Baja California
Central America on a shoestring
Costa Rica
La Ruta Maya
Mexico

North America
Alaska
Canada
Hawaii

Europe
Baltic States & Kaliningrad
Dublin city guide
Eastern Europe on a shoestring
Eastern Europe phrasebook
Finland
France
Greece
Hungary
Iceland, Greenland & the Faroe Islands
Ireland
Italy
Mediterranean Europe on a shoestring
Mediterranean Europe phrasebook
Poland
Scandinavian & Baltic Europe on a shoestring
Scandinavian Europe phrasebook
Switzerland
Trekking in Spain
Trekking in Greece
USSR
Russian phrasebook
Western Europe on a shoestring
Western Europe phrasebook

South America
Argentina, Uruguay & Paraguay
Bolivia
Brazil
Brazilian phrasebook
Chile & Easter Island
Colombia
Ecuador & the Galápagos Islands
Latin American Spanish phrasebook
Peru
Quechua phrasebook
South America on a shoestring
Trekking in the Patagonian Andes

The Lonely Planet Story

Lonely Planet published its first book in 1973 in response to the numerous 'How did you do it?' questions Maureen and Tony Wheeler were asked after driving, bussing, hitching, sailing and railing their way from England to Australia.

Written at a kitchen table and hand collated, trimmed and stapled, *Across Asia on the Cheap* became an instant local bestseller, inspiring thoughts of another book.

Eighteen months in South-East Asia resulted in their second guide, *South-East Asia on a shoestring*, which they put together in a backstreet Chinese hotel in Singapore in 1975. The 'yellow bible' as it quickly became known to backpackers around the world, soon became *the* guide to the region. It has sold well over half a million copies and is now in its 7th edition, still retaining its familiar yellow cover.

Today there are over 130 Lonely Planet titles in print – books that have that same adventurous approach to travel as those early guides; books that 'assume you know how to get your luggage off the carousel' as one reviewer put it.

Although Lonely Planet initially specialised in guides to Asia, they now cover most regions of the world, including the Pacific, South America, Africa, the Middle East and Europe. The list of *walking guides* and *phrasebooks* (for 'unusual' languages such as Quechua, Swahili, Nepali and Egyptian Arabic) is also growing rapidly.

The emphasis continues to be on travel for independent travellers. Tony and Maureen still travel for several months of each year and play an active part in the writing, updating and quality control of Lonely Planet's guides.

They have been joined by over 50 authors, 60 staff – mainly editors, cartographers & designers – at our office in Melbourne, Australia, at our US office in Oakland, California and at our European office in Paris; another five at our office in London handle sales for Britain, Europe and Africa. Travellers themselves also make a valuable contribution to the guides through the feedback we receive in thousands of letters each year.

The people at Lonely Planet strongly believe that travellers can make a positive contribution to the countries they visit, both through their appreciation of the countries' culture, wildlife and natural features, and through the money they spend. In addition, the company makes a direct contribution to the countries and regions it covers. Since 1986 a percentage of the income from each book has been donated to ventures such as famine relief in Africa; aid projects in India; agricultural projects in Central America; Greenpeace's efforts to halt French nuclear testing in the Pacific and Amnesty International. In 1993 $100,000 was donated to such causes.

Lonely Planet's basic travel philosophy is summed up in Tony Wheeler's comment 'Don't worry about whether your trip will work out. Just go!'.